PARIS BLUES

PARIS BLUES

AFRICAN AMERICAN MUSIC
AND FRENCH POPULAR CULTURE,
1920–1960

ANDY FRY

The University of Chicago Press Chicago and London

ANDY FRY teaches in the Music Department at
King's College London.

The University of Chicago Press, Chicago 60637
The University of Chicago Press, Ltd., London
© 2014 by The University of Chicago
All rights reserved. Published 2014.
Printed in the United States of America

23 22 21 20 19 18 17 16 15 14   1 2 3 4 5

ISBN-13: 978-0-226-13878-7 (cloth)
ISBN-13: 978-0-226-13881-7 (paper)
ISBN-13: 978-0-226-13895-4 (e-book)
DOI: 10.7208/chicago/9780226138954.001.0001

Library of Congress Cataloging-in-Publication Data

Fry, Andy, 1974– author.
  Paris blues : African American music and French
popular culture, 1920–1960 / Andy Fry.
      pages ; cm
  Includes bibliographical references and index.
    ISBN 978-0-226-13878-7 (cloth : alk. paper) —
ISBN 978-0-226-13881-7 (pbk. : alk. paper) —
ISBN 978-0-226-13895-4 (e-book)   1. African American
jazz musicians—France.   2. African Americans in the
performing arts—France—History—20th century.
3. Jazz—France—20th century—History and criticism.   4. Musical theater—France—History—20th
century.   5. Musical films—France—History—20th
century.   I. Title.
  ML3509.F7F79 2014
    781.65089′96073044—dc23

                                        2013039183

Contents

Acknowledgments

Paris Blues has occupied me, on and off and in different ways, for rather a long time. Over these years, I've accumulated debts—financial, personal, intellectual—that it would take a forensic accountant to unravel and a lifetime to repay. I can do neither here, only sound the names of some people and institutions it would be truly criminal not to thank, and trust others will know where to come when they need favors in return.

I'm pleased to acknowledge support received at various points from the UK Arts and Humanities Research Council; St John's College, Oxford; both the Academic Senate and the Center for the Humanities of the University of California, San Diego; and the School of Arts and Humanities of King's College London.

Research for *Paris Blues* would not have been possible without the kind assistance provided by staff of many libraries. In Paris, these were the Bibliothèque de l'Arsenal, the Bibliothèque-Musée de l'Opéra, the Bibliothèque de la Ville de Paris, the Médiathèque Musicale Mahler, and three central departments of the Bibliothèque Nationale: Musique, Audiovisuel, and especially Arts du Spectacle. The lattermost, founded on the extraordinary Collection Auguste Rondel, offers unparalleled breadth and depth for research on twentieth-century popular culture, even in these days of full-text search; I couldn't have written this book without it or its helpful staff. In the States, invaluable resources were provided by the Music Department and the Theatre Collection of the Free Library of Philadelphia, the Library for the Performing Arts and the Schomburg Center for Research in Black Culture of the New York Public Library, and the Institute of Jazz Studies at Rutgers. Finally, I've been very fortunate throughout with both the libraries and librarians of the universities where I've been stationed, at Oxford, Penn, UCSD, Berkeley, and London.

Some sections of this book have appeared in earlier or condensed versions, and I am grateful to their editors and publishers for permission to reprint that material here: " 'Du jazz hot à *La Créole*': Josephine Baker Sings Offenbach," *Cambridge Opera Journal* 16 (2004): 43–75 (© 2004 Cambridge

University Press); "Rethinking the *Revue nègre*: Black Musical Theatre in Inter-war Paris," in *Western Music and Race*, edited by Julie Brown, 258–75 (© 2007 Cambridge University Press); and "Remembrance of Jazz Past: Sidney Bechet in France," in *The Oxford Handbook of the New Cultural History of Music*, edited by Jane F. Fulcher, 307–31 (© 2011 Oxford University Press).

Personal debts are much harder to tally. At Oxford, Peter Franklin provided boundless support, wit, and insight in the early stages of my research, and Emanuele Senici shared his kindness and wisdom. A sojourn at Penn was made possible by Cristle Collins Judd and Jeff Kallberg, and Guy Ramsey and Gary Tomlinson went out of their way to advise me. I am grateful to colleagues at UCSD who made my time there enjoyable, especially David Borgo, Nancy Guy, and Mina Yang, as well as chairs Rand Steiger and John Fonville; and to Mary Ann Smart and Bonnie Wade who arranged for me to spend a stimulating semester at Berkeley.

The Music Department at King's College London has been an inspiring home these last few years, and is ever more so as we welcome new colleagues into the fold. I owe an especial debt of gratitude to John Deathridge, who negotiated my move here with his familiar élan, and to my young colleagues Bettina Varwig and Katherine Butler Schofield who always offer a healthy perspective on matters academic and otherwise. Meanwhile, Roger Parker continues to be for me, as for an extraordinary number of my generation, a wise and generous mentor; I appreciate him even more now that we teach in the same institution.

At the University of Chicago Press, I am grateful to Doug Mitchell for believing in this book from early on and for his shuttle diplomacy making my case with readers and committees; to Tim McGovern for going beyond the call of duty to shuffle an overdue manuscript through the system; and to Kelly Finefrock-Creed for turning her fine eye for detail to the text time and again. Other longtime friends, champions, and inspirations I must not fail to thank are Katherine Bergeron, Phil Bohlman, Doreen Cochrane, Joanne Crawford, Melanie Feakins, John Fry, Travis Jackson, Richard Leppert, George Lewis, Art Marsh, Alan Percy, Ruth Rosenberg, Laura Tunbridge, and Ben Walton. Finally, Jennifer Sheppard has lived with this book (or its specter) almost as long as I have. I may never have let her read *Paris Blues*, but her eleventh-hour proofing of footnotes was the very least of her many wonderful contributions to my writing it.

Introduction

FIGURE I.1. Connie (Diahann Caroll) and Eddie (Sidney Poitier), *Paris Blues*, dir. Martin Ritt (1961).

EDDIE. Look, here [in Paris] nobody says Eddie Cook, Negro musician. They say Eddie Cook, musician, period. And that's all I wanna be. [. . .] Musician, period. And I don't have to prove anything else.

CONNIE. Like what?

EDDIE. Like, because I'm Negro I'm different, because I'm Negro I'm not different. I'm different, I'm not different, who cares? Look, I don't have to prove either case. Can you understand that? [. . .]

CONNIE, *shouting.* Eddie, you're wrong, you're wrong. [. . .] Things are much better [in the United States] than they were five years ago, and they're gonna still be better next year. And not because Negroes come to Paris. But because Negroes stay home. [. . .]

EDDIE. Look, are we gonna stand here all day discussing this *jazz*?

The 1961 film *Paris Blues* is remembered primarily for its colorful score by Duke Ellington and Billy Strayhorn.[1] Louis Armstrong's on-screen role as "Wild Man Moore" is less fondly recalled, though his character has

1. Martin Ritt, dir., *Paris Blues* (Los Angeles: Optimum Classic, 2008), DVD.

FIGURE I.2. Eddie (Sidney Poitier), Ram (Paul Newman), Connie (Diahann Carroll), and Lillian (Joanne Woodward), *Paris Blues*, dir. Martin Ritt (1961).

greater depth than was often the case in his movies. "Duke, Satchmo were true heroes to all Parisians," pronounced *Ebony* magazine; during filming, "they were feted and entertained lavishly by artists, poets, actors and intellectuals."[2] On release of the movie, however, sister magazine *Jet* saw only "yet another example of Hollywood's almost chronic inability to fully utilize superlative talent." Although the producer, Sam Shaw, was "a man of progressive ideals and real integrity," *Jet* said, *Paris Blues* "fail[ed] to reflect either the depth of his viewpoint or his superior taste and values."[3] Sure enough, this tale of two American tourists (Joanne Woodward, Diahann Carroll) who fall for expatriate jazz musicians (Paul Newman, Sidney Poitier) is nobody's best effort: its plot is wayward, its dialogue clunky, its performances mixed. But reactions in the black press, like Eddie and Connie's conversation, are in line with a long tradition of viewing the French capital as a hospitable city for African Americans compared to the harsh realities of home.

Certainly, in the cellar bar where Ram and Eddie's band play and mingle with the customers, mutual respect and interracial harmony resound. On a romantic level, however, color coding is enforced. Connie (Carroll), a "socially conscious" African American, prefers saxophonist Eddie Cook (Poitier) to trombonist Ram Bowen (Newman; fig. I.2).[4] Although Eddie enjoys freedom and respect in Paris, he will eventually agree to return

2. Anon., "Paris Blues," *Ebony* 16/10 (August 1961): 46–50 (quote on p. 50).

3. Allan Morrison, "Movie of the Week: Paris Blues," *Jet* 21/6 (30 November 1961): 65.

4. According to the film's producer, Sam Shaw, the pairings were originally interracial (which is still suggested at the film's opening), but the studio forced a switch. See David Hajdu, *Lush Life: A Biography of Billy Strayhorn* (New York: Farrar, Straus, Giroux, 1996), 206–7; and Krin Gabbard, "*Paris Blues*: Ellington, Armstrong, and Saying It with Music," in *Uptown Conversation: The New Jazz Studies*, ed. Robert G. O'Meally, Brent Hayes Edwards, and Farah Jasmine Griffin (New York: Columbia University Press, 2004), 297–311 (esp. p. 302).

to a United States that Connie assures him is transforming. Ram, on the other hand, will disappoint Connie's white friend, Lillian (Woodward). An aspiring composer, whose quest to complete his *Paris Blues* is the film's conceit, he decides at the last moment that he must remain in Paris for the sake of his Art.

A comparison with Harold Flender's 1957 pulp novel, on which the film was loosely based, is instructive.[5] Eddie was originally the central character, not his Jewish bandmate Benny (who becomes the WASPish Ram). Lillian, a spinster chaperone for Connie, was a love interest for neither man. It is hardly a surprise that Hollywood would make Ram the hero, or that it would rejuvenate Lillian as his leading lady. The African American couple may be retained alongside, but their relationship is more or less desexualized, as was customary in Poitier's films (the contrast between the couples is marked in fig. I.3). As if enacting the dynamic to which Eddie fears to return, Connie/Carroll is the viewer's eye candy while Eddie/Poitier is allowed to pose no threat to him [sic]. According to Tyler Stovall, this shift from a black protagonist to a white hero means that "the film both documented the experience of African American musicians in Paris and also symbolized the reasons why the city remained a refuge from America."[6] What the scenario put in question by embracing a black man's story, in other words, narrative logic and Hollywood convention scrambled to reinstate.

Stovall neglects to point out, however, that the film also omits scenes in the book that deal quite bluntly with *French* attitudes to race. For Flender's Eddie, Paris may be "the only place [he has] ever felt at home, accepted, a human being," but, as the story progresses, his experience tarnishes somewhat. A succession of taxi drivers offer tirades against North Africans while insisting that "France is a democratic country. We don't discriminate against Negroes, like they do in America." And Eddie remembers how, when he first arrived in Paris, his warm welcome was less a matter of color blindness than of Negrophilia.[7] Where the book goes so far as to mention the Algerian situation and French anti-Semitism, no such issues cloud the tourist's view of Paris offered by the film.[8]

5. Harold Flender, *Paris Blues* (New York: Ballantine Books, 1957; repr., London: Hamilton, 1961). Subsequent citations refer to the 1961 reprint.

6. Tyler Stovall, *Paris noir: African Americans in the City of Light* (Boston: Mariner Books, 1996), 242.

7. Flender, *Paris Blues*, 26, 66, 81.

8. The movie also makes a telling substitution of the band's guitarist. In Flender's novel, he is a "French Negro" from a wealthy family who experiences a mental breakdown. Mystifying to the African American characters who think he's

FIGURE I.3. French publicity poster for *Paris Blues*, dir. Martin Ritt (1961).

To the extent that the race question still burns in the movie *Paris Blues*, it does so stateside. Can Eddie return to life as a Negro? How much has the

---

had all the advantages they've lacked, his problems seem to result from the psychological violence of colonialism, compounded by the physical violence meted out by the French police. In the film, on the other hand, the guitarist is an altogether more familiar character, comprising two common tropes of jazz lore: "The Gypsy" looks like a member of Django Reinhardt's extended family; he's debilitated not by mental illness but by drug addiction (which, even at the time, critics found clichéd).

country changed in the five years he's been away? As Stovall and others have recognized, in this period African American success abroad ceased to be an automatic cause for celebration at home; it began to look suspiciously like an evasion of duty to the race.[9] But Eddie is not keen to hear Connie's admonitions, reiterating his rather naïve view of colorblind Paris (see the dialogue above). Explaining the film's muted reception, actor Joanne Woodward seemed to agree: "If a picture has a bi-racial cast I guess it's supposed to be a 'problem' picture. Well, there isn't any problem in 'Paris Blues.'"[10] In this sense, the film does not depict France as it actually was (or is), but rather as an idealized vision for the future of America.[11]

The occlusion of race is typical, I suggest, not only of fictional approaches to African Americans in Paris but also of many historical ones: these, too, use France to shine a light on America, while ignoring or downplaying its own "race problem." Take, for instance, William Shack's *Harlem in Montmartre* (2001), one of a number of evocative portrayals in print of black life in Paris. As the author explains, he came from "that generation of African Americans whose first images of France sprang from stories told by fathers who had served in that country . . . during the Great War." These included "descriptions of the hospitality French citizens displayed" and a "refrain . . . that a 'colored man' . . . had to travel . . . to be recognized as 'equal' to a 'white man.'"[12] In this Shack finds his motivating principle.

9. Stovall, *Paris noir*, 216–25, 244–50.

10. William Leonard, "'Paris Blues' Change of Pace for Star," *Chicago Daily Tribune*, 24 September 1961.

11. An important context for *Paris Blues* is found in Poitier's other films of the 1950s and 1960s, which saw him become the most successful African American actor of his time. All, in some sense, concern the struggle for integration but represent it among individuals: from Poitier's assistance to an elderly priest (Canada Lee) in *Cry, the Beloved Country* (1952), through his allegiance to a fellow convict (Tony Curtis) in *The Defiant Ones* (1958), to the ground-breaking interracial romance (with Katharine Houghton) of *Guess Who's Coming to Dinner* (1967). See, inter alia, Donald Bogle, *Toms, Coons, Mulattoes, Mammies, and Bucks: An Interpretive History of Blacks in American Films*, 3rd edition (New York: Continuum, 1997), 175–83, 215–19; and Thomas Cripps, *Making Movies Black: The Hollywood Message Movie from World War II to the Civil Rights Era* (New York: Oxford University Press, 1993), 284–94.

12. William A. Shack, *Harlem in Montmartre: A Paris Jazz Story between the Great Wars* (Berkeley: University of California Press, 2001), xiii. A distinguished Berkeley anthropologist, Shack left *Harlem in Montmartre* unfinished at the time of his death. See my article "Beyond Le Bœuf: Interdisciplinary Rereadings of Jazz in France," *Journal of the Royal Musical Association* 128 (2003): 137–53, on which I draw to some extent in this introduction. Among earlier accounts, see Chris Goddard, *Jazz*

Like Tyler Stovall, who earlier wrote his *Paris noir* "as a success story, without illusions or apologies," "a political statement . . . given the tendency . . . to present blacks as failures or as a 'problem,'" Shack provides a sympathetic account of African American musicians in Paris, primarily from their own reminiscences.[13] His book thus serves as a useful reminder of black Paris's enduring power as a *lieu de mémoire*.

The familiar narrative goes something like this: African American entertainers first came to France as minstrels in the nineteenth century and cakewalkers around the turn of the twentieth (witness Debussy's popular piano pieces "Golliwogg's Cake-Walk" and "The Little Nigar"). During World War I, black servicemen earned a reputation for music as well as fighting, particularly James Reese Europe's 369th "Hellfighters" Division (commissioned to order as "the best damn band in the United States Army").[14] Hot on their tail, early jazz bands such as Louis Mitchell and his Jazz Kings helped France to celebrate victory; Will Marion Cook's Southern Syncopated Orchestra was famously eulogized by conductor Ernest Ansermet.[15] In the twenties, African Americans could be heard in

Away from Home (New York: Paddington Press, 1979); and Bill Moody, *The Jazz Exiles: American Musicians Abroad* (Reno: University of Nevada Press, 1993).

13. Stovall, *Paris noir*, xv–xvi. A generation younger than Shack, Stovall dedicates his book to the memory of his grandfather, who also served as a soldier in France during the First World War. Although, personally, Paris "never impressed [Stovall] as a paradise of racial good feelings" (xv), this is still basically the story he tells. His recent writings, however, have been more critical. See, for example, Tyler Stovall, "Black Community, Black Spectacle: Performance and Race in Transatlantic Perspective," in *Black Cultural Traffic: Crossroads in Global Performance and Popular Culture*, ed. Harry J. Elam Jr. and Kennell Jackson (Ann Arbor: University of Michigan Press, 2005), 221–41; and Stovall, "No Green Pastures: The African Americanization of France," in *Black Europe and the African Diaspora*, ed. Darlene Clark Hine, Trica Danielle Keaton, and Stephen Small (Urbana: University of Illinois Press, 2009), 180–97.

14. Colonel William Hayward, cited in Shack, *Harlem in Montmartre*, 14. For recent accounts, see R. Reid Badger, *A Life in Ragtime: A Biography of James Reese Europe* (New York: Oxford University Press, 1995); and Colin Nettelbeck, "A Different Music: Jazz Comes to France," in *Dancing with DeBeauvoir: Jazz and the French* (Carlton, Victoria: Melbourne University Press, 2004), 16–30.

15. Ernest Ansermet, "Sur un orchestre nègre," in *Écrits sur la musique* (Neuchâtel, Switz.: Baconnière, 1971), 171–78. This much-cited and commonly reproduced text was first published in *La Revue romande* 3/10 (October 1919), then reprinted, with an English translation by Walter E. Schaap, in *Jazz hot*, no. 28 (November–December 1938): 4–9. Among other locations, it is available in English in Ralph de Toledano, ed., *Frontiers of Jazz* (New York: Oliver Durrell, 1947), 115–22; and in Robert Walser,

a variety of venues: exclusive black-run nightclubs in Montmartre such as Gene Bullard's Le Grand Duc (where legendary singer Bricktop started out and where Langston Hughes once washed dishes); music-hall shows, importantly Josephine Baker's (in)famous début in *La Revue nègre*; cafés and nightclubs such as Le Bœuf sur le Toit, the favorite hangout of Jean Cocteau and friends (as several compositions again attest); and, not to forget the decade's new phenomenon, *les dancings*.[16]

In the wake of the depression, the 1930s were quieter, Shack suggests. Yet some of the best musicians—Duke Ellington, Louis Armstrong, and Coleman Hawkins—visited, and the Hot Club de France was established to promote jazz, along with its famous Quintet featuring (almost) home-grown talents Django Reinhardt and Stéphane Grappelli. Less well-known is the paradox of the Second World War: on the one hand, the few African Americans who remained were incarcerated in prison camps; on the other, their music, now naturalized, "blazed as never before." For Shack, at least, jazz's continued presence during the Nazi occupation signaled French resistance, particularly in the hands of the long-haired, zoot-suited youths known as *zazous*.[17] After the war, "Louis Armstrong's gravelly voice symbolized as much Paris liberated as General Charles de Gaulle's victory parade."[18] So not only did African Americans experience a new freedom in France; remarkably they were also able to share it with the French.

Throughout his account, Shack, like many others, views the history of black music and musicians in Paris through rose-tinted spectacles. While it is useful in tracing the role of the American press in France in stoking up racial tensions, for example, it is naïve in denying any role to the locals. "The French public's intolerance of racial prejudice countered white Americans' intolerance . . . of a color-blind French society," he writes.[19]

---

ed., *Keeping Time: Readings in Jazz History* (New York: Oxford University Press, 1999), 9–11. I discuss Ansermet's review at some length in chap. 5 below.

16. See Craig Lloyd, *Eugene Bullard: Black Expatriate in Jazz-Age Paris* (Athens: University of Georgia Press, 2000); Bricktop [Ada Smith], *Bricktop*, with James Haskins (New York: Atheneum, 1983); and Langston Hughes, *The Big Sea* (New York: Hill and Wang, 1933). On Baker, see chap. 3 below. On Cocteau, see, in addition to texts cited later in this introduction, Francis Steegmuller, *Cocteau: A Biography* (London: Macmillan, 1970); and Jann Pasler, "New Music as Confrontation: The Musical Sources of Jean Cocteau's Identity," *Musical Quarterly* 75 (1991): 255–78.

17. Shack, *Harlem in Montmartre*, 117. See Matthew F. Jordan, "*Zazou dans le Métro*: Occupation, Swing, and the Battle for *la Jeunesse*," in *Le Jazz: Jazz and French Cultural Identity* (Urbana: University of Illinois Press, 2010), 185–232.

18. Shack, *Harlem in Montmartre*, 124.

19. Ibid., 67.

In contrast, historian Ralph Schor, in his detailed studies of French immigration and the attitudes it engendered in the interwar period, argues that these egalitarian ideals for the fraternity of races coexisted with an everyday reality of racism. Foreigners were certainly a subject of debate: between 1919 and 1939 there were almost twenty thousand articles on the subject in the eight newspapers he surveyed, and more than three hundred books.[20]

Among the many—sadly familiar—issues Schor found addressed, housing was a particular concern, the blame for a lack of affordable accommodation landing squarely on foreigners. Other fears were that poor sanitation led to disease among immigrants, and poverty and inadequate social conditions to high levels of crime. Most important, there were cultural and physical differences French people were barely able to accept. The general public, Schor argues, spurred on by right-wing parties and the media, felt their society was exposed to "a serious sanitary and moral contamination." Although, for some, foreign performers occupied a special position, for others, they were "signs of an irremediable decadence, such as that of the Roman empire invaded and put to death by the barbarians."[21]

Their New World origins—and money—doubtless granted African Americans some privileges. Coming from segregated America to a country proud of its egalitarianism (albeit an aggressive colonizer), they were also bound to find France a relatively hospitable place. It was not a "discrimination-free environment," however, as Schor's analysis makes plain.[22] Accepting sources whose bias should be self-evident (wartime articles in the black press; recent, ghostwritten memoirs), Shack's book is less a critical history than a nostalgic extension of the story—a compilation of tales sent back home of African American success abroad. Suspicions that such accounts are not telling the whole truth need not challenge one fact: if Harlem in Montmartre is in some ways a myth, it is a lasting and empowering one, which became a historical force in its own right.

Yet more than pedantry sounds the alarm. African Americans' memories of France—themselves more mixed than has often been claimed—

20. Ralph Schor, *L'Opinion française et les étrangers en France, 1919–1939* (Paris: Publications de la Sorbonne, 1985); Schor, *Histoire de l'immigration en France, de la fin du XIXe siècle à nos jours* (Paris: Armand Colin, 1996). The newspapers surveyed were *L'Action française, Le Temps, La Croix, L'Aube, L'Œuvre, Le Populaire, Le Peuple,* and *L'Humanité.*

21. Schor, *Histoire de l'immigration,* 90, 117.

22. Shack, *Harlem in Montmartre,* xvi (quote); Schor, *L'Opinion française;* and Schor, *Histoire de l'immigration.*

must surely be understood in dialogue with the varied forms of segregation, hostility, and violence faced at home; removed from that context,
idealized views too easily become vehicles of French complacency. Even if
there was little direct hostility, black appeal too often relied on exoticist-
racialist thinking that shouldn't be perpetuated, as a number of authors
have by now discussed.[23] More than all this, mythologizing France as a
land of equality rings hollow these days. Recent years have seen a widespread reevaluation of assimilation—in terms both of the legitimacy of
the policy and the success of the practice—in the face of rioting youths
and a resurgent extreme right wing. As the country waits for its minority
groups in the *banlieues* to erupt in protest once more against their cultural
and economic disenfranchisement in the land of *liberté, égalité, fraternité*,
this vision not only proves hard to sustain, it may also have become politically irresponsible.[24]

The apparent disconnect between cultural and sociopolitical history
has been particularly well captured by Carole Sweeney in her book *From
Fetish to Subject*. As rare as it is rich, Sweeney's assessment of the problem
warrants quoting at some length:

> The negrophile aesthetic valorisation of a particular version of black-
> ness [in France in the early twentieth century] did not of course translate
> into enlightened political policies around race and cultural difference
> either domestically or in the colonised territories. . . . The widespread
> popularity of *l'art nègre* and *le jazz hot* in the clubs and salons of bour-
> geois Paris did not make fashionable Parisians aware of the 1919 Pan-
> African Congress in Versailles led by W. E. B. DuBois or the formation of
> the Union Inter-Coloniale in 1921. While black American jazz musicians
> and entertainers were lauded in Paris in the 1920s, in North Africa, for

23. See, for example, Petrine Archer-Straw, *Negrophilia: Avant-Garde Paris and
Black Culture in the 1920s* (London: Thames and Hudson, 2000); Brett A. Berliner,
Ambivalent Desire: The Exotic Black Other in Jazz-Age France (Amherst: University of
Massachusetts Press, 2002); and Elizabeth Ezra, *The Colonial Unconscious: Race and
Culture in Interwar France* (Ithaca, NY: Cornell University Press, 2000).

24. See, for example, Trica Danielle Keaton, "'Black (American) Paris' and the
French Outer-Cities: The Race Question and Questioning Solidarity," in Hine,
Keaton, and Small, *Black Europe and the African Diaspora*, 95–118; and Fred Constant,
"Talking Race in Color-Blind France: Equality Denied, 'Blackness' Reclaimed," in
ibid., 145–60. See also Sue Peabody and Tyler Stovall, eds., *The Color of Liberty: Histo-
ries of Race in France* (Durham, NC: Duke University Press, 2003); and Trica Danielle
Keaton, T. Denean Sharpley-Whiting, and Tyler Stovall, eds., *Black France/France
Noire: The History and Politics of Blackness* (Durham, NC: Duke University Press,
2012).

example, an anti-imperial rebellion, la Guerre du Rif, led by the outlawed Abdel El Krim, was brutally suppressed in 1925 by the French military supporting Spanish forces. As Josephine Baker, the living embodiment of modern primitivism, was taking Paris by storm with her music-hall hit chanson "J'ai deux amours" and her slave-chic attire, the Institut Pasteur hosted a conference on so-called racial hygiene that explained the public health problems of the immigrant population in France. Most striking of all perhaps is the fact that a popular cultural negrophilia existed alongside a gradual resurgence of aggressively xenophobic nationalism.[25]

While the current book is not the place to consider instances of colonial unrest and repression, or conversely the progress of black internationalism and civil rights, I am concerned to locate the reception of African American musicians accurately in terms of the discourses that swirled around them: whether performers became directly aware of them or not, such issues and events as Sweeney mentions often influenced how they were perceived and discussed. A paradoxical effect of cosmopolitanism and internationalism is the provincialism and prejudice they generate as counterforce: these phenomena must surely therefore be understood in both polarities in order to grasp their historical significance.

Not that I intend in this book simply to contest the affirmative view of African Americans in France by reviving their "Paris blues" in any straightforward sense. Rather, what I hope to convey in these pages is something of the complexity of experience that the finest performers in that genre register, particularly by incorporating perspectives gleaned from French reception. I do not attempt to survey the history of black music and musicians in Paris over these forty-odd years. This is a project that has, by now, been attempted several times, and not only in narrative accounts such as Stovall's and Shack's. Ludovic Tournès, Jeffrey H. Jackson, and Matthew F. Jordan, among others, have attended in considerable detail to the geographical, technological, and institutional factors influencing jazz's production and reception in France, as I discuss below. More useful than replicating this approach, I believe, is to offer a series of focused inquiries, which reflect on and engage with these broader narratives but also concentrate in detail on particular cultural events. Thus I pursue case studies of varying kinds (genres, individuals, a work), without attempting to tell a complete or continuous story. To as great an extent as possible, I shape the chapters as critical readings of performances, ones that remain present to a greater or lesser extent, and invite debate.

25. Carole Sweeney, *From Fetish to Subject: Race, Modernism, and Primitivism, 1919–1935* (Westport, CT: Praeger, 2004), 2–3.

The five chapters of *Paris Blues* move broadly chronologically, beginning with two forgotten traditions of the 1920s and 1930s (*revues nègres* and white show bands), continuing through Josephine Baker's shows and films of the 1930s, and concluding with studies of jazz's fortunes during the occupation and postwar years. Importantly, I consider the activities of nonblack musicians, whether American or European, in some detail, as well as African Americans performing music that could scarcely be understood as black. Despite extending as far as the 1950s, however, the book's focus is early jazz and swing: its last chapter considers the revival—reinvention—of these musics alongside modern jazz, and the historiographical consequences of this phenomenon. As *Paris Blues* proceeds, then, it becomes increasingly concerned with the complex intersection of history and memory in the very story it tells. Without wishing to delimit their meanings, in the next section I locate these case studies loosely within the literature, suggesting how they may be understood to advance or intervene in scholarship that bridges several disciplines.[26] This should help readers to navigate the chapters, which may be read individually, or, as I hope, allowed to complement—and sometimes even contest—one another.

*   *   *

Despite the persistence of rose-tinted accounts, I am far from the first to seek to bring a more critical perspective to the study of African Americans in Paris. At least since James Clifford provocatively compared bodies sculpted in flesh with those in wood (the African artifacts known as *art nègre* that became fashionable in the early twentieth century), the black presence in the city has looked newly complex. Railing against the aesthetic autonomy that had seen, for example, Western and non-Western

---

26. At the risk of sounding contrite or, worse, complacent, it may be worth noting that the early chapters of this book were researched and drafted prior to the publication of much of the literature I will discuss here. While I have integrated these authors' insights to as great an extent as possible, the relationship between their texts and mine remains a somewhat oblique one, simply because theirs was not the context in which I conducted my research. On the other hand, the comparative dearth of scholarship at the point I began this project allowed me to pursue my own interests without the implicit constraints inevitably placed on future researchers by the founders of a field. One more text, Jeremy F. Lane's *Jazz and Machine-Age Imperialism: Music, "Race," and Intellectuals in France, 1918–1945* (Ann Arbor: University of Michigan Press, 2013), appeared as this one entered production so cannot unfortunately be considered here.

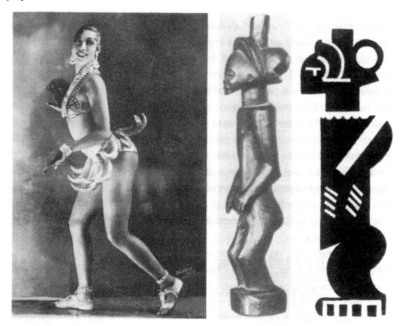

Affinities Not Included in the MOMA "Primitivism" Show.
1. Bodies
(a) Josephine Baker in a famous pose, Paris, ca. 1929
(b) Wooden figure (Chokwe, Angola)
(c) Fernand Léger, costume design for The Creation of
   the World, *1922–23*

FIGURE I.4. A reassessment of artistic primitivism by James Clifford, *The Predicament of Culture* (Cambridge, MA: Harvard University Press, 1988), 199. © ADAGP, Paris and DACS, London 2013.

objects aligned according to formal resemblance alone at the 1984 "Primitivism and Modern Art" show at the Museum of Modern Art, New York, Clifford observed incredulously, "One would be hard pressed to deduce . . . that all the enthusiasm for things *nègre* . . . had anything to do with race." Juxtaposing three examples of the archetypal protruding rear—Josephine Baker's, an Angolan statue's, and a Fernand Léger design's (fig. I.4)—Clifford argued otherwise: "Archaic Africa (which came to Paris by way of the future—that is, America) was sexed, gendered, and invested with 'magic' in specific ways."[27] In short, Clifford saw French *négrophilie* as a weighted

27. James Clifford, "Histories of the Tribal and Modern," in *The Predicament of Culture: Twentieth-Century Ethnography, Literature, and Art* (Cambridge, MA: Harvard

historical phenomenon whose assumptions and implications need to be assessed with critical distance, not naïvely celebrated.

Since then, a substantial literature has grown up, across several disciplines, concerned with such "modernist primitivism."[28] Among authors who were quick to take up the task was musicologist Glenn Watkins whose *Pyramids at the Louvre* offers a thought-provoking reappraisal of African Americans and their music in France.[29] Where this discipline has traditionally viewed jazz in Paris through the eyes of composers—and as a short-lived, frivolous engagement soon thrown off in pursuit of a "purer" neoclassicism—Watkins relocates the phenomenon within a broad primitivism in the arts.[30] Connecting the taste for jazz and ragtime, via Stravinsky, to an older exoticism and Russian primitivism, he encourages readers to consider even Debussy's jazzy (rather, raggy) piano pieces in the wake of *Le Sacre du printemps* (which postdates them). Most important, Watkins proposes jazz as a "tardy but powerful ally" of African art: at last a viable *musique nègre* to join its sister *art*.[31] Situating Milhaud's *La Création du monde* alongside sculptor Constantin Brancusi's ovoid *Beginning of the World*, and Josephine Baker's *La Revue nègre* with Ernst Krenek's "jazz-opera" *Jonny spielt auf*, Watkins adroitly reveals the blurring of "high" and "low," black and white, perhaps even self and other

University Press, 1988), 189–214 (quotes on p. 197) [originally published in *Art in America* (April 1985): 164–77]. The parallel Clifford observes between Baker's familiar posture and *art nègre* had long before been made explicit; see the cover of Joséphine Baker and Marcel Sauvage, *Voyages et aventures de Joséphine Baker* (Paris: Marcel Sheur, 1931) [also reprinted in Jody Blake, *Le Tumulte noir: Modernist Art and Popular Entertainment in Jazz-Age Paris, 1900–1930* (University Park: Pennsylvania State University Press, 1999), 98].

28. See, inter alia, Elazar Barkan and Ronald Bush, eds., *Prehistories of the Future: The Primitivist Project and the Culture of Modernism* (Stanford, CA: Stanford University Press, 1995); Sieglinde Lemke, *Primitivist Modernism: Black Culture and the Origins of Transatlantic Modernism* (New York: Oxford University Press, 1998); and Marianna Torgovnick, *Gone Primitive: Savage Intellects, Modern Lives* (Chicago: University of Chicago Press, 1990).

29. Glenn Watkins, *Pyramids at the Louvre: Music, Culture, and Collage from Stravinsky to the Postmodernists* (Cambridge, MA: Belknap Press of Harvard University Press, 1994).

30. For a solid if traditional musicological account, see Nancy Perloff, *Art and the Everyday: Popular Entertainment and the Circle of Erik Satie* (Oxford: Clarendon Press, 1991); see also James Harding, *The Ox on the Roof: Scenes from Musical Life in Paris in the Twenties* (London: Macdonald, 1972).

31. Watkins, *Pyramids at the Louvre*, 100.

that occurred under the sponsorship of primitivism. Unlike Clifford, he finally retreats from its most troublesome implications, however: while Watkins finds the reason for Baker's "later deconstruction . . . not difficult to determine," for example, he insists, "It is no myth that in Paris she escaped . . . racial prejudice."[32]

Art historian Jody Blake pursues Clifford's lead still further in *Le Tumulte noir*, making African Americans central in the dialogue between "primitive" and "modern" in this period. If authors such as Watkins place the reception of jazz within the context of artistic primitivism, Blake both extends and reverses the formula. Backdating the French discovery of *musique nègre* from jazz to ragtime and cakewalk at the turn of the century, she proposes that American performance arts preceded—and framed—the artists' reactions to African art; she locates them at the heart of artistic movements from the early primitivism of Picasso and others through various versions of futurism to Dada and surrealism. She thus emphasizes the subversive, countercultural quality of modernism's references to popular culture, showing how the impact of an imagined Africa far exceeded formal parameters. After the First World War, however, the influence of African American popular culture on modernism was, Blake argues, transformed if not removed. In the Call to Order, as this period of retrenchment is often called, conservatives reacted against black music and dancing, seeking to promote new French dances such as the neo-traditional *française*; iconic modernists such as Léger and Picasso now composed nostalgic depictions of the *bal musette*. In turn, purists like Le Corbusier reinvented their interest as a primitivism of form in order to mark it as a classicizing project. Thus, the exclusion of context that Clifford bemoaned as late as the 1980s is, for Blake, cause rather than consequence of art history's formalism.

An admirer of her work, I have pointed out elsewhere what seem to me some chronological distortions in Blake's argument.[33] But my concern in this book is not with high culture's appropriation of African American music, whether in visual arts, literature, or "art" music. Taking interest in popular culture only in so far as high culture took interest in it under modernism is, I fear, an academic project that often perpetuates the cultural hierarchy it means to question. Important, though, is an awareness of the historical narrative into which Blake strains to fit her case. For she, like many, accepts a familiar way of parsing the interwar period: ebullient and cosmopolitan at first, France becomes more conservative

32. Ibid., 138.
33. Fry, "Beyond Le Bœuf."

and insular as the years roll on toward the collaborationist Vichy regime of the Second World War, whose cultural politics are anticipated.[34] I intervene in this discussion, among others, in my first chapter by considering one of the genres that bridged the period, black musical theatre.

In 1925, Josephine Baker was famously launched to Parisian stardom by *La Revue nègre*. This show has come to be seen as an end rather than a beginning: the Call to Order supposedly reined in taste for "primitive" *art nègre*, and a revival of French folk traditions accompanied neoclassicism in an era anticipating Vichy. Chapter 1, by contrast, traces a tradition that extends almost the length of the interwar period: far from a single event, the imported "revue nègre" became a genre, embracing such groups as Lew Leslie's Blackbirds (1926, 1929) and Louis Douglas's Black Flowers (1930); they continued, albeit less frequently, into the late 1930s.

The reception of these shows was anything but straightforward, however; I pursue connections to racial theories, both from that time and more recently. Of particular concern were the troupes' apparent hybridity—not always the heuristic concept its prominence in postcolonial theory might lead one to suppose. In "savage" Josephine Baker's wake, other female performers, Florence Mills, Adelaide Hall, Aida Ward, and Valaida Snow, were believed to embody different modes of black womanhood, even varying degrees of civilization. But subtle differences can be found, I argue, between (black) Douglas's presentations of his troupe and that of his white counterpart, "Papa Plantation" Leslie. This reveals a complex negotiation with white expectation—a process that continues today, as I explore in a reading of Spike Lee's *Bamboozled*, which frames chapter 1. Thus I challenge the French press's obtuse insistence at the time of the film's release

---

34. There are several eloquent spokespersons for this position. For example, Romy Golan traces the return to landscape painting and organic forms in *Modernity and Nostalgia: Art and Politics in France between the Wars* (New Haven, CT: Yale University Press, 1995), arguing that the avant-garde began forsaking Paris for New York as early as World War I; far from embracing modernity, the French endeavored to recover land lost to bombs and foreigners and to ward off mechanization. In *True France: The Wars over Cultural Identity, 1900–1945* (Ithaca, NY: Cornell University Press, 1992), Herman Lebovics argues that the first half of the twentieth century saw the invention of a powerful myth of French tradition that simultaneously denied the recent—and ramshackle—establishment of the nation and sought to exclude people and modes of cultural expression now deemed to emanate from outside of it. Lebovics more than Golan, however, is clear that he is telling only part of the story: the myth of true France, if powerful, was not all pervasive; it sometimes met spirited resistance.

that race and racialized representation are of no bearing in contemporary France.

Recent scholarship on jazz in France has increasingly taken on board the unstable formulations of fear and desire located in its early reception. Narratives such as Shack's of the rapturous reception of African Americans tend therefore to be replaced by stories of jazz's gradual and contested assimilation: a tale of progressive integration, in other words, that runs in contrary motion with Blake's account (and others) of increasing opposition. This is, broadly speaking, the approach taken both in Jeffrey H. Jackson's *Making Jazz French* and, most recently, in Matthew F. Jordan's *Le Jazz* (although tellingly they disagree on when assimilation was achieved). For example, Jordan writes: "Today, there is a widespread belief that 'the French love jazz.' But as in all stories of passion, love, and betrayal, this love has been a rocky affair. After jazz was first experienced as a foreign threat to traditional French culture, the initial hostility of listeners and critics waned and, as the French modernized their sense of self, jazz became an accepted and important form of expression that was compatible with most notions of Frenchness and visions of true French culture."[35] This process of integration takes place over a series of "historically situated conversations," ones he reconstructs from the press and particularly the jazz journals.[36] While Jordan frames this assimilation primarily in terms of "modernity," Jackson's keyword is "cosmopolitanism."[37] Both are useful concepts but neither captures the range of meaning jazz was able to signify, nor indeed that these authors discuss. For example, in Jackson's interpretation, interest in jazz throughout this period indicates a continual vein of cosmopolitanism, albeit one that is sometimes constricted. However, a counternarrative emerges just as strongly: a strain of bigoted insularity if not xenophobia that was running almost as fast after the First World War as it was prior to the Second.

While these new conceptualizations of the period thus serve an important function in moving attention away from the 1920s as the highpoint of cosmopolitanism (and the concomitant notion of an ensuing conservatism), I am cautious about some of their effects. One, they slant the

35. Jordan, "Introduction: The Meaning and Function of French Debates about Jazz," in *Le Jazz*, 1–15 (quote on p. 2).

36. Ibid., 11.

37. Jeffrey H. Jackson, *Making Jazz French: Music and Modern Life in Interwar Paris* (Durham, NC: Duke University Press, 2003). See also Denis-Constant Martin and Olivier Roueff, *La France du jazz: Musique, modernité et identité dans la première moitié du XXe siècle* (Marseille: Parenthèses, 2002), which includes a useful selection of articles from the period.

narrative progressively away from contest and toward assimilation. Two, they tend to assume that integration is necessarily a progressive move, rather than one that may itself be directed toward quasi-nationalist or colonialist agendas. Thus Jackson's premise—that "making jazz French" signals an openness to outside influences rather than, say, a desire to absorb and hence defuse them—does not always seem sound. And I am not convinced that the issue of jazz's potential "Frenchness" was settled in the affirmative as soon as Jackson and Jordan think it was (one side or the other of World War II).

For the story of African Americans and their music in France is a process of cultural mediation caught, like French society itself, between conflicting desires: to be "authentic" to racial and national roots, but at the same time to assimilate threatening differences. Throughout the period, otherness fostered both superficial appeal and deep-seated fears about race and nation: "ambivalent desire," as Brett A. Berliner has succinctly captured it.[38] Rather than narrating the story, with Blake, as one of an exotic appeal that subsides and is then rejected, or, with Jackson and Jordan, of an early hostility that progressively gives way to assimilation, I prefer to think of the reception of African American music and musicians as always encompassing multiple contradictory positions. There is change, of course, as the discussion focuses and refocuses on differing musics and issues, but there may also be greater continuity in French reactions than is often suggested.[39]

I take up themes of sameness and difference in chapter 2, in which I turn my attention away from singers and dancers and toward show and dance bands. If the presence in the flesh of performers from the *revues nègres* represented one aspect of jazz in interwar Paris, the circulation of mainly white jazz-band recordings on 78 rpm discs represented quite another. This chapter focuses on the unlikely "King of Jazz" in 1920s and

38. Berliner, *Ambivalent Desire.*

39. Both Jackson and Jordan also have a slightly more abstract sense of discourse than I do. While a belief in the life of written texts beyond their authors and immediate context is obviously essential to a historical study of reception, I try here to keep in quite close contact with specific performers and performances (to the extent that these can be reconstructed). This is why I prefer tracing localized performance histories to surveying broad categories such as "jazz." As well as giving more attention to specific performers and their music, a spotlight helps to reveal how production and reception were involved in a reciprocal relationship. (On the other hand, both Jackson and Jordan pay rather more attention than I do to how and where the music was typically heard: their studies of cultural geography and technologies of transmission in particular reward close attention.)

1930s France, British bandleader Jack Hylton, beginning with his 1931 concert at the Paris Opéra. Re-embodying, then assimilating, Paul Whiteman records, Hylton and "His Boys" toured Europe to great acclaim—a success lost to most research, which focuses on black musicians in the name of authenticity. Mistaken for Americans, however, the band's popularity began to wane as resistance to US dominance mounted. They were then often criticized for their "standardization" of a "dehumanized" musical "formula"—language borrowed from a pervasive anti-Americanism.

Two seemingly paradoxical alternatives conspired to dethrone Hylton, I argue. On the one hand, bands such as Ray Ventura et ses Collégiens offered a "national" jazz with great nostalgic appeal. On the other, African American musicians found support from the influential critic Hugues Panassié and his—more or less racial—distinction between "hot" (black) and "straight" (white) jazz. Audiences learned to perceive in both new models a depth and authenticity in contradistinction from the Hylton "product": an ironic turn given his constant shadowy presence as performer or impresario (for example, when Coleman Hawkins and Duke Ellington visited). In chapter 2, I thus seek to understand how an increasingly international recording industry was experienced at the local level, in a complex interaction with both live performance and French tradition. Its impact, I suggest, was neither all pervasive nor altogether resistible (thus a form of what is sometimes now called "glocalization").

There has, of course, been increasing interest in recent years in the history of American musics outside the United States. I can only give a hint of the diverse literature here, but this diasporic approach is proving powerful in analyzing both the musical transformations that take place across borders and the unexpected significations the music sometimes takes on.[40] Coming in quite large part from outside musicology or ethnomusicology, these studies typically consider jazz in terms of Americanization and modernity, whether experienced by people around the world as liberating forces or imperialistic ones. Closer to my disciplinary base, a

40. Among this literature are E. Taylor Atkins, ed., *Jazz Planet* (Jackson: University Press of Mississippi, 2003); Atkins, *Blue Nippon: Authenticating Jazz in Japan* (Durham, NC: Duke University Press, 2001); Luca Cerchiari, Laurent Cugny, and Franz Kerschbaumer, eds., *Eurojazzland: Jazz and European Sources, Dynamics, and Contexts* (Boston: Northeastern University Press, 2012); Bruce Johnson, *The Inaudible Music: Jazz, Gender and Australian Modernity* (Sydney: Currency Press, 2000); Andrew F. Jones, *Yellow Music: Media Culture and Colonial Modernity in the Chinese Jazz Age* (Durham, NC: Duke University Press, 2001); and Neil A. Wynn, ed., *Cross the Water Blues: African American Music in Europe* (Jackson: University Press of Mississippi, 2007).

utopian impulse is sometimes witnessed in writings on global jazz, one I find difficult to reconcile with even a cursory examination of economic and political power relations.[41] Other scholarship on popular music and dance has been more incisive in its analysis of the transatlantic relationship, and specifically in theorizing ideas of black internationalism and modernism.[42] In the French context, such work naturally intersects with research in colonial arenas, particularly in terms of readings of literature and film. Here, France's unusual proclivity to cast its imperial aggression in cultural rather than religious, political, or capitalist terms has been tested (and usually found wanting).[43]

An almost constant point of reference in this work, bridging African American contexts and French colonial ones, is Josephine Baker: the performer from St. Louis, Missouri, who first visited France, then stayed, and finally adopted French citizenship, while often playing roles as colonial subjects. Her fascinating career—and the large literature already devoted to it—motivates a change of pace in chapter 3. Although contrasting performances from as many as fifty years apart, I focus above all on her unlikely 1934 revival of Offenbach's *La Créole*. Wrapping original and revised texts, reception, and biography together in the operetta's plot, I consider how the same tensions that characterize French reactions to "others" and their music in the previous two chapters play themselves out on the level of theatrical narrative. *La Créole*, I argue, at once completed the construction and tested the limits of a complex redefinition of Baker as French.

If most observers saw Baker's transformation as an affirmation of France's "civilizing mission," the few dissenters paradoxically risked insisting on her difference in terms of an essentialized blackness. A com-

41. For more on this point, see my review of *Jazz Consciousness: Music, Race, and Humanity* by Paul Austerlitz (Middletown, CT: Wesleyan University Press, 2005), *Music and Letters* 88 (2007): 335–40.

42. See, inter alia, Paul Gilroy, *The Black Atlantic: Modernity and Double Consciousness* (London: Verso, 1993); and Jayna Brown, *Babylon Girls: Black Women Performers and the Shaping of the Modern* (Durham, NC: Duke University Press, 2008).

43. Peter J. Bloom, *French Colonial Documentary: Mythologies of Humanitarianism* (Minneapolis: University of Minnesota Press, 2008); Brent Hayes Edwards, *The Practice of Diaspora: Literature, Translation, and the Rise of Black Internationalism* (Cambridge, MA: Harvard University Press, 2003); T. Denean Sharpley-Whiting, *Black Venus: Sexualized Savages, Primal Fears, and Primitive Narratives in French* (Durham, NC: Duke University Press, 1999); Dina Sherzer, ed., *Cinema, Colonialism, Postcolonialism: Perspectives from the French and Francophone World* (Austin: University of Texas Press, 1996); and David Henry Slavin, *Colonial Cinema and Imperial France, 1919–1939: White Blind Spots, Male Fantasies, Settler Myths* (Baltimore, MD: Johns Hopkins University Press, 2001).

parison with other musical treatments of a similar story (*Carmen, Madama Butterfly*) and contemporary Baker films (*Princesse Tam-Tam, Zouzou*) reveal the unhappy logic of their argument. Recognizing both "savage" and "civilized" personas as witty performances relocates Baker's agency. Her virtuosity may even help to move beyond fixed racial categories toward dynamic cultural processes: "creolization." While Baker was highly skilled at mediating audience expectations, however, she was never wholly able to escape them. To this day, celebrations of Baker as an African American heroine contrast with perceptions of her as a sign of successful French assimilation: a tension that may be witnessed in a recent restaging of *La Créole*, presented both in mainland France and in one of its overseas territories, with which I conclude chapter 3.

African American music in France in the middle years of the twentieth century has, rather surprisingly, received less sustained attention than that of the interwar years. (This is in part, no doubt, because composers of art music—for a long time the only ones able to smuggle jazz into musicology—had by this time ceased to engage it so overtly.) Nevertheless, Ludovic Tournès's extraordinary *New Orleans sur Seine*, while ostensibly covering the whole century, is rooted in the 1940s and 1950s. As a historian, Tournès, like Jackson, is particularly attentive to the infrastructure of French jazz (venues, media, education, etc.) and looks past anecdote to match cause with effect. He also provides some quantitative analysis, sharing invaluable statistics (about concert attendance, for example) on which I occasionally draw. Tournès's survey of the development and ideologies of French jazz criticism provides a superb map of the territory, some of which I cover closer to the ground in the pages that follow. In this sense, his strength is also his weakness: Tournès's attention to institutional and critical factors, combined with his sheer scope, constrains the possibility for nuanced musical discussion. Nevertheless, his remains the most profound study of jazz on French soil, and in the latter stages of this book in particular, I owe a huge debt to it.[44]

Tournès's discussion of the "diffusion," "acculturation," and "legitimation" of jazz in France broadly supports Jackson's and Jordan's views of a steady naturalization. The three authors differ on the moment such as-

44. Ludovic Tournès, *New Orleans sur Seine: Histoire du jazz en France* (Paris: Librairie Arthème Fayard, 1999). For a more detailed consideration, see my article "Beyond Le Bœuf." Among other books on this period, see Gérard Régnier, *Jazz et société sous l'Occupation* (Paris: L'Harmattan, 2009), which is the most detailed study of jazz during the war (and is discussed in chap. 4 below); and Colin Nettelbeck, *Dancing with DeBeauvoir*, which focuses on the postwar period from a literary perspective.

similation is supposed to have been achieved, however, in part because Tournès concentrates on institutional and critical factors, where Jordan in particular pays more attention to an assessment of public sentiment. The turning point, Jordan argues, was the war, after which opposition to jazz became virtually impossible for right-thinking French. I disagree on this point, as it happens, for reasons that will become apparent in chapter 4. But more importantly, I disagree with the premise that this assimilation could ever be complete, or that it would be a sign above all of modernity among the French. (Indeed, there's a certain irony in Jordan's description of Jackson's isolation of the interwar period as a "historical fiction," while he apparently takes as axiomatic himself that the post-WWII world was fundamentally different from the prewar one.)[45] Apart from anything else, the hypothesis of jazz's postwar assimilation is impossible to test, since it soon cedes its place in popular culture to rhythm and blues and rock 'n' roll, so the discussion about the influx of (African) American culture simply moves elsewhere.

I tackle aspects of the war, in chapter 4, by means of a sideways glance at France's most celebrated jazz export, Django Reinhardt. I view him first via his surrogate, Emmet Ray, in Woody Allen's "mockumentary" *Sweet and Lowdown* (1999). This movie helps me to unpick one of the riddles of Reinhardt's life: how his greatest success could come during the Nazi occupation of Paris. I borrow a narrative device from the film to present three conflicting versions of jazz's fate at this time: that the music was expelled tout court; that it survived on the margins as the sound of resistance; and that it was tolerated, thanks to careful positioning by critics, but covertly contested the regime. None hold up under scrutiny, I find, linked as they are by what Henry Rousso has called France's "Resistancialist myth."[46] Rather, jazz prospered in wartime France, and the terms in which it was defended evolved naturally out of prewar discourse.

If the nationalistic language that framed Django Reinhardt's success was scarcely original, however, paradoxically his wartime music often sounded newly brassy and American. Some might locate resistance in that gap; others would, on the contrary, recognize a collaborating opportunist. This dispute, I argue, is anachronistic. After France's collapse, jazz was often associated with "national regeneration," a phrase that had no firm political affiliation. Django Reinhardt, then, became an unlikely herald of a reinvigorated New France. The only question was, under whose regime would it be?

45. Jordan, "Introduction," 13.

46. Henry Rousso, *The Vichy Syndrome: History and Memory in France since 1944*, trans. Arthur Goldhammer (Cambridge, MA: Harvard University Press, 1991).

Across chapters 4 and 5, I become progressively more engaged in how the story of jazz itself is remembered and retold. Jazz studies' important ongoing work on historiography and criticism is too big a field to survey here.[47] But it bears restating that the international dimension of early jazz writing has yet properly to be explored.[48] A partial but prescient exception is James Lincoln Collier's controversial *The Reception of Jazz in America*, which does require brief discussion. "The history of jazz," he stated as long ago as 1988, "has been plagued by two myths": "The first . . . says that the American people, until relatively recently, have ignored or despised jazz, . . . the second . . . that it was first taken seriously by Europeans."[49] Collier goes on to complain that he had not found a single comment post-1940 on the popularity of jazz in the States, and nothing since 1935 suggesting that jazz was better treated at home than abroad. As such, he calls attention to the one-sided nature of accounts of jazz in Europe, a characterization that still largely stands twenty-five years later, as I've indicated above.

While recuperating early American critics, however, Collier ignores or brushes over European articles of the early years. For him, there simply was no *real* jazz in Europe from the Original Dixieland Jazz Band's tour of 1919 to Louis Armstrong's first visit in 1932—a restrictive definition that is not only essentialist but ahistorical. Collier's endeavor to explain the "myths" he addresses, then, takes a strange turn: he denounces some of America's most important jazz critics—including John Hammond, Otis Ferguson, and Rudi Blesh—as Communist sympathizers, who promoted the story of the United States' lack of interest in its cultural resources to political ends. Meanwhile, Collier's handling of race issues witnesses a cultivated naïvety.[50] I intervene in this discussion in chapter 5, less by ad-

47. Many issues were initially brought to light by Scott DeVeaux in "Constructing the Jazz Tradition: Jazz Historiography," *Black American Literature Forum* 25 (1991): 525–60 [also reprinted in Robert O'Meally, ed., *The Jazz Cadence of American Culture* (New York: Columbia University Press, 1998), 485–514]. Recent, extended studies include John Gennari, *Blowin' Hot and Cool: Jazz and Its Critics* (Chicago: University of Chicago Press, 2006); and Bruce Boyd Raeburn, *New Orleans Style and the Writing of American Jazz History* (Ann Arbor: University of Michigan Press, 2009).

48. As acknowledged by Gennari, *Blowin' Hot and Cool*, 15–16.

49. James Lincoln Collier, *The Reception of Jazz in America: A New View* (Brooklyn, NY: Institute for Studies in American Music, 1988), 1–2. See also Laurent Cugny, "Did Europe 'Discover' Jazz?," in Cerchiari, Cugny, and Kerschbaumer, *Eurojazzland*, 301–41.

50. As Pete Martin has said: "Anyone who doesn't subscribe to the Ronald Reagan school of historiography is likely to get quite angry" (Pete Martin, "Essay Review," *Popular Music* 9 [1990]: 139–44 [quote on p. 144]). John Gennari similarly de-

judicating between American and European writers than by revealing the broader views and influences behind some critics' positions. I also seek to understand what—contrasting—purposes French writers and African American musicians may have had in perpetuating the idea of European prescience about jazz.

Chapter 5 concerns the unusual career of Sidney Bechet, the New Orleans reedman who occupies a special position among émigré musicians in France. Appearing first in 1919, he is a focus of Ernest Ansermet's celebrated review of the Southern Syncopated Orchestra; in 1925 Bechet helped to launch Josephine Baker to international stardom. Iconic moments in retrospect, but Ansermet's text is not, I show, as trusty a symbol of Europeans' acute perceptions of jazz as historians have long assumed, and Bechet's true rise to fame came not until a Gallic version of the New Orleans Revival Movement in the 1940s and 1950s—"Bechetmania" as it has been called.

No straightforward revivalist, Bechet played versions of old Creole folk songs—or their ur-type—that divided critics. But these tunes struck a chord with French audiences, generating nostalgia for a common past that may never have been. Bechet, too, was busy reshaping history: appropriating an old folktale to write himself into the very foundations of jazz. In the end, though, it is the gap between the musician's and his audience's perspectives that proves most illuminating: Bechet was not reliving the past for its own sake but rather remaking it for the current day—even, in his crazed reception by French teenagers, anticipating the popular music of the future. It is appropriate that Bechet should play the last chorus of *Paris Blues*: bridging my period, his story best exemplifies the range of experience of African American musicians in France, and in turn reveals some of the paradoxes of their music's historiography.

*   *   *

Pulling together the various strands set out above, *Paris Blues* offers an alternative history of African American music and musicians in France, one that looks beyond a few familiar personalities and well-rehearsed stories. It does not dismiss these images, but it asks how they came to be

scribes Collier's as a "quasi-McCarthyite reading" (John Gennari, "Jazz Criticism: Its Development and Ideology," *Black American Literature Forum* 25 [1991]: 449–523 [quote at p. 514n27]). And Amiri Baraka complains that Collier's "various writings give off a distinct aroma of rotting mint julep" (Amiri Baraka, "Jazz Criticism and Its Effect on the Art Form," in *New Perspectives on Jazz*, ed. David N. Baker [Washington, DC: Smithsonian Institution Press, 1990], 55–70 [quote on p. 65]).

so iconic, and what they hide as well as what they preserve. While some chapters actively contest received wisdom, others present complementary stories that complicate current understanding. As Norman Davies has stated recently, "The task of the historian . . . goes beyond the duty of tending the generalized memory. When a few events in the past are remembered pervasively, to the exclusion of equally deserving subjects, there is a need . . . to stray from the beaten track and to recover some of the less fashionable memory sites."[51] Thus familiar figures feature prominently, but in unfamiliar contexts: Josephine Baker singing Offenbach, Django Reinhardt in occupied Paris, Sidney Bechet swinging through the fifties. If these choices surprise today, each I am sure captured the popular imagination at the time, which has been my central guide.

A few more points may usefully be made about my approach. Most important, *Paris Blues* does not pretend to deal with African American lives (or indeed French ones) from the inside out. On the contrary, it considers how those musicians were perceived and represented by audiences in Paris, as this was reflected in public discourse. While I do make a point of engaging in some detail with the qualities of particular performances, my purpose is above all to consider the reception of black music making among the French. Only rarely therefore do I refer to the sources that often constitute the mainstay of jazz writing: the reminiscences of performers. As suggested above, these have already been well represented in the literature. But the value of these accounts, to me, lies not primarily in their accurate representation of events, but in the sense they give of lives lived—or, more exactly, relived. This is not, at a stroke, to discount musicians' memoirs as access points to the past, but simply to observe that the production of these texts has its own historical context, which is frequently ignored when they are marshaled as evidence. Thus in my discussion of Sidney Bechet's autobiography in chapter 5, I am much more concerned with what can be gleaned of the saxophonist's perspective at the time the book was written (and rewritten) than I am in the earlier period he ostensibly describes. Otherwise, confirming or contesting musicians' accounts on a point-by-point basis would seem to me not only churlish but also rather to misunderstand their nature as artifacts.

If personal testimonies are fraught with difficulties as sources of historical knowledge, contemporary documents may be little more transpar-

---

51. Norman Davies, *Vanished Kingdoms: The History of Half-Forgotten Europe* (London: Allen Lane, 2011), 8. I don't, incidentally, share the author's horror at the decline of classical and religious education, which is only the immediate context for these remarks.

ent. Some observations may, however, help to assuage the gravest concerns. As detailed elsewhere, I have benefited in my research from the extraordinary resources of various Parisian archives: the many texts I cite represent a tiny corner of those consulted and that served to shape my views. As well as sheer volume, these collections draw on an unusually wide range of publications. This has helped to widen the scope of this study beyond intellectual or "high-cultural" reactions to popular culture (whose centrality in scholarly accounts is a common problem). In addition, it is sometimes possible to read through reviews to other reactions: negative commentators may chastise an enthusiastic audience; positive writers may berate their indifference—or simply note that people had stayed at home. Of course, my arguments are, no less than others', historical judgments: attempts to fit explanations to evidence, to derive facts from figures. Among a myriad of materials, I identify particular constellations that seem to provide the most illuminating insights into a moment from the past (and to have the weight of evidence on their side).[52]

Nevertheless, there are inherent ethical dangers in my project, ones I've been keenly aware of during research and writing. The extraordinary achievements of African American performers could be diminished or even overwhelmed by the weight of conflicting stories and critical perspectives brought to bear on them. Worse still, my work might serve to reinstitute the objectification of black entertainers that it sometimes decries. As I've indicated, the musicians themselves are rarely the objects of my study here, however. My concern is rather with the ideas that accrued around them, as a record of social attitudes in this period. "It's something, the white imagination, when it comes to blacks," Josephine Baker is once supposed to have said.[53] What I seek to do here is to probe that imagination, as it manifested itself in a particular time and place. If I can offer little by way of simple celebration, I hope at least that there are insights to be found in my lines of inquiry, and that I've made my purpose for conducting them clear throughout.

52. Unlike some studies in French reception history, I engage with politics as only one issue among many, rarely finding it the prime concern. The leanings of particular papers and journalists are not systematically discussed, therefore; only when they become directly relevant do I thematize such issues. On the French press, see Claude Bellanger et al., *Histoire générale de la presse française*, vol. 3, *De 1871 à 1940* (Paris: Presses Universitaires de France, 1972); and Bellanger et al., *Histoire générale de la presse française*, vol. 4, *De 1940 à 1958* (Paris: Presses Universitaires de France, 1975).

53. Baker and Sauvage, *Voyages et aventures*, 16.

I also resist the temptation to impose too grand a narrative on the noisy babble of the past. While the particularities of individual cases may frustrate attempts to generalize, for me they also provide the greatest interest in grappling with history. The peculiarities of given moments are thus awarded as much attention here as are patterns and transitions. To the extent that I engage with theories of cultural contact and change—hybridity, creolization, glocalization, and so on—I do so neither as methodological contexts nor as concluding validations. Rather, I deal with them as ideas, often ideas with their own important lineages, which I hope shed some light on the matter at hand. Meanwhile, other vital recent topics, such as the transatlantic origins of modernism and black internationalism, remain beyond the scope of this study: my focus throughout, and deliberately, is on France and specifically Paris, and on popular culture, primarily music. I would not want to imply a level of generalizability of these experiences that I cannot in fact demonstrate.

I am, however, concerned to highlight the continued relevance of some, ostensibly distant, issues raised in this book. One of the ways I seek to achieve this is by considering their recurrence or representation in recent films—recourse to which I make a number of times, as will already be apparent. This is not, I should point out, to confuse their visualizations with the pasts they purport to show, any more than I mistake recent writings by historians and critics for the sources on which they draw. Nor does it imply that I underestimate how much has changed over recent decades (although I do believe that commonalities across time, considered with caution, can be as revealing as differences). More important, I believe that the historical process is—always and necessarily—one of shuttling between past and present perspectives, in which the researcher desires access to earlier perceptions but always reads them through the lens of current times.

The troubling fact that history is written backward from the present is not, I suggest, something that can be overcome by a heroic act of scholarly re-creation: it is the very condition (and paradox) of history writing, at once its confounding flaw as a scientific enterprise and its greatest asset as a humanistic pursuit. Meanwhile, the imaginative work that movies and other forms of popular chronicling do cannot simply be circumvented. These media are pervasive, so it's more productive to engage them in critical dialogue than to leave them uninterrogated.[54] By discussing

54. For similar arguments, see David Harlan, "Ken Burns and the Coming Crisis of Academic History," *Rethinking History* 7 (2003): 169–92; and Harlan, "Historical Fiction and the Future of Academic History," in *Manifestos for History*, ed. Keith Jenkins, Sue Morgan, and Alun Munslow (London: Routledge, 2007), 108–30.

films—ones I've found myself thinking about a great deal while writing this book—as well as occasionally placing myself on the scene of the research, I endeavor to make my role in the enterprise explicit. This, to me, is a more intellectually honest approach than to seek to remain hidden behind the text.

Whatever the subtexts of the movie *Paris Blues*, argued the great figure of American letters Albert Murray, "Ellington and Armstrong proceeded as if they had simply been provided yet another occasion to play the kind of marvelous good-time music that *keeps the blues at bay in the very process of acknowledging that they are ever present*" (my italics).[55] This is a restatement of Murray's familiar position: that African American music is art(ifice), not the "natural" expression of untutored performers, nor music of primarily sociopolitical significance; it is music of celebration, not of consolation. On the other hand, romantic notions of the autonomy of art, or utopian ones of achieving community through music, risk ignoring the impact of social inequities on the production and reception of black music. My study might therefore occupy a similar paradox to the one Murray identifies: it aims to exorcize some ghosts, but at the same time to commemorate the lives and art of the musicians they haunted. I hope, in sum, to offer a challenging new account of the African American presence in Paris—one that celebrates achievement but does not shirk to identify the complex interplay of race, writing, and power in the construction of history.

A Note on Sources and Translations

This book draws extensively upon the resources of public archives. Collections are cited in full the first time they appear in a chapter; thereafter they are abbreviated. When quoting a source directly from an archive dossier, the file and call number are always specified since the library's own reference may be incomplete, illegible, or occasionally slightly inaccurate. If no such location is given, I have consulted the original publication or its reproduction.

Translations are my own unless otherwise stated. Block quotations are provided in French with English immediately below. Short, in-text

---

55. Albert Murray, "Armstrong and Ellington Stomping the Blues in Paris," in *The Blue Devils of Nada: A Contemporary American Approach to Aesthetic Statement* (New York: Random House, 1996), 97–113 (quote on p. 99). Murray's elegant essay considers how the soundtrack develops tropes of African American vernacular musics, notably trains, as well as the spirit of collaboration rather than of solitary artistic creation; it engages only in passing with the film's narrative.

citations appear in English alone, except where too much is lost in translation. Quotations in footnotes appear in the original language alone. Insignificant errors in French sources have been silently corrected, and accents and capitalization regularized according to current practice. Other aspects of the original typography are preserved wherever possible, particularly in titles, which therefore vary considerably.

Rethinking the *Revue nègre*

Black Musical Theatre after Josephine Baker

"Keepin' It Real": *Bamboozled* in Paris

Arriving in Paris one spring, early in the research for this book, I had a peculiar experience. As I thumbed through the week's entertainment listings in *Pariscope*, eager for a distraction from apartment hunting, two men in blackface stared out at me (fig. 1.1). They were presenting *The Very Black Show*, as Spike Lee's film *Bamboozled* was known in France. This polemic on the representation of African Americans had so far escaped my attention, so its release at the moment I returned to the city to research its history of black musical theatre was unnerving, perhaps even uncanny. Suddenly my subject seemed à la mode.

As its opening lines are anxious to establish, *Bamboozled* is a satire. Meticulously spoken Negro (his term) TV writer Pierre Delacroix (Damon Wayans) prefaces his desperate attempt to lose an insufferable job at ailing corporation CNS with a definition of that dramatic type. Gone are the days when he would write middle-class dramas and situation comedies that his boss Dunwitty (Michael Rapaport) could call "white people with black faces." With his "black wife and two biracial kids," Dunwitty has told Delacroix, "I . . . know niggers better than you": "Brother man, I'm blacker than you. I'm keepin' it real. . . . You're just frontin', tryin' to be white." Under such an edict to dig into his roots, Delacroix will deliver exactly what is expected of him: a very "black" show.

Mantan: The New Millennium Minstrel Show stars two African American street entertainers (tap dancer Savion Glover and comedian Tommy Davidson) whom Delacroix used to pass on his way to work. Renamed after stars of a former era, Mantan (for Mantan Moreland) and Sleep 'n' Eat (Willie Best's moniker) revive minstrel routines, complete with chickens and watermelons, in blackface and comic attire. "Two real coons," they call themselves (in honor of Williams and Walker), from a time when "nigras knew they place" [*sic*]. The studio audience look around nervously before they applaud; the film viewer's position is similarly uncomfortable. When I saw it in Paris, the cinemagoers, primarily people of color,

FIGURE 1.1. French publicity poster for *The Very Black Show* (*Bamboozled*), dir. Spike Lee (2000).

first laughed uproariously then gradually fell into silence. As Delacroix asks when told the network had taken his (supposedly satirical) show and "made it funnier": "Funnier to whom? And at whose expense?"

While the principal target of Lee's ire is the white-dominated entertainment industry, which perpetuates racist stereotypes, *Bamboozled* is by no means singular in its attack. Regardless of his original intent, Delacroix becomes complicit, as does his ambitious assistant, Sloan Hopkins (Jada Pinkett-Smith). She's a "house-nigger" "working hard for the man on the plantation," according to her brother Julius, a.k.a. Big Blak Afrika (hip-hop artist Mos Def). But he and his band of quasi-revolutionary gangsta rappers, the Mau Maus, are also ceaselessly lampooned, particularly in their empty-headed song "Blak iz Blak." While Sleep 'n' Eat and Mantan throw off success in renunciation of the minstrel mask, the Mau Maus turn words into action and execute Mantan (live on TV and the Internet) for his treachery against the race.[1] By now, the viewer might legitimately ask if Spike Lee's satire has not itself lapsed into stereotype. That, of course, is precisely the point: for African American performers (and directors), minstrelsy is at once an unavoidable, sometimes desirable, reference and a dangerous, often destructive, force.[2]

My interest in *Bamboozled* is more than anecdotal. The film asks some important questions that resonate with this chapter. How is "black culture" defined and who may access it? When does "authenticity" become stereotype? To what extent can African Americans control their representation on stage and screen? The history and legacy of minstrelsy is a fraught topic, but one that can now lay claim to a sophisticated literature bridging several disciplines.[3] While raising public awareness of these is-

1. In his director's commentary, Lee is trenchant in his criticism of both gangsta rap and the violent radicalism he, perhaps inadvertently, associates with it (Spike Lee, "Audio Commentary," *Bamboozled*, dir. Spike Lee [Los Angeles, CA: New Line Home Video, 2001], DVD).

2. On *Bamboozled*, see inter alia, Gary Crowdus and Dan Georgakas, "Thinking about the Power of Images: An Interview with Spike Lee," *Cineaste* 26/2 (2001): 4–9; Zeinabu irene Davis, Saul Landau, Cynthia Lucia, Michael Rogin, Greg Tate, and Armond White, "Race, Media and Money: A Critical Symposium on Spike Lee's *Bamboozled*," *Cineaste* 26/2 (2001): 10–17; Stanley Crouch, Eric Lott, Margo Jefferson, Clyde Taylor, and Michele Wallace, "Minding the Messenger: A Symposium on *Bamboozled*," *Black Renaissance / Renaissance Noire* 3/3 (Summer 2001): 9–32; Harry J. Elam Jr., "Spike Lee's *Bamboozled*," in *Black Cultural Traffic: Crossroads in Global Performance and Popular Culture*, ed. Harry J. Elam Jr. and Kennell Jackson (Ann Arbor: University of Michigan Press, 2005), 346–62; Beretta E. Smith-Shomade, "'I Be Smackin' My Hoes': Paradox and Authenticity in *Bamboozled*," in *The Spike Lee Reader*, ed. Paula J. Massood (Philadelphia: Temple University Press, 2008), 228–42; and Ed Guerrero, "*Bamboozled*: In the Mirror of Abjection," in *Contemporary Black American Cinema: Race, Gender and Sexuality at the Movies*, ed. Mia Mask (New York: Routledge, 2012), 109–27.

3. Among the growing literature on minstrelsy, essential volumes include Eric Lott, *Love and Theft: Blackface Minstrelsy and the American Working Class* (New York: Oxford University Press, 1993); Dale Cockrell, *Demons of Disorder: Early Blackface Minstrels and Their World* (Cambridge: Cambridge University Press, 1997); W. T. Lhamon Jr., *Raising Cain: Blackface Performance from Jim Crow to Hip Hop* (Cambridge, MA: Harvard University Press, 1998); William J. Mahar, *Behind the Burnt Cork Mask: Early Blackface Minstrelsy and Antebellum American Popular Culture* (Urbana: University of Illinois Press, 1999); Karen Sotiropoulos, *Staging Race: Black Performers in Turn of the Century America* (Cambridge, MA: Harvard University Press, 2006); and Stephen Johnson, ed., *Burnt Cork: Traditions and Legacies of Blackface Minstrelsy* (Amherst: University of Massachusetts Press, 2012).

sues, *Bamboozled*, some complained, failed to distinguish adequately between different contexts and eras: "who did what to whom," in the words of scholar Michele Wallace.[4] If minstrelsy traded in images that today are unpalatable, it did so in myriad circumstances and their politics were not always the same. Particularly at its nineteenth-century origins, it may have challenged social hierarchies as much as consolidated them, and affection as well as animosity drives the stereotypes; at least in part, minstrelsy functioned as a means to critique mainstream society from a position outside of it. The decline from satire into demeaning comedy seems almost to be topicalized, within the film world of *Bamboozled*, in the fall from grace of Delacroix's show.

These questions may have been well rehearsed in the American context, but in France they are much less frequently raised. Indeed, it is still fondly imagined in some quarters that African Americans escaped prejudice there and were welcomed by everyone as true artists. While the critical response to *Bamboozled* in France was mixed, therefore, most reviewers agreed that its relevance to them was limited if not lacking: they distanced the minstrel mask both geographically (a US phenomenon, ignoring the extent to which it had traveled) and historically (a nineteenth-century theatrical tradition, forgetting *Bamboozled*'s setting in contemporary TV). These "negative and often racist representation[s]," thought one writer, demonstrated "American show business's shameful past"; they were characteristic in particular of late nineteenth-century minstrelsy.[5] Another wondered why Lee rehearsed old grievances rather than taking the next step: the "relative advancement of current practices [mœurs]" would allow him to "mix colors or, better, to ignore them" without risking offense.[6] Race, critics seemed to argue, was an American problem, and at that one of the past.

More egalitarian online discussion lists offered contrasting views—ones in which French attitudes were implicated. One writer thought

4. See, notably, Michele Wallace, "*Bamboozled*: The Legacy," *Black Renaissance/Renaissance Noire* 3/3 (2001): 33–38 (quote on p. 33); and Wallace's contributions to Crouch et al., "Minding the Messenger."

5. Frédéric Bas, "*The Very Black Show (Bamboozled)*," *Chronic'art: Le Webmag culturel*, 18 March 2001, accessed 17 December 2012, http://www.chronicart.com/#!Article/Entree/Categorie/cinema/Id/the_very_black_show__bamboozled_-4899.sls. In fairness to this critic, he does go on to explain how these stereotypes were incorporated into film and TV.

6. Vincent Ostria, "*The Very Black Show* de Spike Lee," *L'Humanité*, 21 March 2001, accessed 17 December 2012, http://www.humanite.fr/node/403770.

Bamboozled the "best film for all self-respecting blacks to see"; a "lucid critique of the current position of blacks in the Western media," which was especially relevant "in France . . . where minorities must still caricature themselves to appear on TV." Another agreed: it represented a profound reflection on "the condition of blacks in France and in the world."[7] The fate of the movie with Parisian audiences, then, comes as little surprise: released in a handful of mainstream houses, it was soon showing in only one, Images d'Ailleurs, "premier espace cinéma black de Paris"—the cinematic equivalent of a ghetto.

Contemporary French representations of people of color are beyond the scope of my project.[8] But I do hope to fill one historical lacuna in the Paris reviews: the black shows of the 1920s and 1930s—a time when, the story goes, African Americans were in vogue in France. A scene eventually omitted from the movie might have made the point: a picture of a naked Josephine Baker adorns the wall of Mantan's dressing room.[9] But, a few stars excepted, memories are short; the connection runs much deeper. In fact, the original Mantan, Mantan Moreland, was among the many black entertainers who performed in the French capital during the *entre-deux-guerres*. Like it or not, the French are implicated in this history, if in different ways to Americans. In this chapter, I study a number of black shows, examining both their production and their reception in Paris in some detail, and endeavoring to understand the dialogue that took place between performers and audience.

Contexts and Controversies: *La Revue nègre*

One moment in particular was notable by its absence from the *Bamboozled* reviews: *La Revue nègre*, Josephine Baker's first Paris show, in 1925. Assembled in New York by white American Caroline Dudley, an all-black troupe famously performed putative scenes of African American life—"Mississippi Steam Boat Race," "New York Skyscraper," "Charleston

7. *"The Very Black Show (Bamboozled),"* *Allocine* online discussion forum, first accessed 1 May 2001, http://www.allocine.fr/film/fichefilm-27060/critiques/spectateurs/recentes/ (archived by author; some comments have subsequently been cut or curtailed).

8. But see, for example, Leora Auslander and Thomas C. Holt, "Sambo in Paris: Race and Racism in the Iconography of the Everyday," in *The Color of Liberty: Histories of Race in France*, ed. Sue Peabody and Tyler Stovall (Durham, NC: Duke University Press, 2003), 147–84.

9. "Deleted Scenes," Lee, *Bamboozled*.

Cabaret," and so on—on the stage of the Théâtre des Champs-Élysées.[10] So successful were they that theatre manager André Daven, director Jacques-Charles, and poster artist Paul Colin would all later be eager to claim a formative role. Baker's biographers have sometimes begun their narratives with *La Revue nègre*, although it was far from the beginning of her career.[11] Writers always give particular attention to Baker and Joe Alex's "Danse de sauvage," barely clad, in feathers—the most shocking routine of all. Certain descriptions—André Levinson's "black Venus that haunted Baudelaire," Janet Flanner's "unforgettable female ebony statue," even Robert de Flers's "lamentable transatlantic exhibitionism which has us reverting to the ape"—signify an almost apocalyptical moment.[12] Less often heard are the reactions of some of Baker's co-performers, who were "horrified at how disgusting Josie was behaving . . . doing her nigger routine": "She had no self-respect, no shame," complained one.[13] Acclaim and horror are juxtaposed, even combined, in the reviews: *La Revue nègre* represented equally "the most barbaric spectacle imaginable" and "the very quintessence of modernism."[14] No account of *les années folles* is complete without it.

Such is the actual and rhetorical importance assigned to *La Revue nègre* that it has come to represent both the apex of African American entertainment in Paris and, paradoxically, the crux of a reaction against it.[15] As

10. Two programs are in Ro 585, "Le Jazz et les spectacles nègres," docs. 9 and 10, Collection Rondel, Département des Arts du Spectacle, Bibliothèque Nationale, Paris (hereafter cited as Rondel), among other locations; a large amount of press material is in Ro 15702(3), "Le Champs-Élysées Music-Hall," Rondel. It is often forgotten that *La Revue nègre* was only the second half of the show: a regular round of variety acts (renewed several times during the run) preceded it.

11. This ploy is used in both Phyllis Rose, *Jazz Cleopatra: Josephine Baker in Her Time* (New York: Vintage Books, 1991); and Jean-Claude Baker and Chris Chase, *Josephine: The Hungry Heart* (New York: Random House, 1993).

12. See, for example, Rose, *Jazz Cleopatra*, 31–32. The sources of these quotations are "Paris ou New-York? Douglas; La Vénus noire," *Comœdia*, 12 October 1925; Janet Flanner, *Paris Was Yesterday: 1925–1939* (New York: Viking, 1972), xx; and Robert de Flers, "La Semaine dramatique," *Le Figaro*, 16 December 1925.

13. Lydia Jones, cited in Baker and Chase, *Josephine*, 6.

14. Martial Perrier, review of *La Revue nègre*, *L'Avenir*, 6 October 1925; Philippe d'Olon, "Au Champs-Élysées Music-Hall: Damia, Gabaroche, La Revue nègre," *Le Soir*, 1 November 1925 (both are in Ro 15702[3], "Le Champs-Élysées Music-Hall," Rondel).

15. For discussions of *La Revue nègre*, see, in addition to the biographical literature on Baker (cited in chap. 3), Ramsay Burt, " 'Savage' Dancer: Tout Paris Goes to See Josephine Baker," in *Alien Bodies: Representations of Modernity, "Race" and Nation*

is well-known, the show was the last all-black affair in which Baker performed, and the only one in France. While she moved on to feature as an exotic star at the Folies-Bergère and Casino de Paris, most of the troupe had soon returned home. *La Revue nègre* thus serves as the mythologized origin of a star who comes to stand for—becomes synonymous with—African American show business in Paris. Typical is a republication of Paul Colin's 1927 lithograph series, *Le Tumulte noir*, renamed *Josephine Baker and "La Revue nègre."*[16] Although it includes several images of Baker, this is not a portrayal of the Champs-Élysées show but a survey of black music and dancing in Paris. More than just marketing, the confusion extends to an introductory essay by Karen Dalton and Henry Louis Gates. Set on a one-track path, they misidentify as Baker the final image, of entertainer Adelaide Hall (about whom more below), and fail to notice that two others are not unknown revelers but familiar figures on the French stage, Joe Alex and Hal Sherman, respectively (the latter was in fact white).[17]

Worse, if Baker was the only real black star in Paris, as the authors suggest, even her appeal was not to last. While acknowledging the images' sometimes questionable connotations, Dalton and Gates insist that they represent a last flowering of racial tolerance: an expression, in their words, of "the communal sigh of relief African Americans exhaled" in this "color-blind land of tolerance" where "they could savor the freedom of feeling like a human being for the very first time."[18] They quickly about-face: "This climate of openness would not last, however. Already in 1921, what became known as 'The Call to Order' . . . [was] admonishing a return

---

in *Early Modern Dance* (London: Routledge, 1998), 57–83; Gerard Le Coat, "Art nègre, jazz nègre, revue nègre," in *Carrefour de cultures: Mélanges offerts à Jacqueline Leiner,* ed. Régis Antoine (Tübingen, Ger.: Gunter Narr Verlag, 1993), 23–34; Jean-Claude Klein, "Swings: *La Revue nègre,*" in *Entre deux guerres: La Création française entre 1919 et 1939,* ed. Olivier Barrot and Pascal Ory (Paris: François Bourin, 1990), 363–77; Carole Sweeney, " 'I'll Say It's Getting Darker and Darker in Paris': Josephine Baker and *La Revue Nègre,*" in *From Fetish to Subject: Race, Modernism, and Primitivism, 1919–1935* (Westport, CT: Praeger, 2004), 37–54; and Glenn Watkins, "Josephine and Jonny," in *Pyramids at the Louvre: Music, Culture, and Collage from Stravinsky to the Postmodernists* (Cambridge, MA: Belknap Press of Harvard University Press, 1994), 134–63.

16. *Josephine Baker and "La Revue nègre": Paul Colin's Lithographs of "Le Tumulte noir" in Paris, 1927,* with an introduction by Henry Louis Gates Jr. and Karen C. C. Dalton (New York: Harry N. Abrams, 1998).

17. No great detective work was required on my part here: the performers' names are penciled on the pictures! A version of this essay also appears as Karen C. C. Dalton and Henry Louis Gates Jr., "Josephine Baker and Paul Colin: African American Dance Seen through Parisian Eyes," *Critical Inquiry* 24 (1998): 903–34.

18. *Josephine Baker and "La Revue nègre,"* 4.

to French 'classical' traditions and a rejection of . . . foreign influences. . . .
Throughout Europe, resentment mounted. . . . And although the National
Socialist party would not come to power in Germany until 1933, the first
volume of Adolf Hitler's *Mein Kampf* had already appeared in 1925."[19] Here
both chronology and geography are distorted in order to locate an incipient conservatism, if not fascism. More judicious but in broad agree-
ment, Jody Blake also thinks *La Revue nègre* was seminal: it "secured the
triumph of African American music and dance and unleashed the back-
lash against it"; it "gave added momentum . . . to a Call to Order in popular entertainment."[20] Both Blake and other authors find support for this
argument in contemporary statements now dismissing jazz by composers
such as Darius Milhaud.[21] In effect, they narrate an end to cosmopolitan
postwar ebullience and an anticipation of the cultural politics of the collaborating Vichy regime.

But was *La Revue nègre* so unique? Less often cited than occasional
writers "slumming" for the "snob" value, the most experienced music-hall
critics, such as Gustave Fréjaville, were more measured in their praise: "It's
a small event, in the history of Parisian music hall. . . . To tell the truth,
we had already seen just about all this in detail, either in variety acts, or
in revues."[22] The originality of *La Revue nègre* came less in nature than in
degree: for the first time, black performers were occupying a French stage
for an entire act (though still not an entire show). Fréjaville could trace
a tradition of African American music and dance in Paris right back to
cakewalkers at the beginning of the century. Aside from jazz musicians
(generally interval entertainment), recent examples multiplied. Two of
Baker's costars in *La Revue nègre*, Louis Douglas and Joe Alex, were already
familiar.[23] Usually, as here, performing in blackface, Douglas had been part
of two duos: first with Fernando Jones, then with his wife Marion Cook;

19. Ibid., 12.

20. Jody Blake, *Le Tumulte noir: Modernist Art and Popular Entertainment in Jazz-
Age Paris, 1900–1930* (University Park: Pennsylvania State University Press, 1999),
91, 100.

21. See, for example, Watkins, *Pyramids at the Louvre*, 161–62.

22. Gustave Fréjaville, "Chronique de la semaine," *Comœdia*, 8 October 1925, in
Ro 16443(3), "Fréjaville, Gustave: Petite Chronique du music-hall, etc.," Rondel.
Among other reviews placing the show in context is Paul Granet, "Une Revue
nègre," unidentified periodical, 18 October 1925, in Ro 15702(3), "Le Champs-Élysées
Music-Hall," Rondel.

23. The program in fact names Douglas as director, although it is hard to determine how much input he had in the face of interference from Dudley, Daven,
Jacques-Charles, and Colin.

according to one critic, he was the true "pioneer of this Negro American civilization" in Paris.[24] Perhaps more significant, the year before *La Revue nègre*, a whole troupe of "Coloured Girls" had provided chimney sweeps and chocolate drops for a Moulin Rouge show that had also featured the "danseur noire burlesque" Tommy Wood.[25] Fréjaville thought that they had "prepared [French eyes] for several of the effects of Josephine Baker and her companions." Among other performers he might have cited are "blacrobats" Mutt and Jeff, Will Garland (and his "troupe de créoles"), "le jongleur mulâtre" Rowland, and the misnamed Peggy Leblanc, "fantaisiste, danseuse nègre et chanteuse acrobatique"; it is unclear if in all cases these were Americans.[26]

If black performers were not a terribly rare sight prior to *La Revue nègre*, neither did they disappear thereafter. Even limiting the field to the larger black troupes—to *revues nègres*—African American performers were a recurrent feature of Parisian music hall throughout the *entre-deux-guerres*, the Call to Order notwithstanding. Far from falling out of fashion, subsequent shows may have infiltrated French *popular* culture more deeply

24. Legrand-Chabrier, "Sous les projecteurs: Cirques—music-hall," unidentified periodical, 6 June 1926, in Ro 18740, "La Revue des Ambassadeurs, 1926," Rondel. On Douglas and Cook, see, for example, material on the music-hall revue *Toute nue*, in Ro 18685, "La Revue du Concert Mayol, 1924," Rondel; and on Douglas and Jones, that on *Bonsoâr* [*sic*], in Ro 18632, "La Revue de Ba-Ta-Clan, 1923," Rondel. On the latter, see also André Levinson, *La Danse au théâtre: Esthétique et actualité mêlées* (Paris: Librairie Blond et Gay, 1924), 218, 224; and Fernand Divoire, *Découvertes sur la danse* (Paris: G. Crès, 1924), 189. Meanwhile, Joe Alex's performances have been traced as far back as 1918, when he appeared in a boxing match of his own choreography at the Olympia Theatre (Denise Pilmer Taylor, "*La Musique pour tout le monde*: Jean Wiéner and the Dawn of French Jazz" [PhD diss., University of Michigan, 1998], 65n).

25. The program for this show, *La Grande Revue du Moulin Rouge*, which includes a scene in "Darktown: Quartier nègre de New-York," is in Ro 15743, "Le Moulin Rouge," Rondel. Reviews, which focus more on a white American troupe, the Hoffman Girls, are in Ro 18688, "La Revue du Moulin Rouge, 1924," Rondel.

26. One of the best sources on the Parisian music hall in these years is Fréjaville's weekly/fortnightly column in *Comœdia* (many of which are collected in Ro 16443, "Fréjaville, Gustave," Rondel; and/or in "Collection Fréjaville," particularly G. F. IX[1–2], "Articles parus dans divers journaux," Département des Arts du Spectacle, Bibliothèque Nationale, Paris, hereafter cited as AdS). Cited here are, respectively, "Petite Chronique du music-hall," 16 September 1920, 23 June 1920, and 31 December 1919; and "Chronique de la semaine," 12 March 1925 (all are in Ro 16443, "Fréjaville, Gustave," Rondel).

than the original.[27] Sketching their history opens an illuminating window on race and representation in Paris, specifically a process of cultural negotiation between African Americans and the French. In what follows, I begin by showing how primitivist stereotypes of old were confronted and gradually displaced by alternative models of "civilized" and "spiritual" black people. I then consider how this range of behaviors came to be theorized in terms of discourses of hybridity (not, historically, the panacea contemporary theory would sometimes wish it to be). I conclude by exploring some attempts by African American performers and directors to gain a greater hold on their representation, as the tradition of black shows extended into the 1930s.

Establishing a Tradition: *Revues nègres*, 1926–1930

In the half decade following the Baker show, *revue nègre* ceased to denote a particular show and became a generic description. "Each year, on the return of Spring," the great music-hall critic Legrand-Chabrier wrote in 1930, "we offer a *revue nègre*, if not two!"[28] On another occasion, he spotted a duo of black dancers whom he deemed "worthy . . . of our *revues nègres* of yesterday, today and tomorrow."[29] Legrand-Chabrier was not exaggerating: every year from 1925 to 1930 there was at least one all-black show. If not all were of the same high profile as Josephine Baker's, a few may even have reached wider audiences than did hers.

First among these troupes, in 1926, were the Blackbirds. Their manager-director was another white American, central to black revues both at home and abroad: Lew Leslie (formerly Louis Lesinsky, of Russian Jewish parentage), a performer turned producer who promoted black talent, first in nightclub shows and later in the theatre. Versions of the *Blackbirds of 1926* had already been successful in London and New York.[30] In Paris

27. Klein, "Swings: *La Revue nègre*," 370–71, addresses the mixed modernist and populist signals emanating from *La Revue nègre*. Only recently converted into a music hall, the Théâtre des Champs-Élysées had been considered an avant-garde venue and retained a whiff of past controversies (most famously the premiere of Stravinsky's *Le Sacre du printemps* in 1913).

28. Legrand-Chabrier, "Du promenoir à la piste: Introduction à la revue nègre," *La Volonté*, 26 June 1930, in Ro 585, "Le Jazz," doc. 116, Rondel.

29. Legrand-Chabrier, "Music-Hall d'amateurs et music-hall professionnel," *La Volonté*, 3 June 1929, in Ro 14770, "Les Cafés et cabarets de Montparnasse," Rondel; the dancers were Bob Jackson and Ralph Thompson.

30. *Blackbirds of 1926* had a lengthy gestation. Its origins lay in a floor show at the Plantation Club, New York, in 1922; this was subsequently presented as the *Plantation Revue* at the Forty-Eighth Street Theatre and at the Lafayette Theatre,

the Blackbirds played the Ambassadeurs, newly redesigned as a "théâtre-restaurant," moving only later to the nearby Théâtre des Champs-Élysées.[31] Thus several skits—"The Heart of the Jungle," "The Wrong Cop," "Treasure Castle"—were dropped in favor of song-and-dance acts, more accommodating of digestion. Favorites were the opening plantation number, "Down South," in which a homecoming Florence Mills (star of the show) burst out of a huge cake on her mammy's birthday; a jungle dance for Mills and her "Zulus"; Johnny Hudgins's "In Silence" in which he, in blackface and white gloves, mimed a song whose notes were supplied on a

---

Harlem. A version (preceded by white acts) played London (but not Paris, as some maintain) in 1923 as *From Dover* [or *Dover Street*] *to Dixie*. The all-black New York edition, *Dixie to Broadway*, appeared at the Broadhurst Theatre, New York, in 1924–1925, and then went on a national tour. The show was revamped first as *Blackbirds of 1925* at the Plantation Club, then as *Blackbirds of 1926* at the Alhambra Theatre, Harlem, before heading to Paris, then London. A program for *Dixie to Broadway*, Broadhurst Theatre, New York, week beginning 3 November 1924, is in the "Dixie to Broadway" file, Theatre Collection, Philadelphia Free Library, Philadelphia (hereafter cited as Philadelphia); similar programs are reproduced or transcribed in several of the sources listed below. Information on these and many of the shows and performers discussed in this chapter is gleaned from the following sources: Stephen Robert Alkire, "The Development and Treatment of the Negro Character as Presented in American Music Theater, 1927–1968" (PhD diss., Michigan State University, 1972); Robert Kimball and William Bolcom, *Reminiscing with Sissle and Blake* (New York: Viking Press, 1973; repr., New York: Cooper Square Books, 2000); Bernard L. Peterson, *A Century of Musicals in Black and White: An Encyclopedia of Musical Stage Works by, about, or involving African Americans* (Westport, CT: Greenwood Press, 1993); Bernard L. Peterson, *Profiles of African American Stage Performers and Theatre People, 1816–1960* (Westport, CT: Greenwood Press, 2001); Henry T. Sampson, *Blacks in Blackface: A Source Book on Early Black Musical Shows* (Metuchen, NJ: Scarecrow Press, 1980); Marshall Stearns and Jean Stearns, *Jazz Dance: The Story of American Vernacular Dance* (New York: Macmillan, 1968; repr., New York: Schirmer Books, 1979); Allen Woll, *Dictionary of the Black Theatre: Broadway, Off-Broadway, and Selected Harlem Theatre* (Westport, CT: Greenwood Press, 1983); and Allen Woll, *Black Musical Theatre: From Coontown to Dreamgirls* (Baton Rouge: Louisiana State University Press, 1989; repr., New York: Da Capo, 1991).

31. One writer effectively summed up the attendant sense of disorientation: "Cette revue, qui est plutôt une exhibition dans un théâtre lequel est plutôt un restaurant, plaira énormément aux Parisiens qui seront plutôt des étrangers" (A. de Montgon, "'Les Oiseaux noirs' aux Ambassadeurs," unidentified periodical, 29 May 1926, in Ro 18740, "Ambassadeurs, 1926," Rondel). As well as many reviews, two programs for the Ambassadeurs show are in Ro 18740; one for the slightly shorter version that played the Théâtre des Champs-Élysées (where, as had *La Revue nègre*, it occupied only the second half) is in Ro 585, "Le Jazz," doc. 25, Rondel.

FIGURE 1.2. Newspaper cartoon of Florence Mills and Johnny Hudgins in *Blackbirds of 1926* (*Comœdia*, 30 May 1926).

cornet (fig. 1.2); and a parody of Russian dance troupe La Chauve-Souris's "Parade of the Wooden Soldiers" (which, reviewers agreed, brought not only humor to the number but greater precision). Original music for the show had been provided by a team of Leslie's white colleagues: composers Geo(rge) W. Meyer and Arthur Johnson and lyricists Grant Clarke and Roy Turk.

A few critics, particularly in the right-wing press, took up the mantle of Robert de Flers to attack the whole enterprise. There was much they could protest. The show was presented in English at a historic venue that had recently been subjected to a brutal modernization. As a sign of American "colonization," its tastelessness risked sapping the French of their superior culture. Finally, with the falling franc and prices in dollars, few locals could afford to enter let alone dine—small comfort indeed for those fearful of cultural pollution.[32] Still, there was a significant change:

32. Among such responses, consider the following: "Je ne nie point l'attrait singulier de ces spectacles. Mais serons-nous, après quelques années du régime noir, capables encore de goûter un vers de Racine ou de Mallarmé, une suite d'accords de Fauré, un dégradé argenté de Corot? Ou, abrutis par le balancement des deux notes obsédantes, autour desquelles se crispe, tournoie, piétine et rugit toute la musique de jazz, finirons-nous par nous regarder, dans un bout de miroir cassé, parmi des

Blackbirds of 1926 was berated more as a sign of American modernity than as a descent into primitive barbarity; if *La Revue nègre* had still seemed to retain a whiff of the jungle, there was no doubting that this was New York chic—especially after Paul Whiteman and His Orchestra joined the bill, rivaling the show's own Plantation Orchestra (led by violinist Ralph "Shrimp" Jones) as the best jazz band yet heard in Paris.[33]

Even in New York (as *Dixie to Broadway*, in 1924), opinion had been divided as to how black—or rather "black"—the Blackbirds were. Where one critic bemoaned a lack of "the fundamental jokes of blackface comedy, and . . . but fleeting references to razors, craps and chicken stealing," another noted "a passionate fidelity to the eternal verities of tempo not in the inheritance of Nordics."[34] This conversation continued in Paris,

---

débris de bananes, portant dans nos pauvres yeux humides la nostalgie des temps civilisés et de la beauté perdue?" (Robert Kemp, "Aux Ambassadeurs: Black Birds 1926, danses et chansons," *La Liberté*, 31 May 1926); "Mais où sommes-nous? À Paris, en 1926? Ou dans la Rome du cinquième siècle, celle qui n'était plus Rome que de nom? Et tout cela pendant que le franc cède et roule? Quelle tristesse!" (Marcel Boulenger, "Charmante soirée en Île-de-France," *Le Figaro*, 16 July 1926). See also René Bizet, "La Revue Black Birds aux Ambassadeurs," *Candide*, 3 June 1926; Colin-Muset, untitled article, *L'Avenir*, 7 June 1926; and Auguste Villeroy, "Au royaume du jazz et du nègre," *Le Soir*, 4 July 1926. Despite this constellation of unsympathetic responses on the right, it would be wrong to assume consistent editorial positions. Compare, for example, Jacques Patin's two enthusiastic reviews in *Le Figaro* ("Avant-Première: Les Nouveaux Ambassadeurs," 29 May 1926; "Au Théâtre-Restaurant des Ambassadeurs: La Revue américaine Black Birds 1926," 31 May 1926) with Boulenger's above. All articles cited are in Ro 18740, "Ambassadeurs, 1926," Rondel.

33. Indeed, *Blackbirds of 1926* was often advertised as a "revue américaine." From July 1926 the show was renamed *Dixie to Paris*, after the earlier New York title, *Dixie to Broadway*. Whiteman's band appeared for the first two weeks of July, during which time they also played the Théâtre des Champs-Élysées; I discuss their reception briefly in chap. 2. Another white American band, Irving Aaronson and the Commanders, subsequently replaced Whiteman's at both venues.

34. Percy Hammond, "The Talented Colored Folks Make a Lively Show of 'From Dixie to Broadway,'" *Tribune* (New York), 30 October 1924; Heywood Broun, "The New Play: At the Broadhurst: 'Dixie to Broadway,'" *World* (New York), 30 October 1924 (both, and many more, are in the "Dixie to Broadway" file, Billy Rose Theatre Collection, Performing Arts Division, New York Public Library, New York, hereafter cited as Billy Rose). Even when the show, as *Blackbirds of 1926*, played the Alhambra Theatre in Harlem for six weeks prior to departure for Europe, one critic complained that sometimes "they make the sad mistake of going white" (Anon., "That Mills Girl: 'Black Birds' Flutter at the Alhambra Theater," *New York Sun*, 13 April 1926, in "Blackbirds of 1926" file, Billy Rose).

where *La Revue nègre* was the primary reference point. Critics disagreed on their favorite show but not on the terms of the discussion: *La Revue nègre* was "wild and impromptu," "barbaric and hot," "so raw and of such a discordant savagery";[35] *Blackbirds* was "tempered," "most civil and most civilized"—perhaps "too civilized"—"less fantastic [and] less eccentric."[36] Having "taken off their African and American rags," one writer noted, the Blackbirds had become "altogether Parisianized"; another referred to the troupe as "cannibales débonnaires."[37]

The comparison between the shows extended, too, to their female stars: Josephine Baker (now idol of the Folies-Bergère, in her famous banana skirt) faced her first serious competition from the Blackbirds' Florence Mills.[38] A performer since childhood, Mills was already hugely popular with black and white audiences in New York; she'd also been well received in the earlier version of Leslie's show in London in 1923. But while Mills was not unknown to don a wig and grass skirt for a jungle number (fig. 1.3), her real appeal lay elsewhere. It was less her looks that attracted Europeans—"a monkey-like profile," one critic put it; a "little bulldog" another—as the dignity and force of personality she projected on stage.[39] There was a tragic side to Mills's comedy, one that her sudden death a year later, aged thirty-two, has done nothing to dispel.

Even Mills's signature song, "I'm a Little Blackbird Looking for a Blue-

35. Pierre Lazareff, "Aux Ambassadeurs: Lew Leslie présente 'Black Birds 1926,'" *Le Soir*, 30 May 1926; Les Sept Dames du 3e rang [pseud.], "Aux Ambassadeurs: Black-Birds 1926," *Minerva*, 13 June 1926; Gustave Fréjaville, "Aux Ambassadeurs: 'Black Birds 1926,'" *Comœdia*, 30 May 1926 (all are in Ro 18740, "Ambassadeurs, 1926," Rondel).

36. Les Sept Dames, "Aux Ambassadeurs"; René Bizet, "Ambassadeurs," *L'Intransigeant*, 31 May 1926; Fréjaville, "Aux Ambassadeurs" (also Bizet, "La Revue Black Birds"); Legrand-Chabrier, "Sous les projecteurs" (all are in Ro 18740, "Ambassadeurs, 1926," Rondel).

37. Jane Catulle-Mendès, "Ambassadeurs: The Black Birds," *La Presse*, 2 June 1926, in Ro 18740, "Ambassadeurs, 1926," Rondel (the paper printed "passionnés" in place of "parisianisés," which the author corrected the following day); André Levinson, "Aux Champs-Élysées Music-Hall: La Vengeance des dieux," *Comœdia*, 1 August 1926, in Ro 15702(5), "Le Champs-Élysées Music-Hall," Rondel, where some other reviews of the show at the Champs-Élysées are located.

38. On Mills, see Bill Egan, *Florence Mills: Harlem Jazz Queen* (Lanham, MD: Scarecrow Press, 2004); and Jayna Brown, "Translocations: Florence Mills, Josephine Baker, and Valaida Snow," in *Babylon Girls: Black Women Performers and the Shaping of the Modern* (Durham, NC: Duke University Press, 2008), 238–79.

39. Pierre Brisson, "Chronique théâtrale: Une Soirée aux Ambassadeurs," *Le Temps*, 31 May 1926, in Ro 18740, "Ambassadeurs, 1926," Rondel; Paul Achard, "Music-

FIGURE 1.3. Florence Mills in *Dixie to Broadway*, New York, NY, 1924.

bird" was scarcely an obvious hit. Borrowing on blues tropes, it opens, to a
disconcertingly jaunty rhythm, "Never had no happiness." But more than
presenting "Just a lonesome bit of humanity . . . / In search of some-one
to feather my nest," the song engages in social commentary: "Tho' I'm of
a darker hue," Mills sang, "I've a heart the same as you"; she was "Buildin'
fairy castles, same as all the white folks do." The music is typical of the
innocuous syncopated numbers white composers liked to write for black
shows (ex. 1.1). But the lyrics' odd switching between ideas suggests that
Mills's happiness was bound up with a search not just for love but for a
freedom denied her as a person of color.[40]

Hall: The Commanders Band, Black Birds," *Paris-Midi*, 21 July 1926, in Ro 15702(5),
"Le Champs-Élysées Music-Hall," Rondel.

   40. The French words that Didier-Gold and Pierre Darius provided for the
chorus, although not a translation, pick up on this tendency: "Je suis pour votre

EXAMPLE 1.1. First eight bars of verse of "I'm a Little Blackbird Looking for a Bluebird" (music, Geo. W. Meyer and Arthur Johnson; lyrics, Grant Clarke and Roy Turk), sung by Florence Mills in *Blackbirds of 1926*.

As the *Baltimore Afro-American* wrote, "It would be hard to miss the forces that caused Miss Mills to write and sing this song. It is the spirit of youth struggling against oppression. This is another instance of use of talent to touch a more serious phase of racial contact, and Miss Mills has succeeded in doing it deftly."[41] The song was not in fact her own, but the sentiment seems to have been. As Mills's biographer Bill Egan has shown, the performer used her fame to advance the African American cause. She had already turned down a role as a rare black star in the *Ziegfeld Follies*,

---

goût, Hélas! / Peut-être un peu trop brune?" Mills does not appear to have sung in French, but this text was given in the program and circulated widely in the press, often as a way to characterize her personality.

41. Anon., "Florence Mills Seeks Her Bluebird," *Baltimore Afro-American*, 10 October 1924, cited in Egan, *Florence Mills*, 113.

because she felt she "could best serve the Colored actor by [instead] accepting Mr. Leslie's offer" to headline an all-black cast on Broadway.[42] Mills later published an article called "The Soul of the Negro" protesting racial injustice.[43]

In Paris, one writer thought Mills a "chaste and modest" "black fairy" compared to the "demon" Baker; with her "deliberate sense of decency" (volontaire décence), he said, "she could dance at the Vatican."[44] Legrand-Chabrier put it more bluntly: "In Josephine Baker, there is Africa. In Florence Mills, there is only America."[45] For another reviewer, it was as if Baker had been " 'laminated' by some conservatory, which imparted more expertise but diminished some of her gifts."[46] Émigré Russian intellectual and dance critic André Levinson explored the matter in greater depth:

> Josephine Baker . . . is an extraordinary creature of simian suppleness. . . . Thanks to her carnal magnificence and her impulsive vehemence, her unashamed exhibition comes close to pathos. . . . Dainty Florence Mills gives a sweetened travesty of this type of dancing. There is not the slightest trace of the wild thing in this rococo Creole. . . . It is no longer the tigress who stands before us but the marquise, who has rubbed a little burnt cork on her cheeks, instead of her customary rouge, before dancing a Court Charleston "ad usum Delphini."[47]

42. Anon., "Florence Mills Turned Down Offer to Appear in *Ziegfeld Follies*," *Chicago Defender*, 23 August 1924, cited in Egan, *Florence Mills*, 107.

43. Florence Mills, "The Soul of the Negro," *Sunday Chronicle* (London), 10 October 1926, cited in Egan, *Florence Mills*, 178.

44. Pierre Varenne, "Aux Ambassadeurs: Black Birds 1926," *Paris-Soir*, 1 June 1926, in Ro 18740, "Ambassadeurs, 1926," Rondel.

45. Legrand-Chabrier, "Sous les projecteurs."

46. Louis Léon-Martin, "Aux Ambassadeurs: Black Birds," *Paris-Midi*, 29 May 1926; see also Gérard Bauer, review of *Blackbirds of 1926*, *Annales politiques et littéraires*, 13 June 1926 (both are in Ro 18740, "Ambassadeurs, 1926," Rondel).

47. I.e., "purified." André Levinson, "The Negro Dance: Under European Eyes," *Theatre Arts Monthly*, April 1927, reprinted in Joan Acocella and Lynn Garafola, eds., *André Levinson on Dance: Writings from Paris in the Twenties* (Hanover, NH: Wesleyan University Press, 1991), 69–75 (quote on pp. 74–75). Levinson's writings often saw publication in several forms. This article, published in English, drew extensively on at least three earlier French pieces: "Paris ou New-York?"; "Le Ballet et le charleston: Le 'Step' et le rythme," *Comœdia*, [15?] September 1926; and "Le Ballet et le charleston II: Black and White," *Comœdia*, 20 September 1926 (both the latter are in Ro 9805[2], "Levinson, André: La Danse et les danseurs," Rondel). A version of "The Negro Dance" subsequently appeared as "Steps nègres," in Levinson, *La Danse d'aujourd'hui* (Paris: Duchartre et Van Buggenhoudt, 1929), 271–80. This com-

For Levinson, Mills's performance began to suggest a permeability of boundaries of race and culture on which he was otherwise rather insistent. Just a page earlier, he had described how "the undeniable rhythmic superiority of these Negro dancers is nothing less than an adjunct of their irrepressible animality." But Mills instead provided evidence of race's performance: that "the Negro dancers of today are no longer beings possessed by devils, but merely professionals."[48]

One might suppose that Levinson, a conservative (if eclectic) critic well-known for his staunch opposition to the Ballets Russes' divergence from classical tradition, would have been delighted by black dancers' "progress."[49] He was more ambivalent, however. For Levinson, the acculturation of black styles, as well as their adoption by white society, signaled a regrettable loss of purity, albeit of a pure savagery: cultural contact, he seemed to fear, threatened traditions with extinction—and this was as true of the "primitive" meeting "civilization" as it was of his precious classicism under attack from barbarian hordes.[50] Another critic went further: the Blackbirds' apparent melancholy reminded him of monkeys peeling nuts in a zoo.[51] While Mills and the Blackbirds had begun to stretch expectations of African American performance, therefore, Paris was far from the utopia imagined by Dalton and Gates. Even with the show's American pizzazz and the venue's Parisian elegance, a crass racial slur was never far away.

Not until Lew Leslie returned, with *Blackbirds of 1929*, did another *revue nègre* have the same profile as Florence Mills's. Before turning to that, I want to mention several smaller productions, to give a sense of their plenty. Two played the Apollo in Montmartre. The first, *Black-Bottom Follies*, opened in November 1926; it was a "dîner-spectacle" modeled on the Ambassadeurs' *Blackbirds*. Featuring Sam Wooding's band, an African

---

pilation of articles has confused some writers (including Acocella and Garafola in their introduction to the text) into thinking that Florence Mills appeared alongside Josephine Baker in Paris, which she did not.

48. Levinson, "The Negro Dance," 73, 75.

49. On Levinson, see, in addition to Acocella and Garafola, *André Levinson on Dance*, Garafola's "Politics in Paradise: André Levinson's Classicism," *New Dance Review* 6/3 (Spring 1994): 12–18.

50. This is especially apparent in the new ending Levinson wrote for this article after Mills had died: "Autant le Yankee noircit au contact des bateleurs nègres, autant ces derniers blanchissent par le frottement. Et c'est peut-être bien au tout dernier moment que nous avons été mis en présence de cette ultime floraison des saturnales noires" (*La Danse d'aujourd'hui*, 280).

51. Kemp, "Aux Ambassadeurs."

American outfit that had been touring Europe for several years (notably with the show *Chocolate Kiddies*, which never made it to France), *Black-Bottom Follies* claimed to present the latest black dances, although its dancers may have been white.[52]

More significant was the second, *La Revue nègre: The Dark Town Serenaders*—main act on a variety program the same time the following year. Boasting, doubtless fallaciously, "1600 représentations à l'Hippodrome de New-York," thirty-six—or sometimes forty—"artistes nègres," and, of course, an "orchestre nègre," the show appeared first at another music hall, Concert Mayol, a little south in the tenth arrondissement, as *Black Follies* or *Colored Charleston* (fig. 1.4).[53] It featured "la nouvelle Étoile Nègre" Betty Rowland (daughter of "jongleur fantaisiste" Rowland, she was feather-clad like Josephine Baker but lacked her overt sexuality); "le meilleur danseur-fantaisiste nègre" Willy Robbins (performing in blackface, his turn included an imitation of Johnny Hudgins's "In Silence"); "le colored fantaisiste" Seth Jones; and singer Joë Boyd and his jazz band, the Cracker Jacks.[54] The show seems to have been assembled among black entertainers already in Paris, some of whom may have been of French colonial origin. Making conspicuous efforts to align itself with the imported *revues nègres*, however, it raises the curious possibility of French-speaking Africans imitating black Americans pretending to be Africans—and all this for the sake of a purported authenticity. Critics agreed that the Apollo show did not rival those of the Champs-Élysées or Ambassadeurs, but it served as a pleasant reminder: "the two 'revues nègres' ... concentrated into a variety act," in Fréjaville's words, recognizing the new genre.[55]

In August 1928, a "revue musicale nègre," *Dance, dance!*, directed by Earl B. Granstaff, took place at the Gaity Theatre in Montmartre. Little

52. A handful of reviews are in Ro 15692(1), "L'Apollo," Rondel. On Wooding, see Hugues Panassié, "Sam Wooding à l'Embassy," in *Douze années de jazz (1927–1938): Souvenirs* (Paris: Corrêa, 1946), 39–43; Samuel Wooding, "Eight Years Abroad with a Jazz Band," *Étude* 57/4 (April 1939): 233–34, 282; and Chip Deffaa, "Sam Wooding: Bringing Big Band Jazz to Europe," in *Voices of the Jazz Age* (Urbana: University of Illinois Press, 1990), 1–27.

53. A handful of advertisements and reviews are in Ro 18800, "La Revue du Concert Mayol, 1927," Rondel.

54. A program (week beginning 25 November 1927) is in Ro 15692(6), "L'Apollo," Rondel. A handful of advertisements and reviews are in Ro 15692(1), "L'Apollo," Rondel.

55. Gustave Fréjaville, "La Semaine au music-hall," *Comœdia*, 1 December 1927, in Ro 16443(4), "Fréjaville, Gustave," Rondel.

FIGURE 1.4. Double-sided advertising flyer for a little-known *revue nègre: Black Follies,*
Paris, 1927.

more is known: it was so poorly publicized that the few critics who attended found themselves among the only people there. Wherever the performers hailed from, the essentials were familiar: four song-and-dance
tableaux located in ur-Africa, on a southern plantation, among a jazz
band, and at a cabaret. The show had, enthused one reviewer, "un je ne
sais quoi de primitif et de pimenté"; another thought it possessed "all the

naivety, all the charming puerility, all the nostalgia, all the throbbing and colorful movement" of Josephine Baker's 1925 revue.[56]

More successful with the public was a floor show at the "restaurant-dancing-cabaret" the Embassy in May 1930: *Revue noire: Hot Stuff*, advertised as "Harlem aux Champs-Élysées." Directed by S. H. Dudley, the show included singers Louis Cole and Elisabeth Welch (all three familiar from *Blackbirds of 1929*), as well as much new talent: singers El Brown (*en travestie* until the end); dancers Livina Mack, Jacky Young, and Glennie Chessman; and comic Snow Fisher. Unusually, the band accompanying their songs and dances was *un jazz français*, Andy Jordan's. One critic thought that Parisians should, by rights, have become blasé about *revues nègres* by now, but in fact the excitement remained.[57] For some, however, the genre's blackness was in question: Legrand-Chabrier believed it "une revue blanche à la manière noire."[58] Indeed, Parisian audiences, in common with white directors, were eager to use their newfound experience of African American music theatre to judge who was still "keepin' it real."[59] One

56. P. D., "Un Nouveau Spectacle nègre," *La Rumeur*, 11 August 1928; Hanry-Jaunet, "Au Gaity-Theatre: 'Dance, Dance!' Revue musicale nègre en quatre tableaux, de M. Earl B. Granstaff," *La Presse*, 15 August 1928 (both are in Ro 585, "Le Jazz," doc. 58, Rondel, where a few other reviews are located).

57. Louis Léon-Martin, "À l'Embassy: 'La Revue noire,'" *Paris-Midi*, 18 May 1930, in Ro 585, "Le Jazz," doc. 110, Rondel, where a few other reviews are located.

58. Legrand-Chabrier, "Le Music-Hall au dancing," *Le Carnet de la semaine*, 1 June 1930, in Ro 585, "Le Jazz," doc. 110, Rondel.

59. Black acts also continued to perform in variety shows during this period. Singers (Turner) Layton and (Clarence) Johnstone had a successful recording career that at once was driven by and promoted their music-hall appearances (e.g., Empire Theatre, fortnight beginning 24 February 1928: see program, in Ro 15718[3], "L'Empire," Rondel; press, in Ro 15718[8–9], "L'Empire," Rondel). Others male duos included "Coon dancers" Mutt and Jeff (e.g., Empire, fort. beg. 20 May 1927: prog., in Ro 15718[2], "L'Empire," Rondel; press, in Ro 15718 [6–7], "L'Empire," Rondel); and "The coloured aristocrats" (Rufus) Greenlee and (Thaddeus) Drayton (e.g., Empire, fort. beg. 27 December 1929: prog., in Ro 15718[4], "L'Empire," Rondel; press, in Ro 15718 [11–15], "L'Empire," Rondel). Among other acts were the Three Eddies (e.g., "Show of 1928," Ambassadeurs Theatre, May 1928: in Ro 15690[2], "Les Ambassadeurs," doc. 18, Rondel); and Little Esther (e.g., Moulin Rouge, month beg. 22 March 1929: in Ro 15743[5–10], "Le Moulin Rouge," Rondel). See also Fréjaville's regular reviews, as cited above; and his colleague Legrand-Chabrier's similar column, many of which are collected in Ro 16444, "Legrand-Chabrier: Piste et plateaux," Rondel. Relevant, too, is the "fantaisie-opérette" *Olive chez les nègres, ou Le Village blanc*, music by Jean Wiéner on a libretto by Henri Falk, which was performed at the Théâtre des Champs-Élysées during November and December 1926. En route to Africa, Marseilles industrialist

show in particular illuminates the crosscurrents between artistic, scientific, and political discourses of race as they were circulating in France at the turn of the decade.

Body and Soul: *Blackbirds of 1929*

For the first time, claims for *Blackbirds of 1929*'s authenticity were, in a limited sense, correct: the revue was presented more or less as on Broadway where, the year before, it had been the most successful black show of all time (running for an extraordinary 518 performances, as *Blackbirds of 1928*; fig. 1.5).[60] Minor changes were made for the Moulin Rouge but no more than might take place during a normal run: Eddie Rector replaced Bill "Bojangles" Robinson in his famous stair dance; dance team the Berry Brothers came on board; a skit was cut; several minor roles changed hands.[61] Constants were the rapid-fire alternation of singing and dancing around some familiar themes—a prologue "Way Down South," a "Scene in Jungle Land"—along with the occasional skit of no greater originality: a poker game, a boxing match, a spooky graveyard scene. Comedian Mantan Moreland (remembered in *Bamboozled*) had made the trip, occupying roles as "Billy the Dope" and "Do Little Jackson" alongside the bill-topping blackface comic Tim Moore. The music, by white composer and

M. Olive Cadolive (Roger Ferreol) and his companions are shipwrecked and captured by the natives. Cannibals (of course), they would eat them, but their king (Joe Alex) prefers to make them suffer the same humiliation as had he at the 1922 Exposition coloniale de Marseille: exhibition. The show also featured Jessie Crawford and Allegretti Anderson (the "Crawford Sisters") as "princesses noires," and several other dancers as their "troupe africaine." On stage as well was a jazz band led by African American Vance Lowry (famous for his performances at the Bœuf sur le Toit) representing the Africans, and an *orphéon*, playing in contrast in a French folk-song idiom, to represent the Marseillais. While not exactly belonging to the genre in question, *Olive* witnessed, according to one critic, "l'intelligente assimilation des originalités des différents spectacles nègres" (René Bizet, "Champs-Élysées," *L'Intransigeant*, 29 November 1926, in Ro 15702[5] "Le Champs-Élysées Music-Hall," Rondel, where many reviews are located), and clearly aimed to benefit from the vogue for them.

60. Allen Woll, *Black Musical Theatre*, 125.

61. Description based on program for week beginning 11 June 1928, Liberty Theatre, New York, in the "Blackbirds of 1928" file, Philadelphia; and program for week beginning 29 July 1929, Moulin Rouge, Paris, in Ro 15743, "Le Moulin Rouge," Rondel. Two other, slightly different, Paris programs are available: one dated 4 July, in Ro 15743, "Le Moulin Rouge," Rondel; and one dated 7 June, in Ro 585, "Le Jazz," doc. 74, Rondel. The New York show itself was by no means a stable entity; there was also a second, touring company starring Harriett Calloway.

FIGURE 1.5. Paul Colin's poster for *Blackbirds of 1929*, Paris (© ADAGP, Paris and DACS, London 2013).

lyricist team, Jimmy McHugh and Dorothy Fields, has proved unusually lasting: the show popularized such numbers as "I Can't Give You Anything but Love, Baby," "I Must Have That Man," and, for the stair dance, "Doin' the New Lowdown." If the reason for their success was not, as Lew Leslie insisted, that whites "understand the colored man better than he does himself," it may be the case that they better understood their white audiences' expectations of African American performers.[62]

One scene above all fascinated the French critics: a gloss on DuBose Heyward's play *Porgy* (some years before Gershwin's *Porgy and Bess* of 1935).[63] As far as it can be reconstructed, there were two main numbers: one a song for Bess, which I come to below; the other a wake scene for Robbins (killed by Crown) turning into a celebration—in effect, a telescoping of what would become Gershwin's act 1, scene 2. Accompanying this in the program (and slavishly reiterated in the press) was a quasi-ethnographic "explanation" whose origins are obscure:

62. Anon., "Prefers to Stage All-Negro Shows: Lew Leslie Declares No White Girls Work So Hard as Do the Harlem Belles," unidentified clipping, n.d., in the "Lew Leslie" file, Philadelphia.

63. A useful discussion of antecedents of *Porgy and Bess*, including Lew Leslie's show, is found in John Andrew Johnson, "Gershwin's 'American Folk Opera': The Genesis, Style, and Reputation of *Porgy and Bess* (1935)" (PhD diss., Harvard University, 1996).

Dans les États du Sud, le pays est au même niveau que la mer et lorsqu'un nègre meurt, s'il n'est pas assez riche pour être inhumé dans les montagnes, il est enterré dans les marais où l'eau fait revenir son corps à la surface. Quand un nègre meurt et qu'il est pauvre, tous les nègres du village se réunissent autour de son cercueil et créent, par leurs chants, une sorte d'hystérie qui pousse les hommes à voler et les femmes à se vendre aux blancs, pour réunir l'argent suffisant à l'inhumation du défunt.

In the southern states, the land is at the same level as the sea and when a Negro dies, if he is not rich enough to be laid to rest in the mountains, he is buried in the swamp where the water forces his body back to the surface. When a Negro who is poor dies, all the Negroes in the village get together around his coffin and create, by their songs, a sort of hysteria that pushes the men to steal and the women to sell themselves to whites, to get together enough money for the interment of the deceased.

An imperfect idea of the music can be gained from a recording made several years later in which celebrated blues singer Ethel Waters replaces the Blackbirds' Geneva Washington in the role of the mourning Serena but the Cecil Mack Choir is retained.[64] Into the brief duration of a "78" are squeezed three contrasting sections: a doleful call and response between leader and choir as the people of Catfish Row raise money for Robbins's burial ("Sing, brother sing"; fig. 1.6); an up-tempo section in which the mortician demands swift action, the choir again responding in harmony ("What dat you say?"); and a variant on the "St. Louis Blues" featuring Serena singing in impassioned counterpoint with her community ("Oh, Lordy, Lordy"), first lamenting Robbins's death then gaining strength to go "on her way" (a coda quotes the last bars of Gershwin's *Rhapsody in Blue*). The religio-sexual intoxication invoked by this scenario, as well as the huddled mourners on stage and the repetitive interlocutions of the music, acted very powerfully on the French imagination. According to one critic, it was "certainly the most beautiful thing that *art nègre* has yet sent us"; another had "never seen anything more moving in the world."[65] Describing the spectacle in which the singers, seated, alternately prostrated themselves before the coffin and flung their arms rapturously into the air, this writer continued:

64. Cecil Mack Choir with Ethel Waters, "St. Louis Blues," 23 December 1932 (B12790–A, Brunswick 6521), reissued on *Lew Leslie's Blackbirds of 1928* LP (Columbia, Mono OL6770 [1968]).

65. In DuBose Heyward's original novel, published in 1925, and in *Porgy and Bess*, the concern is a more "modern" one: that the Board of Health will take Robbins's body for use by medical students.

TIM MOORE   FUZiER

FIGURE 1.6. Newspaper cartoon of Tim Moore as the preacher in the "Porgy" scene from *Blackbirds of 1929* (*Le Soir*, 10 July 1929).

Ah! ce balancement régulier des têtes crépues, ces mains aux paumes blanchâtres, tendues vers les dieux qui ne répondent pas, ces voix graves, féminines, enfantines, qui se confondent en une lamentation générale, et ces visages enfouis dans l'ombre et qu'on devine brûlés par les larmes, quel spectacle! On est bouleversé.[66]

Ah! this steady swaying of frizzy heads, these hands with off-white palms, outstretched toward the gods who do not respond, these voices, solemn, feminine, childlike, which merge in a general lamentation, and these faces buried in the darkness and that one supposes stung by tears, what a spectacle! One is overwhelmed.

André Levinson was also struck by this scene, casting his net widely in search of a comparison: first, Ravel's *Boléro* of the previous year, which similarly achieved its effect through insistent repetition rather than variation; next, dramatic vocal works such as Honegger's *Le Roi David* and Stravinsky's *Oedipus Rex*, whose power derived from a ritualistic quality

66. Hanry-Jaunet, "La Revue des Lew Leslie's Blackbirds," *La Presse*, 13 June 1929; Pierre Varenne, "Au Moulin Rouge," *L'Œuvre*, 14 June 1929 (both are in Ro 585, "Le Jazz," doc. 74b, Rondel, where a huge number of reviews are located).

that paradoxically bordered on stasis; finally, the stylized melodramas of Russian Jewish theatre, which revealed for him the common ground between these two exiled races, between "the discerning intellectual [such as Levinson himself] with his ancient dialectic and the naïve primitive acting on dim instinct and atavistic fears."[67] In this way, "Porgy" had brought the music hall into line with more highbrow genres. Yet Levinson did not believe the Blackbirds had achieved the status of "art," quite the contrary. As he wrote of their rhythmic skills in particular, African American musical talent was for him "an innate gift, not a conscious art—a gift that has more or less atrophied in the cultivated human being" (or, of Josephine Baker: "Elle exprime *supérieurement* une manière d'être *inférieure*").[68] Music critics should not, Levinson implied, repeat the process in which art critics had for some while been engaged: the co-option of the ritual objects of *art nègre* as artistic ones. Yet his concern was not, of course, about the misappropriation of foreign cultures; rather it was for the Western tradition's integrity and uniqueness, a cause he would defend to the last.

Ironically, Levinson was joined on this point—that the Blackbirds and their kin did not represent art, still less Art—by a writer coming to the problem from the opposite direction: "surrealist-ethnographer" Michel Leiris, in the renegade journal *Documents*. No defender of the classical ballet, he found the Blackbirds "very much short of art, at a point of human development where this bastard idea has not yet hypertrophied," their entry to the ranks of art not only denied but scorned.[69] Instead, Leiris took the show as a model for escaping the conventions that held the arts—and society—in an ever more suffocating grasp, a view that was widely shared among his iconoclastic circle.[70]

67. André Levinson, "Aframérique," in *Les Visages de la danse* (Paris: Bernard Grasset, 1933), 259–64 (quote on p. 263). In this section, Levinson combines two reviews: " 'Porgy' et la revue des 'Oiseaux noirs,' " *L'Art vivant*, 15 July 1929, in Ro 585, "Le Jazz," doc. 79, Rondel; and "Encore les 'Oiseaux noirs,' " *Candide*, 15 August 1929, in Ro 585, "Le Jazz," doc. 74b, Rondel.

68. Levinson, "The Negro Dance," 73; Levinson, "L'Année chorégraphique," *Le Temps*, 16 August 1926, in Ro 9805(2), "Levinson, André," Rondel (italics original).

69. Michel Leiris, "Civilisation," *Documents* 1/4 (July 1929): 221–22 (quote on p. 222) [also translated by Lydia Davis, in *Sulfur*, no. 15 (1986): 93–96]. The term *surrealist-ethnographer* is James Clifford's; see his "Tell about Your Trip: Michel Leiris," in *The Predicament of Culture: Twentieth-Century Ethnography, Literature, and Art* (Cambridge, MA: Harvard University Press, 1988), 165–74 (esp. p. 168).

70. In the same issue of his journal, Georges Bataille provided a definition of "Blackbirds" for his "Dictionnaire" (*Documents* 1/4 [July 1929]: 215); and André Schaeffner contributed a laudatory review, "Les 'Lew Leslie's Black Birds' au Moulin Rouge" (ibid., 223). See also Matthew F. Jordan, "*Amphibiologie*: Ethnographic Sur-

The break of *Documents'* editor Georges Bataille with the surrealist movement's leader, André Breton, had turned on politics as well as, perhaps, a definition of their project: Bataille desired not a *sur*-realism (above or beyond reality) but a *sous*-realism (under or beneath it), to borrow Petrine Archer-Straw's apt term.[71] Instead of a free life of the mind, Bataille and his closest associates were concerned with the very real business of the body and its urges—sex, defecation, violence—which he summed up as *la bassesse* (baseness): a position that put them at odds with Breton's comparatively conservative notions and with his more orthodox communism.

For Leiris, even "civilized" life offered flickers of existential clarity incited by moments of such rawness (often sexual) that they broke through to the savage inside: "Civilization," he suggested, "can be compared to the thin layer . . . that forms on the surface of calm waters . . . until an eddy comes along and unsettles everything."[72] He found one such moment in his unexpected encounter, on a Montmartre street, with one of the Blackbirds troupe, wet roses in her hand—a lascivious image.[73] Another, less complete, he found in "Porgy," whose scenario was of a "hysteria so intense that it should be capable of pushing the audience to the immediate realization of sordid acts and extravagant debaucheries," but whose effect was partly lost on an audience who could not completely vanquish their "spinelessness" (veulerie).[74]

As his diary shows, Leiris's attraction to African Americans, as later to Africans, was often of a frankly erotic nature, and his writings repeat in inversion tropes of primitive physicality and spirituality opposing Western celebralism: a more or less unhelpful form of "positive racism," as he later came to realize.[75] So much is evidenced by the proximity of Leiris's

---

realism in French Discourse on Jazz," *Journal of European Studies* 31 (2001): 157–86; and Jordan, *"La Revue Nègre*, Ethnography, and Cultural Hybridity," in *Le Jazz: Jazz and French Cultural Identity* (Urbana: University of Illinois Press, 2010), 102–40.

71. Petrine Archer-Straw, "The Darker Side of Surrealism," in *Negrophilia: Avant-Garde Paris and Black Culture in the 1920s* (London: Thames and Hudson, 2000), 134–57 (esp. p. 143).

72. Leiris, "Civilisation," 221.

73. Michel Leiris, "Alberto Giacometti," *Documents* 1/4 (July 1929): 209–10 (esp. p. 209) [also translated by James Clifford, in *Sulfur*, no. 15 (1986): 38–40].

74. Leiris, "Civilisation," 222. See also Leiris's diary, where he praises *Blackbirds of 1929* as a "spectacle admirable" in which everything is "pur et naïf," comparing the "Porgy" scene to Stravinsky's *Les Noces* and another one to Marinetti (Michel Leiris, *Journal, 1922–1989*, ed. Jean Jamin [Paris: Gallimard, 1989], entry for 11 June 1929, p. 190; that for 15 August, p. 196, notes that he attended again).

75. For example, his diary entry for 21 August 1929: "M'occupe presque exclusivement . . . de faire l'amour. Un nom: celui de Ruth Johnston" (a member of the

position to Levinson's (the one attacking Western art, the other anxious to defend it): even attempting to reverse polarities—to regard the primitive above the civilized, use value over art value—it fails to break down their binary logic, inadvertently perpetuating the very hierarchies it had intended to destroy.

More down to earth, other critics similarly saw an implicit critique of recent music-hall offerings in the Blackbirds' show. Compared to a typical revue, theirs was positively sparse: the cast was small; scenery and props were at a minimum; even the costumes were relatively basic (although never so as to forget the performers' modesty). Yet their show packed an emotional punch that left others seeming hollow, their spectacle superficial. In short, African American artists seemed to achieve so much more with so much less—a model the French would have to learn from in these difficult days for the music hall. "Une leçon d'intelligence donnée par les noirs!" one critic exclaimed, acknowledging an ironic sign of the times.[76]

As their investment in the primitive religiosity of "Porgy" reveals, writers thus often imagined a simplicity and purity in African American theatre that was lacking in their own garish enterprises. These, paradoxically, were full of modern staging tricks learned from the States. In this way, French interest in black shows sometimes combined curiously with an ill-defined anti-Americanism. Pierre Varenne, for example, considered the Negroes "poets among 'businessmen.'"[77] Whatever their origins, white Americans were now "all mass-produced . . . on the same model" whose only function was making money. Among Negroes, however, "black blood" remained strongest, allowing them to retain their "roving spirit"

Blackbirds); 24 August: "Les *coloured girls* américaines . . . ont des voix qui dépassent tout ce qui peut s'exprimer. . . . Ce sont des images pour moi inoubliables que les images de celles qui ont ainsi chanté. . . . Les baisers dont je garde le plus aigu sont des baisers anonymes, ou quasi anonymes, en tout cas jamais répétés ni suivis d'autre chose. Ainsi . . . Ruth Johnston au 'Music Box'"; 25 August: "Je regrette que tant d'aventures qui, j'en suis sûr, auraient pu être délicieuses aient si piteusement avorté. Je pense aux événements récents avec les Blackbirds. Je pense aussi à une très ancienne histoire . . . avec une femme de chez Maxim's" (Leiris, *Journal*, 196–97). For Leiris's mature reflections on his youthful obsessions, see "Michel Leiris: 'L'Autre qui apparaît chez vous,'" in "Jazz en France," ed. Michael Haggerty, special issue, *Jazz Magazine*, no. 325 (January 1984): 34–36 [also translated by Michael Haggerty, as "Jazz," in *Sulfur*, no. 15 (1986): 97–104].

76. Louis Léon-Martin, "Au Moulin Rouge: La Revue des 'Blackbirds' de M. Lew Leslie," *Paris-Midi*, 12 June 1929. For similar, see Léon-Martin, "Au Moulin Rouge: Blackbirds," *Le Petit Parisien*, 12 June 1929; and René Bizet, "Moulin Rouge," *L'Intransigeant*, 8 August 1929 (all three are in Ro 585, "Le Jazz," doc. 74b, Rondel).

77. Varenne, "Au Moulin Rouge," *L'Œuvre*; he uses the English.

(âme vagabonde). Proclaiming his love for this vibrant race, Varenne continued to express concern for their welfare:

> Chers et doux nègres! Pourquoi rester dans ce pays que le morne puritanisme n'a pas rendu moins cruel! . . . Vous possédez les trésors qu'ont eus des poètes de chez nous, Baudelaire, Verlaine, et bien d'autres, des trésors près de quoi la fortune d'un Rockefeller ou d'un Vanderbilt n'est rien.[78]

> Dear, sweet Negroes! Why stay in this country [the United States] that dreary Puritanism has not made less cruel! . . . You possess treasures that our poets have had, Baudelaire, Verlaine, and many others, treasures alongside which the fortune of a Rockefeller or a Vanderbilt is nothing.

As these words suggest, sympathetic critics occasionally went so far as to claim solidarity with African Americans in opposition to white America—at least its prudish, racist, cultureless caricature. This remained, of course, a one-sided, paternalistic affair. But interwar French society felt increasingly beholden to (and alienated by) the mechanized, industrialized vision of the future it associated with the States, as I discuss in chapter 2. In these reactions to *revues nègres*, then, a hint may be recognized of the subversion and social radicalism that some writers have located in the origins of minstrelsy. A certain solidarity across barriers of race may even be recovered in the French tendency to locate in black shows a respite from American modernity, to sympathize with the performers as fellow victims rather than laugh at their clumsy misfortunes. At the same time, however, the power dynamic in this relationship was grossly uneven, and French writers have rarely hesitated to cast themselves as racially liberal and socially conscious compared to Americans, any evidence to the contrary notwithstanding.

Similar observations can be made of a curious book published a year later by a critic and sometime novelist: Jean Lasserre's *Auprès de ma noire*.[79] Described as a "roman" (novel), it depicts the experiences of a French man

78. Varenne expresses similar ideas in another article (with the same title): "Au Moulin Rouge," *Paris-Soir*, 16 June 1929, in Ro 585, "Le Jazz," doc. 74b, Rondel.

79. Jean Lasserre, *Auprès de ma noire: Roman* (Paris: Éditions de France, 1930). Lasserre was a critic for *Gringoire: Le Grand Hebdomadaire Parisien politique et littéraire*, among other publications. See his reviews of the show: "Au music-hall: 'Black Birds' (Les Oiseaux noirs)," *L'Ami du peuple du soir*, 11 June 1929; and "Au music-hall: Black Birds," *Gringoire*, 14 June 1929 (both are in Ro 585, "Le Jazz," doc. 74b, Rondel).

(the author?) temporarily resident in Harlem and has at least some basis in fact: Lew Leslie, his shows, and their stars are discussed; Lasserre signs off the preface "J. L. New York, N.-Y." Yet the story often seems little more than an imaginative re-creation of African American life derived from scenes of a black show: stock situations, such as poker and crap games, trips home to the South, even the stealing of chickens and watermelons, are played out in prose. The book is full of the crassest stereotypes: Negroes are so lazy that as soon as they wake they try to go back to sleep; Negroes live for the present for they have no sense of a past or a future; Negroes carry large razors, particularly when they are playing cards; Negroes are natural performers and live for the stage. Yet Lasserre also repeatedly attacks America's treatment of blacks, and with some knowledge and sophistication: from the segregation of housing to the inadequate policing of black neighborhoods, to the hypocrisy of using their labor but denying them rights; in places, particularly a lengthy section on lynchings by the Ku Klux Klan, his writing assumes an emotive force that is hard to reconcile with his complacent perpetuation of racist images. As with Varenne—and countless other writers—Lasserre blithely contrasts the tolerance of his land of "liberté, égalité, fraternité" (France's own colonial malpractices and massacres are forgotten). He shares the pain of African Americans at the abuses inherent in American modernity, but he studiously avoids any implication of the French, viewing them not as modernity's exploiters but as its exploited.

The reception of African American performance away from home, then, surprises in both its richness and its contradictions: the most flagrant stereotypes may contain a nub of good intention (albeit a naïve one), but superficial resonance with familiar notions of cultural difference may, on the contrary, imply a belief in racial separatism. Certain is that *revues nègres* remained slightly troubling to audiences: the comic (and tragic) stereotypes the entertainers performed were unstable and, for some at least, turned their critique back on the West. At the same time, however, French writers could shield themselves from these charges, insisting that the prejudice was American and that they, uniquely, had African American interests at heart. As I continue, I want to consider how quasi-scientific notions of racial intermixture came, increasingly, to influence discussion of black shows.

Colonial Desire and Hybridity: The Female Stars

No longer content with one female star, *Blackbirds of 1929* had two: Aida Ward (who had a minor role in the earlier show) and Adelaide Hall (who would go on to be Duke Ellington's favored "girl singer" and later

FIGURE 1.7. Publicity still of Aida Ward in *Blackbirds of 1928*, New York, NY (White Studio / © The New York Public Library).

FIGURE 1.8. Publicity still of Adelaide Hall in *Blackbirds of 1928*, New York, NY (White Studio / © The New York Public Library).

a European cabaret star; figs. 1.7 and 1.8). Artistes in different styles, their repertoires were carefully tailored to their stage personalities. Ward's understated distinction and delicate voice added to the charm of sentimental airs such as "I Can't Give You Anything but Love" and "Porgy" (a love song for Bess from the scene already addressed). While author DuBose Heyward's Bess was no angel, to be sure, there is scant sign of worldliness in McHugh's song: Bess redeems herself through love for the crippled Porgy; her new respectability and contentment find expression in music that is syllabic and lacks any hint of syncopation, whose typically stepwise movement and simple sequences form regular arch-like phrases (ex. 1.2). (The duet "Bess, You Is My Woman Now" from *Porgy and Bess* act 2, scene 1, is Gershwin's rough equivalent, although its undercurrent of passion is lacking in "Porgy.") Adelaide Hall, on the other hand, demanded satisfaction in the lusty "I Must Have That Man"; she titillated the audience in up-tempo song-and-dance numbers such as "Bandanna Babies" and the jungle scene's "Diga Diga Doo" (ex. 1.3).[80]

A 1932 Duke Ellington recording of the latter number gives an idea of

80. On Hall, see Stephen Bourne, *Sophisticated Lady: A Celebration of Adelaide Hall* (London: Ethnic Communities Oral History Project, 2001); and Iain Cameron Wil-

EXAMPLE 1.2. First eight bars of chorus of "Porgy" from *Blackbirds of 1928/29* (music, Jimmy McHugh; lyrics, Dorothy Fields), sung by Aida Ward.

the effect: A mysterious, vocalized "clarinet" sails over a trudging bass figure answered by pleas from a muted trumpet in the brief introduction. The piano enters driving forward into a first statement, on the trumpet, complete with the glissandi and growls characteristic of the "jungle" genre. Colorful lyrics leave little to the imagination—"You love me and I love you / And when you love it is natural to / Diga Diga Doo Diga Doo Doo / Diga Diga Doo Diga Doo"—with language eventually giving way to scat. The rhythm section and singers jostle the beat impatiently, adding to the music's edginess.[81] What the disc does not capture was more provocative still: a troupe of scantily clad female dancers performing wild, "African" steps (fig. 1.9). They were "the most attractive tribe of little savages" one critic could imagine; another compared them to "young wildcats in the bush."[82] The same writer found "Diga Diga Doo" "one of the

liams, *Underneath a Harlem Moon: The Harlem to Paris Years of Adelaide Hall* (London: Continuum, 2002).

81. Mills Brothers with Duke Ellington and his Famous Orchestra, 22 December 1932 (B12781–A, Brunswick 6519), reissued on *Lew Leslie's Blackbirds of 1928* LP.

82. Edouard Beaudu, "Moulin-Rouge: La Revue des Lew Leslie's *Black Birds*," *Le Petit Journal*, 15 June 1929; Anon., "D'où viennent les 'Oiseaux noirs,'" *L'Intransigeant*, 30 June 1929 (both are in Ro 585, "Le Jazz," doc. 74b, Rondel).

EXAMPLE 1.3. First sixteen bars of chorus of "Diga Diga Doo" from *Blackbirds of 1928/29* (music, Jimmy McHugh; lyrics, Dorothy Fields), sung by Adelaide Hall.

CHORUS

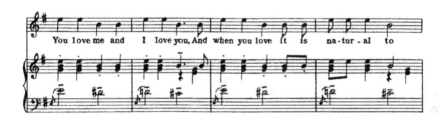

most (a)rousing [troublantes] dance scenes, which our imagination can locate in the savannahs, in the distant jungles."

The contrast between the two stars—which re-embodied on one stage, many noted, that between Mills and Baker—was genuinely somewhat baffling to the French writers; the variety of expression now apparent frustrated their attempts to essentialize. "[Ward] doesn't have—or

FIGURE 1.9. Newspaper cartoon of *Blackbirds of 1929* (*Le Quotidien*, 16 June 1929).

doesn't any longer have—the specifically Negro character of her companions," noted one critic: "She is, in a word, perfectly civilized. Adelaide Hall, on the other hand, has remained completely primitive."[83] For another, Ward expressed the melancholic, "*Uncle Tom's Cabin* side of the Negro character," while Hall offered instead its "truly seductive animal litheness."[84] If Mills had seemed to follow Baker's savagery with civilization, now they had joined hands; critics no longer knew what to think (fig. 1.10).

For some, the female stars' behavior was symptomatic of a broader condition. As far back as *La Revue nègre* (1925) reports exoticizing the performers' blackness contrasted with those acknowledging their often very light skins; reviews locating the shows deep in the African jungle competed with those recognizing them as all-American affairs. In response to *Blackbirds of 1929*, a formulation touched on before was developed at some length: that African Americans might represent neither a pure native culture nor a modern American one, but a mix of the two—a hybrid in other words. If theirs was a mixed race, the logic went, this could explain their lack of uniformity, in character as much as in skin

83. P. Loiselet, "Les Black Birds au Moulin-Rouge," *Le Soir*, 12 June 1929, in Ro 585, "Le Jazz," doc. 74b, Rondel. The association of Ward with Mills was completed by a scene in tribute to the late star, "Voici venir mon oiseau noir," in which she was personified by the young singer.

84. G. de Pawlowski, "La Revue des 'Oiseaux noirs' au Moulin-Rouge," *Le Journal*, 13 June 1929, in Ro 585, "Le Jazz," doc. 74b, Rondel. Michel Leiris remembered the striking contrast between the stars more than fifty years later: "À Paris au Moulin-Rouge, la revue de Blackbirds 1929 avait deux vedettes féminines: l'une élégiaque, Aïda Ward, l'autre trépidante, Adelaïde Hall" (Leiris, *Journal*, 203 [note dated 22 November 1983 appended to a picture of Hall in Leiris's 1929 diary]).

LES BLACK-BIRDS AU MOULIN-ROUGE

Aïda WARD   Adelaïde HALL   Earl FUCKER

FIGURE 1.10. Newspaper cartoon of three of the stars of *Blackbirds of 1929*. (Earl Tucker's hip-gyrating "snaky" dancing, recognized as an antecedent of Elvis Presley's, is perhaps captured a little too well in the misspelling of his name.)

tone. One critic was anxious to point out that "by *nègres* I scarcely mean [Africans] . . . but these descendants of slaves mixed with the white population that compose the artificial Negro American race"; the historical happenstance of this people's development was commonly noted.[85] Other writers suggested that, while African Americans could pass for civilized in everyday life, music brought out their black blood: "Seeing the Blackbirds dance," one concluded, "one cannot doubt the effect of atavism."[86]

Replacing essentialized blackness with hybridity in this way, French reportage may even begin to chime superficially with today's criticism. Yet as postcolonial scholars such as Robert J. C. Young and, more recently, Tavia Nyong'o have warned, the local contexts in which such notions have their grounding are vital to understanding them: one must not assume that such—at root biological—ideas are inherently progressive, even as they have a ring of antiessentialism.[87] Historically, hybridity has tended to suppose that races were distinct species ("polygenism"). It thus often represented a more reactionary position than either "monogenetic"

85. Pawlowski, "Revue des 'Oiseaux noirs.'"

86. Anon., "D'où viennent les 'Oiseaux noirs.'"

87. Robert J. C. Young, *Colonial Desire: Hybridity in Theory, Culture and Race* (London: Routledge, 1995); Tavia Nyong'o, *The Amalgamation Waltz: Race, Performance, and the Ruses of Memory* (Minneapolis: University of Minnesota Press, 2009).

view: the religious doctrine of races with a single origin that split, or the evolutionist argument that races mark points along a scale of civilization. Hybrids, like mules, were infertile, many argued, and thus would soon die out. If, as was often self-evident, they were able to procreate, then a process of degeneration would follow, commonly understood in cultural as well as biological terms. However, theorizations of hybridity were also, Young argues, marked by "colonial desire": an obsessive rehearsing of the consequences of the guilty appetite for—and, often forced, union with—the other that was a feature of colonial movements the world over. They are thus ambivalent: "contradictory, disruptive and already deconstructed," in his words.[88]

Even Count Gobineau's four-volume *Essai sur l'inégalité des races humaines* of 1853–1855, which remained central to racial thinking as late as the Third Reich, can be considered a theory of hybridity.[89] Civilizations (of which, he argued, there were few), were built by whites intermixing with other races; all great cultures were hybrid. But located within their vitalizing mix was an instability that would eventually lead to their degeneration, Gobineau maintained. This process would be hastened if miscegenation continued after the racial balance a national culture required to establish itself had been reached. The life and death of a society were bound up in its hybrid race.[90]

As has been common, Gobineau's work was misunderstood by Maurice Muret in his 1925 *Le Crépuscule des nations blanches* as a complete injunction on interbreeding. Instead, Muret restated another widespread theory most influentially made in the French context by Pierre Paul Broca in 1860: mixing between proximate races was beneficial; that between distant ones dangerous.[91] "The more primitive the human type," Muret ar-

88. Young, *Colonial Desire*, 27. For an excellent survey of nineteenth-century racial theory in France, see Claude Blanckaert, "Of Monstrous Métis? Hybridity, Fear of Miscegenation, and Patriotism from Buffon to Paul Broca," in *The Color of Liberty: Histories of Race in France*, ed. Sue Peabody and Tyler Stovall (Durham, NC: Duke University Press, 2003), 42–70.

89. Joseph Arthur comte de Gobineau, *Essai sur l'inégalité des races humaines*, 4 vols. (Paris: Firmin Didot, 1853–1855).

90. See Young, *Colonial Desire*; and Michael D. Biddiss, *Father of Racist Ideology: The Social and Political Thought of Count Gobineau* (New York: Weidenfeld and Nicolson, 1970).

91. Maurice Muret, *Le Crépuscule des nations blanches* (Paris: Payot, 1925) [translated by Lida (Miller) Touzalin as *The Twilight of the White Races* (London: Fischer Unwin, 1926)]; Pierre Paul Broca, *Recherches sur l'hybridité animale en général et sur l'hybridité humaine en particulier considérées dans leurs rapports avec la question de la plu-*

gued, "the more considerable its power of absorption. As the black is the most primitive . . . cross-breeding between . . . negro and . . . white has been more injurious to the whites."[92]

This view increasingly found support among the French Eugenics Society. According to William Schneider, greater immigration in the 1920s encouraged a move from the "positive eugenics" that had sought to promote the growth of a healthy population before the war toward a "negative eugenics" based in part on racial selection. Georges Vacher de Lapouge, who in 1909 had controversially urged his countrymen to replace "Liberty, Equality, Fraternity" with "Determinism, Inequality, Selection," came back into fashion; in 1926, he set up and wrote the preface for a French translation of the American eugenicist Madison Grant's *The Passing of the Great Race* (1916). René Martial adopted the biochemical indexes that had relocated race from anatomy to biology to propose a model of immigration based on tree grafting: the closer the match, the more chance the cutting would take (or the immigrant assimilate); flanking the French on the index were, conveniently enough, other nonthreatening Western Europeans. Like Gobineau, Martial accepted that races had long been hybrid but insisted that this gave all the more reason to supervise how they were mixed.[93]

Where race mixing was of most pressing concern, of course, was not in the metropolis but in overseas territories. French colonial ideology is as multifarious as the theorists and ministers who decided policies and, no less important, the powerful governors who implemented—or ignored—them on the ground. But, broadly speaking, France moved away from its original notion of assimilation (in any case, realized in only very small part) toward a looser, so-called association of colonies, which was theorized in the late nineteenth century and put into practice in the early twentieth.[94] One lens through which this shift can be viewed is the treatment

---

ralité des espèces humaines (Paris: J. Claye, 1860) [translated by Charles Carter Blake as *On the Phenomena of Hybridity in the Genus Homo* (London: Anthropological Society, 1864)].

92. Muret, *Twilight of the White Races*, 169.

93. William H. Schneider, *Quality and Quantity: The Quest for Biological Regeneration in Twentieth-Century France* (Cambridge: Cambridge University Press, 1990), 208–55.

94. Raymond F. Betts, *Assimilation and Association in French Colonial Theory, 1890–1914* (New York: Columbia University Press, 1961); Alice L. Conklin, *A Mission to Civilize: The Republican Idea of Empire in France and West Africa, 1895–1930* (Stanford, CA: Stanford University Press, 1997).

of mixed-race children born in the colonies to white men and colonial women. As Owen White, Emmanuelle Saada, and others have shown, in the nineteenth century relationships with natives were not only accepted but also often encouraged as a tool of assimilation ("making French" in a peculiarly biological manner).[95] They also served to produce a colonial elite who could aid with administrating the colonies: French-educated like their fathers, the children would gain from their mothers sufficient knowledge of native culture to serve as go-betweens.

This policy arguably suffered from its own success: people of mixed race were soon of sufficient number to form a distinct ethnic identity; closer to the ruling class, they demanded political representation and the right of relocation to the metropolis, neither of which French authorities intended to grant in great numbers. The worst fear of opponents of race mixing seemed to have been realized: the creation of a group of dangerous *déclassés* hybrids who contested the regime's power. In an effort to reestablish a simpler binary division between colonizers and colonized, policymakers ceased to regard their overseas possessions unsuitable for French women (as they long had) and began encouraging administrators to take their wives. In theory at least, *métissage* would cease as the white blood already mixed among the local population was diluted across generations; henceforth both natives and Europeans would procreate solely among themselves.

Returning from the colonies to the Parisian theatre, it should come as no surprise that traces of the scientific, moral, and political debates about hybridity—in which barely disguised desire intermingled with apprehension about its consequences—are found in reactions to *Blackbirds of 1929*. Pierre Brisson, a future editor of *Le Figaro*, for example, described the troupe in the following terms:

> Aucun de ces produits humains n'est vraiment noir, et vous avez l'échantillonnage le plus complet de mulâtres . . . tercerons, nègres caraïbes ou coyotes . . . , les croisements imprévus d'une grande ville-carrefour. . . . Les filles décolorées sont plus belles et tentantes; les hommes, musclés et nerveux. . . . Et il y a tout de même le vieux tam-tam des grands-

---

95. Owen White, *Children of the French Empire: Miscegenation and Colonial Society in French West Africa, 1895–1960* (Oxford: Oxford University Press, 1999); Emmanuelle Saada, *Empire's Children: Race, Filiation, and Citizenship in the French Colonies*, trans. Arthur Goldhammer (Chicago: University of Chicago Press, 2012). See also Elisa Camiscioli, *Reproducing the French Race: Immigration, Intimacy, and Embodiment in the Early Twentieth Century* (Durham, NC: Duke University Press, 2009).

parents, la vieille odeur des festins sanglants qui tourmente leurs reins en délire.[96]

None of these human products is really black, and you have the most complete range of mulattos . . . quarteroons, Caribbean Negroes or mongrels . . . , the unexpected crossbreeds of a crossroads-city. . . . The lightened girls are more beautiful and tempting; the men, muscular and vigorous. . . . And there is all the same the old tam-tam of the grandparents, the old smell of a bloody feast that racks their loins into a frenzy.

André Levinson, meanwhile, took Brisson's basically positive (if hardly flattering) exercise in the exoticization of a vital hybridity—and in the sublimation of desire—and tacitly transmogrified it into a much more disturbing phenomenon he called "métissage au théâtre." As if précising Brisson, he argued:

C'est le métissage, croisement fantasque de races, mélange capricieusement dosé, greffé, altération violente, contamination, transfusion de sève, qui multiplient, exaspèrent—et minent, comme chez cette adorable Florence Mills, morte, fleur maladive, à vingt-quatre ans—la vitalité de "l'homme de couleur" d'Amérique.

It's *métissage*, whimsical crossing of races, capriciously proportioned and grafted mixing, violent distortion, contamination, transfusion of sap, which multiplies, exasperates—and drains, as with this lovely Florence Mills, dead, sickly flower, at twenty-four [sic]—the vitality of America's colored man.

Any lingering notion of this tradition's purity had to be dispelled:

Chez ces *afro-américains*, nous sommes en présence non d'une tribu indigène à l'état de sauvagerie paradisiaque, mais . . . mixte, bigarrée au possible . . . l'explosion suprême et ultime d'une singularité ethnique en décomposition.[97]

96. Pierre Brisson, "Au music-hall," *Le Temps*, 17 June 1929, in Ro 585, "Le Jazz," doc. 74b, Rondel.
97. André Levinson, "Le Métissage au théâtre," *Comœdia*, 21 July 1929, in Ro 9805(2), "Levinson, André," Rondel [also reprinted in *Les Visages de la danse*, 270–73 (quote on pp. 270–71)].

Among these Afro-Americans, we are in the presence not of an indigenous tribe in a state of heavenly savagery, but of . . . as motley a mix as possible . . . the supreme and final explosion of an ethnic singularity decomposing.

These are strong statements, but as with his earlier reflections on Florence Mills, Levinson's position as a whole is ambivalent: he reviewed the show three times elsewhere in largely positive terms.[98] The source of his ire here can be located partly in Brisson's article, which had criticized Levinson's unmodulating defense of the classical tradition. Levinson hits back by inverting Brisson's concept of a vigorous hybridity to make African American culture—people—an aberration about to implode (both possibilities, of course, that could be found in Gobineau). But even Levinson was not immune to "colonial desire" and its attendant anxiety. In the same article, he argued: "We are in the hold of this hybrid art, bastard, but all the more intense"; it was an "aphrodisiac love potion," "which burns us as it wastes away."

Thus it was that the Blackbirds found themselves caught up in a debate about the French "race" and its culture. More familiar now, African Americans had come to represent not only a source of a vitalizing (or terrifying) primitiveness but also an example of racial mixing. Since *métissage* was, at this time, a real concern to many French both at home and in the colonies, reactions to the Blackbirds and their kin lack historical charge until relocated in that specific context. On the topic of hybridity, Emmanuelle Saada writes:

In opposition to an ahistorical and often functionalist vision of *métissage*, which posits the "hybrid" as a universal type fulfilling the role of social mediator—a *Homo métis* produced by all societies—the example of colonial France shows that the very existence of the *métis* category depends on the way in which social identities are defined, and therefore on power relations. . . . [Recalling this] is a valuable exercise at a time when French politicians and social scientists are celebrating a "*métis* France" and thereby reinforcing the very racial identities they claim to be undermining.[99]

In other words, and as I have attempted above, historical discourse about hybridity must be understood in terms of its own biological and colo-

98. André Levinson, "Exotismes américains," *Candide*, 19 June 1929, in Ro 585, "Le Jazz," doc. 74b, Rondel; "Encore les 'Oiseaux noirs'"; "'Porgy' et la revue des 'Oiseaux noirs.'"

99. Saada, *Empire's Children*, 9–10.

nial frame of reference: *métissage* is a function of, not an escape from, racialized discourse. As I continue into the 1930s, I will ask how African American performers—and their audiences—responded to the controversy swirling around them.

Getting Serious: Black Flowers (1930)

While I focus here on the reactions of French observers to the Paris shows, contrasting responses to the *Blackbirds of 1929* in the *Baltimore Afro-American* provide a rare opportunity to engage with opinion among some African American audience members. The activities of the community's artists at home and abroad were always of great interest in the black press. Rarely, however, did this coverage diverge from a strict party line: the success of performers was celebrated as a sign of black achievement; recognition in Europe, in particular, conferred prestige and suggested opportunities lacking in the States. The importance of entertainers, like sportspeople (and increasingly writers and intellectuals in this period) in generating race pride cannot be overestimated. Moreover, as Jayna Brown writes in an important study of touring female performers, "Recognition from abroad was leverage, legitimating black claims to full citizenship in the United States."[100]

So much is clear in a report by the troupe's stage manager, who boasted that "'Blackbirds' is still the hit of Paris. Adelaide Hall . . . is another Josephine Baker"; he continued to list the show's many high points.[101] On the same page, however, a member of the famous university choral group the Fisk Jubilee Singers, who were touring Europe at the time, gave an altogether different take: "Watermelon eating on stage shocks American traveling abroad"; "Razors, pistols, cops, dishonesty riles visitors." Not altogether dismissive—he admires in particular the "Porgy" scene and the men's dancing—this writer concludes with a warning: "All in all 'Blackbirds' is probably doing more harm than good. It is giving to Paris the wrong idea of the typical American Negro. . . . The danger in such

100. Brown, "Translocations," 248–49.

101. S. H. Dudley, "S. H. Dudley Writes from Paris," *Baltimore Afro-American*, 24 August 1929. In the same newspaper, see also Anon., "'Blackbirds' Acclaimed Season's Hit at Moulin Rouge," 13 July 1929; J. A. Rogers, "Adelaide Hall Rivals Jo Baker on European Stage," 3 August 1929; Anon., "Home Town Turns Out for Star: Aida Ward Crowds Church Twice on Sunday," 5 October 1929; and Anon., "Aida Ward Liked Paris Hats, Lovemaking and Monuments," 12 October 1929. Harlem Renaissance writer and campaigner James Weldon Johnson gives a sympathetic account of the New York shows in his *Black Manhattan* (New York: Alfred A. Knopf, 1930), chaps. 16 and 17, 182–230, but refrains from discussing their particulars.

shows . . . is that they will give generally to white people, the [derisive] attitude [toward Negroes] of the southerner."[102]

In many ways, this reaction is unsurprising: the Fisk Jubileee Singers were—and still are today—dedicated to "cultivated" a capella performance. Already of sixty years' standing by the time of the *Blackbirds*, they had formed at a time when minstrelsy was the only form of black performance most white audiences would have experienced, and were anxious to challenge those preconceptions. The student's response is thus characteristic of a period in which the "talented tenth" charged with uplifting the race were more commonly imagined as writers and composers than as tap dancers and jazz musicians. But the article's laying of blame for perpetuating stereotypes at least in part with the performers themselves begs a question: how much scope did African American entertainers have in this era to control their depiction on stage?

At once borrowing on the success of *Blackbirds of 1929* and, perhaps, proposing an alternative model came African American director (and dancer) Louis Douglas's Black Flowers in their show *Liza* the following year.[103] For the first time, one critic marveled, this was "a show entirely created and played by blacks without the slightest contribution from whites."[104] Not that the controversy around hybridity had entirely disappeared. Pierre Brisson's position was ambivalent, located between evolutionism—"their uncertain race is no longer black [but] it is not yet white"—and a process of intermixture that would have made some shudder: "old blood renewed by animal sap." Levinson had been wrong, however, to suggest that African American performers were degenerate: "Decadence is not among

102. L. K. McMillan, "McMillan in Paris sees 'Blackbirds,'" *Baltimore Afro-American*, 24 August 1929.

103. See program dated 3 June 1930, in Ro 585, "Le Jazz," doc. 111, Rondel. As far as I can establish, this show was not related to the musical comedy *Liza* (book by Irvin C. Miller, music and lyrics by Maceo Pinkard) that was presented in New York in 1922–1923. For an attempt to document Louis Douglas's extraordinary life, see Rainer E. Lotz, "Louis Douglas," in *Black People: Entertainers of African Descent in Europe and Germany* (Bonn, Ger.: Birgit Lotz Verlag, 1997), 297–390, which indicates that he presented a similar show to this elsewhere in Europe. Lotz is frequently inaccurate with respect to Douglas's time in France, however (and sometimes places him elsewhere when he was there). See also Leroy Hopkins, "Louis Douglas and the Weimar Reception of Harlemania," in *Germans and African Americans: Two Centuries of Change*, ed. Larry A. Greene and Anka Ortlepp (Jackson: University Press of Mississippi, 2011), 50–69. For *Liza* (sometimes called *Louisiana*) in other French towns, see Ro 585, "Le Jazz," docs. 107–8 and 125–27, Rondel.

104. Anon., "Avant-Première: À la Porte Saint-Martin: Le Spectacle nègre des Black Flower [*sic*]," *L'Œuvre*, 31 May 1930, in Ro 585, "Le Jazz," doc. 111, Rondel.

them, it is in us," Brisson maintained.[105] Another critic disagreed: the troupe had "an imperfect structure and legs that are too fat or too spindly, as is the case among those of mixed blood"; one more was amused by the "contradictions between [their] monkey-like faces and [their] smart clothes [toilettes d'apparat]."[106] For most, however, the presence of Douglas as director indicated a cultural authenticity whatever the makeup of the race. His role alongside Josephine Baker in the first *Revue nègre* was well remembered, but whereas she had since been "naturalized white," one writer argued, Douglas had "remained Negro."[107] Such troupes having become commonplace (poncif), another noted, only "le magicien noir" Louis Douglas could create something new, with the "naïve and unsullied [frais] charm . . . of primitive cultures," in the words of a third.[108]

What, if anything, was different about this revue? The location was notable: the Théâtre de la Porte Saint-Martin was no frivolous music hall or cabaret but a venerable institution (still there today, near the Place

105. Pierre Brisson, review of Black Flowers' *Liza*, *Le Temps*, 9 June 1930, in Ro 585, "Le Jazz," doc. 111, Rondel. The passage reads: "Derrière ces nègres en frac, plus minces et plus agiles que les sportsmen d'un club anglais, il y a le tam-tam des grands-parents, la sanglante odeur des festins primitifs. Leur race douteuse n'est plus noire, elle n'est pas encore blanche, elle est une transaction, une sorte de sous-produit de la civilisation industrielle. On pressent le règne du métissage: le vieux sang renouvelé par des sèves animales, quelque chose d'obscur et d'inquiétant. . . . À l'origine de leurs exercices, il y a une joie animale soutenue par l'exubérance de dons physiques anormaux. La décadence n'est pas chez eux, elle est en nous."

106. A. de Montgon, "Spectacle nègre à la Porte-Saint-Martin," *Le Petit Parisien*, 5 June 1930; Paul Reboux, "Porte-Saint-Martin: *Liza*," *Paris-Soir*, 6 June 1930 (both are in Ro 585, "Le Jazz," doc. 111, Rondel). As ever, the varied skin tones among the troupe generated considerable interest: "La compagnie des Black Flowers présente toutes les nuances du noir depuis le mulâtre, produit du blanc et du noir, à égalité: deux sous de lait, deux sous de café; passant par le gris, produit du mulâtre et du noir: un sou de lait, trois sous de café; le marabout, produit du gris et du noir: trois sous et demi de café et un demi-sou de lait; jusqu'au quarteron, produit du mulâtre et du blanc: trois sous de lait, un sou de café, et jusqu'au tierceron, produit du quarteron et du blanc: trois sous et demi de lait pour un demi-sou de café" (Jean Bastia, "Fantaisie métissée sur 'Liza': Opérette nègre," *Comœdia*, 5 June 1930, in Ro 585, "Le Jazz," doc. 111, Rondel).

107. Bastia, "Fantaisie métissée sur 'Liza.'"

108. George Stuart, "Au théâtre nègre: 'Black Flowers' Liza," *Le Soir*, [5?] June 1930; Gerard Missaire, "À la Porte Saint-Martin (théâtre nègre): *Liza* opérette-revue à grand spectacle en deux actes, huit tableaux et quarante-cinq scènes, de M. Louis Douglas," *Journal des débats*, 5 June 1930 (both are in Ro 585, "Le Jazz," doc. 111, Rondel). On changing perceptions of Josephine Baker, see chap. 3.

de la République); the preceding production had been Edmond Rostand's *Cyrano de Bergerac*. As Brisson noted: "This time the acclimatization is definitive."[109] Doubtless this explains the company's billing as "théâtre nègre: The Black Flowers," with the title of their show, *Liza*, sometimes appended as an afterthought. Genres multiplied: *Liza* was an "opérette-revue nègre à grand spectacle" ("revue à grand spectacle" being the conventional designation for glamorous shows such as those at the Folies-Bergère). The message was simple: this was not an ordinary black revue.

Nor was it, although it drew liberally on their conventions. In effect, Douglas had assembled stereotypically black scenes into a more or less coherent narrative that could legitimately be termed "opérette." Following the fortunes of Liza (another dynamic female entertainer and jazz musician, Valaida Snow), the show opens and closes on a cotton plantation. Liza is about to marry Rastus (Douglas) when she is swept off to New York by a dandy (Douglas's former partner, Fernando Jones): cue Harlem low life and high jinks. Rastus follows, fights the dandy—the time-honored boxing scene—and then he, like Liza, finds a job at a Negro theatre: the Plantation Cabaret (where Snow could stun the audience, as she was apt, by playing trumpet and piano, among other instruments, as well as singing and dancing; fig. 1.11).[110] In between rehearsal and performance, they pass the time shooting craps. Back together, Liza and Rastus return to the real plantation in time for her mammy's birthday and marry: an all-purpose Negro celebration embracing homecoming, birthday, and wedding—conventional tropes of the black stage.

To be sure, none of this rewrote the book of black theatre, but the effort to coalesce standard topoi into a coherent drama was significant: it recalled the heyday of New York in the early twenties, when black musical comedies such as *Shuffle Along* involved not only African American performers but directors and composers. What is more, the play within a play could be said to signify on stereotypes even as it reproduced them: the last two scenes juxtaposed two plantations, the cabaret's and the play's own, the one no more real than the other. Other conventions were broken. For one, most of the time the performers remained conspicuously fully attired. Only in the cabaret was nudity tolerated, focusing fetishization of the black body on that one "artificial" scene. Valaida Snow, noted a critic, has "an elegant body which she offers much less generously to

109. Brisson, review of Black Flowers' *Liza*.

110. On Valaida Snow, see Mark Miller, *High Hat, Trumpet and Rhythm: The Life and Music of Valaida Snow* (Toronto: Mercury Press, 2007), which includes a discography, 143–52; Snow's recordings have been rereleased in several volumes on both Classics and Harlequin labels among others. See also Brown, "Translocations."

FIGURE 1.11. Valaida Snow, ca. 1930 (White Studio / © The New York Public Library).

view than Josephine Baker." Once a joke, "le noir est toujours habillé" ("the black is always dressed," i.e., in his or her skin color) had become a fact, another complained.[111] Further, while the two principal male characters might suggest rural and urban minstrel figures, Jim Crow and Zip Coon, Douglas played his character with such poignancy and melancholy that he brought to mind no demeaning stereotype but a *commedia dell'arte* character, "un pierrot romantique." He was

111. Unidentified review of Black Flowers' *Liza*, 7 June 1930, in Ro 585, "Le Jazz," doc. 111, Rondel; Bastia, "Fantaisie métissée sur 'Liza.'"

un délicieux et bel amoureux, passionné, tendre à la voix étrangement chantante et mélodieuse. . . . Et tous ceux qui l'entourent aujourd'hui, sans renier ces rythmes originaux, sans abandonner cette frénésie presque mystique qui leur sont propres, nous montrent le même cœur. . . . Ces nègres jusqu'ici sur la défensive, se montrent à nous, tels qu'ils sont.[112]

a charming and handsome lover, passionate, tender, with a strangely lilting and melodious voice. . . . And all those who surround him today, without renouncing these original rhythms, without abandoning this almost mystical frenzy which is their own, show us the same heart. . . . These Negroes, up to now on the defensive, reveal themselves to us, such as they are.

In both its plot—a woman caught between good and bad men who leaves her southern home for the city—and its ambition to climb the ladder of genres, *Liza* represents a sort of *Porgy and Bess* avant la lettre (except, of course, that its writer-director was black). While no music is available, the program and press reviews suggest it leaned heavily on spiritual-type numbers featuring the Utica Jubilee Singers (a group modeled on that of Fisk, from a black college in Mississippi) as well as, of course, fast-paced songs and dances, led by Booker T. Wingfield and his Black Flowers Jazz. Particular attractions included an early demonstration of the Lindy Hop during a rehearsal scene, the cabaret featuring some titillating drum majorettes, and Louis Douglas's version of the "Stair Step Dance" (borrowed from Bill "Bojangles" Robinson via Eddie Rector's rendition in *Blackbirds of 1929*). The variety was capable of representing, one critic thought, the different "états d'âme" of the American Negro: vitality matched with sadness.[113] In sum, *Liza* reveals an unexpected power for African Americans in this period to modify their representation on stage, but it also indicates, no less clearly, that they worked within an externally determined range of possibilities in order to ensure their success. I take up this question again, and in much greater detail, in chapter 3, in which I consider Josephine Baker's transition from exotic music-hall star to almost homely singer of French operetta in Offenbach's *La Créole*: a role in which she,

112. Hanry-Jaunet, "À propos de: Spectacles nègres," *Le Soir*, 8 June 1930, in Ro 585, "Le Jazz," doc. 111, Rondel. See also René Bizet, "Revue nègre," *L'Intransigeant*, 6 June 1930, in Ro 585, "Le Jazz," doc. 111, Rondel; and Michel Leiris, "Folklore théâtral: 'Liza,' opérette de Louis Douglas," *Documents* 2/4 (1930): 306.

113. Robert Le Bret, "À la Porte Saint-Martin: Les 'Black Flowers' dans une opérette nègre: 'Liza,'" *L'Ami du peuple du soir*, 5 June 1930, in Ro 585, "Le Jazz," doc. 111, Rondel.

like the Black Flowers, both acquiesced to and challenged expectations of African American performance, without quite being able to wrest control of them.

A Tradition Continued: The 1930s

It would be wrong to suggest that black revues continued with such pace through the 1930s. The economic slowdown led by the Wall Street crash made risky ventures such as European tours impossible. Even in France, where instability was slower to take effect, labor laws restricting the number of foreigners employed were increasingly cited (if rarely enforced) as French performers felt the pinch.[114] To make matters worse, many music-hall directors, facing spiraling costs and competition from movie theatres, gave up the fight: even the Moulin Rouge converted to the silver screen as soon as the Blackbirds had departed. All the same, the early thirties saw the first visits of important jazz musicians (Louis Armstrong and Coleman Hawkins among them) and even bands (Cab Calloway's and Duke Ellington's, for example), as I will discuss in chapter 2. Requiring few props and costumes, and paying only short visits, their concerts were more practically and economically viable than music-hall shows. Meanwhile, black entertainers continued to grace the French stage in the more modest variety shows, as they had done for many years.[115]

A surprise, though, comes with a minor resurgence of black shows in the later 1930s: *Harlem Black Birds 36* at the Alcazar Theatre and *Cotton Club* the following year at the Moulin Rouge (now reconverted). The first, again produced and directed by Louis Douglas, bore a suspicious resemblance to *Liza*: a loose plot moved the performers between a mythical southern plantation and a no less mythical Harlem.[116] This time they managed to

114. See Jeffrey H. Jackson, "Making Enemies: Jazz in Inter-war Paris," *French Cultural Studies* 10 (1999): 179–99; and Jackson, "New Bands and New Tensions," in *Making Jazz French: Music and Modern Life in Interwar Paris* (Durham, NC: Duke University Press, 2003), 143–53.

115. These included "the coloured comedian dancers" the Five Spillers (e.g., Empire Theatre, fortnight beginning 21 August 1931: program, in Ro 15718[4], "L'Empire," Rondel; press, in Ro 15718[11–15], "L'Empire," Rondel); Roy Atkins, Alma Smith, and "neuf girls noires" in *Ambassadeurs 1933* (Ambassadeurs Theatre, May 1933: in Ro 15690[2], "Les Ambassadeurs," doc. 24, Rondel); and "trois coloured gentlemen" the Midnight Steppers (e.g., Empire, fort. beg. 2 October 1936: prog., Ro 15718[29–31], "L'Empire," Rondel; press, in 8° Sw 95, "Empire, 1933–1954," AdS). See also Fréjaville's regular reviews, as cited above.

116. Insurance salesman Dandy Dan (Lewis Hardcastle) returns from Harlem to the cotton plantation; he meets Lulu who wants to search for her long lost mother.

insert not only rehearsal, cabaret, and wedding scenes, but also a concert, by the Southern Jubilee Singers. Although advertising a specious connection with the Cotton Club ("1000 représentations à New-York, 800 à Londres"), the show appears to have been assembled from performers already resident in France, who may have hailed from the Old World as much as from the New.[117] Critics agreed on a sense of déjà vu but typically enjoyed it, even if the female dancers again left rather much to the imagination: another example of Douglas's stricture on the white audience to focus on black talent rather than on black physicality alone.[118] An exception in this respect was Charles Delaunay (an important early jazz critic and discographer, who will feature prominently in subsequent chapters) writing in the recently established magazine *Jazz hot*. *Harlem Black Birds 36*, he complained, was a "scandal" and a "lamentable spectacle" that profited from the publicity of Lew Leslie's *Blackbirds of 1936* in London to present "Negroes recruited in the working-class districts of [Paris] . . . miserable wretches . . . walking the boards . . . for the first time."[119]

More completely successful was the second show, which reopened the Moulin Rouge as an upscale nightclub.[120] This time it *was* a real Cotton Club affair. Again black-directed, by dancer and choreographer Clarence Robinson, it featured Teddy Hill's Orchestra: one of "the poorest bands to come out of Harlem in the Swing Era," in Gunther Schuller's opinion, but cradling a young John Birks ("Dizzy") Gillespie nevertheless.[121] For some, the revue, which still included a jungle number among much high-paced

Dandy Dan takes her to the North, but her lover Boule de Neige (Douglas) and his friend Beausoleil (Joe Alex) pursue them. Predictably enough, this duo scrapes together a living on the stage, before the evening concludes with a "mariage nègre." The program is transcribed in Lotz, *Black People*, 377–79.

117. The wording, presumably from a press release, appears in "Harlem Black Birds 1936," *La Volonté*, 29 April 1936; and André Lénéka, "À l'Alcazar de Paris: Hamlem [sic] Black Birds 1936," *L'Avenir*, 2 May 1936, both in 8° Sw 79(2), "Cabarets: L'Alcazar de Paris, 1933–1939," AdS.

118. A. de Montgon, "À l'Alcazar: 'La Revue nègre,'" *Le Petit Bleu de Paris*, 7 May 1936, in Ro 19105, "Les Revues de l'Alcazar, 1936," Rondel.

119. Ch. D., "En France: Le Scandale de 'Blackbirds 36' de Paris," *Jazz hot*, no. 8 (May 1936): 16. For uncertain reasons, *Blackbirds of 1936* did not visit France. On the London show, see Jeff R. Aldam, "En Angleterre: Les Blackbirds 1936," *Jazz hot*, no. 7 (April 1936): 13; and Aldam, ". . . En Angleterre," *Jazz hot*, no. 11 (September–October 1936): 18.

120. A program is in R. Supp. 655, "Revues représentées en 1937," Rondel.

121. Gunther Schuller, *The Swing Era: The Development of Jazz, 1930–1945* (New York: Oxford University Press, 1989), 422. See also Dizzy Gillespie with Al Fraser, *To Be or Not . . . to Bop* (New York: Doubleday, 1979), 73–78.

dancing by the likes of Bill Bailey and the Berry Brothers (well-known for performances with Duke Ellington), lacked somewhat in "nostalgic laments" revealing the "primitive soul." But another, aware of society opinion, simply insisted: "You must have seen these Negroes."[122] Hugues Panassié, France's foremost jazz critic in this period and tireless propagandist for the cause of "jazz hot," recalled the show—and provided photographs—in a 1946 book; it was the "biggest event of the season," and he went fifteen or twenty times.[123] He had reviewed it at least twice, once in *Jazz hot* and once, more remarkably, in the extreme right-wing if not protofascist paper *Insurgé*. Panassié prefaced his detailed descriptions of the revue's glories with the following statement:

> Tout le monde devrait aller voir la revue du Cotton-Club. . . . Il faudrait que ce courant de sang frais et vigoureux serve à arracher les Européens aux divertissements amollis dans lesquels ils sont de plus en plus embourbés. . . . Il n'est nullement anachronique de souhaiter qu'une revue comme celle du Cotton-Club ait sur nous une influence salutaire.[124]

> Everyone should go to see the Cotton Club revue. . . . This current of fresh and vigorous blood ought to serve to drag Europeans away from the limp amusements in which they are more and more bogged down. . . . It is not at all anachronistic to wish that a revue like the Cotton Club one has a beneficial influence on us.

Panassié's denial of anachronism reveals an anxiety that is easily located: his argument—that Europeans should renew themselves by recovering the depths of primitive expression—resonates most strongly of all with the surrealist-turning-anarchist Michel Leiris. This is hardly an obvious view to find, in late-1930s France, in a paper that vehemently opposed the Popular Front, demonized Russian Communism, and maintained an ambivalent respect for German National Socialism. It was not just op-

122. Pierre Varenne, "Au Moulin Rouge: Le Cotton-Club," *L'Intransigeant*, 21 June 1937; Anon., "Le Cotton-Club au Moulin-Rouge," *Le Temps*, 15 June 1937; and André Warnod, "La Revue de Cotton-Club au Bal du Moulin-Rouge," *Le Figaro*, 17 June 1937 (all are in 8° Sw 103[1], "Cabarets: Bal du Moulin Rouge, 1937–1960," AdS).

123. Panassié, *Douze années de jazz*, 209, 211.

124. Hugues Panassié, "La Revue du Cotton-Club," *Insurgé* 1/23 (16 June 1937). See also Panassié, "Teddy Hill's Orchestra," *Jazz hot*, no. 18 (June–July 1937): 3–4; Madeleine Gautier, "Le Cotton-Club de New-York à Paris," *Jazz hot*, no. 18 (June–July 1937): 5; and J. H., "Teddy Hill et le 'Cotton Club Orchestra' au 'Moulin Rouge,'" *Jazz-Tango-Dancing* 8/78 (July 1937): 9.

portunism that found Panassié writing in such a venue, however: his own Catholic monarchism, which went as far as opposition to suffrage, was little less reactionary.[125] An interesting compound, he exploits the right's language of decadence but proposes a radical solution: not at all the recovery of national spirit through a revival of folklore that is associated with the closed nationalism of Vichy, but rather a continued reference to outside cultures—African Americans of all people. André Levinson, who died in 1933 correcting proofs of a book including his thoughts on "métissage," would not have approved.[126]

Panassié's comments help me to draw to a temporary close: they explode several of the assumptions with which I have taken issue in this chapter. African American music theatre was not chased out of France in the mid-1920s, as the story of high culture's engagement with it has sometimes supposed. Interest did not even peak among the general public for another few years. Nor did cosmopolitanism cede to conservatism in discrete, successive moments. A wider view—one interested in popular culture in and for itself—tells a different story: an ambivalent coexistence of liberal and reactionary tendencies, on music, race, and culture, throughout the interwar period. In this way, I seek to locate, more evenhandedly, the roots not just of Vichy ideology but also of its discontents; or, rather, to understand how Vichy itself could come to be characterized less by a coherent cultural policy than by a set of rhetorical strategies, which did not, even then, exclude jazz.

Certainly, French opinion on African Americans and their music was not straightforwardly political: extremes of right and left sometimes met at the opposition they constructed between black and white musics, cultures, and peoples. On all sides a pungent mix of half-absorbed theories (themselves equivocal) were brought to bear on questions of race. To their enormous credit, performers from Florence Mills to Louis Douglas did not just perpetuate stereotypes but used their strength and versatility to make a chink in the armor of race, racism, and racialism. If the challenges they embodied led hybridity to replace purity (i.e., savagery) as a paradigm, however, detailed investigation reveals that it too spanned the gamut from *re*generation to *de*generation.

As *Bamboozled* makes plain, this process of black negotiation with

125. Pertinent discussions include Tom Perchard, "Tradition, Modernity and the Supernatural Swing: Re-reading 'Primitivism' in Hugues Panassié's Writing on Jazz," *Popular Music* 30 (2011): 25–45; and Philippe Gumplowicz, "Musicographes réactionnaires des années 1930," *Le Mouvement social*, no. 208 (2004): 91–124. See also chaps. 2 and 4 below.

126. Levinson, *Les Visages de la danse.*

white expectation continues even today—a fact the mainstream media, in France as elsewhere, too often refuse to acknowledge. Although they date from long ago, these shows cannot be consigned to the past as period curiosities, for this would assume that racist stereotypes no longer held any charge today. At the same time, the passionate discussions about authenticity and hybridity I locate in the reception of these *revues nègres* suggest that their meanings to contemporary audiences mutated even more quickly than did the shows themselves: the music and images tell only part of a story that was as much bound up with conceptualizations of race circulating in the contexts of colonialism and immigration. If *Bamboozled*'s critique may thus feel heavy-handed, its history not sufficiently nuanced, it was intent nevertheless on fostering a dialogue between past and present, one that sadly the French press was disinclined to hear. Recovering this forgotten history indicates yet again how deeply musical and theatrical representations have, for better and worse, engaged the racial imagination. It is not only naïve but reckless to consider that they have ceased to do so.

2 *Jack à l'Opéra*
Jazz Bands in Black and White

An Unlikely Alliance: Stravinsky and the Boys

When British bandleader Jack Hylton (and "His Boys") played the Paris Opéra in 1931, controversy was inevitable (fig. 2.1). The organizers sought to turn it to their profit—and, no doubt, to hasten its demise—with a spoof "Opéra-jazz," *Jack à l'Opéra*, circulated as publicity. In act 1, regular patrons gather denouncing "Jack the barbarian": "Horror! Horror! My Robert, my Lucia! My Samson, Faust, Thaïs. . . . Shame and Damnation! . . . You will be avenged!!!" In act 2, they confront the management about this sacrilege. But in act 3, the band's performance wins over even the most recalcitrant; the chorus sing "Jack Hylton is a God."[1]

Other people had different ideas. The day before the concert, the Opéra's new ballet director, Serge Lifar, premiered a "fantaisie chorégraphique" on a scenario by Paul Gsell and the celebrated Wagnerian tenor Franz-Gautier. In *L'Orchestre en liberté*, instruments of the orchestra come to life, showing off and making merry. When a Negro jazz band launches a surprise attack, the orchestra does battle against this "péril noir" until "the darkies [moricauds] are vanquished" (fig. 2.2).[2] A funeral march leads to a joyous *bourrée* and the descent of a celestial harp: "the return to harmony."[3]

---

1. *Le Valmaletav: Bulletin mensuel d'informations du bureau de concerts Marcel de Valmalète*, no. 4 (31 January 1931), in Ro 586, "La Musique nègre et les chefs d'orchestre de jazz," p. 219, Collection Rondel, Département des Arts du Spectacle, Bibliothèque Nationale, Paris (hereafter cited as Rondel).

2. E. V. [Émile Vuillermoz?], "Théâtre de l'Opéra," *Excelsior*, 18 February 1931, in Ro 3648, "Laparra, Raoul: *L'Illustre Fregona*, Zarzuela en 3 actes," Rondel (Laparra's was the main work on the program).

3. Dominique Sordet, "Théâtre national de l'Opéra: Trois créations," *L'Action française*, 20 February 1931, in Ro 3648, "*L'Illustre Fregona*," Rondel. The *livret* for *L'Orchestre en liberté*, which includes the scenario, etc., is available at both Ro 4365, Rondel, and LIV.929, Bibliothèque-Musée de l'Opéra, Département de la Musique, Bibliothèque Nationale, Paris (hereafter cited as Opéra).

FIGURE 2.1. *Above*, Jack Hylton and His Boys during a rehearsal at the Paris Opéra, February 1931 (Keystone-France/Gamma-Keystone via Getty Images).

FIGURE 2.2. *Left*, Paul Colin's design for Le Jazz Nègre in the "fantaisie chorégraphique" *L'Orchestre en liberté* (music, Henry Sauveplane; choreography, Serge Lifar), Paris Opéra, 1931 (© ADAGP, Paris and DACS, London 2013).

L'Orchestre's composer, Henry Sauveplane, was little known, but critic André Cœuroy could speculate: Sauveplane was from central France (witness the celebratory *bourrée*), was in his forties, and read the conservative *Revue des deux mondes*.⁴ Ironically, it was not the ballet's reactionary moral but its "modernistic" construction that made it unpopular. Despite one critic's insistence that its "parodic dissonances" served only the "triumph of classicism," the audience protested at its "barbaric" sounds and "music-hall acrobatics."⁵ Some writers even spoke up for the demonized jazz, complaining that Sauveplane lacked the talent for its pastiche let alone its parody.⁶

Hylton's concert thus occurred at a particularly heated moment: the most appropriate response, some thought, to *L'Orchestre en liberté*. Upping the stakes, the "King of Jazz" was taking an unusual step: including among the fox-trots and novelty numbers a special arrangement of a selection from Stravinsky's *Mavra*, advertised as the "principal attraction."⁷ The origin of the idea and exact motivation of the two parties are impossible to establish reliably, but the arrangement was sanctioned, possibly suggested, and certainly encouraged by the composer, who was present (fig. 2.3).⁸

4. André Cœuroy, "À l'Opéra: *Prélude dominical* de Henry Sauveplane," *Paris-Midi*, 18 February 1931, in Ro 3648, "*L'Illustre Fregona*," Rondel (the article's title mistakenly names a work by Guy Ropartz, also on the program, in place of *L'Orchestre*).

5. Unidentified review of *L'Orchestre en liberté*, 21 February 1931; J. F., "La Danse à l'Opéra," *Paris-Midi*, 6 March 1931 (both are in Ro 3648, "*L'Illustre Fregona*," Rondel).

6. For reviews see, in addition to Ro 3648, "*L'Illustre Fregona*," Rondel, the *dossier d'œuvre* for Laparra's *L'Illustre Fregona*, in Opéra. A printed short score (A. I. D. Mus. 1145), manuscript full score (A. 785a), and manuscript orchestral parts ("Matériel") for *L'Orchestre en liberté* are also in Opéra.

7. For concert announcements, see, for example, *Le Temps*, 8 February 1931.

8. Extracts of letters exchanged between Hylton and Stravinsky are provided in a somewhat confused passage of Robert Craft, ed., *Stravinsky: Selected Correspondence*, vol. 2 (London: Faber and Faber, 1984), 123–24n. While Craft states that Hylton approached Stravinsky for permission to make the arrangement, Hylton's reference to "the music which you have honored me by asking me to play" (123n) seems to imply that the idea originated with the composer. As far as I have been able to ascertain, the recording of *Mavra* mentioned here and in other sources did not take place. For an attempt to piece together the evidence and a useful account of the concert in general, see Pete Faint's article "Hylton and Stravinsky" at his website on the bandleader, http://www.jackhylton.com (accessed 19 August 2013), to which I am indebted. For more on the arrangement itself, see Deborah Mawer, "Jazzing a Classic: Hylton and Stravinsky's *Mavra* at the Paris Opéra," *Twentieth-Century Music* 6 (2009): 155–82.

FIGURE 2.3. Stravinsky at a rehearsal of *Mavra*, with Hylton to his right (Mary Evans / SZ Photo / Scherl).

It is almost as hard to find out what happened on the night. The first half, presented to a full, notably young, and well-heeled house had so far been a great success.[9] A hush fell as the promoter, Marcel de Valmalète, stepped forward to explain the piece Hylton and His Boys would perform (stagehands meanwhile furnishing the band and its leader for the first

9. On the audience, see Émile [Vuillermoz?], "Jack Hylton à l'Opéra," *Excelsior*, 24 February 1931, in Ro 586, "La Musique nègre," p. 222, Rondel.

time with parts and music stands).[10] Although the selection from *Mavra* was well rehearsed (sometimes in Stravinsky's presence), the bandsmen's recollections suggest the performance did not go well.[11] (According to one, a petrified Hylton, accustomed only to remembering if tunes were in two, three, or four, was heard to murmur, "Take no notice of me: I'm bloody lost!")[12] Whether owing to this or unfamiliarity with the music, the audience reaction was cool. On one account, the composer stamped out, "telling Hylton, his Boys and jazz to go to the devil."[13]

However receptive they were to the concert as a whole, the press agreed that the Stravinsky project had been ill-advised. One reviewer, otherwise sympathetic, judged it "one of the most pitiful failures" he had witnessed in a long time.[14] Another thought it achieved the "complete failure" that it "perfectly merited," its only function having been to highlight how "essentially musical" was the rest of the concert.[15] Less outspoken, French jazzman Ray Ventura—about whom much more below—thought it a "half-success" despite the incomprehension of much of the audience.[16] And this is the point: the concert had largely failed to attract people beyond the usual crowd of fans and record collectors. Far from crossing boundaries, Hylton's concert, like Lifar's ballet, had shown how clearly cultural demarcations continued to exist.

10. Ray Ventura, "Le Triomphe du jazz: Jack Hylton à l'Opéra," *Jazz-Tango* 2/6 (1 March 1931): n.p.

11. According to Vera Stravinsky's diary, the composer attended rehearsals in London on January 29, 1931, and in Paris on February 17, the day of the concert; see Robert Craft, ed., *Dearest Bubushkin: The Correspondence of Vera and Igor Stravinsky, 1921–1954, with Excerpts from Vera Stravinsky's Diaries, 1922–1971* (London: Thames and Hudson, 1985), 51, 53. The *Times* (Anon., "Stravinsky and Jack Hylton: Jazz Version of Operatic Excerpt," 29 January 1931) also put Stravinsky at a rehearsal with the band on January 28.

12. Les Carew, "How are the Mighty. .?," *Nostalgia* 10/40 (n.d.): 19–21 (quote on p. 21).

13. Anon., "L'Humeur de Jack," *Le Carnet de la semaine*, 1 March 1931. But compare a British source: "Stravinsky himself did not attempt to disguise his pleasure and was most open with his praise" (Anon., "Shades of Grand Opera: Hylton Makes More History," *Melody Maker* 6/63 [March 1931]: 217). The notoriously unreliable (and mediated) elderly Stravinsky placed responsibility for the idea squarely with Hylton, describing the performance as "an awful flop" and the concert as "the most bizarre . . . I have ever attended" (Igor Stravinsky and Robert Craft, *Expositions and Developments* [London: Faber and Faber, 1962], 82n).

14. Pierre Leroi, "Jack Hylton à l'Opéra," *L'Édition musicale vivante*, no. 37 (February 1931): 12–13 (quote on p. 12).

15. Émile Vuillermoz, "La Musique: Les Concerts," *Excelsior*, 23 February 1931.

16. Ventura, "Le Triomphe du jazz."

On reflection, *Mavra*, even in a bowdlerized version, was not the wisest choice. Stravinsky had never had much luck with it, and there was no reason to suppose that Hylton would fare any better. According to Richard Taruskin, the failure of *Mavra*, which had premiered in the same hall almost a decade earlier, was "without a doubt the most painful experience in Stravinsky's career."[17] The Russian had pinned on this piece his hopes for "naturalization" as a European classical composer. In the event, even Diaghilev (who had in one sense inspired this assimilation) disliked *Mavra*. Though Stravinsky remained an iconic figure, his "neoclassical" compositions had not received the acceptance and popularity of his "exotic" Russian works.

Thus when Émile Vuillermoz complained that Stravinsky's genius, unlike Hylton's, was "not of a strictly musical order," he was harking back not least to the "veritable cry of pain" that was his original *Mavra* review.[18] In an early statement of what became, says Taruskin, "a time-honored cliché," Vuillermoz had exposed Stravinsky's supposed failure as a melodist: having divested himself of Russian folklore, the line went, Stravinsky had not the natural musical gifts with which to replace such a resource.[19] "Let this great musician desist forthwith from wasting his time on such useless jokes!" he concluded; a defiant, if wounded, Stravinsky stuck Vuillermoz's article into his score.[20] In 1931, one writer was scarcely more cautious: he didn't want to be accused of "Stravinsky-phobia" but thought "thank God, [the composer had] enough great works [œuvres géniales] . . . not to hesitate to underline the triviality of a so-called comic opera."[21] The project, which may have originated in Stravinsky's last-ditch attempt to save a few snippets of *Mavra* from complete public indifference, had only confirmed it.

"King of Jazz": Jack Hylton and the French

Mavra did Hylton no more favors than it did Stravinsky: while the bandleader may have hoped for greater cultural prestige, he had no need of

17. Richard Taruskin, *Stravinsky and the Russian Traditions: A Biography of the Works through "Mavra,"* vol. 2 (Berkeley: University of California Press, 1996), 1591.

18. Vuillermoz, "La Musique"; Taruskin, *Stravinsky and the Russian Traditions,* 2:1596.

19. Taruskin, *Stravinsky and the Russian Traditions,* 2:1597.

20. Émile Vuillermoz, "Mavra," *Excelsior,* 12 June 1922, cited and translated in Taruskin, *Stravinsky and the Russian Traditions,* 2:1596–97 (quote on p. 1597); Darius Milhaud, *Notes without Music,* trans. Donald Evans (New York: Alfred A. Knopf, 1953), 131, cited in Taruskin, *Stravinsky and the Russian Traditions,* 2:1596.

21. Leroi, "Jack Hylton," 13.

extra publicity. In France, he was already a serious contender for the title "King of Jazz," fighting off Americans both black and white. What is more, he had recently been recognized by the state, as *Officier de l'instruction publique*.[22] The pivotal role Hylton played in the history of jazz in France is difficult to take on board: the sight and sound of a canon of American musicians is too ingrained in historical imagination. Respect for critical orthodoxy, as well as a focus on jazz as a site of primitivism, has led to his absence from histories of jazz in Europe, which often imply that African American performers were more central there than was the case. In this chapter, Hylton's changing fortunes are the focal point of a survey of bands in French popular culture in the 1920s and 1930s, as well as of the incipient specialist jazz culture spearheaded by the young critic Hugues Panassié.

The band's story also tells much about the circulation of music in the age of mechanical reproduction. Picking up jazz from American records, which at first Hylton just transcribed, the Boys in turn recorded heavily (often with Decca, in which Hylton was a major shareholder).[23] By 1930, it was claimed that they had made more than one thousand discs, or a total fifty hours of music.[24] The Boys' sonic trace thus long preceded their presence "in the flesh" in Paris—a new and unsettling phenomenon. Given the preeminence that "Anglo-Saxon" recording companies quickly assumed, however, this experience was one that would often be repeated.[25]

While a record-buying culture was growing fast, the precise standing of recordings, and their relationship to live music, remained in flux in the

22. On or about August 14, 1930; see Alasdair Fenton, "Jax Bax: The Story of British Bandleader Jack Hylton" (published in twenty-five parts most months between April 1966 [no. 11] and October 1968 [no. 41]), pt. 7, *RSVP* [*Record Sales Various Prices*], no. 17 (October 1966): 48. In 1932, Hylton was awarded the *Légion d'honneur* (Pete Faint, "Full Biography," accessed 17 December 2012, http://www.jackhylton.com).

23. See Jack Hylton, "The High Finance of Jazz," *Rhythm* 13/136 (January 1939): 3–7, for Hylton's personal recollections; Faint, "Full Biography"; and Fenton, "Jax Bax."

24. Anon., "Jack Hylton," *La Vie Marseillaise*, 22 March 1930, in Ro 586, "La Musique nègre," p. 210, Rondel. The calculation is not correct for double-sided discs—1,000 discs at 3 minutes per side equals 100 hours—but I am more interested in the perception of their huge output than in the accuracy of accounting. On Hylton's repertory and arrangements, for the French tours in particular, see Deborah Mawer, "'Parisomania'? Jack Hylton and the French Connection," *Journal of the Royal Musical Association* 133 (2008): 270–317.

25. Among other performers to build a music-hall career in France on the back of recording success were the African American singing duo (Turner) Layton and (Clarence) Johnstone and the white vocal quartet the Revellers.

twenties and thirties. André Cœuroy summarized the issues in his book *Le Phonographe* of 1929. As he describes it, recording was a fickle process, whose results were unpredictable. For example, it was frequently supposed that Anglo-Saxons, whatever their intrinsic merits, were superior as recording artists to their continental colleagues. Explanations varied from familiarity with the medium—American artists had grown up with the microphone whereas Europeans were adapting to it with difficulty—to linguistic if not physiological difference: Cœuroy himself supposed "elective affinities between the Anglo-Saxon larynx and the personality of the phonograph."[26]

That the phonograph had a personality, like any other instrument, was not in doubt; Cœuroy insisted that it be respected. Thus efforts to make records sound ever more like live performances were mistaken, for "the truth of art is not a servile copy of reality."[27] In effect, Cœuroy was invoking age-old aesthetic arguments about the superiority of effective mimesis over trompe l'œil—or, in this case, *trompe l'oreille*: the job of the phonograph, he insisted, was to transpose and not to copy.[28] There was another element: the phonograph, if it were to meet its full potential, should not only reproduce but originate; responsible artists would create a new music for it, an aesthetic alliance with the technological age.

In the case of bands such as Hylton's, which were known first from record, the problem presented itself the other way up. As was commonly noted, hearing recording artists live held the same curiosity value as seeing a movie star in person. But while little was required of film actors except glamour and outrage, musicians—whose appeal was rarely visual—had to give something new. When music-hall critic Gustave Fréjaville first heard Hylton and His Boys play in London in 1925, he praised the band but questioned the merit of assigning them so long on stage: a music hall's attractions were supposed to be at once ocular and auricular.[29] In Paris, the convention was for (smaller) bands to accompany dancers or else to play on stage—or in the bar—only during the interval. When Paul

26. André Cœuroy, *Le Phonographe* (Paris: Kra, 1929), 104 (the first explanation is drawn from an unreferenced quotation from critic Dominique Sordet).

27. Cœuroy, *Le Phonographe*, 128.

28. Strange as they may sound today, there is historical truth in Cœuroy's words: the most successful early recordings of classical repertory modified instrumentation, as well as instituting cuts. See, inter alia, Timothy Day, *A Century of Recorded Music: Listening to Musical History* (New Haven, CT: Yale University Press, 2000).

29. Gustave Fréjaville, "Chronique de la semaine," *Comœdia*, 31 December 1925, in Ro 16443(3), "Fréjaville, Gustave: Petite Chronique du music-hall, etc.," Rondel.

Whiteman's band played the Théâtre des Champs-Élysées in 1926, this unwritten rule was broken—to Fréjaville's great disquiet. While the critic did not doubt for a moment the performers' virtuosity, he thought that "something altogether different would be required to sustain attention for more than a quarter of an hour." For the moment, their performance was "a lot of noise for nothing," which placed in jeopardy "all [the music hall's] character and all its attraction."[30]

More was the surprise, then, when on Hylton's arrival in Paris in 1927, Fréjaville announced his hearty support. The British band was now "un véritable numéro de music-hall," he said, and his objection no longer stood:

> Voici une "attraction" de tout premier ordre, dont la musique, il est vrai, est la base et le prétexte, mais qui nous intéresse et nous amuse par mille trouvailles spirituelles, chaque musicien devenant à son tour l'un des acteurs d'une comédie ingénue, où les instruments eux-mêmes sont des personnages et tiennent leurs rôles bouffons ou ironiques avec une très vivante fantaisie.[31]

Here is an act of the very first order, whose music, it is true, is its foundation and pretext, but that interests and entertains us with a thousand witty new ideas, each musician becoming in turn one of the actors in a

---

30. Gustave Fréjaville, "La Semaine au music-hall," *Comœdia*, 8 July 1926, in Ro 16443(4), "Fréjaville, Gustave," Rondel. Fréjaville persisted with his argument when another white American band, Irving Aaronson and the Commanders, appeared at the Théâtre des Champs-Élysées later in the year, despite confessing that the public seemed to disagree; see "La Semaine au music-hall," *Comœdia*, 17 August 1926, in ibid. Jazz's ambiguous position at this time is indicated by other Whiteman reviews, some of which complained in complete contrast that the band had played militaristic and novelty numbers rather than the "better" music known from record. See, for example, André Messager, "Théâtre des Champs-Élysées: Paul Whiteman et son jazz-band," *Le Figaro*, 4 July 1926; and Émile Vuillermoz, "L'Orchestre Paul Whiteman," *Candide*, 8 July 1926 (both are in Ro 15702[5], "Le Champs-Élysées Music-Hall," Rondel). As I noted with regard to the Blackbirds in chap. 1, the varied opinions are explained in part by critics' differing expectations of this avant-garde venue turned music hall.

31. Gustave Fréjaville, "La Semaine au music-hall," *Comœdia*, 5 January 1928, in Ro 16443(5), "Fréjaville, Gustave," Rondel. Fréjaville reiterated his enthusiasm when the band returned to the Empire a few months later; see "Les Attractions de la quinzaine," *Comœdia*, 12 April 1928, in ibid.

broad comedy, in which the instruments themselves are characters and fill their comical or ironical roles with a very lively imagination.

As Fréjaville observed, the Boys had worked hard to turn their sojourning dance band into a fully fledged music-hall act; they had learned to sing, dance, and clown around, topping it off with costumes and scenery, lights and technological tricks. For example, the band took the tune "Bye, Bye, Blackbird" on a tour of the world, synchronizing film of countries from China to Scotland in case musical cues were not enough. And in "Hello Swannie" they sat in a train carriage through whose windows one saw projected the passing countryside. Other numbers found them dressed as boy scouts or guardsmen on parade; finally they wished each other good night and disappeared to bed![32] In short, the Boys were now so much more than their records would suggest.

Most critics agreed with Fréjaville's upbeat assessment. Celebrated commentator Legrand-Chabrier thought it a red-letter day in the history of the music hall.[33] Writers were happy to see Hylton in flesh and blood at last, and agreed that his stage show made all the difference. Some had no doubt that Hylton's band was "the best in the world."[34] If others thought Whiteman had the technical edge, Hylton's act still won out over the American's "perfection un peu académique."[35] Only the music critics repeated a caveat made earlier about Whiteman: the band played better—and better music—on record. For some, it appears, recording artists were never as effective in person as they were in the privacy of one's own home: "Inflexible admirers [admirateurs stricts] of the phonograph," reported Cœuroy, "prefer Hylton . . . invisible on disc."[36] For a very few, the spectacle—and the audience's evident enjoyment of it—was just too

32. See, in addition to Fréjaville, Yvon Novy, "A l'Empire: Jack Hylton et son jazz," *Chantecler*, 7 January 1928, in Ro 15718(7), "L'Empire," Rondel (fortnight beginning 30 December 1927).

33. Legrand-Chabrier, "Du promenoir à la piste: Jack Hylton et son jazz à l'Empire," *La Volonté*, 2 January 1928, in Ro 15718(7), "L'Empire," Rondel.

34. Jacques Patin, "Empire: Le Jazz Jack Hylton," *Le Figaro*, 2 January 1928, in Ro 15718(7), "L'Empire," Rondel.

35. Maurice Verne, "Peindre l'époque par le jazz," *La Rumeur*, 4 January 1928, in Ro 15718(7), "L'Empire," Rondel.

36. Cœuroy, *Le Phonographe*, 63. For example, Jean Lasserre: "Si Jack Hylton était resté caché dans le mystère de ses disques, si nous ne l'avions jamais vu avec ses boys, nous l'aimerions certainement beaucoup plus. Comme les Revellers, comme Layton et Johnston, Jack Hylton a eu tort de se montrer" ("Jack Hylton à l'Empire," *L'Ami du peuple du soir*, 15 December 1928, in Ro 15718[9], "L'Empire," Rondel).

FIGURE 2.4. Newspaper cartoons of Jack Hylton (*Gringoire*, 21 December 1928; *L'Ami du peuple du soir*, 23 December 1928).

much: one writer thought the act of such "foolish bad taste" that "it would be necessary to invent the term 'anglo-saxon' if it didn't exist already."[37] But for music-hall critics (and, it seems, the general public) this was just what was required to negotiate successfully the transition from recording artists to live entertainers (fig. 2.4).

The King Dethroned: American Jack

For the next few years, the success of Hylton and His Boys went from strength to strength. Far from reducing interest in public performance, as had sometimes been feared, their discs served as an elaborate—and profitable—form of concert promotion; the two became mutually reinforcing. Year by year, Hylton made steady progress toward the central space of Parisian musical life: from the Empire and Palace music halls (1927–1928) to the Salle Pleyel and Théâtre des Champs-Élysées (1929–1930), and finally, of course, to the Opéra (1931). But he then beat a retreat, via the Salle Pleyel and Empire (1931–1932), to a less celebrated role as intermission entertainer in the new temples of celluloid (Rex and Gaumont Palace

37. Pierre Bost, *Revue hebdomadaire*, 11 January 1928, in Ro 15718(7), "L'Empire," Rondel. It was the musical equivalent, he thought, of "peinture sans dessin," the charge that was often leveled by academic painters on modern artists.

cinemas, 1933–1935). Whatever the Boys' aspiration to cultural status, it could not be sustained.

Reactions to Hylton on his return to the Empire a few weeks after the Opéra concert provide several clues why. Whether for practical reasons, or through a genuine desire to reshape the band's act toward a more highbrow aesthetic, is not clear, but the extramusical components of their performance were drastically reduced: fewer costumes, pranks, and lighting effects, and not a single major prop such as the musical train. Although, ironically, Fréjaville remained sure that "if any jazz-band justifies . . . its presence on stage, it is . . . Jack Hylton's," others were no longer convinced: the audience, they said, was as listless as the Boys themselves.[38] Legrand-Chabrier feared that "a certain austerity," even "an air of superiority" had replaced the band's good-humored frivolity.[39] A further writer wanted "a little more spontaneity, a little more real gaiety" in place of this "cold perfection."[40]

Another way of expressing this was that the Boys' performances had become, like Whiteman's, no more or less than their discs. Stravinsky, who had spent the day of Hylton's Opéra concert recording the *Symphony of Psalms*, was the wrong model: his insistence that discs' accuracy in representing the composer's intentions made them "the best instrument of transmission of the thinking of masters of modern music" seemed to portend the death of live music.[41] And like Stravinsky, Hylton's band had failed to acknowledge that their exoticism (albeit expressed via English schoolboy humor) was an important part of their appeal. The public, at least in the music hall, still expected a level of spontaneity and frivolity from live performance that was not available on 78 rpm discs.

Recorded music itself was just a corner of the issue, however. One critic grumbled that the Boys' performance was now "more mechanical than spontaneous," a far cry from when jazz was "the last cry of primitive man." Following "general standardization," he thought, "M. Jack Hylton"

38. Gustave Fréjaville, "Jack Hylton à l'Empire," *Comœdia*, 7 April 1931, in Ro 15718(11–15), "L'Empire," Rondel.

39. Legrand-Chabrier, *Le Carnet de la semaine*, 12 April 1931, in Ro 15718(11–15), "L'Empire," Rondel.

40. L.-R. Dauven, "Jack Hylton à l'Empire," *L'Ami du peuple du soir*, in Ro 15718 (11–15), "L'Empire," Rondel.

41. Igor Stravinsky cited in Cœuroy, *Le Phonographe*, 85. The quotation is from Florent Fels, "Un Entretien avec Igor Stravinsky à propos de l'enregistrement au phonographe de *Pétrouchka*," *Les Nouvelles littéraires*, 8 December 1928 [reprinted in François Lesure, ed., *Stravinsky: Études et témoignages* (Paris: Jean Claude Lattès, 1982), 248].

made his music with "the same methods and the same results as M. Ford his cars."[42] In this the writer was allying himself with a thread of criticism that had already begun to develop; his article bears comparison with one a few months earlier in the right-wing *Action française*. Following a 1930 concert at the Salle Pleyel, columnist André Villeneuve tellingly counted Hylton and His Boys among citizens of the New World. He noted with horror how this "American orchestra" that played "American music" with what "they call in America 'humor' " entertained a well-heeled audience with an "acrobatic virtuosity" in which "emotion and beauty are forbidden." Villeneuve remembered an early black band fondly, if paternalistically, but he continued:

> Maintenant, imaginez la gambade nègre imitée par le puritain du *Mayflower* devenu industriel: c'est le *jazz band* américain, offense à la race blanche et à la musique. . . . Le genre est devenu mécanique et industriel . . . et [comme] l'on dirait en américain . . . standardisé. . . . C'est une scène de la vie future.[43]

> Now, imagine the Negro caper imitated by the puritan of the *Mayflower* become industrial: it's the American jazz band, offense to the white race and to music. . . . The genre has become mechanical . . . and [as] they say in American . . . standardized. . . . It's a scene from life in the future.

This last phrase (also the article's title) was a reference to Georges Duhamel's book *Scène de la vie future* published earlier in 1930. It could not have been missed: this urtext of French antimodernism and anti-Americanism had gone through an astonishing 150 editions in its first five months.[44] Fanning the flames of popular sentiment, Duhamel provided an almost hysterical depiction of industrialized American society as a vision of Eu-

42. R. Fuzier, "Le Nouveau Programme de l'Empire," *Le Soir*, 9 April 1931, in Ro 15718(11–15), "L'Empire," Rondel.

43. André Villeneuve, "Scène de la vie future," *L'Action française*, 5 December 1930, in Ro 586, "La Musique nègre," p. 218, Rondel.

44. Pascal Ory, "De Baudelaire à Duhamel: L'Improbable Rejet," in *L'Amérique dans les têtes: Un Siècle de fascinations et d'aversions*, ed. Denis Lacorne, Jacques Rupnik, and Marie-France Toinet (Paris: Hachette, 1986), 57–69 (esp. p. 65). Duhamel's book ran to 187 editions in 1930, reaching 243 in 1931 (Romy Golan, *Modernity and Nostalgia: Art and Politics in France between the Wars* [New Haven, CT: Yale University Press, 1995], 82). See also Jean-Philippe Mathy, *Extrême Occident: French Intellectuals and America* (Chicago: University of Chicago Press, 1993); and Philippe Roger, *The American Enemy: The History of French Anti-Americanism*, trans. Sharon Bowman (Chicago: University of Chicago Press, 2005).

rope's future; reading the book now—when anti-Americanism is scarcely unknown—one can only be astonished by the depth of bile he spreads across 250 pages. For Duhamel, America represented a greater threat to Europe than communism: its ostensible apoliticism made it impossible to perceive—hence resist—as ideology; it was truly hegemonic.[45] Futurist America, thought Duhamel, was pushing society from human to "entomological morals: the same effacement of the individual, the same rarefaction and progressive unification of social types, the same organization of the group into specialized castes, the same submission of all to the obscure demands of . . . the beehive or of the anthill" (224). In the United States he thus felt "dépaysé" (out of his element) less in space than in time (18).

Duhamel was reacting in large part to principles set out some twenty years earlier in American engineer Frederick Taylor's influential *The Principles of Scientific Management* (1911): productivity and efficiency could be achieved by the analysis and rationalization of respective tasks of manufacture. So behind every American luxury Duhamel saw an automated system of production and distribution whose effect was dehumanization. Most striking is his account of the industrialized process of death in a Chicago abattoir: a process so mechanized that each worker on the conveyor belt conducted a single operation, be it animal slaughter or meatpacking, half-asleep, like an automaton. As carcasses were first butchered and then melted down for every possible by-product, one thing only was left over: the animals' cries of terror as they met their death. In an entirely rational procedure such wastefulness was clearly absurd; Duhamel imagined that these screams must go to make music, "de beaux airs de jazz-band" (*Scène de la vie future*, 129). Similarly, he was deeply disturbed by the "false music" that one heard but did not listen to; discs, he thought, were "canned music" (musique en boîtes de conserve) from the "musical abattoir" where "they kill the music . . . carve it up [dépèce], salt, pepper, and cook" (52–53). Duhamel preferred to re-create music himself than to hear it in a record's cold accuracy: "living faults rather than all this dead perfection" (65). At the end of a long day, this "Français de France" took inspiration from his forebears, "paysans français," to conduct a private ritual: foregoing the convenience of America's "immoderate and inharmonious civilization," he washed and mended his clothes by hand (39, 216–17).

For Duhamel, American culture, itself standardized, consisted not of objects for contemplation by free will but of commodities forced on consumers by advertisers. He describes at length his reaction at an American

45. Georges Duhamel, *Scène de la vie future*, 107th ed. (Paris: Mercure de France, 1930), 240–45 (subsequent references in text); Mathy, *Extrême Occident*, 80.

cinema: the apparent passivity of the crowd, the banality of the movie, his horror that the score is assembled from fragments of masterpieces. Jazz was no better: the "triumph of barbaric stupidity" that "whines, whimpers, scratches and squawks over the whole face of the earth" (147). The effect of this music was both physically stimulating and intellectually debilitating; as in Adorno's later analysis, the mindless gyrations it encouraged served to keep the masses in their place. But even more than Adorno's, Duhamel's apparent concern for the effect of mass culture on the collective psyche is impossible to separate from what is fundamentally an elitist defense of humanist education: nothing riles him more than intellectuals pandering to the masses. Tocqueville had long before coined the phrase that best captures the threat America posed to French intellectuals: the "tyranny of the majority."[46]

Duhamel fan Villeneuve was not the only one to focus such widely shared concerns on Jack Hylton's honorary Americans. Jacques Janin, a composer and conductor for film and chanson, had been troubled for some while that the Boys commonly omitted composers' names from their programs, a custom that for him signaled a horrific depersonalization: the tunes were so generic that it ceased to matter which of the "hundreds of artisans Taylorized and rationalized to the core [who] each year make the same fox-trot" had written it; "nothing is more impersonal, unindividual" than jazz, he thought.[47] For Janin, the Boys' tightly rehearsed ensemble, in its lack of individualism, represented nothing less than an American rejection of humanism; their multiple tasks (singing, playing, dancing, and comedy) were a ghastly example of a rationalization of the workforce. Elsewhere, he and other writers bemoaned the "Taylorization" of music with "formulae," or the "industrialized" production of records "manufactured in series, like cars."[48] For one last critic, Hylton was a "bu-

46. Alexis de Tocqueville, *De la démocratie en Amérique* (1835–1840). Duhamel's book was far from the only anti-American tract in these years, if the most widely read. Others included André Tardieu, *Devant l'obstacle: L'Amérique et nous* (1927); André Siegfried, *Les États-Unis d'aujourd'hui* (1927); Lucien Romier, *Qui sera le maître? Europe ou Amérique* (1927); and Robert Aron and Arnaud Dandieu, *Le Cancer américain* (1931). However, there were also positive responses: for example, Philippe Soupault, *The American Influence in France* (1930); and Paul Morand, *New York* (1930).

47. Jacques Janin, "Le Jazz, lumière de l'occident? Les Nouveautés de la 'nationale,'" *L'Ami du peuple du soir*, 26 March 1929, in Ro 585, "Le Jazz et les spectacles nègres," doc. 68, Rondel.

48. Jacques Janin, "Jack Hylton," *L'Ami du peuple du soir*, 19 October 1929, in Ro 586, "La Musique nègre," p. 206a, Rondel; Lucien Rebatet, "Jack Hylton," *Ric et rac*, 5 July 1930, in ibid., p. 215; Émile Vuillermoz, untitled article, *Excelsior*, 17 January 1932, cited in Hugues Panassié, "Revue de la presse," *Jazz-Tango-Dancing* 3/18

reaucrat" whose "wildest fantasies he manufacture[d] like a clerk."[49] Embodying Taylor's principles of production and management, therefore, Hylton and His Boys had come to symbolize the grave danger of Americanization to the French way of life.

Hylton was nothing if not a canny showman, and even during his two-week stint at the Empire, he reacted to critics, reviving some of his old act.[50] Returning at the end of the year, the Boys took further precautions: their show was advertised as *La Renaissance du jazz*, "especially conceived for the music hall."[51] But this moment of resistance to Hylton by the press and public exposes a vein of sharp criticism. With the rise of Hollywood (and the consequent decline of the local film industry) many overworked French were already complaining that even their free time was regulated by international industry—an animosity that could only increase when foreign recording stars invaded cultural institutions such as the Paris Opéra. In Hylton's hands, jazz was far from the primitivism that is often imagined to be its primary appeal in France; on the contrary, for some it had come to represent the very worst excesses of modernity.

The Gallic Touch: Jazz Turns French

What, then, to do? The first of two, seemingly paradoxical, solutions lay in the "naturalization" of jazz. In this way, the global market of mass-produced commodities might be replaced by a cottage industry supplying customized, homemade goods. Among several pretenders, Grégor et ses Grégoriens gained widespread publicity as "the first French jazz band." Their adverts boasted twenty talented musicians who were "young, stylish [élégants], able to dance and sing, and who—astonishing, unbeliev-

(March 1932): [15?]; and Rêve [pseud.], "Critique de jazz," *Jazz-Tango* 1/3–4 (25 December 1930): 18.

49. Jean Lasserre, "Ted Lewis," *Gringoire*, 5 September 1930, in Ro 15718(11–15), "L'Empire," Rondel. From his first appearance in 1928, the white American bandleader and "grand romantique" Ted Lewis sometimes rivaled Hylton at his own game (see programs, in Ro 15692[7], "L'Apollo," Rondel; and press, in Ro 15692[2], "L'Apollo," Rondel [fortnight beginning 14 September 1928]). Another critic noted that, in comparison with Lewis, Hylton was "mécanique, comique parfois, mais rarement très original" (Jacques Monteux, review of Ted Lewis, *Paris-Presse*, 11 August 1930, in Ro 15718[11–15], "L'Empire," Rondel).

50. Legrand-Chabrier, "À l'Empire: Variétés et récital de jazz," *La Volonté*, 8 April 1931, in Ro 15718(11–15), "L'Empire," Rondel.

51. See program, in Ro 15718(4), "L'Empire," Rondel; and press, in Ro 15718(11–15), "L'Empire," Rondel (fortnight beginning 25 December 1931).

FIGURE 2.5. Grégor et ses Grégoriens.

able novelty—[were] all French" (fig. 2.5).[52] That this was not strictly true of their polyglot ensemble would, they hoped, be overlooked; banners hanging from their music stands prudently formed a tricolor. Although but "French by adoption," former dancer Grégor (Krikor Kélékian) bravely claimed to be leading the "emancipation" of French jazz; his style was "more colorful, more nuanced and . . . more musical" than the Anglo-Saxons', he said.[53] Sometimes the strategy worked: "It suffices for me to prefer them," said Pierre Varenne, "that Grégor et ses Grégoriens tell us that they are from *chez nous*."[54] Perhaps Grégor would achieve his ambition of acting as "musical ambassador for France."[55]

Alas, many found the Armenian-born bandleader an unlikely candidate to create a "Latin formula of jazz."[56] Fréjaville thought that this was "misplaced nationalism"; besides, he said, the band's "names and M. Grégor's profile [are not] so French [as to be] a characteristic

52. Advertisement for Grégor et ses Grégoriens at the Empire Theatre, fortnight beginning 16 May 1930, in Ro 15718 (11–15), "L'Empire," Rondel.

53. H. R., "La Nouvelle Formule du jazz latin va enfin occuper la place qu'elle mérite" [interview with Grégor], *Comœdia*, 28 February 1930, in Ro 585, "Le Jazz," doc. 101, Rondel.

54. Pierre Varenne, "À l'Olympia," *Paris-Soir*, 6 June 1930, in Ro 585, "Le Jazz," doc. 113, Rondel. The program for this run at the Olympia Theatre is in ibid., doc. 112.

55. H. R., "La Nouvelle Formule du jazz latin." Grégor was also behind France's first, short-lived jazz magazine, *La Revue du jazz*, in 1929.

56. H. R., "La Nouvelle Formule du jazz latin."

Le chef d'orchestre Grégor

Gregor
Dessin de H. Kett.

FIGURE 2.6. Newspaper cartoons of Grégor (*Comœdia*, 4 November 1930; *Le Soir*, 22 May 1930).

example of our race and our national temperament" (fig. 2.6).[57] Others were plainer: they believed Grégor had "Levantine features" and the accent of a Polish Jew.[58] In any case, the band failed to match up to the standards set by Hylton. Many critics felt it misguided to appeal to nationalism when the band was not yet up to scratch: the audience, one noted, were torn between patriotism and taste, and "an over-exuberant claque" was not sufficient for the former to win out over the latter.[59] For others the whole idea of French jazz seemed an oxymoron, particularly as the band had done little to acculturate the music.[60] Aside from one old song, "Les Fraises et les framboises," their music evinced, one critic protested, "nothing specifically 'Latin'"; only by pursuing that isolated

57. Gustave Fréjaville, review of Grégor et ses Grégoriens, *Comœdia*, 21 May 1930, in Ro 15718(11–15), "L'Empire," Rondel.

58. Pierre Loiselet, "À l'Empire: Grégor et ses Grégoriens," *Le Soir*, 20 May 1930; Jacques Chabannes, "Les Jours se suivent: Nationalisme déplacé," *La Volonté*, 26 May 1930 (both are in Ro 15718[11–15], "L'Empire," Rondel).

59. Chabannes, "Les Jours se suivent"; Legrand-Chabrier, review of Grégor et ses Grégoriens, unidentified periodical, 25 May 1930, in Ro 15718(11–15), "L'Empire," Rondel.

60. See, for example, Legrand-Chabrier, "À l'Empire: Cette quinzaine, qu'y voit-on?," *La Volonté*, 22 May 1930, in Ro 15718(11–15), "L'Empire," Rondel.

FIGURE 2.7. Ray Ventura et ses Collégiens.

example could they hope to be a success.[61] Otherwise they were but a poor imitation of an American model—the ultimate indignity for the French.

More acceptable on all counts were Ray Ventura et ses Collégiens. Schoolboy chums (or so they long claimed), their pasty young faces were comfortingly familiar to a Parisian audience (fig. 2.7). And their humor was considered a witty French riposte to Hylton's rude Anglo-Saxon comedy. Besides, one writer thought, the Boys had become so serious that their band now seemed "out of place in the music hall, in the very setting for which it was originally conceived"; Ventura's intervention was required to return jazz to its rightful place.[62] Unlike the Grégoriens, however, the Collégiens had "something graceful, sound [juste], clear [aéré], balanced, sensible even in whimsy [fantaisie]," which showed, according to Fréjaville, "the mark of the French spirit."[63] They had learned from Gré-

61. Loiselet, "À l'Empire"; Legrand-Chabrier, "À l'Empire."

62. L.-R. Dauven, "À l'Empire: Le Jazz de Ray Ventura," *L'Ami du peuple du soir,* 29 June 1931, in Ro 15718(11–15), "L'Empire," Rondel (fortnight beginning 26 June 1931).

63. Gustave Fréjaville, "À l'Empire," *Comœdia,* 30 June 1931, in Ro 15718(11–15), "L'Empire," Rondel.

gor's experience and were attempting to carry it forward by forging a native approach to jazz.[64]

Ventura sought to position his efforts quite carefully in an article of 1931 (mindful as well of the jazz "purists" I shall turn to in a moment). The band's music was not jazz per se, he argued, but then neither were Louis Armstrong's performances of popular songs "of Judeo-American origin." Invoking the now familiar anti-American, antimodern rhetoric—and not forsaking anti-Semitism although his father was a Jew—Ventura argued that Jewish composers had "commercialized [popular music] so much that . . . there is a saturation owing, in large part, to over-production." Better, he thought, to play one's own country's music, which "corresponds to its temperament and to its mentality"; in this way all nationalities could contribute to the evolution of jazz.[65] The Collégiens began their first big concert, at the Salle Gaveau in 1931, with a similar gloss: In front of the curtain, one of their number narrated jazz's development, the unseen band cynically evoking earlier hits. Now, their spokesman explained, jazz had "grown up" and "established itself," the curtain rising triumphantly for the Frenchmen to demonstrate their superiority.[66]

What was their formula? A typical early example was the "Vieilles Chansons de France," a medley that appealed to nostalgia, syncopating familiar tunes. Better still, in the "Tour de France en chansons," the Collégiens located traditional ditties for the audience on a huge map—a peculiarly didactic gesture toward the thirties' budding folklorism and regionalism—and in the "Promenade imagée à l'exposition coloniale" they provided a similar survey of the empire, this time in musical caricature. In still other numbers, Ventura made fun of the imperfect devices that were taking his tunes, like Hylton's, into people's homes: the record player that got stuck or the radio that was hard to tune. If the Boys' perfunctory performances had become mere replicas of their perfect, mechanical representations, the Collégiens, at once more accurate and less respectful, refused to sacrifice their souls to a machine.

Their strategy paid off. One critic thought Ventura's band had successfully "adapted jazz to the French temperament."[67] Another found in

64. For general accounts of Ventura and Grégor (plus many excellent photographs), see Jacques Hélian, *Les Grands Orchestres de music hall en France (souvenirs & témoignages)* (Paris: Filipacchi, 1984).

65. Ray Ventura, "Non . . . Le Jazz ne meurt pas! Il évolue . . . ," *L'Édition musicale vivante* 4/43 (September 1931): 7–9 (quote on p. 9).

66. Hélian, *Les Grands Orchestres*, 74.

67. Louis Léon-Martin, "À l'Empire," *Le Petit Parisien*, 9 February 1932, in Ro 15718(16–18), "L'Empire," Rondel (fortnight beginning 5 February 1932).

their performance "a youthfulness, a real gaiety that [he was] happy to exchange for [the] stiff manner [and] mechanical humor" of Hylton's Boys.
Ventura, he argued, did "not believe in formulae" and had "taste, a sense
of artistic nuance and balance"—"doubtless because he [was] a Latin."
Before the Collégiens, he continued, "the Americans could . . . imagine
that jazz had colonized us" but Ventura had "naturalized it"; it was still "a
product of foreign manufacture, but [one] retouched by French hands."[68]
International but national: was this a form of glocalization?[69] Of course,
any theorization of such an idea was many decades off, but the model of
a global practice reinvented locally was already developing, even if the
evidence for it in this case was as much rhetorical as musical.

A mode of French jazz now established, other bands soon followed:
Fred Adison et son Orchestre, Roland Dorsay et ses Cadets, Jo Bouillon
et son Orchestre (Bouillon would later marry Josephine Baker and with
her adopt the multiracial "Rainbow tribe"). Even Grégor, who had fled the
country in 1930 to avoid imprisonment for dangerous driving, reestab-
lished his band in 1932 and operated successfully for several years. With
many changes of personnel, Ventura maintained an ensemble until 1947
(disbanding during the *drôle de guerre*, they soon reformed and spent the
rest of the war in South America). "American" sellout Jack Hylton could
now surely be forgotten, his lessons both learned and transcended by
French big bands.

Ironies abound, however. Not only was the paradigm of American
commercialization actually a Brit from Lancashire, but the new French
jazz owed more to mass culture, and specifically to Hylton, than many
liked to admit. The first pretender, Grégor, had a hard time coming out
from Hylton's shadow, despite an appeal to patriotism. One critic was on
to him: "Any conductor with half a mind [un peu habile] could form such
an ensemble by drawing inspiration from Hylton records."[70] More successful, Ray Ventura had no right to boast: still more or less amateur, the
Collégiens experienced the revelation of their future while watching the
Boys' music-hall show; their act was consciously modeled on it, adding
a Gallic twist.[71] Even that was not as original as one might think: Hylton

68. L.-R. Dauven, "À l'Empire: La Rentrée de Ray Ventura," *L'Ami du peuple du soir*,
9 February 1932, in Ro 15718(16–18), "L'Empire," Rondel.

69. This paradoxical combination of the global and the local was first theorized
by Roland Robertson; see his *Globalization: Social Theory and Global Culture* (London: Sage, 1992).

70. Robert Le Bret, "Beaucoup de bruit, peu d'effet," *L'Ami du peuple du soir*, 24 May
1930, in Ro 15718(11–15), "L'Empire," Rondel.

71. Hélian, *Les Grands Orchestres*, 71.

himself had long made a specialty of his French numbers, as Deborah Mawer has shown.[72] In 1932, Hylton went further and booked the Collégiens for London, winning their enthusiastic support.[73] French bandsman Michel Emer thought Hylton's troupe was "remarkable"; he enjoyed a trip in his Rolls Royce and a "soirée charmante" spent listening to his recent discs.[74] Indeed, patriotism did not stop several of the best French jazz musicians of the era from signing lucrative contracts to join the British band: Léon Vauchant (trombone); André Ekyan (saxophone); and, longest of all, Philippe Brun (trumpet, 1930–1936) whose defection left Grégor bitter, particularly with Hylton.[75] The origins of French jazz were located less in Harlem, it seems, than they were in Hackney or Hammersmith.

Critical Defense: French Critics and Jazz

In retrospect the realization of a French jazz was belated; critical attempts to naturalize the music had been active for some time. The nationality of jazz was far from self-evident in the twenties—so much so that (ethno)musicologist André Schaeffner noted wearily on Hylton's arrival that Britain was another possible fount.[76] Following publication of his book (with André Cœuroy) *Le Jazz* of 1926, he found himself engaged in a dialogue with composer-critic Arthur Hoerée. Previously serialized as "Notes sur la musique afro-américaine," Schaeffner's work was one of the first serious attempts to trace (rather than simply to suppose) the African roots of jazz. An armchair project, it makes eccentric reading today: lengthy dissertations on rhythm, timbre, and instruments drawing on sources dating back to seventeenth-century colonists. But in its time it was a major reassessment of the extent and nature of musical retentions from the Old World into the New.[77]

72. Mawer, " 'Parisomania'?"

73. See, for example, Solange Duvernon, "Ray Ventura nous revient avec ses Collégiens," *L'Intransigeant*, 1 February 1932, in Ro 15718(16–18), "L'Empire," Rondel.

74. Michel Emer, "Voyage à Londres," *Jazz-Tango-Dancing* 3/22 (July 1932): 15.

75. Grégor, "Un Scandale," *La Revue du jazz*, nos. 6–7 (7 January 1930), cited in Hélian, *Les Grands Orchestres*, 52.

76. André Schaeffner, "Jack Hylton et son jazz," *La Revue musicale* 9/4 (1 February 1928): 67–68.

77. André Schaeffner and André Cœuroy, *Le Jazz* (Paris: Claude Aveline, 1926; repr., with a preface by Frank Ténot and postfaces by Lucien Malson and Jacques B. Hess, Paris: Jean-Michel Place, 1988); and, with more comprehensive notes, Schaeffner, "Notes sur la musique afro-américaine," *Le Ménestrel* 88/26 (25 June 1926): 285–87; 88/27 (2 July 1926): 297–300; 88/28 (9 July 1926): 309–12; 88/29 (16 July 1926): 321–23; 88/30 (23 July 1926): 329–32; 88/31 (30 July 1926): 337–39; 88/32 (6 August

Although he expounded his theory at great length in *La Revue musicale*, Hoerée's conclusions are not difficult to summarize. Taking as his point of departure reactionary writer and art historian Camille Mauclair's stark rejection of jazz, "J'appartiens à la race blanche" ("I belong to the white race"), Hoerée argued that the terms of this objection were misguided: jazz, he maintained, was "located at the intersection of many races," having "but two-sixths provided by Negroes," of which one, "rhythm, is common to Arabs."[78] So much was indicated, he thought, by the fact that jazz's arrival in France was preceded by dances such as the fox-trot, which veered little from European musical vocabulary. Where Schaeffner had studied only the black contribution to jazz, for Hoerée it was better described as a part-black appropriation of white music: "Contrary to the widespread idea, I do not consider jazz an essentially Negro expression, but a Negro interpretation of an art of white stock [de race blanche] and of European origin."[79] He went on to show, through analysis, how—how little—the basic components of the fox-trot were transformed in jazz. The black contribution, Hoerée argued, had been made primarily in performance, but even this had been understood and adopted by Jewish composers (Gershwin, Berlin, Youmans, Kern, etc.), "whose assimilative powers we know," to create a "perfected, civilized jazz."[80] "Those who hate *art nègre*," he concluded, "do not therefore have to hate jazz."[81]

1926): 345–47. Schaeffner's opinions have been rather confused by a later section of the book eulogizing Paul Whiteman, which was in fact authored by Cœuroy; see the latter's "Le Jazz," *L'Art vivant* 2/40 (15 August 1926): 615–17. Compare Schaeffner's (less than laudatory) reviews of the band: "Orchestre Whiteman," *La Revue musicale* 7/11 (1 October 1926): 252–53; and "La Semaine musicale: Music-Hall du Théâtre des Champs-Élysées: Orchestre de Paul Whiteman," *Le Ménestrel* 88/28 (9 July 1926): 312–13. A version of the last chapter of *Le Jazz*, "Le Jazz et nous," appeared as Schaeffner and Cœuroy, "Romantisme du jazz," *La Revue musicale* 7/11 (1 October 1926): 221–24. On Schaeffner, see James Clifford, Arthur Hoerée, Michel Leiris, Claude Lévi-Strauss, et al., "Les Fantaisies du voyageur," special issue, *Revue de musicologie* 68/1–2 (1982).

78. Arthur Hoerée, "Le Jazz," *La Revue musicale* 8/11 (1 October 1927): 213–41 (quotes on p. 215). Mauclair's reaction comes from a survey conducted by Schaeffner and Cœuroy in the pages of *Paris-Midi*, from 8 May 1925 to 1 July 1925 (many of which are collected in Ro 585, "Le Jazz," doc. 7, Rondel); his, 16 May 1925. Selected responses (not Mauclair's) were reprinted as "Le Jazz devant les juges," in Schaeffner and Cœuroy, *Le Jazz*, 113–36.

79. Hoerée, "Le Jazz," 221.

80. Ibid., 237. Darius Milhaud and Jean Wiéner, "les deux Français ayant pénétré le plus l'esprit du jazz," were also Jewish, he noted (ibid.).

81. Ibid., 239–40.

In his reply, Schaeffner concurred that there were many components to jazz but not on their relative importance: for him, the black elements were defining. Hoerée was wrong to see jazz as a black appropriation of European music: this ignored that white composers already drew on a black idiom in their popular songs; it was rather a reappropriation. "If the Negro borrows," said Schaeffner, "it is because a laziness, perhaps native in him, benefits from it [y trouve un certain compte]," but he bears such natural musicality that the result will be more his own than his model's.[82] Schaeffner emphasized the performance aspect of jazz that had been lost in Hoerée's analysis: you only had to compare Whiteman's band and that of *La Revue nègre*, he said, to know the difference between white and black jazz.

The debate continued with both men using reviews to reiterate their positions. For Hoerée, Gershwin's Piano Concerto in F was more proof that "the Negroes . . . have been carried along in a 'white' if not to say European adventure" and that this composer, like the others, "owes to Israel his power of assimilation."[83] Meanwhile Schaeffner noted with satisfaction that two recent books on jazz (one German, one British) "both rely on the hypothesis of an Afro-American origin."[84] Hoerée was unmoved: in a later article he accepted that ragtime and American dances had preceded the fox-trot, but insisted that jazz was located at "the intersection of many races" and that all such music known today was "uniquement de race blanche."[85]

If Hoerée was determined to prove that jazz traced more of its ancestors to Europe than to Africa, other writers were concerned specifically with

82. André Schaeffner, "Réflexions sur la musique: Le Jazz," *La Revue musicale* 9/1 (1 November 1927): 72–76 (quote on p. 74).

83. Arthur Hoerée, "Concerto en fa, pour piano et orchestre, par Georges Gershwin (Concert Tiomkin)," *La Revue musicale* 9/9 (1 July 1928): 293–94.

84. André Schaeffner, "Les Livres: Paul Bernhard: *Jazz, eine musikalische Zeitfrage* (. . . Munich: Delphin-Verlag, 1927); R. W. S. Mendl: *The Appeal of Jazz* (. . . Londres: Philip Allan and Co., 1927)," *La Revue musicale* 9/10 (1 August 1928): 405–6 (quote on p. 405).

85. Arthur Hoerée, "Le Jazz et la musique d'aujourd'hui," *Le Courrier musical et théâtral* 30 (1928): 671–72 (quote on p. 671). The same article also appeared as "Le Jazz et son influence sur la musique d'aujourd'hui," *Le Ménestrel* 91/33 (16 August 1929): 361–63; and under the original title, in *Europe*, no. 84 (15 December 1929): 593–96. Among articles suggesting a similar position to Hoerée's, see Henri Monnet, "Le Nègre et la musique américaine," *Cahiers d'art*, no. 7–8 (1927): 259–60. A later article witnesses a moderation of his views: Arthur Hoerée, "Le Jazz," in *La Musique des origines à nos jours*, ed. Norbert Dufourcq (Paris: Librairie Larousse, 1946), 473–80.

its relationship to France. *Académicien* Fortunat Strowski offered a new hypothesis, "Et si le jazz était français?," a question that seemed to be on many lips. In New York, Strowski had found listening to jazz a strangely nostalgic experience. If one could discount jazz's rhythm, he maintained, one would find "some old French *chanson* or one of those *airs galants* of the seventeenth and eighteenth centuries." So much was explained, he thought, by jazz's roots along the Mississippi, where former slaves were still in the service of old French families: further proof that America was created by "the French genius as much as the [Anglo-]Saxon genius, the gallant, amiable, gay spirit of our civilization as much as the puritanical, grave spirit of old England."[86] Composer Maurice Delage was among those who agreed, finding nothing anachronistic about Europeans playing jazz: the music had merely "brought back from Louisiana an old stock [fond] of French love song [romance] heightened by its passage on the strings of the plantation banjo."[87] For these writers, jazz's roots in (French) Louisiana were far from a coincidence; the new music could be celebrated as another of France's many contributions to world culture.

Two further strategies were commonly employed in attempts to appropriate jazz. First, among possible etymologies (which still compete today), one was favored by many French.[88] *Jazz*, they said, derived from their own word *jaser* meaning "to chatter," "to babble," "to gossip." This, it was thought, was a way to describe the relationship between players engaged in collective improvisation: they did not recite, as do classical musicians, but conducted more free-form discourse. "The word jazz is of French origin and its application to music is the faithful reflection

86. Fortunat Strowski, "Petites Hypothèses: Et si le jazz était français? Nous aurions apporté aux nègres les mélodies, et eux leur auraient donné le rythme," *Paris-Midi*, 20 March 1928, in Ro 585, "Le Jazz," doc. 50, Rondel.

87. Maurice Delage, "La Musique de jazz," *Revue Pleyel*, no. 31 (April 1926): 18–20 (quote on p. 19). Delage was discussing the French piano duo (Jean) Wiéner and (Clément) Doucet, who anticipated to some extent the establishment of a mode of French jazz and (at least in their reception) the nationalistic discourse that accompanied it. See, for example, Robert Brisacq, "Les Concerts: Wiéner et Doucet," *La Rumeur*, 16 February 1928, in Ro 585, "Le Jazz," doc. 47, Rondel; and Brisacq, "Wiéner et Doucet," *La Volonté*, [16?] May 1929, ibid., doc. 73. See also Denise Pilmer Taylor, "*La Musique pour tout le monde*: Jean Wiéner and the Dawn of French Jazz" (PhD diss., University of Michigan, 1998), particularly chap. 4, "*Jazz à deux pianos*: Wiéner and Doucet Embrace Accessibility," 191–239.

88. See Alan P. Merriam and Fradley H. Garner, "Jazz—the Word," *Ethnomusicology* 12 (1968): 373–96 [also reprinted in Robert G. O'Meally, ed., *The Jazz Cadence of American Culture* (New York: Columbia University Press, 1998), 7–31].

of its literal sense,"[89] wrote an American correspondent in Paris, Irving Schwerké. The second strategy was concerned less with origins than with contemporary realities. Wasn't the saxophone the sine qua non of the jazz band, people asked, and weren't that instrument's origins French? In fact, Adolphe Sax's birth in Belgium in 1814, the year before France ceded it to the Netherlands, makes this rather tenuous; still, the instrument was patented in Paris (in 1846) and Berlioz was among several prominent French supporters. For one writer, this was proof enough that jazz was beholden to "the French genius whose mark is almost always found at the origin of . . . Art"; for another, it even signaled that "jazz is a French invention!"[90] Contrary to popular belief, jazz's arrival in France, these writers maintained, was actually its homecoming.[91]

Back to Roots: "Hot" and "Straight" Jazz

It was into this muddy field—in which jazz's origins could be located anywhere from Madagascar to Le Midi—that a precocious teenager called Hugues Panassié (1912–1974) entered the fray. More determined than any to rid France of Hylton, he took an altogether different tack. Beginning in articles in 1930 and culminating in his famous book *Le Jazz hot* (1934), Panassié sought to distinguish between so-called "hot" and "straight" jazz (terms for which, he insisted, there were no adequate French equivalents). According to him, the roots of jazz were not Anglo-Saxon, as Hylton had led some to suppose, still less Latin; they were specifically American, and at that African American.[92] The original, "hot" jazz was

89. Irving Schwerké, "Le Jazz est mort! Vive le jazz!," *Le Guide du concert*, 12 and 19 March 1926, reprinted in Schwerké, *Kings Jazz and David (Jazz et David, rois)* [bilingual] (Paris: Presses Modernes, 1927), 13–30 (quote on p. 22).

90. Responses to the survey "Aimez-vous le jazz?," conducted in *Le Soir*, from 15 June 1926 (collected in Ro 585, "Le Jazz," doc. 24, Rondel), by Gabriel Astruc (15 June 1926), and Adolphe Sax (16 June 1926; subtitled "Le Jazz est né d'une invention française: Ce que dit M. Adolphe Sax fils de l'inventeur du saxophone").

91. Also common, less to claim ownership of jazz than to deny any genuine originality to it (and its African American creators), was comparing its syncopation to that of medieval and renaissance composers such as Jannequin and Josquin. See, for example, René Dumesnil, "La Musique: Le Jazz," *La Femme de France*, 22 March 1931, in Ro 585, "Le Jazz," doc. 129, Rondel; Dumesnil, *La Musique contemporaine en France* (Paris: Librairie Armand Colin, 1930), 98; and, most curiously, Jean-Gustave Schencke, "Réflexions sur le rythme du plain-chant et du jazz-band," *Le Courrier musical* 26 (1924): 516–17.

92. See, for example, Hugues Panassié, "Revue de la presse," *Jazz-Tango* 2/13 (October 1931): 12.

the dynamic, improvised music played primarily by blacks—the beginning of the jazz canon as it is known today. "Straight" was its commercial appropriation, usually white, that had seen a move from extemporization to arrangement.

In straight bands such as Hylton's, Panassié argued, musicians adhered strictly to arrangements; worse, these were "all built on the same model" with "the same interchangeable formulae"—the familiar language of anti-Americanism and anti-industrialism, as encountered above. In hot bands, on the other hand, players "improvise[d] . . . on a given theme . . . in a syncopated style"; they soloed "according to [their] inspiration" in line with a practice that came "directly from the Negro tradition."[93] While this distinction between the two styles often seemed more or less racial, it was not straightforwardly so. Panassié cited both black and white bands and soloists, and he insisted that it was "an error to believe that whites are inferior to Negroes." Whites, too, could play hot by assimilating the Negro style; in fact, some were so good that it was "difficult to tell them apart."[94] Similarly, not all black bands and players were hot, although they were more naturally inclined to be.

While Panassié's descriptions of straight jazz often borrowed—and sometimes created—the industrial vocabulary common to other critics, he did not share their suspicion of music on disc. On the contrary, recordings not only captured fleeting moments of improvisational inspiration, they allowed them to be heard thousands of miles away in Europe, where hot jazz was barely known.[95] As Panassié alludes to above, it was in part records that succeeded in moving race from the biological to the performative (or even exposing it as imaginary): when blues singer Sophie Tucker first performed in France, for example, critics confessed to sharing the audience's astonishment when a buxom blond—more, a Jewess—came on stage.[96]

93. Hugues Panassié, "Le Jazz 'hot,'" *La Revue musicale* 11/105 (June 1930): 481–94 (quotes on p. 483). An earlier Panassié piece stating the same case in brief is Philorythmos [pseud.], "Sam Wooding nous quitte: Le Roi du jazz 'hot,'" *La Volonté*, 14 [January?] 1930, in Ro 585, "Le Jazz," doc. 96, Rondel.

94. Panassié, "Le Jazz 'hot,'" 488. Panassié made the same point in his later article "Blancs et noirs," *Jazz-Tango-Dancing* 4/39 (December 1933): 7. Here he dismissed arguments both that only blacks can play real jazz and that whites can play better. The first was "a prejudice"; the second, "absurd." While both races could attain an equal standard, however, he thought talented blacks would always be more numerous and play with more ease.

95. See, for example, Panassié, "Le Jazz 'hot,'" 487.

96. See reactions to her performance at the Empire Theatre, fortnight beginning 20 February 1931, in Ro 15718(11–15), "L'Empire," Rondel. See also Peter An-

Endeavoring to establish hot's supremacy, the authoritarian Panassié was quick to denounce others who mistook straight jazz for the real thing or otherwise failed to uphold (his) critical standards.[97] In his regular "Revue de la presse" in the magazine *Jazz-Tango(-Dancing)*, he not only quoted but responded to other writers' articles, taking them to task for what he perceived as misinformation, misunderstanding, or misjudgment.[98] Time and again, Panassié insisted that his own opinion was not partial but an objective assimilation of the taste and learning of the finest (black) jazz musicians; to disagree was evidence of a failure to grasp the music's fundamental aesthetics.[99]

For Panassié, "mistakes" were especially reprehensible when Jack Hylton and his band were concerned. His favorite whipping boys, they offered, he would say, "no trace of the Negro spirit," "general bad taste," and "jazz commercialized for . . . the general public."[100] In one of their records, he complained, "the character of jazz is completely neglected"; another was "too vulgar" to discuss.[101] He was flabbergasted when a critic proposed adding a Louis Armstrong record to one's collection alongside Jack Hylton's version—worse later when a dealer suggested a Hylton recording

telyes, "Red Hot Mamas: Bessie Smith, Sophie Tucker, and the Ethnic Maternal Voice in American Popular Song," in *Embodied Voices: Representing Female Vocality in Western Culture*, ed. Leslie C. Dunn and Nancy A. Jones (Cambridge: Cambridge University Press, 1994), 212–29.

97. See, for example, Hugues Panassié, "La Situation actuelle du jazz," *Jazz-Tango-Dancing* 3/17 (February 1932): 7–8; and Panassié, "Revue de la presse," *Jazz-Tango-Dancing* 4/32 (May 1933): 11, 13.

98. Launched on October 15, 1930, as *Jazz-Tango*, this monthly magazine was renamed *Jazz-Tango-Dancing* in issue 2/15 (December 1931) and continued under this name until 9/94 (November 1938), which I believe was the last.

99. For example, the first page of Panassié, "Le Jazz 'hot'": "Je demande au lecteur de noter que ce n'est pas ma compréhension du jazz que je vais exposer ici, mais celle des techniciens les plus autorisés" (481).

100. Hugues Panassié, "Autour d'un article de M. Wiéner," *Jazz-Tango-Dancing* 3/18 (March 1932): 6–7 (quotes on p. 7); Panassié, "Critique de jazz: Jack Hylton et son orchestre," *Jazz-Tango-Dancing* 2/15 (December 1931) 15; Panassié, "La Malentendu du jazz hot," *L'Insurgé* 1/3 (27 January 1937). On another occasion, Panassié complained: "[Hylton] se présente partout comme orchestre de jazz. En réalité, la musique qu'il joue n'a le plus souvent aucun rapport avec celle qui nous intéresse. . . . Tout cela ne peut continuer à s'appeler jazz qu'à la faveur de la confusion qui règne dans l'esprit du public, pour qui porte ce nom tout ce qui est joué avec des cuivres, des saxophones, une batterie, un banjo" ("La Situation actuelle du jazz," 7).

101. Hugues Panassié, "Critique de jazz," *Jazz-Tango* 2/6 (1 March 1931): n.p.

as an *alternative* to Armstrong's.[102] These discs, he argued, were "not only ridiculous but [wear] terribly on the nerves."[103] Most damning, he knew that Hylton would be indifferent to these criticisms so long as his discs were a commercial success.[104] The band had the ability to play hot, Panassié maintained, but not the artistic commitment. Still railing against Hylton—and fellow writers—in his book *Le Jazz hot*, Panassié argued that the Boys owed their success to "publicity and the incompetence of critics, who were not even able to discern that this orchestra was concerned only with commercial success and almost never played real jazz music."[105]

A patriot, however, Panassié praised individual French musicians whom Hylton had hired; similarly he exempted Grégor's and Ventura's ensembles from the worst attacks on straight jazz. This frequently involved him in critical sleight of hand. In listings of the best jazz musicians, Panassié excluded French players on the grounds that they lacked "points of comparison" with the Americans, but he still insisted that several deserved a place.[106] In a review of a concert by Ventura, he acknowledged that the band could be criticized for placing too much emphasis on spectacle, but appealed for an explanation to "the incomprehension of a large part of the public" with regard to pure jazz: a leniency he would have never allowed Hylton.[107] This is indicative of the duplicity in which Panassié's main vehicle, *Jazz-Tango(-Dancing)*, was constantly engaged. Since it was conceived as much as a trade journal as a forum for critical discussion, articles complaining about foreign musicians taking French jobs (and the authorities turning a blind eye) sat uneasily alongside Pa-

102. Hugues Panassié, *Le Jazz hot* (Paris: Corrêa, 1934), 27.

103. Hugues Panassié, "Critique de jazz," *Jazz-Tango* 2/12 (September 1931): 14.

104. Hugues Panassié, "Critique de jazz," *Jazz-Tango-Dancing* 3/16 (January 1932): 14.

105. Panassié, *Le Jazz hot*, 21. For other examples of invective directed at critics who praise Hylton, see Panassié's "Revue de la presse," in *Jazz-Tango* 2/8 (May 1931): 15, 19, in *Jazz-Tango* 2/14 (November 1931): 33, and in *Jazz-Tango-Dancing* 4/31 (April 1933): 9; and Panassié, "Mise au point," *Jazz-Tango-Dancing* 4/37 (October 1933): 6.

106. Hugues Panassié, "Les Meilleurs Musiciens hot étrangers," *Jazz-Tango-Dancing* 3/27 (December 1932): 5; Panassié makes the same point in "Blancs et noirs."

107. Hugues Panassié, "Ray Ventura et ses Collégiens," *Jazz-Tango* 2/7 (April 1931): n.p.; see also Panassié, "Ray Ventura à la Salle Pleyel," *Jazz-Tango-Dancing* 3/22 (July 1932): 14. In his article "Non . . . Le Jazz ne meurt pas!," Ventura was careful in return how he handled Panassié: he at once accepted the critic's formulation of jazz's past and origins, and tried to locate a space for French musicians to contribute to its present and future.

nassié's calls for critical standards and arcane discussion of the latest hot jazz from America.[108] Following a dispute in 1935, he left the magazine to found *Jazz hot*, whose interests were from the start more narrowly defined.[109]

Panassié's attitude toward audiences was curious (although perhaps not out of place among modernist aesthetics). On the one hand, he ceaselessly proselytized for what he understood as real jazz. On the other, his contempt for mass culture was such that he regarded popularity with suspicion.[110] Le Hot Club de France, a fan association established in 1932, thus provided his perfect forum. Activities included small concerts by musicians resident in Paris or passing through, record evenings in which rare performances were shared and discussed, and a mail-order service for procuring discs. Gradually assuming the guiding hand, Panassié enjoyed the attention of a captive audience whose membership implied a willingness to interiorize his aesthetic predilections. As spreading the news of jazz became more and more a quasi-religious mission (on which more below), this surprisingly undemonstrative man grew to be most comfortable preaching to the converted. Indeed, the Hot Club movement may best be thought an attempt not only to promote hot jazz but also to find a space for it apart from the pressures of market forces and musicians' livelihoods—where music that was spiritual by essence could come into its own.[111] From time to time, though, events beyond the Hot Club's control pushed discussion back into the public domain.

108. For the former see, for example, Maurice Bedouc-Ermonchy, "La Main-d'œuvre étrangère," *Jazz-Tango* 1/2 (15 November 1930): 3; Jazz-Tango [pseud.], "À MM. les chefs d'orchestre," *Jazz-Tango* 2/6 (1 March 1931): n.p.; and Louis Dor, "La Page corporative: Organisons la corporation," *Jazz-Tango* 2/9 (June 1931): 5. See also Jeffrey H. Jackson, "Making Enemies: Jazz in Inter-war Paris," *French Cultural Studies* 10 (1999): 179–99.

109. As shown by the opening editorial: "Il n'existait jusqu'à présent aucune revue, aucun journal dans le monde qui fut *exclusivement* consacré à la véritable musique de jazz. Cette lacune devait être comblée. C'est pourquoi *Jazz-Hot* a été fondé" (Anon., "Présentation," *Jazz hot*, no. 1 [March 1935]: 3).

110. While he had nothing good to say about the rest of the concert, for example, Panassié took the absence of applause following Hylton's performance of *Mavra* at the Opéra as "irrefutable proof" that it was not as dreadful as some critics held; see "Revue de la presse," *Jazz-Tango* 2/7 (April 1931): n.p.

111. For much more on the founding and history of the Hot Club de France, see Ludovic Tournès, *New Orleans sur Seine: Histoire du jazz en France* (Paris: Librairie Arthème Fayard, 1999); and Anne Legrand, *Charles Delaunay et le jazz en France dans les années 30 et 40* (Paris: Layeur, 2009).

Test Case: Duke Ellington in Paris

That Panassié's views were gaining notoriety was indicated by reaction to Duke Ellington and His Orchestra's first Paris concert, at the Salle Pleyel in July 1933.[112] "Straight jazz or hot jazz?" one critic demanded: "It is essential ... to have an opinion." Another thought the average Frenchman with little musical knowledge was well aware of this distinction.[113] All knew that Ellington's band (like Hylton's, preceded by their recordings) were the most celebrated hot performers yet to visit France. Reviving a primitivism that had been rather forgotten since the twenties' all-black revues, Émile Vuillermoz heard in their music "something so profoundly human [that it] seem[ed] to be the language of our subconscious"; another critic was amazed by their "primitive musicality" in which "the melancholy of the plantations alternate[d] with the brutal poetry of the jungle."[114] One more writer placed the band in comparative perspective: "Poles apart from Ray Ventura's ... Latin art ... of measure and gaiety," he argued, Ellington's was alternately primitive and melancholy, vehement and sweet. It was not a savage art for it possessed "a degree of perfection," but with its rejection of subtlety and intellect in favor of instinct, the music remained primitive.[115]

If Panassié and his growing coterie had hoped that this concert would be the winning strike in a propaganda war of hot over straight, they

112. The band performed three times: July 27 and 29 and August 1. The last concert was added due to overwhelming demand (possibly the last two).

113. Vincent Breton, "Duke Ellington," *Paris-Soir*, 30 July 1933; Émile Vuillermoz, "Duke Ellington," *Candide*, 3 August 1933 (both are in Ro 585, "Le Jazz," doc. 154, Rondel).

114. Émile Vuillermoz, "Duke Ellington et son orchestre," *Excelsior*, 29 July 1933; Carol-Berard, "Duke Ellington à la Salle Pleyel," *L'Écho de Paris*, 29 July 1933 (both are in Ro 585, "Le Jazz," doc. 154, Rondel).

115. Louis Aubert, "La Semaine musicale," *Le Journal*, 1 August 1933, in Ro 585, "Le Jazz," doc. 154, Rondel. The full passage reads: "Aux antipodes de l'art de Ray Ventura, art latin, tout de mesure et de gaîté contrôlée par l'esprit, l'art d'Ellington est primitif, véhément, truculent, hyperbolique, avec des oppositions de douceur mélancolique et méditative d'une adorable suavité. Certes, on ne peut appeler cela un art sauvage, car il est poussé à un degré de perfection qui est le signe d'une évidente civilisation, mais art de primitif car il ignore la demi-teinte, le sous-entendu, le complexe. Tablant sur l'instinct sous tous ses aspects, il étonne et séduit, parfois même il émeut, mais jamais il ne s'adresse à l'esprit." Henry Prunières disagreed that the music had left the wilderness: "Art sauvage sans doute, mais d'une richesse et d'une spontanéité incomparables" ("Les Concerts de Duke Ellington," *La Revue musicale* 14/139 [September–October 1933]: 208–10 [quote on p. 210]).

were mistaken. By a bizarre twist that must have left them reeling, Ellington's 1933 posters began with the words "Jack Hylton presents . . ." Perhaps sensing that his band-leading days were numbered, Hylton had started on a second career as impresario (in which he would again triumph). That he of all people would bring hot jazz to France threatened to blur a distinction Panassié had been eager to maintain. In an interview, the British bandleader maintained that this new departure did not signal a change in his own "aesthetic conceptions" but represented a commitment to honor—and doubtless to profit from—all forms of jazz.[116] (The following year, Hylton would provide Coleman Hawkins with a band for Paris.) Still, when on the first night Hylton came on stage to introduce the Ellington band, Panassié was proud to be among those who whistled him (the French sign of disapproval) and sent him scuttling back to the wings.[117] The jazz critic failed to record, however, that others had been applauding. "Two aesthetics confronted one another," a different writer noted: Hylton may have been "the initiated's bête noire" but he was still "the general public's favorite."[118] To the members of the Hot Club, there seemed no end to his sins. According to Panassié, Hylton had tried unsuccessfully to make the band play "commercial."[119] Another critic thought he had barred the band from jamming at Bricktop's nightclub later, except on payment of an extortionate fee.[120] Much later, Panassié remembered with horror the "chubby face . . . of [this] English pork butcher" alongside whom the Duke looked more like a prince (fig. 2.8).[121]

Although there were claims to the contrary, the program Ellington presented does not strike as exceptional for the band in this era.[122] Familiar numbers such as "Dinah" and "Tiger Rag" combined with Ellington originals like "Creole Love Call" and "Mood Indigo," plus longer pieces such as the "Black and Tan Fantasy" and a "Blackbirds Medley" (compiled from

116. Anon., "Du Jazz 'hot' au jazz 'straight': Jack Hylton nous parle de Duke Ellington," *Excelsior*, [24?] July 1933, in Ro 585, "Le Jazz," doc. 154, Rondel.

117. Hugues Panassié, "Duke Ellington à Paris," *Jazz-Tango-Dancing* 4/36 (September 1933): 4.

118. Prunières, "Les Concerts de Duke Ellington," 208.

119. Panassié, "Duke Ellington à Paris."

120. E. D., "Duke Ellington à Paris," *Jazz-Tango-Dancing* 4/35 (August 1933): 18.

121. Hugues Panassié, *Douze années de jazz (1927–1938): Souvenirs* (Paris: Corrêa, 1946), 116.

122. Contrary to those who thought Ellington had "dumbed down" his program, American critic John Hammond believed that the attention of a European audience had allowed the bandleader to present a more "arty" concert; see "Duke Ellington à la Salle Pleyel," trans. Mme Hugues Panassié, *Jazz-Tango-Dancing* 4/35 (August 1933): 4.

FIGURE 2.8. Jack Hylton with Duke Ellington in London, 1933 (Popperfoto/Getty Images).

the show that played in France as *Blackbirds of 1929*). Singer Ivie Anderson joined the band for "Stormy Weather" and "It Don't Mean a Thing," and—perceived as a concession to the audience—dancers Bessie Dudley and "Bailey and Derby" accompanied numbers such as "Ducky Wucky" and "I Got Rhythm."[123] This corporeal intrusion upon the music prompted a spat between the important American critic and promoter John Hammond, in town for the concert, and his friend and collaborator Panassié: Hammond complained that the Hot Club members' stoic refusal to clap the dancers ignored an integral part of the show; Panassié replied that their (in)action was motivated by the general public's disproportionately enthusiastic reaction to these numbers, while the band alone had failed to garner as much applause as was customary even for Hylton.[124]

Despite filling the enormous Salle Pleyel three times, Ellington's con-

123. Hugues Panassié, "Duke Ellington à la Salle Pleyel," *Jazz-Tango-Dancing* 4/35 (August 1933): 5.

124. Hammond, "Duke Ellington à la Salle Pleyel" (and note appended by Panassié); Panassié, "Duke Ellington à Paris."

cert had been a "failure," Panassié concluded. Hylton was again to blame: the publicity was grotesque; the program empty, lacking in any information on how to listen to hot.[125] True enough, there was some confusion: one critic discerned—on the sole grounds that the music stands were removed during the interval—that the first half had been straight, the second half hot.[126] But others contested the distinction more legitimately. Like those who, earlier, had questioned the authenticity of shows such as the Blackbirds', not all would accept that hot and straight jazz were so simply opposed. Some writers thought that Ellington's concert had shown there was nothing new in hot; another refused to believe that the players were really improvising (for the most part, of course, they were not).[127] André Schaeffner reverted to industrial metaphors (adding a comparison with the "artificial" Ravel) to show that Ellington's music was now far from the rawness of hot: "Between *Boléro* and this," he said, "what difference is there, apart from that which marks a few years in the manufacture of automobiles?"[128] Transgressing a boundary between art and commerce that Panassié had so eagerly policed, Schaeffner had returned, on four wheels, to familiar anti-American territory.

Authenticity in Print: *Le Jazz hot*

Perhaps in response to these criticisms, Panassié began subtly to change his definition of jazz, specifically his view of straight. By the time of *Le Jazz hot* in 1934, both straight and hot styles could aspire to authenticity. The qualifying criterion was now the presence of "swing nègre," a concept that obstinately resists definition but "is, however, objective."[129] If racial-

125. Panassié, "Duke Ellington à Paris."

126. Henry Malherbe, "À la Salle Pleyel: Duke Ellington et son orchestre," *Le Temps*, 2 August 1933, in Ro 585, "Le Jazz," doc. 154, Rondel.

127. Georges Devaise, review of Duke Ellington and His Orchestra, *Gringoire*, 4 August 1933, cited in Hugues Panassié, "Revue de la presse," *Jazz-Tango-Dancing* 4/36 (September 1933): 9, 12 (esp. p. 9).

128. André Schaeffner, review of Duke Ellington and His Orchestra, *Beaux-Arts*, 11 August 1933, cited in Panassié, "Revue de la presse," *Jazz-Tango-Dancing* 4/36 (September 1933): 12.

129. Panassié, *Le Jazz hot*, 29. Although Panassié occasionally used the term *swing* beforehand, his first attempt at any form of definition appears to have been a few months after the Ellington concert: "Le swing qui est toujours présent dans les exécutions de jazz authentiques, est le swing nègre, qu'il ne faut pas confondre avec le balancement des diverses musiques de danses, car il est essentiellement différent. Il ne faut donc pas s'étonner que les noirs soient plus doués que les autres races" ("Blancs et noirs," 7). A discussion of the phenomenon had, how-

ization was this time more explicit, it was neither complete nor exclusive: swing was a characteristic of Negro music (even perhaps of the Negro body), but talented whites could learn it and incompetent blacks might lack it. In fact, though jazz's essence was Negro, white musicians had also contributed "certain qualities of a purely musical order as a result of their superior training [provenant de leur culture supérieure]."[130] Subsequent generations, black and white, assimilated earlier musicians' advances. Thus, while Louis Armstrong most completely embodied hot jazz for Panassié, what seems now a surprising number of white Chicago musicians were among his favorites (a fact he later attributed to inexperience).[131]

Not that this conceptual shift did anything to aid Hylton; it deliberately served to rebut any blurring of commercial and authentic jazz. With "straight" now reserved for tunes such as Ellington's "Mood Indigo," Hylton's offerings were no longer jazz at all: "straight without swing (Jack Hylton)" represented but "the outer form of jazz without its substance, the peel without the fruit"; elsewhere Panassié referred to the "faux disques de jazz (genre Jack Hylton)."[132] The critic illustrated his point with two recordings of the same tune, comparing the "superficial force" of Hylton's

---

ever, been provided by French pianist Stéphane Mougin: "Le Swing," *Jazz-Tango-Dancing* 4/37 (October 1933): 4. And J. P. Van Praag may have introduced the notion of "swing nègre": "Le Style dans la musique de jazz écrite," *Jazz-Tango-Dancing* 4/38 (November 1933): 5.

130. Panassié, *Le Jazz hot*, 59.

131. See, for example, Panassié's letter to Jean Reldy, 16 August 1946, reprinted in Christian Senn, *Hugues Panassié: Fondateur, president du Hot Club de France* (Lutry, Switz.: privately published, 1995), 113: "Quand j'ai écrit 'Le Jazz hot,' en 1933–1934, j'étais loin de savoir sur le jazz autant de choses qu'à présent, j'étais presque un novice en la matière, et—c'est le plus grave—je l'entendais encore avec l'état d'esprit et l'oreille d'un blanc. D'où de multiples erreurs, et de nombreuses injustices à l'égard des musiciens de race noire qui sont infiniment supérieurs aux blancs pour cette musique—et c'est bien naturel, puisque c'est *leur* musique."

132. Hugues Panassié, "La Vraie Physionomie de la musique de jazz," *La Revue musicale* 15/146 (May 1934): 359–71 (quotes on p. 367); Panassié, *Le Jazz hot*, 358. Panassié was frank that he had erred on straight jazz: "Nous devons faire amende honorable et nous excuser d'avoir eu trop de complaisance pour un préjugé qui consistait à dénier tout caractère de jazz aux exécutions *straight*, sous prétexte qu'un orchestre comme celui de Jack Hylton ne pouvait être considéré comme un orchestre de jazz authentique. Il était bien vrai que Jack Hylton ne produisait pas de la vraie musique de jazz, mais il aurait fallu ajouter qu'en dehors de lui existait des exécutions *straight* se rattachant réellement au jazz" ("La Vraie Physionomie," 359–60). This article is, in effect, a summation of the "theoretical" component of *Le Jazz hot*, with whole paragraphs borrowed from (or perhaps contributing to) it.

band with the "irresistible swing" of Ellington's.[133] While the instrumentation and repertoire were enough to persuade ill-informed listeners that the former was jazz, the absence of swing determined that it was not. A new tool was now at hand to separate the wheat from the chaff.

In one sense, then, Panassié's critical method relied on a process of othering, such as has been commonplace in processes of canon formation. It had the usual hallmarks: a norm was defined or codified by a critic and other styles judged according to their concordance with or deviation from it.[134] A learned art, performing or even appreciating the model did not come easily; the deviant style was its popular derivation, which catered to mass taste and was straightforwardly understood. The market was the enemy, encouraging musicians to play to the lowest common denominator; real art was created elsewhere, in spaces where business was replaced by the cultural capital of connoisseurs, where an aristocracy of taste prevailed. Musicians' need to earn their livelihood was respected to a certain degree: the occasional commercial recording would not damage a reputation as long as serious output continued (implicitly indicating contempt for the industry and its consumers). Securing the boundary stood the critic who, more than the musicians (but often in their name), exercised his, or occasionally her, judgment in determining which side a given record, concert, performer, band, or style would fall. In this sense, Panassié's critical practice was in line with his authoritarian social and political beliefs.

Yet, in one important respect, Panassié's judgments were unusual: far from defending established privilege, he spoke out for black musicians. One immediately suspects, of course, that his air of detachment hid a virulent primitivism, but his early criticism is unusual in attributing to jazz not only spirit but form, and to its performers not only instinct but intellect. Equally uncommon, Panassié valued improvisation over composition where many writers assumed that jazz would "evolve" toward full notation. He thus fought against the increasing tendency in music criticism to see loyalty to a text as more or less synonymous with artistic worth. Problematic as Panassié's writings are, his early work in particular certainly aided African American music to gain critical respect in Europe: at a time when it was still an unusual step for writers on either side of

133. Panassié, *Le Jazz hot*, 34; and "La Vraie Physionomie," 362. The number in question was "Limehouse Blues," recorded by Hylton on Gramophone B 5789, and by Ellington on Gramophone K 6429.

134. A panegyrical review praised the "normative character" of Panassié's book, accepting the critic's own view of the objective quality of his judgments; see Georges Hilaire, "Hugues Panassié," *Jazz hot*, no. 1 (March 1935): 14.

the Atlantic, he unequivocally positioned the black performer's rendition above the white composer's score.[135]

A desire to legitimate his position only in part explains Panassié's increased reference in *Le Jazz hot* to the neo-Thomist scholasticism of Catholic philosopher Jacques Maritain. Hardly an obvious contact point for a jazz critic, these allusions are not as unlikely as they first sound. Maritain and his 1920 book *Art et scolastique* were widely known in Parisian artistic circles; Cocteau and Stravinsky both acknowledged a debt to him.[136] *Le Jazz hot* opens with an epigraph from Maritain, along with one from Louis Armstrong. Prior to the pope's denunciation of the reactionary organization Action Française (with which Maritain had been associated) in 1926, the philosopher and the jazz critic would also have agreed on politics: Maritain then moderated his views, coming to believe in democracy; Panassié never veered from monarchism or from opposition to suffrage.[137]

Le Jazz hot was not the first time that Panassié deferred to Maritain. As early as 1930, he cited the theologian's definition of classicism as the subordination of material to form, the sacrifice of the exterior to the interior. Arguing that hot jazz, like Bach, was concerned with the imaginative working out of inner processes, Panassié's purpose was as ever to separate out a core of authentic jazz: he wanted to direct attention away from its novel instrumentation and unusual timbres toward the musical ingenuity of its improvisational method, and to show, in short, that jazz was "une musique intellectuelle."[138]

135. For a stimulating reexamination of Panassié that at once seeks to locate his primitivism in its specific conservative, Catholic tradition and to recognize his quasi-ethnographic approach to meanings circulating among musicians as—to some degree at least—progressive, see Tom Perchard, "Tradition, Modernity and the Supernatural Swing: Re-reading 'Primitivism' in Hugues Panassié's Writing on Jazz," *Popular Music* 30 (2011): 25–45.

136. See Jean Cocteau, *Lettre à Jacques Maritain* (Paris: Stock, 1926).

137. In a book of conversations published the year after his death, Panassié spoke of democracy and universal suffrage as "véritable superstitions des temps modernes," which, beholden to the will of the majority, failed to allow superior individuals to rise above inferior ones (Panassié, *Monsieur Jazz: Entretiens avec Pierre Casalta* [Paris: Stock, 1975], 131). On Panassié and Maritain, see Tournès, *New Orleans sur Seine*, 38–40. This section is based in part on my review of Tournès in "Beyond Le Bœuf: Interdisciplinary Rereadings of Jazz in France," *Journal of the Royal Musical Association* 128 (2003): 137–53. See also Jean-Luc Barré, *Jacques et Raïssa Maritain: Les Mendiants du ciel* (Paris: Stock, 1996).

138. Panassié, "Le Jazz 'hot,'" 493. Panassié reiterated this argument, quoting the same section of Maritain, in both "Le Jazz hot," *Orbes*, no. 4 (Winter 1932–1933): 69–83 (esp. pp. 80–81), and *Le Jazz hot*, 359–60. He also quoted Maritain in his ac-

By 1934 he could go further. Although it is uncertain how closely Panassié had studied *Art et scolastique* (equivocal in its references to music), the last chapter of *Le Jazz hot* cites it several times. Maritain's view of music is invoked to show that playing and listening to hot jazz is not a matter merely of technique and visceral attraction but of transmitting and accessing a quasi-spiritual message that resists translation into words. As a corollary, learning to play, recognize, or understand hot jazz should not be taught by academies but through informal apprenticeship (jam sessions, musicians and listeners sharing knowledge, and so forth). To this end, Panassié approvingly cited Maritain's dismissal of the École des Beaux-Arts in favor of the familial master-student relationships of prerevolutionary years (a result of the philosopher's belief that the arts involved "practical" rather than "speculative" orders of knowledge).[139]

As Ludovic Tournès argues, Panassié even translated this method into his teaching of jazz appreciation at the hot clubs.[140] In his "conférence-auditions" (lectures illustrated with records), members were taught to imitate the bodily gestures of the players. This was, Tournès suggests, Panassié's version of the ancien régime's "apprentissage corporatif."[141] Harmless enough in itself, this eccentric practice may therefore stand as a sign of a counterrevolutionism that was far less benign: as the industrialization of culture was also its democratization, so one of the benefits of the Enlightenment was mass education. With a curious combination of primitivist and patrician values, Panassié found in the African American community a prerevolutionary microcosm alive and well within the paradigmatic nation of industrialism and democracy.

This begins to explain, then, why two models—one French, one Af-

ceptance of the presidency of the Hot Club de France; see "Hot-Club Magazine," *Jazz-Tango-Dancing* 5/40 (January 1934): 30.

139. Panassié, *Le Jazz hot*, 343–47.

140. Tournès, *New Orleans sur Seine*, 44–45.

141. Jacques Maritain, *Art et scolastique* (Paris: Librairie de l'Art Catholique, 1920), 69, cited in Panassié, *Le Jazz hot*, 346. Panassié had previously made the same case for learning jazz by example, almost to the word, in "L'Enseignement du style hot: L'Exemple de Milton Mesirow," *Jazz-Tango-Dancing* 5/41 (February 1934): 5, 7. Panassié's lifetime support for white American clarinetist Milton Mesirow, or Mezz Mezzrow, one of his principal early informants about jazz, has often mystified other critics—not least Nat Hentoff who thought Mesirow was "so consistently out of tune that he may have invented a new scale system" (Hentoff, "Counterpoint," *DownBeat*, 11 February 1953, 5, cited in *The Encyclopedia of Jazz*, ed. Leonard Feather, new ed. [London: Arthur Baker, 1961], 332). See also Hugues Panassié, *Quand Mezzrow enregistre* (Paris: Robert Laffont, 1952); and Mezz Mezzrow with Bernard Wolfe, *Really the Blues* (New York: Random House, 1946).

rican American—paradoxically found favor during the same years: at least rhetorically, both fitted into the same anti-American, antimodern agenda. The naturalization of jazz as French was the obvious solution, but returning to the source still extant within the heartland of mass culture was a viable alternative. Both proposed local, authentic traditions as replacements for industrial, standardized commodities; this was how they could form an (admittedly uneasy) alliance. They eventually came together in the creation of the Quintette du Hot Club de France: still the best-known hot French band.[142]

That it took a Gypsy born in Belgium (Django Reinhardt) and a poor Italian immigrant's son (Stéphane Grappelli) to bring hot jazz home to France has a degree of irony. But the combination of melodically gifted soloists and the unusual timbres of the all-string ensemble (violin, three guitars, and bass), in which contrasts were subtle and nuance great, provided a unique formula that many were happy to identify as French. Disagreement crept in, however, regarding how far it might lead away from the "jazz tradition" beginning to be defined. Henry Prunières, respected critic of La Revue musicale whose predilections were unusually well-honed toward jazz, thought it presaged a style of "white hot" that dispensed with aggressive wind instruments to cultivate jazz's sensitive side.[143] But Panassié dismissed any such idea as a "contradiction in terms": white Americans and Europeans could learn to play hot perfectly well, but this did not change the fact that its origins—and its prospects—were black.[144]

While on one hand, then, the Quintette resolved a tension between nationalist and purist attitudes toward jazz, on the other it encouraged fissures to grow. Since Panassié's departure from Jazz-Tango(-Dancing), the magazine no longer covered hot records; Jazz hot rarely dealt with anything else. Many were the critics who had always thought hot simply too barbaric for France. And now that the Hot Club had its own national ensemble, specialists such as Panassié no longer felt obliged to defend French musicians on grounds of citizenship alone. Notwithstanding their continuing prestige, or their future success, the Quintette did not yet match the popular appeal of Ray Ventura's band, which now moved squarely into the mainstream.

As Hylton's Opéra concert had failed to reconcile "high" and "low," now a subset of jazz was admitted to the citadel of culture only at the expense

142. See William H. Kenney III, "The Assimilation of American Jazz in France, 1917–1940," American Studies 25 (1984): 5–24.

143. H. P. [Henry Prunières], "Hot-Club," La Revue musicale 15/143 (February 1934): 162.

144. Panassié, "La Vraie Physionomie," 367.

of much other music. The crossings-over and unlikely collaborations that Panassié had always denied or downplayed actually began to cease. When the Ellington band made a return visit to Europe on the eve of war in 1939, for example, they were presented not by a promoter such as Hylton but by the Hot Club; critics' desire for hot to occupy an autonomous realm removed from the decadence of society and the corruption of public discourse had to some extent been achieved. Yet *Jazz hot* found even this concert too commercial.[145] One begins to wonder, then, whether the goal of a pure jazz experience, as it had come to be defined, were more than a pipe dream.

Here again, Panassié's reliance on Maritain may prove interesting; it returns me, by a roundabout path, to that other great antimodernist, Stravinsky. The philosopher's influence on Stravinsky's aesthetics—at least, his aesthetic statements—has been established.[146] Louis Andriessen and Elmer Schönberger also suggest him as the source of a familiar Stravinsky pose: the artisan who crafts his music for the glory of God without thought of expression or innovation. In Panassié's hands, this nostalgia for the religious truths of the Middle Ages merges into a primitivist myth: black musicians should channel spiritual energy from their ancestors to replicate styles within the tradition rather than remaking it. Similarly, Stravinsky's denunciation of modernism as "in its most clearly defined meaning . . . a form of theological liberalism which is a fallacy condemned by the Church of Rome" could just as easily have come from the jazz critic.[147] In Panassié's hands, African American music had fallen into line with an extreme conservatism; hot jazz had become, in effect, another form of (neo)classicism.[148]

---

145. Anon. [Hugues Panassié?], "Duke Ellington à Paris," *Jazz hot*, no. 32 (July–August 1939): 17–18.

146. In particular, Stravinsky's 1939–1940 Harvard lectures, published as *Poétique musicale (sous forme de six leçons)* (Cambridge, MA: Harvard University Press, 1942), echo both Maritain's ideas and his rhetoric. See Louis Andriessen and Elmer Schönberger, *The Apollonian Clockwork: On Stravinsky*, trans. Jeff Hamburg (Oxford: Oxford University Press, 1989), 86–96. *Poétique musicale* was ghostwritten by Alexis Roland-Manuel and Pierre Souvschinsky, from Stravinsky's notes.

147. Stravinsky, *Poétique musicale*, cited in Andriessen and Schönberger, *The Apollonian Clockwork*, 94–95.

148. French neoclassicism has been aligned to similarly traditionalist (and politically conservative) agendas. See Scott Messing, *Neoclassicism in Music from the Genesis of the Concept through the Schoenberg/Stravinsky Polemic* (Ann Arbor, MI: UMI Research Press, 1988); and, particularly, Richard Taruskin, "Review: Back to Whom? Neoclassicism as Ideology," *Nineteenth-Century Music* 16 (1993): 286–302.

Center of the Periphery: "Jack's Back"

Among Hylton's best publicity ploys was a cartoon announcing his return to town: baton in hand, as viewed from the audience, the bandleader wears a jacket emblazoned "Jack's Back." How often Hylton has crept back into my story is a function in part, of course, of my desire to critique certain assumptions about jazz in interwar France: truisms about the centrality of American performers, the color blindness of the French, and their innate ability to appreciate real "jazzistic" genius. But it is more than that.

As I have shown, once Hylton had established himself as King of Jazz in France, attempts to topple him were many; his name became synonymous with vapid commercialization even as he retained his extraordinary popularity. However hard critics and musicians tried to rid themselves of the trace of Hylton, only self-delusion could convince them they had been successful. Panassié was eager to banish the specter precisely because he knew what jazz in France owed to this figurehead become grotesque (in his younger days, Panassié too had enjoyed the Boys' records).[149] In this case, one is tempted toward a psychological explanation of his contempt for mass culture: before contracting the polio that left him partially paralyzed, Panassié had been a keen dancer (and sportsman); it was during convalescence that his interest in jazz proceeded beyond that of passing familiarity. French musicians, less intransigent than the critic, nevertheless felt the need to disavow the British bandleader: to forget how much they had learned from him and to overestimate the distance they had traveled since. Yet there Hylton was: promoting Ellington, backing Coleman Hawkins—still selling records.[150] In order to remove this seeming fixture, Panassié twice split jazz into halves that could not easily be prized apart: first "hot" and "straight," then more simply "true" and "false."

While one can of course describe styles as more or less commercial (in the sense that they appeal to differing extents to the large buying public), any attempt to drive a wedge between the two is both historically and aesthetically naïve: these are differences of degree, not of kind. As I have

---

149. The opening sentence of Panassié's 1946 book of recollections reads: "C'est en 1927 que je pris contact avec le jazz, avec le *vrai* jazz, du moins, car je connaissais déjà les Jack Hylton, Revellers et autres ersatz" (Panassié, *Douze années de jazz*, 11).

150. As late as 1937, Panassié felt the need to reiterate his complaint with Hylton: "Le jazz pratiqué par un Jack Hylton n'a aucun rapport avec [le jazz hot]. Ce n'est même pas du jazz "straight" authentique. C'est du jazz commercialisé pour le goût du gros public, particulièrement du public européen" (Hugues Panassié, "Le Malentendu du jazz hot," *Insurgé* 1/3 [27 January 1937]).

indicated, bands of all sorts learned from one another, exchanged players and music—and performed in no single style. Perhaps more important, at least in Europe (where no overt distinction was made along racial lines), all swam in the same water, fighting for an audience whose fickle desires they—and their promoters and recording companies—did their best to satisfy. Any perceived autonomy for the music could only be relative; any professed escape, merely an illusion (or delusion).

This unlikely story—of the British bandleader who became *Roi du jazz*—may thus have broader implications. Reviewing contemporary discourse, one witnesses not only the emergence of canonical musicians but also the decline of others, who in their time were much more popular. While the "survival of the fittest" doubtless plays a role in this process, aesthetics and the musics that inform or result from them cannot be separated from national, racial, and cultural ideologies, and music's participation in the market economy is a fact that is escaped only in certain extreme forms of modernist theory. As I have shown, the aestheticist attention to African American music for which European critics are often praised was a corollary of a movement against the industrialization of culture that was vehemently anti-American. In other words, proudly ascribing to jazz (as do many) the title "America's classical music" may, ironically, risk participating in an un-American activity.[151]

The mixed messages jazz generated in France suggest that it may more accurately lay claim to two contradictory premiers: as the first truly global popular music (whose function rests on its multivalent universality), but also as the first "world music" (which paradoxically trades internationally on its exotic particularity). Circulated as much by white musicians on record as by black performers in person, jazz proved remarkably versatile. If its so-called Americanized manifestation, commodified and industrialized, became tiresome, then older traditions could reinvigorate it. Whether recovering or, conversely, superimposing folk material, jazz traded again on its authenticity, its New World origins forgotten as it dug deep into local soil. Big bands in interwar France thus make an intriguing early case study. The fearful discourse about mass production and Americanization swirling around them was more or less independent of the homespun music from Britain and later France that was mostly heard. And the African American performers who were most reliant on the recording industry and modern travel to bring their music and bands to Paris were those commonly understood to exhibit a "primitive" au-

151. See, for example, Grover Sales, *Jazz: America's Classical Music* (Englewood Cliffs, NJ: Prentice Hall, 1984).

thenticity. In other words, the models that come most easily to hand—of center and periphery, or global and local—don't capture this process well: the movement was in large part around the periphery, and the center was finally construed as the most peripheral of all.

A similar ambiguity pervades discussion and marketing even today: jazz is seen at once or alternately as a folk-derived African American music, as America's classical music (perhaps especially as it is no longer popular), and as an international language with distinct national dialects. Its multiple appropriations and reappropriations are a historical, theoretical, and sometimes even ethical minefield. "French jazz" is, then, a case in point. In France, even recent accounts can see the naturalization of the music as a victory over its creators: self-righteously taking and "reforming" jazz, this strikes the outsider as an appropriation informed by colonialism.[152] But the Gallic attitude also marks a distant trace of another, venerable argument: French jazz can be—and has long been—seen quite differently, as a form of counterhegemonic resistance against global markets and normalizing technologies.

It is perhaps surprising how often discussion about culture returns to the same unresolved tension: on the one hand, fears of a stagnating homogenization, and on the other, the conspicuous fact of ever-expanding possibilities. At least so far, the presence of American popular musics in Europe, Africa, or Asia has not aborted local traditions; like jazz in France, it has often inspired vital hybrids. But neither does the authenticity billed as a counterpoise offer a genuine alternative: in an era of world music and tourism, escape from international trade and culture can never be complete. As this curious story from interwar Paris reveals, cultural exchanges that may have distant origins and far-reaching consequences take place on the ground in complex and contested territory. Then as now, actions and products are neither globally identical nor locally unique; they are rather the result of the complex interaction of more or less localized practices. Such processes are hard to recognize from on high, since it is down there, in the thick of it all, that musicians and listeners negotiate the sense and sound of place.

152. For more on this point, see the epilogue and my article "Beyond Le Bœuf," 148–50.

3 "Du jazz hot à *La Créole*"

Josephine Baker Sings Offenbach

Joséphine: A Life in the Theatre

By the time of Josephine Baker's final Paris show, in 1975, her first, *La Revue nègre*, was a distant memory. *Académicien* Robert de Flers had thought: "It's an insult to French taste. We are reverting to the ape more quickly than we descended from it!" Fifty years on, his words, which were quoted in the new show, had become thick with irony: his doomsday prophecy had not come to pass, and African American Baker was, by then, an institution in France.[1] Her sudden death a matter of days after the show's opening offered further proof: crowds lined the street to glimpse Baker's memorial cortège; a televised state funeral commemorated her life with full military honors, twenty thousand people overflowing around the church, La Madeleine.

The reviews and obituaries (sometimes as one) presented a confused picture of Baker's racial and national allegiances.[2] For many, her father was Senegalese; for others, it was her mother. One parent was surely white; whether it was a Spanish father or an American mother was unclear. But Baker's patriotism for *la France*, her adopted home for much of her last half century, was well-known: of the number "Paris, mes amours" one critic noted, "For Josephine, *who is French*, this song is a profession of faith!"[3] Detailing her lineage more imaginatively, an obituary made her

---

1. This line from the show at the Bobino Theatre, Montparnasse, was reported in Jacqueline Cartier, "Joséphine, 72 heures avant le jour J. . . . et 50 ans après ses débuts," *France-Soir*, 23 March 1975; and Anne de Gasperi, "Joséphine, cinquante ans de rêve et de lumière," *Le Quotidien de Paris*, 1 April 1975. The original review on which it was based is Robert de Flers, "La Semaine dramatique," *Le Figaro*, 16 December 1925, a response to *La Revue nègre* at the Théâtre-Music-Hall des Champs-Élysées.

2. A collection is found in 4° Sw 4754(1–3), "Baker, Joséphine: Biographie, carrière, nécrologie," Département des Arts du Spectacle, Bibliothèque Nationale, Paris (hereafter cited as AdS), from which I draw the quotations and references here.

3. Gilberte Cournand, "Rencontre avec Joséphine Baker," *Le Parisien*, 24 March 1975 (my italics).

the "granddaughter of slaves originally from Senegal who had stopped off in Martinique before being sold in the South," presumably in the former French colony of Louisiana that the show assumed was Baker's American home.[4]

It is true that this 1975 retrospective, *Joséphine*, which staged supposed scenes from Baker's life, did little to unravel contradictions. After a comic, fairy-tale introduction, three scenes portrayed the performer prior to her (in)famous Parisian debut. The first, featuring "sorcerers" (dancers costumed as wild animals) in Africa conjuring up the phenomenon that would be Josephine Baker, was a focus of particular confusion: while some papers recognized that she was at least a couple of generations removed from this continent ("pays de ses grands-parents"), another referred to "her childhood in Africa, where she was born."[5] The second scene, in which three child actors played Baker growing up in Louisiana, preferred to forget that her hometown, St. Louis, now lies in Missouri: it would have failed to summon up the requisite nostalgia for *la plus grande France*. The third marked Baker's last New York stop before she was swept off to Paris. Next, for "La Revue nègre," a young dancer stood in for Baker; to the sound of "le jazz-band," she danced topless in a skirt of perkily phallic bananas, invoking the rebuke of de Flers.[6] In "Les Débuts de Joséphine aux Folies-Bergère," however, Baker herself sang some of her most enduringly popular songs; if her appeal remained always "exotic," she had quickly learned to play that role with peculiarly Parisian finesse.

The extent to which de Flers had misjudged the performer was soon made clear: in "Joséphine chant la France," Sous-Lieutenant Baker sat in uniform on the "Josie-Jeep," singing patriotic songs and recounting her wartime adventures. Active in the French resistance, Baker had trafficked military secrets using an artist's freedom to travel without suspicion. Later, recovering from an almost fatal illness that left her hospitalized

4. Jean Prasteau, "Joséphine Baker: Un Demi-Siècle de panache," *Le Figaro*, 14 April 1975. Baker was born Freda McDonald in St. Louis, Missouri, in 1906, daughter of African American Carrie McDonald and an unknown (possibly Caucasian) father. On her marriage to Jean Lion in 1937, she took French citizenship.

5. Maurice Rapin, "Joséphine revue de André Levasseur," *Le Figaro*, 4 April 1975 (also Cartier, "Joséphine"); André Ransan, "À Bobino: 'Joséphine,'" *L'Aurore*, 4 April 1975. This scene does not appear on the various audio releases (none currently available) of *Joséphine à Bobino 1975*. My (selective) description is based on a souvenir program, "Jean-Claude Dauzonne présente *Joséphine*, un grand spectacle de André Levasseur," at 4° W 1613, AdS, and on reviews.

6. In fact, Baker's legendary banana skirt did not appear until her first Folies-Bergère show, *La Folie du jour*, in 1926: in *La Revue nègre*, she was feather clad.

over a year in Casablanca, she toured widely in Africa to entertain allied troops. When, in 1963, Baker spoke prior to Martin Luther King Jr. at the March on Washington, she did so in the uniform of the Free French Army. Now, ironically, a review in the left-wing *Libération* denounced her as a "vestige of the past and notorious Gaullist": Baker's continued support for de Gaulle in 1968 suggested that her politics had not aged as well as she had herself.[7] President Valéry Giscard d'Estaing, however, sent a telegram of support, "paying homage to [her] vast talent and expressing France's gratitude."[8] Baker also received a long-service medal from the Paris council to add to her *Rosette de la résistance*, *Croix de guerre*, and *Légion d'honneur*; within a few days they would be laid out on her coffin.

Joséphine was but one episode in the mythologization of Baker's life, not by any means the first or last. In addition to retrospective shows, constant media attention, and even her own waxworks museum, Baker had published four (elaborately ghostwritten) autobiographies by the time of her death and another appeared a year later; an additional book recounted her wartime experiences.[9] Biographies—which now number around a dozen—soon followed, as did television documentaries.[10] A 1991

7. André Viso, "Pipi de chat et vieille rosette," *Libération*, 5 April 1975.

8. Cited in Anon., "Cette nuit à Bobino: Un Télégramme de V. G. E. et Grace de Monaco pour le gala de Joséphine Baker," *L'Aurore*, 9 April 1975.

9. Retrospectives of Baker's life go back at least to her 1956 "farewell" show at the Olympia, Paris (the first of many retirements and comebacks); the Bobino show in 1975 was itself based on one given at a Red Cross gala in Monte Carlo the previous year. The "Jorama" waxworks museum was one of the original exhibits at Baker's château, Les Milandes; it was re-created for the house's reopening several years ago as a tourist attraction—see http://www.milandes.com (accessed 7 August 2012). The texts in question are: Joséphine Baker and Marcel Sauvage, *Les Mémoires de Joséphine Baker* (Paris: Kra, 1927); Baker and Sauvage, *Voyages et aventures de Joséphine Baker* (Paris: Marcel Sheur, 1931); Baker and André Rivollet, *Joséphine Baker: Une Vie de toutes les couleurs* (Grenoble, Fr.: B. Arthaud, 1935); Jacques Abtey, *La Guerre secrète de Joséphine Baker* (Paris: Siboney, 1948); Baker and Sauvage, *Les Mémoires de Joséphine Baker* (Paris: Corrêa, 1949); Baker and Jo Bouillon, *Joséphine* (Paris: Robert Laffont, 1976) [translated by Mariana Fitzpatrick as *Josephine* (New York: Harper and Row, 1977)]. These "official" accounts were themselves in part responsible for the confusion over Baker's parentage and background: they offer several imaginative versions.

10. Among the biographies are Lynn Haney, *Naked at the Feast: The Biography of Josephine Baker* (New York: Dodd, Mead, 1981); Phyllis Rose, *Jazz Cleopatra: Josephine Baker in Her Time* (New York: Vintage Books, 1991); Jean-Claude Baker and Chris Chase, *Josephine: The Hungry Heart* (New York: Random House, 1993); Ean Wood, *The Josephine Baker Story* (London: Sanctuary Publishing, 2000); and Em-

film also told *The Josephine Baker Story*. More recently, scholars across a number of disciplines have become interested in Baker: as a performer, as a campaigner, and as a remarkable symbol of social and cultural change.[11] If the majority of this attention still attaches to her early appearances as an alluring yet dangerous other, Baker's subsequent transformation into a national icon in France is increasingly recognized as at least as rich a site of investigation.[12]

My focus here is a moment that was, I think, seminal to Baker's assimilation but has so far received scant attention: her 1934 revival of an Offenbach operetta, *La Créole*, unperformed for sixty years then, and little heard since. *La Créole*'s racial and national subtexts are several and speak to the complex process by which Baker came to be accepted in France. Examining it in detail reveals much, I suggest, about both Baker and the society in which she lived. For this, as one flamboyant critic put it at the time, was "the strange and wonderful rendezvous of the old man from Cologne and the granddaughter of Uncle Tom."[13]

A Tale of Black and White: Revising *La Créole*

Offenbach's 1875 opéra-comique *La Créole* is not a weighty affair. On a libretto by Henri Meilhac and Albert Millaud, it tells of two couples (René and Dora, Frontignac and Antoinette) forced into amorous deceit. A sailor, René, meets Dora, "la créole," when he is stationed in the colonies. Returning to France, he finds that his uncle, a naval commander, has arranged for him to marry Antoinette. In the Commandant's absence, however, she instead forms a union with her lover Frontignac. Meanwhile, Dora's father dies and the Commandant, an old friend, brings her to France. Unaware of her relationship with René (and Antoinette's secret marriage), he decides she should wed Frontignac. Both couples now mismatched,

---

manuel Bonini, *La Véritable Joséphine Baker* (Paris: Pygmalion, 2000). I have derived the basic biographical information outlined in the previous paragraphs from these sources.

11. In particular, see Bennetta Jules-Rosette, *Josephine Baker in Art and Life: The Icon and the Image* (Urbana: University of Illinois Press, 2007); and Anne Anlin Cheng, *Second Skin: Josephine Baker and the Modern Surface* (New York: Oxford University Press, 2011).

12. See, for example, Jayna Brown, "Translocations: Florence Mills, Josephine Baker, and Valaida Snow," in *Babylon Girls: Black Women Performers and the Shaping of the Modern* (Durham: Duke University Press, 2008), 238–79.

13. Carlo Rim, review of *La Créole, Vu*, 26 December 1934. *La Créole* opened at the Théâtre Marigny, Paris, circa 15 December 1934; it played for at least two months.

a great tangle ensues. It is not resolved until the final act, on board ship, when love wins out and the Commandant is forced to rescind.[14]

Revived as a vehicle for Baker in 1934, *La Créole* underwent significant revision at the hands of Albert Willemetz and Georges Delance, librettists of contemporary operettas both. As well as importing some songs and swapping around others, they made the piece substantially longer: the three-act format of the original now embraced five tableaux; in particular a new first section was added from scratch to act 1, focusing attention immediately on Baker's interpretation of Dora.[15] Audiences were also more apt to take her romance with René (played by René Charles) seriously: his part, formerly a trouser role, had been rewritten to remove the (then conventional) bending of gender on stage. Among several new characters, a second interracial couple was added: quartermaster Cartahut (M. Dréan) and Dora's black nanny, Crème fouettée (Carmen Lahenz).[16] These were only the most explicit ways in which the racial implications of the story (barely apparent in the original) were brought to the fore. One new song above all serves to make the point.

Offenbach's comic number, "Les Fariniers, les charbonniers" (ex. 3.1) tells the tale of a woman with two men: her dusty husband is a coalman (charbonnier) and her flour-covered lover is a miller (farinier). They are alike in all but one respect: "C'est que l'charbonnier est tout noir / Et que l'farinier est tout blanc." She spends life brushing herself down to avoid discovery (fig. 3.1 gives the idea). In its original context (another little-known Offenbach operetta, *La Boulangère a des écus*), the song's meaning is clear: it refers to a series of love triangles. However, "Les Fariniers" stands at some distance from the situation it reflects: it displaces the infidelity onto characters not part of the operetta; even those who sing it are

14. Vocal scores of both versions of *La Créole* were published by Choudens. A printed libretto of the original (1875) version is at LIV.19 360a(5), Bibliothèque-Musée de l'Opéra, Département de la Musique, Bibliothèque Nationale, Paris (hereafter cited as Opéra). The (manuscript) *livret de mise en scène* is at C52 (II), Archives de l'Association de la Régie Théâtrale, Bibliothèque Historique de la Ville de Paris, Paris (hereafter cited as BHVP). For the 1934 version, a typescript libretto with detailed staging directions (and many handwritten annotations) is at C52 (I), BHVP; this includes some set plans and photographs. Except where my source could be unclear, I draw on these without further reference.

15. In addition, an extension to the finale of act 2 formed a second tableau to that act, which includes no spoken dialogue.

16. There was a minor character called Cartahut in the original operetta but his role was not the same. I have yet to find a satisfactory explanation for the name "Crème fouettée" ("whipped cream"), but it is obviously a racialized allusion of one form or another.

FIGURE 3.1. Nineteenth-century English sheet music edition of Offenbach's "Les Fariniers, les charbonniers," from *La Boulangère a des écus* (courtesy of the Bodleian Library,
Oxford).

EXAMPLE 3.1. Offenbach, "Les Fariniers, les charbonniers," *La Créole* (1934 version), act 2, opening stage song (originally from *La Boulangère a des écus*, 1875).

EXAMPLE 3.1. *continued*

EXAMPLE 3.1. *continued*

Millers, coalmen, / Have the same bag, the same big hat / Coalmen, millers, / Look as alike as two drops of water / However for those who can see well, / There's a very important detail: // It's that the coalman is all black (All black) / And that the miller is all white (All white) / All white, All white, All white, All white / Millers are good sports // I know a little woman who was, / Who was the wife of a coalman / And this little woman had, / A lover who was a miller / Her husband came to kiss her, / Then it was the turn of her lover / She spent her life brushing herself, / So as not to have any trouble in disguise.[17] Imported into the revised *Créole*, this setting apart from the main narrative is emphasized: curtain-raiser to act 2, it is performed alone on stage by Frontignac and Antoinette (doubling at the keyboard), between (and for) themselves.

If the coalman and the miller are obviously out of place in this nautical drama, the choice of stage song is scarcely a coincidence. Aside from a pun on the star's name—she was a *boulangère* with some *écus* of her own—it is again reflexive of the story.[18] One level on which "Les Fariniers" signifies in *La Créole* is its original function of marking deceit (or at least confusion) among lovers. Another is obviously now race. In an operetta that recounts journeys across the sea, lost foreign lovers, titillating *couleur locale*, this prominent song contrasts the "tout noir" with the "tout blanc." If the 1875 version had barely considered race, then, the 1934 one would often approach it indirectly.[19] *La Créole* also calls to mind Baker's first, silent film, *La Sirène des tropiques* (1927), in which she plays a native Antillaise who falls in love with a visiting colonist and follows him to France. Seeking to evade capture on board ship, she topples first down a coal chute and then into a flour vat—surely another point of reference for "Les Fariniers, les charbonniers" several years later.[20]

I come to some of Baker's films below, but I want to remain in the theatre long enough to locate the revision of Offenbach's work in its musicodramatic context. For *La Créole* shares some basic characteristics with a group of stage works concerned, as James Parakilas defines them, with

17. *La Boulangère a des écus* dates, like *La Créole*, from 1875. A (printed) libretto (B7 [III]) and a (manuscript) *livret de mise en scène* (B7 [II]) are in BHVP. The miller and coalman are actually policemen searching for a crook; the *boulangère* took the fugitive in as a favor to his lover but now wants him for herself. Adding to the deceit, one policeman is having an affair with the other's wife, and she as well with their boss, and the *boulangère's* faithful servant (who exchanged clothes with the crook) is secretly in love with her.

18. I owe the point about the work's title to Carlo Caballero. Carolyn Abbate's discussion of the "reflexive narrative," of course, informs my discussion; see Abbate, *Unsung Voices: Opera and Musical Narrative in the Nineteenth Century* (Princeton, NJ: Princeton University Press, 1991), particularly chaps. 1 and 3.

19. In contrast to "Les Fariniers," the number that occupied its place at the opening of act 2 in 1875, although already a form of stage song, functioned straightforwardly: René (not Frontignac) and Antoinette's "Je croyais que tu m'aimais" was directly concerned with their romance that never was.

20. Mario Nalpas and Henri Étiévant, dir., *Siren of the Tropics* [original title, *La Sirène des tropiques*, 1927] (New York: Kino Video, 2005), DVD.

"Europeans who go to an exotic world."[21] The most familiar examples are *Carmen* (though the setting is among the Gypsies of Seville) and *Madama Butterfly* (though Pinkerton is only European by descent). Indeed, Parakilas sees *Carmen*—premiering in the same year as *La Créole* (1875) and sharing a librettist, Henri Meilhac—as the first fully fledged example of a new variation: the "soldier and the exotic." This plot type distinguishes itself from the earlier "age of discovery" story in at least three ways: its setting is more contemporary (the nineteenth century rather than the fifteenth or sixteenth); its music is more distinctly exotic (particularly in portrayal of the foreign character herself); and its ending is tragic (usually the death of the heroine).[22] These changes of mode, he argues, come as a recognition of cultural differences separating the parties and as a response to essentializing racial theories; they problematize the earlier operas' assumption that true love will triumph in the end—that is, that the exotic woman will adapt to the colonizing man's superior culture.[23]

In its first version *La Créole* is closer to the age of discovery model than to the soldier and the exotic, but it is not a perfect fit.[24] As Parakilas notes, such operas may already feature incipient soldier/exotic stories, as is the case here. Indeed, outside of the telling of a love story in a colonial setting, *La Créole* has none of the military action one would expect: set in 1685 (fifty years after France took Guadeloupe, where it is set) it already functions as the plot type's parody or sequel. Moreover, Dora's arrival in

21. James Parakilas, "The Soldier and the Exotic: Operatic Variations on a Theme of Racial Encounter (part 1)," *Opera Quarterly* 10/2 (1993): 33–56 (quote on p. 33). Part 2 appears in *Opera Quarterly* 10/3 (1994): 43–69.

22. Of the earlier type, Parakilas cites, for example, Spontini's *Fernand Cortez, ou la conquête du Mexique* (1819) and Félicien David's *La Perle du Brésil* (1851) ("The Soldier and the Exotic [part 1]," 36).

23. Parakilas further distinguishes between earlier works of this type, such as *Carmen*, and later ones, such as *Madama Butterfly*: the first, though they concern the relationship between two individuals, do so from the perspective of the European male, who dreams of escaping into the exotic; the second, if they retain Eurocentric principles, nevertheless focus on the fantasized escape of the "exotic" into the "mainstream" and the West's complicity in the establishment (and inevitable failure) of that dream ("The Soldier and the Exotic [part 1]").

24. As with many such taxonomies, Parakilas's categories are easy to fault. In particular, it is notable that no single opera reveals all the characteristics of its supposed type. However, I have found this schema a useful way to think about the process of revision in *La Créole*. At the least, it's reasonable to consider *Carmen* and *Madama Butterfly*, both repertory operas in Paris by this time, as part of the dramatic context for the revised operetta.

France reverses the standard story (if not its colonial premise): it is the return of the exotic to Europe rather than her discovery on foreign soil. Yet the original *Créole* may still usefully be termed an age of discovery piece: it confidently assumes that Dora will assimilate and, excepting a few "creolesque" syllables, has her speak the same language—verbal, musical, corporeal—as the French, a language assumed to be universal.[25]

The new version of *La Créole* is more of a hybrid. Its first tableau focuses attention on Dora's (the exotic's) experience like later operas in the soldier/exotic mode. A change in the era of the drama, from Louis XIV to Louis-Philippe (to just two decades after *Carmen*), almost suggests a deliberate decampment.[26] Yet *La Créole*'s denouement lacks the tragedy that, in another work, would arise from irresolvable cultural differences: for Dora and René at least, the story has a happy ending. This apparent contradiction—a focus on the female's experience but a resolution of the ensuing conflict—is key to the operetta's novelty, and to Baker's special position. To discover more, I need to consider each act in turn, alongside related texts and contemporary discourse. Reconstructing *La Créole*, in both its production and its reception, reveals how Baker at once gratified and challenged what Elizabeth Ezra has called the "colonial unconscious" of interwar France;[27] doing so on the broader scale of an operetta allows greater nuance than often is possible in the quick fire of a revue.

A New Opening for Dora (Baker): Act 1, Tableau 1

As it stood, *La Créole* would never have worked for a star of the French music hall such as Josephine Baker: her character, Dora, did not even appear in the first act. Adaptations would give Baker more to sing, to dance, and even to act; she had to appear from the beginning. Thus the whole first tableau (seven numbers) was assembled as a prologue. Where the 1875 operetta had begun in La Rochelle with preparations for Antoinette's undesired marriage to René, the revised version begins at an earlier stage: in Jamaica (where now, nonsensically, these French colonials are located)

25. Parakilas writes: "In opera after opera on the Age of Discovery theme, there is no difference of inalienable nature between the explorer and the exotic, no difference that they cannot overcome. Furthermore, when the lovers do in the end overcome what separates them, they do so on the explorer's—the European's— terms" ("The Soldier and the Exotic [part 1]," 37).

26. According to the 1934 *Créole* libretto, the action takes place in 1845; *Carmen* is set circa 1820.

27. Elizabeth Ezra, *The Colonial Unconscious: Race and Culture in Interwar France* (Ithaca, NY: Cornell University Press, 2000).

FIGURE 3.2. Josephine Baker in "native" finery, *La Créole*, Théâtre Marigny, Paris, 1934 (© Boris Lipnitzki / Roger-Viollet).

the navy are bidding the natives farewell.[28] After an opening number (borrowed from the third act) in which a choir of sailors imagine "Les Dames de Bordeaux," René and Cartahut are in conversation; they break up and hide when they hear Dora coming, singing her "Chanson créole" (fig. 3.2).

28. Why the overseas location was changed from French Guadeloupe to British Jamaica, I do not know. Perhaps the authors, in Paris in the mid-1930s, preferred to detach the piece from (always contentious) French colonialism, or possibly Baker's French was too obviously that of an Anglophone. The geographical shift is thematized in the piece to some small degree, but the fact remains that the French navy has been stationed on her island and that Dora is brought to France to marry.

Here, for the moment, is the original text (as it still appears in act 2), Dora proclaiming her love for René first in French and then in "Creole":

Je l'aim', l'aim', l'aim', l'aim',
Je l'aim' comme une folle
Je l'aim', l'aim', l'aim', l'aim',
Comme on n'aima jamais
Je viens d'vous l'dire en Français,
Faut-il vous le dire en Créole,

Ah! Ma t'aimé ma zamais te quitter
Toi cé çandell' et ma cé zozo,
Et ma cé zozo, zozo
Moi, brûler mon aile à li zoli z'amour
Ah! qué mi aime à vous coco
Cari, carilalo

I love him, love him, love him, love him, / I love him like a fool / I love him, love him, love him, love him, / like no one has ever loved / I just told you in French, / Must I tell you in Creole? // Ah! / Me love you me never leave you / You are candle [chandelle] and me bird [oiseau], / And me bird, bird / Me, burn my wing on pretty love, / Ah! how much me love you coco / Cari, carilalo

To include this song at the beginning is to make a significant change. In the later act, Dora is owning up that she cannot marry Frontignac because she is still in love with René. Relocating it to the prologue has three important effects. First, it focuses attention immediately on Baker as the Creole: while in 1875 Dora had to wait until the second act for her entrance (and was then restricted to a few numbers), now it is her story from the start. Second, by reversing the stanzas so that Dora sings first in "Creole" as she comes on stage (switching to French only when she meets René), an early emphasis is placed on her difference.[29] Third, it gives great priority to Dora and René's relationship: "Je l'aim'" becomes "Je t'aim'" as a love song is made from one intended to clear up a misunderstanding.[30] Where formerly Antoinette and Frontignac had been first to proclaim

29. She also repeats the "créole" chorus, where previously it had been heard only once.

30. The change from "him" to "you" had also taken place at the repeat in 1875, but this, of course, was not until the second act.

their love, here René and Dora take center stage: theirs is sanctioned as a loving alliance between a native and a metropolitan.[31]

The nature of René and Dora's partnership is explored further in a third number, derived from the same operetta as "Les Fariniers." Unlike it, however, the verse of this song did not survive its transfer from *La Boulangère*, where it too had concerned a relationship:[32]

> Un homm'd'un vrai mérite aimait,
> Un' dame indign'de son hommage
> Quand il apprit qu'ell'le trompait,
> Il l'en aima bien davantage

A man of real merit loved, / A woman unworthy of his tribute / When he learned that she tricked him, / He loved her even more

Transformed into "Le Ramier et la tourterelle" (The Ringdove and the Turtledove), Dora sings it to René in contribution to a discussion of their future: while René attempts to broach his departure, Dora disarms him with a story her nanny taught her:

> Un ramier tomba, en volant,
> Amoureux d'une tourterelle
> Elle était noire, il était blanc,
> Ils n's'en aimer'nt que de plus belle!

A ringdove fell, in flying, / In love with a turtledove / She was black, he was white, / And they were even more in love![33]

Although Dora's tale is displaced even further from the drama than was "Les Fariniers," her relationship with René is again the real concern. In effect, the moral distinction of the original version is replaced by one of

---

31. This despite the new colonial policies discouraging interracial relationships discussed in chap. 1.

32. In *La Boulangère*, the song concerns the baker's servant: for love of his mistress, he has refused to identify the crook to the police, even though it was her plan to have the two men swap places that had led to the servant's arrest.

33. The chorus, on the blindness of love, remains more or less the same in both versions: "Qu'y voulez vous faire, / C'est comm' ça, [x3] / Quand on aime, on aime quand même, / Il faut bien en passer par là [*La Créole*: L'amour ne se raisonne pas] / Qu'y voulez vous faire, / C'est comm' ça, [x3] / Il faut bien, il faut bien en passer par là!"

race. Like the relocated "Chanson créole," this song at once focuses on Dora and endorses publicly her partnership with René; it reveals the refreshing naïvety of her attitude to a relationship that might be considered taboo.

Concluding the new first tableau is the song that will come to represent Dora in the new version of the opera, "À la Jamaïque."[34] She and René sing of their time together, salaciously swimming under the moonlight "Sans pudeur, sans pudeur aucune!" (Without any modesty). René tells Dora that his heart will remain forever in Jamaica; she bids him remember her love and not succumb to others' charms. The song is immediately recalled, first by her alone, reminding René of his promise, and then by the orchestra in the interlude that bridges the tableaux; it will recur several times more, providing a musical cue for Dora that was lacking in the original *Créole*.[35]

In the revised *Créole*, of course, René and Dora are no longer the only mixed couple. At the time of parting, the contrast between their relationship and Cartahut's with Crème fouettée could not be more marked: where René kisses Dora passionately, Cartahut will not even allow Crème to cry into his handkerchief as he laughs off her suggestion she accompany him. The two men have already discussed Cartahut's strategy as a form of warfare. In "Fidèle à la consigne," he disingenuously tells "pirate" Crème that he must turn his cannon against her—a double entendre—in loyalty to *la France*.[36] The first stanza below shows the tragicomic fashion in which Crème misunderstands Cartahut, reinterpreting his words as the sweet nothings of love:

CARTAHUT.
    Soyons fidèle à la consigne,
    Courage, honneur, Patrie, devoir
CRÈME FOUETTÉE.
    Je ne vais plus jamais te voir!

34. This was derived from another source: the "Chanson béarnaise" was the only song from a play, *Le Gascon*, for which Offenbach had, in 1873, written some of the incidental music (the rest was by Albert Vizentini). Here, the text is replaced outright and bears no notable relationship to the original. The manuscript score for *Le Gascon* is at ♭5405, Opéra; this song was published separately.

35. The superimposition of texts in the 1934 typescript libretto indicates that it was originally intended for Dora to recall not "À la Jamaïque" so quickly but the up-tempo "C'est comme ça" refrain from "Le Ramier et la tourterelle." The revision highlights the romantic melancholy of the situation rather than Dora and René's resignation to it; it also affirms the association of this music with Dora and the memory of her and René's happiness together in the colonies. This song was often praised in the press.

36. I have been unable to locate the origin of this song.

CARTAHUT.
    Que doit faire un vaisseau de ligne,
    sous le vent d'un pavillon noir?
CRÈME FOUETTÉE.
    C'est moi ton p'tit papillon noir
CARTAHUT.
    Il doit charger ses caronades,
    En démasquant toutes ses bouch's à feu!
CRÈME FOUETTÉE.
    Oui ma bouche est en feu
CARTAHUT.
    Et déclancher la canonnade,
    L'honneur l'exige et le devoir le veut!
    Il faut que je sois bien courageux
CRÈME FOUETTÉE.
    Donn'moi ton z-yeux ton joli z-yeux bleu
    Viens je te veux
CARTAHUT.
    L'honneur le veut, l'honneur le veut

Car.: Being loyal to orders, / Courage, honor, homeland, duty / C.F.: I am never going to see you again! / Car.: What must a ship-of-the-line [i.e., warship] do, / downwind of a black flag [Jolly Roger]? / C.F.: It's me your little black butterfly / Car.: It must charge its carronades [small cannons], / Unmasking all its cannon mouths! / C.F.: Yes my lips are on fire / Car.: And open cannon fire, / Honor demands it and duty requires it! / I need to be very courageous / C.F.: Give me your eyes your pretty blue eyes / Come I want you / Car.: Honor requires it, honor requires it

In response to Cartahut's faux patriotism, all Crème fouettée can do is to affirm her own commitment to the French navy and express her sadness at his loss.[37] In a different context, Cartahut would enthusiastically endorse Dora's liberal sentiments regarding love across borders, but he does not extend them to Crème fouettée; while later it is he who keeps up René's correspondence with Dora, in the same letters he feigns his own death in order to free himself of Crème. A distinction thus emerges between the two exotic women: while great efforts had been made to give Dora (Baker) a strong presence (and to affirm her relationship with René), at the same time a new native was introduced whose portrayal was derogatory and

37. "J'aim' la marine, / Mais c'est vraiment bien ennuyeux / Par discipline, / Que tu doives me dire adieu."

comic (and whom Cartahut would disown).[38] In several ways, then, this new first tableau sets up the central tenets of *La Créole*'s revision. Far from simply adding a prologue derived from the existing story, it adds new layers, complicates meaning, perhaps even renders the text unstable. As I continue through the operetta, I will tease out these alternatives, with the aid of contemporary reception.

Racial Distinctions: Act 1, Tableau 2

If the second tableau was more involved than the original first act (on which it was based) the result was much the same: the wedding preparations in the Commandant's La Rochelle mansion lead not, as he proposes, to Antoinette's marriage to his nephew René, but, after the Commandant's sudden departure, to her union with Frontignac. The musical content would also have been similar had not a series of last-minute cuts in 1934 again served to sharpen the focus on René and Dora's relationship, even as "la créole" herself does not appear; they eliminate, in particular, the distraction of numbers featuring René with Antoinette.[39]

René's role (and his attitude to Dora) is ambiguous. He enters boasting of his womanizing in the rondeau "Je pars de Paris"; it is this that has decided the Commandant (played by entertainer M. Urban) to take his nephew's welfare into his own hands. Reminded by a reminiscence of "À la Jamaïque" in the orchestra, however, René describes Dora as "the only woman who has made off with a piece of my heart." We do not doubt his sincerity; until, that is, he meets beautiful, blond Antoinette (Rose Carday) and decides that their wedding should go ahead after all. A tension is

38. It would be wrong to suggest, however, that Dora was seen to equal the French men. She is sometimes portrayed as having an endearing, but childlike, simplicity: Dora, too, is given to misunderstandings and, for example, plays with (and talks to) a "poupée négrillonne" (black doll).

39. In the published scores, the only significant change was the addition of a "Marche des garde-marines" providing a spectacular show of the chorus' military muscle; I have been unable to locate its origin. (A short quartet, "C'est lui qui vient! que l'on s'empresse," was removed to accommodate it.) However, three songs that continue to appear in the 1934 published score are indicated as cut in the typescript libretto. They are the Commandant's "On connait notre nom partout" ("Romance des Feuilles Mortes"), in which he sings of the importance of protecting the family name; the trio "Embrassez-vous!," in which the Commandant urges René and Antoinette to acquaint themselves hurriedly prior to their wedding; and "C'est une chose," in which René and Antoinette discuss their predicament and René makes advances, rejected by Antoinette.

apparent between this return to the original scenario and the prologue of the new version.[40] The audience would now be disappointed by René's betrayal of Dora; in 1875 (not having met the Creole, let alone seen her with René) they would have had no such empathy. In this way, too, *La Créole* had fallen into line with the new model of exotic drama: if it lacked the tragedy of a *Madama Butterfly*, it succeeded in generating sympathy for the heroine; it no longer allowed the philandering René (or his audience) to escape with conscience clear.

Reviews of the operetta provide an insight into French opinion on the racialized subtext of this love triangle. For several critics, Dora's apparent competition from Antoinette suggested something of a race war. A rare female writer, Madeleine Porter, noted the contrast achieved with the other women by the "supple voice [and] subtle charm" of the "ravishing" Rose Carday.[41] More bluntly, a male counterpart thought the singer "as blond as one could wish between these two negresses."[42] Another agreed that she had successfully defended the merits of white women—"which means a lot when the colored rival is of such a rare quality."[43] One last reviewer believed that Carday displayed, "with dignity beside the famous Creole, qualities of the white race."[44]

But black and white may be too polarized a distinction for *La Créole*. Cartahut and René's opening conversation (back in the first tableau) seems keen to add some nuance: Dora is termed "cette petite Créole"; Crème fouettée, "la dame noire," "la négrillonne" (piccaninny). In some lines tardily cut from the second tableau, the same point is made: René tries to explain that he met his partner of choice abroad. "Une négrillonne?" accuses the Commandant. René replies, "[Non,] une ravissante créole."[45] The

40. It may have been in an effort to reduce this strain on the plot (as well as to save time) that Antoinette and René's numbers together were ultimately cut.

41. Madeleine Porter, review of *La Créole*, *Comœdia*, 18 December 1934.

42. Pierre de Regnier, "'La Créole' à Marigny," *Gringoire*, 21 December 1934, in Ro 3969, "Offenbach: *La Créole*," Collection Rondel, Département des Arts du Spectacle, Bibliothèque Nationale, Paris (hereafter cited as Rondel).

43. Léo Ryk, "'La Créole' au Théâtre Marigny," *Avant-Scène*, 22 December 1934, in Ro 3969, "Offenbach: *La Créole*," Rondel.

44. Gustave Bret, "Théâtre Marigny: La Créole," *L'Intransigeant*, 18 December 1934 (incorrectly dated 17 December in A. I. D. 2025, "Offenbach: *La Créole*" [a typed volume of extracts from reviews compiled by the Association Internationale de la Danse], Opéra).

45. Annotations in the typescript libretto indicate that this line (which matched, more or less, one from 1875) was cut prior to performance in 1934. The distinction remains implicit in the text on a number of levels, however.

difference between the two was a hot topic in the press. Madeleine Porter noted Carmen Lahenz's "good humor [in portraying] the classic negress, with silk turban and gold rings."[46] Another writer concurred that hers was "an authentic negress."[47] More critics thought she was a "pretty black artist" whose "dark-skinned charms" would be hard to resist.[48]

Whether Baker was a suitable choice for "la créole" was rather less clear. For many reviewers she was indeed "in the skin of her role."[49] "A real Creole" like her, they observed, could play it "au naturel."[50] A number of times, Baker was compared favorably to the original "créole," the celebrated Anna Judic, who had had to blacken up. Despite her best efforts she "could not evoke exotic islands like Madame Josephine Baker," wrote one critic, judging the latter the real creator of the role.[51] Others simply asserted that "she is made for the role and the role is made for her"; it had been "predestined for her for all eternity."[52]

A number of writers, however, raised a slippery issue: was a "créole" genuinely dark-skinned (a "mulâtresse") or was she simply a white from the colonies? According to one, there was a common mistake "that consists of identifying 'Creole' with 'half-caste' [métisse] when the first of these two words means, on the contrary, a 'white' of pure blood, born in a . . . tropical country."[53] Another insisted: "A Creole is not a negress, nor even a woman of mixed blood."[54] One magazine went as far as to invent a rhyme:

46. Porter, review of *La Créole*.

47. Raoul Brunel, review of *La Créole*, *L'Œuvre*, 18 December 1934.

48. Gustave Fréjaville, "Théâtre Marigny: *La Créole*, opérette en trois actes d'Albert Millaud, musique de Jacques Offenbach," *Journal des débats*, 20 December 1934; Regnier, "'La Créole' à Marigny."

49. R. M., review of *La Créole*, *Les Annales coloniales*, 18 December 1934, in A. I. D. 2025, "Offenbach: *La Créole*," Opéra.

50. Henri de Curzon, "Revue musicale: Trois Opérettes, anciennes et nouvelles: 'Mandrin,' de M. Szulc; 'La Créole,' d'Offenbach; 'Le Petit Faust,' d'Hervé," *Journal des débats*, 27 December 1934; Brunel, review of *La Créole*.

51. Henri de Curzon, review of *La Créole*, *La Métropole* (Anvers), n.d., in A. I. D. 2025, "Offenbach: *La Créole*," Opéra. See also Rim, review of *La Créole*.

52. Gaston-Gérard, review of *La Créole*, *Comœdia*, 30 December 1934; Robert Dezarnaux, review of *La Créole*, *La Liberté*, 18 December 1934.

53. Jane Catulle Mendès, "Théâtre Marigny: 'La Créole,' opérette en trois actes et cinq tableaux, d'Albert Millaud. Version nouvelle de MM. Albert Willemetz et Georges Delance. Musique d'Offenbach," *L'Ancien Combattant*, 13 January 1935.

54. Regnier, "'La Créole' à Marigny."

À Paris comme à La Réole
L'ignorance règne en maîtresse;
Et le livret confond Créole
        Et Mulâtresse![55]

In Paris as in La Réole / Ignorance rules supreme, / And the libretto confuses Creole / And mulatto!

Given Baker's evident facility in the role, however, few took the objection seriously. Émile Vuillermoz knew that this usage was strictly incorrect but thought Baker's "delicious light bronze body tone . . . [should put] an end to the discussion."[56] Or, to quote another writer: "The negress, who should not be a negress, will, for our greater enjoyment, really be a negress."[57]

Yet the array of words to describe Baker—*créole, métisse, mulâtresse, négresse*—suggests that her body was not easily read. Noting that the organizers had "made the 'Creole' a mulatto," one critic conceded "that this mulatto who is Josephine Baker has a lot of milk in her coffee."[58] Another, observing powder on Baker's skin, ventured that she had "lightened her long supple body as much as Judic . . . had tanned hers."[59] Most intriguing was Edmond Le Page:

Il ne pouvait être fait meilleur choix pour le rôle de Dora, que celui de l'ex-créole authentique: Joséphine Baker. Je dis "EX" car la charmante artiste, reine du music-hall, est devenue aujourd'hui presque . . . "une blanche." J'ajouterai que je le regrette car Joséphine Baker créole, était Joséphine Baker l'inimitable, tandis que Joséphine Baker mi-blanche, mi-créole, n'est plus la Joséphine Baker intégrale.[60]

55. Ragotin, "À travers la vie parisienne: Couloirs et coulisses," *La Vie parisienne,* 9 February 1935, 172 (incorrectly dated 9 January 1935 in A. I. D. 2025, "Offenbach: *La Créole*," Opéra).

56. Émile Vuillermoz, "La Musique: 'Mandrin' et 'La Créole,' " *Candide,* 20 December 1934, in Ro 3969, "Offenbach: *La Créole*," Rondel.

57. André Frank, "Au Théâtre Marigny: Le Retour d'Offenbach . . . ," *L'Intransigeant,* 16 December 1934.

58. A. de Montgon, "Au Théâtre Marigny, 'La Créole,' " *Le Petit Bleu de Paris,* 20 December 1934, in Ro 3969, "Offenbach: *La Créole*," Rondel.

59. Anon., review of *La Créole, Aux Écoutes,* 22 December 1934, in A. I. D. 2025, "Offenbach: *La Créole*," Opéra.

60. Edmond Le Page, review of *La Créole, Journal d'Anvers,* 4 January 1935, in A. I. D. 2025, "Offenbach: *La Créole*," Opéra.

There could not have been a better choice for the role of Dora than that of the authentic ex-Creole: Josephine Baker. I say "EX" because the charming artist, queen of the music hall, has become today almost... "a white." I will add that I regret this because Creole Josephine Baker was the inimitable Josephine Baker, whereas half-white, half-Creole Josephine Baker is no longer the complete Josephine Baker.

Despite Le Page's concern, most critics celebrated Baker's "evolution" toward French operetta. Sometimes this manifested itself in the benign form of a respect for her growing versatility, particularly as singer and actor.[61] Often, however, there was an added implication: Baker's work to develop her act was conflated with a broader process of "civilization," or at least acculturation. Consider, for example, Gérard Bauer, whose enthusiasm for Baker verges on incredulity: "She is charming. Seeing her today so acclimatized, how can one not remember her arrival in Paris, when she was a grimacing little black, with a banana belt, exhibiting her wild frenzy in *La Revue nègre*?"[62] Although Bauer was critical of de Flers for attacking Baker in 1925, he was content with her recent transformation; this, he felt, was an appropriate response to the changing times and to earlier criticism: "That was ten years ago. We have got a bit whiter, Josephine Baker too, and Offenbach's *La Créole* responds to Robert de Flers."[63] Her performance was not perfect—Bauer thought, in particular, that her French still left something to be desired—but this only suited Baker to the role: "If she still re-

61. Respected music-hall critic Gustave Fréjaville observed: "La petite danseuse excentrique ... est devenue une étonnante artiste; elle chante, joue, danse, avec un naturel délicieux" (Fréjaville, "Théâtre Marigny: *La Créole*"). Another writer exclaimed: "Que de chemin parcouru depuis [ses débuts]! Que de progrès accomplis!" (Octave Plagal, review of *La Créole*, *La Griffe*, 30 December 1934, in A. I. D. 2025, "Offenbach: *La Créole*," Opéra). Discourse of this kind dates back at least as far as Baker's 1930–1931 show at the Casino de Paris, *Paris qui remue*, timed to coincide with the Exposition Coloniale. For examples of this, see Pepito Abatino, ed., *Joséphine Baker vue par la presse française* (Paris: Isis, 1931); and Ro 18937, "La Revue du Casino de Paris, 1930," Rondel. Such descriptions peaked with *La Créole*, however.

62. Gérard Bauer, "Les Pièces nouvelles: Théâtre Marigny—La Créole, opérette en trois actes et cinq tableaux, d'Albert Milhaud [sic]," *L'Écho de Paris*, 17 December 1934. See also Jacques Daltier, review of *La Créole*, *L'Indépendance belge*, 22 December 1934, in A. I. D. 2025, "Offenbach: *La Créole*," Opéra.

63. Bauer observed here that de Flers had ignored Baker's connection to a long French tradition of "un romantisme de couleur." A few years earlier Bauer had presented "D'un romantisme à l'autre: Le 'Romantisme de couleur' d''Atala' à 'Magie Noire,'" lecture, Université des Annales, 14 November 1930, published in *Conferencia* 24/20 (5 October 1930): 389–400, in which de Flers's attack on Baker was discussed.

tains some imperfections of her race, here they give her some advantages
. . . : she is very *couleur locale*," he said, adding "This little *café au lait* devil
delights me."[64] She had come to represent, as a different writer put it, a
"delightful compromise of a young savage brought up *à la parisienne*."[65]

For some, it even seemed that Baker's skin had faded in line with the
transition in her art (as Bauer's transition from "noire" to "café au lait" already suggests). One paper made just such a connection, recognizing this as
a "radical transformation but one that was not made instantaneously":

> A ses dernières apparitions, nous devinions bien qu'il se passait quelque
> chose. Joséphine, la négresse, n'était plus si noire, Joséphine pâlissait. . . .
> Et elle commençait à moduler de ravissantes chansons des îles tropiques.
> À présent, son teint est plus clair. . . . Et Joséphine chante à ravir. Elle
> chante avec un art profond.[66]

> In her last appearances, we suspected that something was happening.
> Josephine, the negress, was no longer so black. Josephine was growing
> paler. . . . And she was starting to change her delightful exotic songs. Now
> [in *La Créole*], her skin is [even] lighter. . . . And Josephine sings delight-
> fully. She sings with a profound art.

Of course, writers may not have intended their biological suppositions to
be taken altogether seriously. But race and culture were often perceived
as so tightly intertwined that one could become the sign of the other.
The flattery accepted for France (and colonial politics) in this "civilizing"
process was considerable. To believe one critic:

> Dans *La Créole*, Joséphine Baker dépasse tout ce qu'on pouvait espérer et
> attendre d'elle. Arriver à parler notre langue comme elle la parle, à jouer
> comme elle joue, à mimer comme elle mime, enfin à chanter comme elle
> chante, dénote un tel amour de notre pays et de l'art que tout succès qui

64. Bauer had made his point about Baker's efforts to accommodate traditional
French taste before. In a review of her 1930–1931 Casino de Paris show, he noted
that de Flers (and his fears for the future of French civilization) could now rest in
peace, for the line of influence was running the right way: "Ce n'est pas nous qui
avons fait le chemin, c'est Mlle. Baker qui s'est approchée de nous" (Gérard Bauer,
review of *Paris qui remue* [Casino de Paris], *Gironde-Bordeaux*, 19 October 1930, in
Abatino, *Joséphine Baker*, 28).

65. Jacques Soubies, "Le Théâtre," *L'Hygiène sociale* 7/135 (25 February 1935):
124–25 (review of *La Créole* on p. 125).

66. Anon., review of *La Créole*, *Le Cri de Paris*, 21 December 1934 [also reprinted as
"La Métamorphose de Joséphine Baker," *Le Progrès de Saône-et-Loire*, 25 December
1934].

ne serait pas un triomphe serait insuffisant. . . . Joséphine Baker incarne toutes les grâces de la divette exotique, tout en s'adaptant merveilleuse-ment au classicisme latin.[67]

In *La Créole*, Josephine Baker surpasses all that one could have hoped and expected of her. Coming to speak our language as she speaks it, to act as she acts, to mime as she mimes, finally to sing as she sings, denotes such a love of our country and of art that any success that were not a triumph would be insufficient. . . . Josephine Baker embodies all the grace of an exotic star, all while adapting marvelously to Latin classicism.

André Rivollet, collaborator on one of Baker's "auto"biographies, dis-cussed her transformation in a joint presentation for the Université des Annales, a public lecture series.[68] In order to trace her "progress," he first established Baker as emblematic of *jazz hot*. He traced the roots of jazz (in Africa and America), its popularity in Paris and the dances it had helped create, and finally its appropriation by French composers. But now, Rivol-let argued, the tide was turning; Paris was returning to a gentler syncopa-tion, an elegant dancing, something more distinctly French: "It is this that the sensitive Josephine Baker has so marvelously understood in perform-ing this operetta that Offenbach had written in 1875." Rivollet explained:

67. Jean-Marie de Fontaubert, "Joséphine Baker dans 'Zouzou' et 'La Créole,'" *L'Intermédiaire forain* (Avignon), 16 March 1935 (incorrectly dated 16 February 1935 in A. I. D. 2025, "Offenbach: *La Créole*," Opéra). Louis Jean Finot was in a similarly self-congratulatory mode when he observed the effect on Baker of the city of light: "Quels progrès magnifiques elle a réalisés depuis son arrivée à Paris. Ses piaille-ments d'oiseau des îles sont devenus des notes qu'elle file avec art; ses gestes en-fantins et primitifs sont devenus jeux de scène que peuvent lui envier les vedettes classées" ("La Rentrée de Joséphine Baker dans 'La Créole' à Marigny," *La Semaine à Paris*, 21 December 1934). Indeed, even those, such as Jacques Soubies, who at-tended the theatre anticipating a transgression of French taste in the event were quite charmed: "Non sans quelque inquiétude je m'étais rendu au théâtre Marigny pour les débuts de l'opérette de Mme Joséphine Baker. . . . Avec quelle heureuse sur-prise j'ai vu une actrice respectueuse du style, propre à l'ouvrage, jouant à l'unisson avec la fantaisie la plus charmante mais aussi la mieux surveillée. . . . Quels progrès Joséphine Baker a-t-elle fait depuis ses débuts cependant sensationnels dans une revue nègre. La voici acclimatée, ayant travaillé, plus gaie, plus entraînante que jamais, une vedette de Paris!" (Soubies, "Le Théâtre," 125).
    68. André Rivollet, "Du jazz hot à 'La Créole,'" lecture, Université des Annales, 21 March 1935, published in *Conferencia* 29/9 (1 July 1935): 101–11; I take Rivollet's title as my own. Baker and Rivollet's *Joséphine Baker: Une Vie de toutes les couleurs* was also published in 1935.

Après avoir été un sujet de surprise, de curiosité, Joséphine Baker a tempéré cet instinct bondissant qu'elle laissait aller aux rythmes des premiers *jazz hot* en improvisant des danses avec une frénésie . . . presque sauvage. Depuis, [elle] s'est disciplinée. Elle s'est laissé séduire . . . par le gai Paris.

After having been a cause for surprise, for curiosity, Josephine Baker has tempered this wild instinct that she released to the rhythms of the first *jazz hot* by improvising dances with a frenzy that was . . . almost savage. Since, [she] has learned self-discipline. She has let herself be seduced . . . by gay Paris.

Finally, he introduced Baker (who would sing a mixture of popular songs and Offenbach): "The star who symbolizes . . . the journey from hot jazz to *La Créole*."[69]

That Baker, of all people, would turn her back on jazz for French operetta was, for many, telling: it marked a reassertion of national cultural values after a period of foreign influence. Far from rejecting the star, however, France had helped the eager Baker to transform and to assimilate. If *La Créole* became another vehicle for the debate about racial hybridity, the fears of degeneration sounded quite seriously with respect to the African American troupes were not here any concern. Baker's skin color may have remained the titillating sign of miscegenation, but her performance left no doubt that she was on the path to naturalization. In other words, to invoke colonial terms, Baker evinced the continued effectiveness of France's *mission civilisatrice*.

Performance as Resistance? Act 2, Tableau 1

Deviations from nationalistic triumphalism in response to Baker's performance were few, but they did exist. As shown above, Edmond Le Page preferred "la Joséphine Baker intégrale" to "l'ex-créole authentique."[70] Most notable among other critics was Stefan Priacel in the communist journal *Monde*. For him, *La Créole* was something of a challenge: many had asked "how [it was] possible to discover in so trifling and innocuous an entertainment material for a [social] critique."[71] With the music and

69. Rivollet, "Du jazz hot à 'La Créole,'" 105–6. The published version of Rivollet's talk reproduced four songs: the "Berceuse créole" from the operetta (discussed below), Vincent Scotto's "J'ai deux amours" and "Haïti" (the latter from the movie *Zouzou*), and Cole Porter's "Miss Otis Regrets." This is presumably indicative of the repertoire Baker performed.

70. Page, review of *La Créole*.

71. Stefan Priacel, "Le Cinéma et le théâtre—La Créole (au théâtre Marigny)," *Monde: Hebdomadaire international*, 11 January 1935, 13. This journal is not to be

dancing, Priacel was forced to agree, it was hard to find fault. But he disapproved of the plot's pandering, in 1875, to the taste for exoticism and colonial adventure of a so-called "tout Paris" that represented only the rich bourgeoisie. Although Dora's portrayal was tender, she was "greatly inferior to the conquering white nobles," he complained: "She is not a thinking being, is she? this half-negress—but at the most a beautiful exotic animal." He continued to consider the context of the "love story" and to question the militaristic and colonial ideology it proposes.

In a curious turn, Priacel compared the performance to one of *Uncle Tom's Cabin* in Leningrad. There, he felt, the drama was not enjoyed for its exotic charm alone (and as an implicit affirmation, in this way, of the West's superiority) but carried revolutionary potential for "the struggle against slavery and . . . the abjection of colonialism." *La Créole*, on the other hand, was but a "punch à la sauce coloniale," as a different writer put it.[72] Interestingly, however, Priacel was not critical of Baker herself: she, he thought, was able to transcend or even to subvert the plot. Where his bourgeois counterparts thought "civilization" had quite absorbed her, he believed that she sometimes escaped it, momentarily recovering her "true" nature:

> Elle retrouve par endroits des accents dont la violence et la vérité dépassant le cadre "bonbon fondant" de l'opérette fait, pendant de trop rares secondes songer à l'impression de force et de magnifique révolte qu'elle dégageait, voici dix ans, dans *La Revue nègre* où elle n'était pas encore une vedette, mais déjà une très grande artiste.

> She regains in places tones whose violence and truthfulness go beyond the sugary context of the operetta, making one think, for too rare seconds, of the impression of force and magnificent rebellion that she emitted, ten years ago, in *La Revue nègre*, where she was not yet a star, but already a very great artist.

While admiring Baker's apparent resistance, Priacel was unaware how much the text had been revised. A new opening tableau had, of course, remade Dora for Baker. In act 2 she was given specific moments of revolt, as some scenes from the first tableau will serve to illustrate.[73]

---

confused with the postwar national daily, *Le Monde*. Subsequent quotations from Priacel all derive from this review.

72. Frank, "Au Théâtre Marigny."

73. The music of this act survived revision reasonably intact: the only major changes were the substitution of "Les Fariniers, les charbonniers" for Antoinette and René's song, "Je croyais que tu m'aimais," as the opening number, and the di-

Arriving back from a trip, the Commandant surprises Antoinette, René, and Frontignac, who must all pretend to have obeyed his wishes as a matchmaker. With the Commandant is Dora, announced in the new version by another return of "À la Jamaïque." Following introduction to Antoinette, "femme de René," Dora sings "Il vous souvient de moi, j'espère" in melancholy recognition of the fact that René is lost to her, just as in 1875.[74] The next scene, however, was the site of a dramatic alteration. The Commandant requests tea in the antique Chinese tea service to celebrate Dora's arrival. As he explains René's philandering and subsequent marriage, Dora infuriates the Commandant by casually dropping first her own cup and then his in reaction to what she is told.

The destruction continues in the next scene, in which Frontignac cryptically tries to explain to Dora that her dispute is not with Antoinette, contrasting the hot-blooded colonial to the cool, collected European. As if to prove the point, Dora soon sends an oriental vase crashing to the ground.[75] When Frontignac laughs at Dora's plea that she now cares only for him, he becomes the target of more than her affections: the flight of a lamp and then other missiles have him hiding behind the sofa. It was, according to Cartahut, "une colère noire" (black temper); or, better, from the program synopsis, "une colère . . . créole." Returning to her European lover only to find him married and she about to be passed on to another, Dora takes out her frustration on trinkets of imperialism. By refusing to accept the polite conventions of the bourgeois drawing room—failing to maintain "civilized" decorum—she is, the operetta implies, letting out her true self. "What a startling type of savage thrown into a European salon!" one enthusiastic reviewer exclaimed.[76]

It is hard to imagine a simple theatrical device causing such a stir, but the critics were in raptures. Acclaimed music-hall reporter Gustave Fréjaville experienced "pure joy" watching this "little savage battling with

---

vision of an extended version of the finale as a separate second tableau, with the addition of extra dances. The dialogue and action, however, were transformed: a new scene was added for Cartahut and Crème fouettée, and, in particular, Dora's role was carefully tailored.

74. The 1934 libretto described the scene: a Louis XV–style room full of exotic trinkets the Commandant had brought back from his travels. For practical reasons or otherwise, members of the company appear to have thought better of the original idea (new in 1934 but crossed out in the typescript libretto) of having Dora arrive with a marmoset on her shoulder and a parrot in a cage.

75. At the equivalent moment in 1875, Dora hammered down the keys of the harpsichord, the closest she got to the destructive outbursts found in 1934.

76. J. Delini, "'La Créole' au Théâtre Marigny et Joséphine Baker dans l'opérette," *Comœdia*, 16 December 1934, in Ro 3969, "Offenbach: *La Créole*," Rondel.

civilized life, whose conventions her simple and tender heart does not very well understand"; she looked to him like "a young wildcat in a rage."[77] Another writer wished the audience, too, had brought their crockery "for the joy of seeing her wrinkle her cruel little nose again, and stamp her fine high-spirited yearling's legs."[78]

A further scene, surrounding Dora and Frontignac's song "Si vous croyez que ça m'amuse," reveals a different side to this newfound aggression. Accepting that she has lost René's affections, Dora decides that her future husband, Frontignac, must woo her instead. In 1875, this was a rather pitiful affair, with Dora concluding that Frontignac's reticence arose from a simple fact: "I haven't got white skin, you find me ugly, you find me horrid."[79] Frontignac kisses Dora, feeling sorry for her. In 1934 it is Dora who kisses Frontignac—by force. During the song, she makes Frontignac sit down and rests on his knee; at the end she pulls him up by his hair.

In the revised *Créole*, then, Dora can confront—contest—her treatment by European society in a way unthinkable in the original. As one critic pointed out, "Her violent temperament could have exploded the character of the sentimental little Creole pictured sixty years ago by [Meilhac] and Millaud."[80] Another tension thus becomes apparent in the text: an imperial fantasy confronts a native who refuses to yield to it. The operetta proved that "Creoles are not Rarahu, still less Madame Chrysanthème," Dora's violent anger and sexual aggression giving the lie to Pierre Loti's notorious depiction of the deferential colonial woman.[81] The revised version seemed to give Dora an unexpected power to affect or even subvert the forward movement of the narrative.

There's a danger, of course, in locating resistance to colonial structures in Dora's outbursts: while it contests mistreatment, her tempestuousness risks invoking another stereotype—replacing the submissive "oriental" of the original *Créole* with a "primitive" African. A contrast is drawn be-

77. Fréjaville, "Théâtre Marigny: *La Créole*."

78. Jacques d'Antibes, review of *La Créole*, *Paris-Sport*, 20 December 1934, in A. I. D. 2025, "Offenbach: *La Créole*," Opéra.

79. This was the only original line indicating, incontrovertibly, that Dora was dark-skinned (and therefore that singer Anna Judic had to blacken up). A similar line—"Oh, je sais bien pourquoi vous ne pouvez pas m'aimer. . . . J'ai pas la peau blanche. Vous me trouvez laide"—appears in the 1934 libretto, but the reference to her color (in italics) is crossed out.

80. Anon., review of *La Créole*, *L'Action française*, 21 December 1934. I have corrected this author's misplaced ascription of the original libretto to Ludovic Halévy.

81. Gaston-Gérard, revue of *La Créole*.

tween the Europeans and Dora: with the exception of the Commandant, they understand the situation and proceed by reason to try to resolve it; she is kept ignorant, and, in protest, reverts to barbarity, lashing out violently or exhibiting a hypersexual nature.[82] In this sense, an apparent subversion of the colonial narrative may itself be complicit with a myth of fundamental racial difference.[83]

The interpretative difficulties of these reversions are heightened as soon as it's acknowledged that there was more than a fictional character at stake. As already observed in Priacel's text, these moments of revolt were often considered a return of the real, "authentic" Baker (defined, usually, by *La Revue nègre*) as well as of Dora, whom she played. Describing this moment in the scenario, for example, one critic forgot himself:

> Ne croyez pas . . . que l'ancienne *Joséphine Baker* soit tout à faite morte. De temps à autre, elle ressuscite, elle se déchaîne. Et alors elle saute comme une panthère, elle trépigne, elle fait voler en éclats les tasses et les potiches.[84]

> Don't believe . . . that the old *Josephine Baker* is altogether dead. From time to time, she revives, she breaks loose. And then she leaps like a panther, she stamps her feet, she breaks cups and oriental vases into pieces.

Exchanging Baker for her character in a plot summary was telling: as was the case with Dora, critics suggested, Baker's newly "civilized" exterior hid a deeper, darker truth. If the story as a whole thematized a reconciliation with France that Baker's performance in operetta itself seemed to stage, these moments marked a struggle to find the terms on which such a settlement could be made; it was then that the true Baker shone through. This assumption made explicit an odd complicity that had developed between the story told by *La Créole* and that forming of Baker's life: the plot of the

---

82. These tropes have been particularly well explored by Sander Gilman: see Gilman, *Difference and Pathology: Stereotypes of Sexuality, Race, and Madness* (Ithaca, NY: Cornell University Press, 1985); and Gilman, "Black Bodies, White Bodies: Toward an Iconography of Female Sexuality in Late Nineteenth-Century Art, Medicine and Literature," *Critical Inquiry* 12 (1985): 204–42 [also reprinted in Henry Louis Gates Jr., ed., *"Race," Writing, and Difference* (Chicago: University of Chicago Press, 1986), 223–61].

83. This is the paradox that Parakilas observes of the soldier and the exotic plot type, as seen already in the opening tableau of *La Créole*: on the one hand, it makes the exotic a real subject; on the other, it constructs her subjectivity by means of her difference ("The Soldier and the Exotic [part 1]").

84. Anon., review of *La Créole*, *Le Cri de Paris* (my italics).

operetta (Dora's arrival from the colonies and her progressive assimilation to France) was Baker's own supposed tale, just as it would be told in the Bobino show days prior to her death. Before continuing with *La Créole*'s story, then, I want to pursue that connection a little further, for this was far from the first time that Baker's role had seemed to intersect with her life.

Life and Art: Tragic Mulattoes and Marian Motifs

In a recent book, *Josephine Baker in Art and Life*, sociologist Bennetta Jules-Rosette offers a rich examination of the correlations between Baker's stage and offstage roles, suggesting that the two are finally inseparable. She argues, "The search for the true Baker, while compelling, is less fecund than an exploration of the constructed images and nested narratives that constitute her persona and the social strategies that she used to bring these images to life."[85] The basic tale is very often a Cinderella-like rags-to-riches story (sometimes crossed with Pygmalion) whose happy ending is replaced by a sacrifice for the greater good ("the Marian motif"). This narrative bridges Baker's several autobiographies, her fictional writings, and her performances. Given that her white male collaborators at the very least mediated Baker's ideas, Jules-Rosette is rightly cautious about overstating the performer's agency. Whether, as she ultimately insists, "[Baker's] voice was [nevertheless] evident in every piece," I am unsure.[86] But Jules-Rosette's observation (made with specific regard to successive variants on the famous banana skirt) that Baker's career witnesses "the evolution of artistic agency within a framework of social control" encapsulates both Baker's considerable achievements and the no less considerable constraints upon them.[87]

The Cinderella/Pygmalion thread of Baker's narrative is, of course, a generic convention of show-business stories, as they find expression on and off the stage and screen. But her sacrifice of personal happiness for the greater good (and a saintly glow) is far more unusual. Jules-Rosette finds it first in the 1927 film *La Sirène des tropiques*, mentioned above, in which Baker's character's mishap-laden journey from the Antilles to France ends with her giving up her lover to his fiancée: she asks only to keep his prayer book, wherein she learns that "sacrifice is the purest form of joy on earth."[88] A similar trope appears in Baker's novella, *Mon Sang dans tes veines* (*My Blood in Your Veins*; 1931), in which a young mulatto, Joan, saves the life of the man she idolizes with a blood transfusion; when her

85. Jules-Rosette, *Josephine Baker in Art and Life*, 4–5.

86. Ibid., 157.

87. Ibid., 50.

88. Nalpas and Étiévant, *Siren of the Tropics*, DVD.

hero is horrified to discover he has become "un nègre blanc," Joan simply runs away.[89] Eventually, after all her success, sacrifice becomes a trope of Baker's personal life, as she works for France during the war, fights against racism in various capacities, and adopts children from around the world to form her multiracial Rainbow Tribe.

While Jules-Rosette is deeply insightful on the conflations of life and art in the Josephine Baker persona, some distinction between the performer's own decisions and narrative types must surely be retained. Baker made a choice at various points in her life to stand up for her principles, and to sacrifice her personal well-being for the greater good. These situations were real, as was Baker's bravery, even if in subsequent retelling fact is often lost to fiction. Conflicts in her dramas unfold differently, and not only because they're normally couched in terms of relationships. There she typically acquiesces to society's expectations rather than contesting them. Baker's characters may be martyrs, but that status is somewhat unearned, since they do not fight long for their causes. At worst, this repeated enactment of powerlessness may, rather than protesting inequality, (re)constitute and normalize it in the world: sacrifice becomes synonymous with capitulation.

Tyler Stovall is among other scholars who have asked "why the women Baker portrayed never got the guy." As he says, "Time and time again, when we see Baker on stage and screen, she is eating her heart out for a white Frenchman who generally remains completely ignorant of her desire, and who ends up instead with a white Frenchwoman, leaving Baker sad and alone."[90] In this respect, *La Créole* is somewhat of an exception, as here she does fight and does get her way in the end. Before returning to her performance of Offenbach's operetta, then, I want to consider two Baker movies that were contemporary with it, *Zouzou* and *Princesse Tam-Tam*.[91] The three

89. Felix de la Camara and Pepito Abatino, *Mon Sang dans tes veines: Roman d'après une idée de Joséphine Baker* (Paris: Isis, 1931), 178, cited in Jules-Rosette, *Josephine Baker in Art and Life*, 166.

90. Tyler Stovall, "The New Woman and the New Empire: Josephine Baker and Changing Views of Femininity in Interwar France," in "Josephine Baker: A Century in the Spotlight," ed. Kaiama L. Glover, double issue, *S&F Online* 6/1–6/2 (2007–2008): n.p., accessed 10 November 2012, http://sfonline.barnard.edu/baker/stovall_01.htm.

91. See Elizabeth Coffman, "Uncanny Performances in Colonial Narratives: Josephine Baker in *Princess Tam Tam*," *Paradoxa* 3 (1997): 379–94; Elizabeth Ezra, "A Colonial Princess: Josephine Baker's French Films," in *The Colonial Unconscious*, 97–128; and Kathryn Kalinak, "Disciplining Josephine Baker: Gender, Race, and the Limits of Disciplinarity," in *Music and Cinema*, ed. James Buhler, Caryl Flinn, and David Neumeyer (Hanover, NH: Wesleyan University Press, 2000), 316–35.

FIGURE 3.3. Josephine Baker and Jean Gabin as "twins" in *Zouzou*, dir. Marc Allegret (1934; courtesy of Michael Everson).

stories together illustrate well the conflation of life and drama in Baker's career. But their great similarities are not sustained to their conclusions: with its happy ending, *La Créole* appears finally to be exempted from the dangerous logic of racial essentialism that the films follow through.

In *Zouzou* (1934), Baker plays the sister to a young Jean Gabin (one of the most celebrated French actors of his generation).[92] As we see in a prologue, the siblings were adopted as children and brought up by a circus performer, earning their keep as "the two most extraordinary twins of all Creation;"[93] here she is even described as "la créole." As they grow older, Jean (Gabin), like René, leaves Zouzou (Baker) for the navy; she is secretly in love with a brother she realizes is not her own (fig. 3.3). But in Manila he is seen surrounded by women: he is a womanizer in the mode of René.

When, subsequently, Jean leaves the navy and takes a job as an electrician in a music hall, the scene is set for the rags-to-riches story that was Baker's life.[94] Zouzou is a laundress; in one scene her coworkers wonder if

92. Marc Allegret, dir., *Zou Zou* (New York: Kino Video, 2005), DVD.

93. Lucien Ray, "Zouzou avec Joséphine Baker et Jean Gabin," *Film complet* 14/1618 (28 March 1935): 2–14 (quote on p. 2).

94. Anticipating the film, Baker herself is reported to have said: "Mon manager, M. G. Abatino qui me connaît comme lui-même, en a écrit le scénario. Je

it is because she wishes to whiten her skin that she works in a "blanchisse-rie." Returning clothes to the music hall, she dances on stage, secretly ob-served by the director. Recognizing a star, he chases Zouzou, who bites her captor to escape; he describes her as a "cannibal." Eventually she does take to the stage in order to raise money for Jean, who has been wrongly im-prisoned for murder. But released from jail he walks out not with Zouzou, who looks on, but with her white friend, Claire. As Zouzou returns pas-sively to her performance—in one scene she sings the song "Haïti" as an exotic bird swinging on a perch in a huge cage—and Jean takes his white lover, the distinction between the races is restored. Mirroring almost ex-actly comments about *La Créole*, *Le Film complet* explained: "This girl of free nature bore the fetters of civilization badly."[95]

More gratuitously racialized, *Princesse Tam-Tam* (1935) has some un-cannily similar moments. Filmed in part in Tunisia, it tells the tale of an author, Max; driven crazy by his socialite wife and experiencing writ-er's block, he decides to seek inspiration in Africa: "Let's go among the savages. The real savages! Yes, to Africa!" he tells his friend.[96] On arrival, he is charmed by "native" Alouina's (Baker's) gambades as she steals fruit in a restaurant. The author decides he will take her to his villa, "train" her, and write about the dawning on her of "civilization." In fact, he will pre-tend to fall in love with her in order to observe her reactions and to study her "progress" more closely: "An interracial story," he exclaims, "it could be a contemporary novel."

In one scene whose clumsiness of metaphor exceeds even that of the revised *Créole*, a French gardener notes, of the indigenous flowers: "They'll be even lovelier once I transplant them. Now they're too wild. They're not ready for the parlor yet." African servant Tahar, who will eventually settle down with Alouina, foretells the end of the story: "African flowers aren't meant for the parlor." Later, Max, tired of Alouina's eating habits, informs her: "The stomach gets used to eating at mealtimes. The stomach can be-come civilized. Alouina, you know, civilization is beautiful." She, however, prefers to eat (with her hands) when she is hungry, and turning down a bed, she sleeps on the floor; she cannot wear shoes.

Max, meanwhile, is tiring of Africa and missing his wife, whom he hears is accompanying a maharajah in Paris (a second interracial pair). He decides he must finish his book quickly; the picture fades to the action of

---

n'interprèterai pas un rôle. . . . Je vivrai, ce sera moi" (quoted in René Vlamant, "Du cinéma . . . Enfin, je vais faire du cinéma . . . ," *Avant-scène*, 19 May 1934).

95. Ray, "Zouzou," 6.

96. Edmond Gréville, dir., *Princess Tam Tam* (New York: Kino Video, 2005), DVD. For ease of reference, I quote here from the subtitles on the Kino video.

his novel. In his story he takes Alouina back with him to Paris, masquerading her as Indian royalty, Princesse Tam-Tam.[97] She is taken to society events and, despite unseemly enthusiasm at the horse racing, carries off the charade well—until one night a black band playing in a local bar induces her to return to her "savage dance." At the next society event, Max's wife plies the princess with alcohol and then asks her to perform; stripping off her fancy clothes to dance, Alouina's true identity is revealed. Extraordinarily, to mark the return of the native, the movie flashes back to a scene from an ethnographic film, which had appeared in the opening credits—an African beating his drum.

Now, in "real life," Max has finished his story and leaves Africa for France. His villa is left to Alouina; we see her, Tahar, and their baby there, animals roaming the house. Despite her spacious surroundings, Alouina has returned to her "primitive" life with an African man: this, rather than French sophistication, was her destiny. In the final scene, her donkey chews on the pages of the new book—Max is seen signing copies in Paris—whose title is *Civilisation*.

The type Baker played in these movies is close to one that literary and film critics term the "tragic mulatto." She is a character whose ambiguous racial characteristics (her *café au lait* skin) allow her certain privileges in society, even perhaps to pass for white. However, the revelation of her identity and racial difference ultimately bars her from assimilation, particularly from a relationship with a white man. Donald Bogle writes: "Usually the mulatto is made likeable—even sympathetic (because of her white blood, no doubt)—and the audience believes that the girl's life could have been productive and happy had she not been a 'victim of divided racial inheritance.'"[98]

Baker's two tragic mulattos work together as retellings of her own supposed story: in *Zouzou* she comes up from nothing to become a music-hall star; in *Princesse Tam-Tam* a journey from Africa leads to a scandalous performance despite her attempt to be "civilized." In both, reversions to "authentic" racial characteristics (especially in dancing) prevent her from achieving a full transformation; belying her "Frenchness," they incite a break in her relationships. These stories could almost be seen as forms of the soldier and the exotic: while their tragedy is not as extreme as *Car-*

97. The range of Africanist and Orientalist signifiers in *Princesse Tam-Tam* is well discussed in Ezra, "A Colonial Princess," particularly pp. 124–26.

98. Donald Bogle, *Toms, Coons, Mulattoes, Mammies, and Bucks: An Interpretive History of Blacks in American Films*, 3rd ed. (New York: Continuum, 1994), 9. See also pp. 31–33, 147–54, 166–75, and 191–92.

men or *Madama Butterfly* (and Max is no soldier), it is in the same way the realization of unbridgeable difference that drives the couples apart. This poses a question: why in *La Créole*, despite similar reversions to an unmediated otherness, can a happy ending with René be achieved?[99] Answering this question may also help to explain why another black character, Crème fouettée, had been brought on board.

Civilized Singing or Dancing Fever? Act 2, Tableau 2, and Act 3

The latter part of *La Créole* also saw a refined Josephine Baker several times let herself go in dance. In the second tableau of act 2 (developed from the old finale) a "ballet" was added in premature celebration of Dora and Frontignac's wedding.[100] More important, Dora's "Chanson créole" (repeated here in its original location, following their refusal to marry) continues as a dance. Adding an extra touch of "authenticity," a staging instruction explains: "During Dora's dance, Crème squats; she claps her hands, like the natives do." In effect, Crème fouettée replaces the African drummer spliced into *Princesse Tam-Tam* to signal the primitive instinct taking hold of Baker's character. The Commandant is having none of it. Protesting vainly as Dora removes her wedding garb to dance (as Alouina had her fancy gown), he resorts to issuing orders: sailors take Frontignac, Crème fouettée, and Dora, still dancing, by force; her bare legs kicking high in the air, she is carried off to sea (fig. 3.4).[101]

A parallel moment occurs in act 3. Temporarily freed from bondage aboard ship, Dora sings "Les Dames de Bordeaux" with Cartahut and the sailors; it too now concludes in a dance (fig. 3.5). Returning, the Commandant not only orders Dora tied up immediately but arrests her feeble-

99. The generic context of a comic opera does of course demand this. What interests me is the strategy employed to reconcile Dora's difference with her assimilation, allowing at once for continued exoticism and the expected happy ending.

100. This "Marche nuptiale et divertissement" was directed by choreographer Robert Quinault and featured a children's dance troupe, in addition to Baker and the cast.

101. A photograph of this scene is among those included with the libretto of *La Créole*, at C52 (I), BHVP. In both versions, the third act transpires on board ship, en route for the colonies. In 1875, the Commandant has both couples brought on board and locks them in the partnerships he wishes to keep. In 1934, he instead tries to separate the couples by distance, taking with him only Frontignac and Dora; René and Antoinette embark anyway, disguised respectively as Queen Victoria's cousin, the Duke of Birmingham [*sic*], and his kilt-clad Scottish orderly with (the Commandant remarks) unexpectedly appealing thighs.

FIGURE 3.4. Josephine Baker in less modest costume, *La Créole*, Théâtre Marigny, Paris, 1934 (Michael Ochs Archives / Getty Images).

minded guard. That Dora is twice captured during her dancing indicates both an anxiety about a "return of the native" and an effective policy to control it: the Commandant, in the name of colonial authority, sees that her limbs are put in chains. Given Baker's close association with her role, it almost suggests that she herself was policed for resisting her transformation. In disciplining the native for dancing, in other words, the Commandant may have been reclaiming Baker for France.

It is here in the third act that the issue of assimilation comes to a head; the racial discourse that has been a permanent undercurrent of the new version surfaces for all to see. Among substantial dramatic and musical revisions, a baby (Crème fouettée's) was added, to the great surprise of its apparent father, Cartahut. One of two numbers originally sung to a sleepy Commandant but now to the baby was the "Berceuse créole," which Dora chirps kneeling by his crib.[102] While critics typically considered this one of the operetta's most touching moments, Priacel was right, in his anticolonialist review, that it trades in racist stereotypes: describing a

102. The other, "Il dort faisons silence," was now squeezed into the opening "Barcarolle" at the moment when Cartahut entered with his newly discovered child.

FIGURE 3.5. Josephine
Baker in her sailor outfit,
La Créole, Théâtre Mari-
gny, Paris, 1934 (© Gaston
Paris / Roger-Viollet).

"négrillon" with "frizzy hair," the song concludes "Son corps est noir, son
âme est blanche, / Il est gentil comme un p'tit blanc" (His body is black,
his soul is white, / He is as nice as a little white).[103]

Still, in terms of the (re)construction of Baker's persona, the "Berceuse créole" (less so other numbers such as "À la Jamaïque") played an
important role: it established both her vocal credentials and her ability
to sustain a more "civilized" (and more conventionally feminine) persona.
For Madeleine Porter, for example, it was in this song, rather than in her
feistier moments, that Baker created "the most astonishing image" and
showed "what the new Josephine is capable of."[104] Another writer found
her "pure and supple voice simply ravishing" in the lullaby. André Cœuroy
agreed that, musically, moments such as these were the finest in an operetta he considered a "turkey." In an essentialist move, however, he found
it ironic that Baker would shine (vocally) in "the sentimental and the
pretty-pretty, exactly the opposite of Josephine's nature."[105] Most interesting, Louis Laloy had a racialized interpretation even of Baker's sound:

103. In the original, this "native" lullaby was the only song to address race directly; in the absence of a baby, it was significant only of Dora's race. The words
(which did not change) had therefore become a lot more fitting since, in 1875, Dora
sang it to put the Commandant to sleep.

104. Porter, review of *La Créole*.

105. André Cœuroy, review of *La Créole*, *Paris-Midi*, 17 December 1934.

Sa voix colorée comme son teint dans le registre ordinaire possède dans la quinte aiguë, entre le sol et le ré au-dessus de la portée, des notes d'un éclat et d'une fraîcheur incomparables. Elle en use avec art, et rien n'est plus touchant que . . . la berceuse en murmure.[106]

Her voice, which is colored like her complexion in the normal register, possesses in the upper fifth, between G and D above the stave, notes of an incomparable brilliance and purity. She uses them skillfully, and nothing is more touching than . . . the murmured lullaby.

If Baker's high notes lost color, as had her skin, she was more perfect than ever for the role: even her voice, it seemed, could manifest the hybridity of a Creole.[107]

Preceding the "Berceuse créole" and forming a contrast, "Le Sang créole!" was based on an incomplete manuscript withdrawn from the original operetta.[108] Having finally agreed (as a ploy) to marry Frontignac, Dora is caught by the Commandant kissing René. René and his coconspirators try to explain away her behavior as a result of her hot Creole blood:

RENÉ.
J'exciouse cette attitioude [sic],
Quand le thermomètre est si haut,

106. Louis Laloy, review of La Créole, Revue des deux mondes, 1 January 1935, 228–29 (quote on p. 229). Laloy makes a similar point in his review of La Créole, Sélection, 5 January 1935, in A. I. D. 2025, "Offenbach: La Créole," Opéra.

107. Unfortunately, no recordings of Baker in La Créole are available. Two numbers, "À la Jamaïque" and the "Berceuse créole," were recorded by Columbia on February 15, 1935, but were never released and are believed lost. The most complete discography and filmography for Baker are found in Bonini, La Véritable Joséphine Baker, 349–61.

108. These sketches are in Ms. 20655, Département de la Musique, Bibliothèque Nationale, Paris. It is impossible to identify how or where this number was originally intended to fit in, or even who sang it. However, it was presumably to this song that Georges Delance (who revised the work with Albert Willemetz) was referring when he said: "Nous avons fait, dans les archives des Bouffes-Parisiens, une riche trouvaille qui nous a permis de doter la partition originale d'un air inédit d'Offenbach où l'on retrouve l'exquise légèreté et en même temps le brio inimaginable de l'auteur de la 'Vie Parisienne'" (Jean Pages, "Le Théâtre: On découvre dans les archives des Bouffes-Parisiens une partition inédite d'Offenbach," Le Petit Journal, 28 November 1934). The 1934 version uses a new text.

FRONTIGNAC.
   C'est très normal sous ces latitudes,
   Qu'elle ait un peu le sang chaud

R.: I apologize for this attitude, / When the thermometer is so high, / F.:
It's very normal at these latitudes, / That she's a bit hot blooded

Dora concedes their explanation ("C'est le sang créole qui veut ça") before
continuing to exercise her impetuousness in a dance to the same music.[109]
Eager for the titillation anticipated of her shows, a risqué journal noted
with some relief that Josephine Baker was at last au naturel, "that's to
say just about nude and dancing a frenzied jig in which her long sinewy
thighs and her wiggling buttocks perform wonders."[110] Another writer
thought Baker's reversions revealed in sharp relief the civilized performer
she had become, "permit[ting] us to measure the distance covered and the
experience gained, all without . . . [her] native qualities . . . having been
lost, spoilt or weakened."[111]

As in the films, it is in Baker's dancing, as well as in her violent or
hypersexual behavior, that her "authentic" character shines through. The
introduction of dances to *La Créole*, though their music is not exotic, replaces the musical orientalisms one might find in another version of this
plot. As to the status of these revelations, however, "Le Sang créole!" is
ambivalent. While the root cause is biological, the song's concentration
on environmental conditions affecting Dora (the temperature, the lati-
tude, the sea air) leaves open a possibility: under the grey skies of France,
her behavior (like Baker's) might be tamed.[112] Could the same be said of
Crème fouettée's "sang noir"?

*   *   *

In a new, greatly extended finale, several numbers are reprised, sometimes realizing implications that had not at first been manifest. When

109. Although the song was new in 1934, the 1875 libretto similarly put Dora's
behavior down to her "sang créole."
110. Pierre Dargile, "La Vie théâtrale: La Créole," *La Vie Parisienne*, 5 January
1935.
111. Ryk, " 'La Créole' au Théâtre Marigny."
112. Parakilas has remarked on "the contradiction that has always been at the
heart of the theme of the Soldier and the Exotic: the contradiction between the desire to escape from the world one belongs to and the belief that one's nature is ines-
capably bound up with one's people" ("The Soldier and the Exotic [part 2]," 66–67).

Cartahut recalls "Le Ramier et la tourterelle," for example, its theme of race in love must now embrace Crème fouettée's dream (and Cartahut's fear) of uniting, as well as René's and Dora's aspirations. In another song, however, Crème provides Cartahut his way out. Taking up the music of "Les Fariniers" (ex. 3.2), she explains her response to his (feigned) death: she replaced him with another. Continuing into the refrain, Dora makes explicit the meaning of her tale of black and white. If there remained any doubt that the "tout blanc . . . tout noir" now referred beyond the dusty discoloration of "Les Fariniers, les charbonniers" to natural pigmentation, it is here dispelled as the song becomes unequivocally a matter of race: Crème fouettée, too, had two lovers, and here black replaces white.

The news that he is not the baby's father gets Cartahut off the hook. At the end of the operetta, Frontignac and Antoinette's marriage is out in the open and the Commandant agrees Dora and René may wed. In contrast, the final scene finds Cartahut climbing the ship's mast to escape a similar union for him. As the chorus intones words that will lead to rapturous applause for Baker as Dora, Crème fouettée gives up her pursuit in tears: Creole Dora might assimilate to France, but dark-skinned Crème is irredeemably other. Akin to the roles Baker herself played on film, Crème fouettée's story reinstates the racial division that the plot had seemed to transgress; like Princesse Tam-Tam, she must return home with her black baby and leave "civilization" to the French. In other words, the problematic hybrid status of the revised *Créole* (an exotic heroine treated as if it were still the age of discovery) is resolved by the displacement of difference onto Crème: in the system the revised operetta operates, she serves as a foil to "la créole." If Baker's character had, at very long last, "got the guy," the story still demanded a sacrifice.

Performing the Creole: Concerns and Consolations

Despite Baker's great success with *La Créole* in 1934, the piece retains a troubling edge: even as it was revised to be actively discursive of race, it fails to live up to its (and Dora's) sometimes utopian ideals. Although transformed "for" Josephine Baker, modifications construe her character primarily in terms of difference, which the plot then endeavors to control. Even moments when Dora seems to escape an imperial narrative are complicit with a malignant notion: reversions to an inferior racial essence. Besides, the Creole's final assimilation is bought only at the expense of black Crème fouettée. Given a tendency to conflate Baker's life and drama, her presentation in French operetta may itself be a colonizing gesture, as a sign of her "progress" in assimilating French culture. Yet to resist

EXAMPLE 3.2. Reminiscence of "Les Fariniers, les charbonniers," *La Créole* (1934 version), act 3 finale.

EXAMPLE 3.2. *continued*

EXAMPLE 3.2. *continued*

C.F.: Me lie when say that it was, / That it was Cartahut's child / Car.: If it's not me who made it for you, / Then who did you have it with? / C.F.: When you thought dead, / Great despair / Me such grief, / Such such such such / Car.: You such grief? / René: You such grief? / C.F.: Me such grief took replacement // Dora: Doudou [i.e., C.F.] takes a love all black (All black), / To console a love all white (All white) / All white (All white) All white (All white) / And black gives a little child not white / (*All repeat*)

by means of a retrogression in performance style is merely to adhere to a stereotype. If the outcome is problematic whether Dora/Baker should endeavor to be the "same" (marry into France, learn its musical idiom) or settle to be "different" (go home, retain a putatively African or African American style), what option could remain?

La Créole, like Baker's life in France, is situated on the cusp of an insoluble dilemma: between the preservation of cultural inheritance and the assimilation of minority groups. The compromise attempted between plot types here is in some ways a quixotic ideal: it represents the notion that difference should not bar acceptance; it suggests that genuine "exotics" (unlike those, indistinct from metropolitans, of earlier operas) should be accepted at home. If the 1934 *Créole* must remain unsettling on certain levels, then, there may at least be more positive ways to understand Baker's role.

One last review of *La Créole*, by Marc Fabrel, reads:

> Extraordinaire créature que cette Baker, capable à quelques années de distance d'incarner deux âmes si diverses et toutes deux si personnelles. L'école "nègre," promotrice en Europe du Charleston endiablé et lubrique, de la danse de l'instinct déchaîné . . . et aujourd'hui . . . La Créole . . . puérile et fine, spontanée et distinguée, ardente et délicieusement femme. . . . Sans renoncer à rien de ce qui fit jadis son succès sans égal elle corrige, affine, transforme son sex-appeal.[113]

> What an extraordinary creature this Baker is, capable of embodying a few years apart two souls so diverse and both so personal. [First,] the "Negro" school, promoter in Europe of the wild and lewd Charleston, of the dance of unfettered instinct . . . [and now,] La Créole . . . childish and keen, spontaneous and elegant, passionate and deliciously womanly. . . . Without renouncing anything of what formerly made her unequalled success she corrects, refines, transforms [the nature of] her sex appeal.

On one level, this account is familiar: it reiterates the transformation in Baker's persona that many critics discussed. Yet for Fabrel, although Baker embodied these different identities on stage, her metamorphosis was artistic rather than personal: he did not confuse her stage roles with her own "civilization" but recognized them as the performances of an actor. In the context of the French reviews seen above, this apparently trivial observation was most unusual. So imbued had Baker's life story become

113. Marc Fabrel, review of *La Créole*, *Paris Spectacles*, 10 January 1935, in A. I. D. 2025, "Offenbach: *La Créole*," Opéra.

with colonialist narratives that the fact a talented American actor lay behind these roles risked to be altogether lost.[114]

Revisiting the question today—when it has become increasingly commonplace to consider race and gender both as learned, and learnable, behaviors—it is easier to recognize that the identities Baker personified were all, in some sense, "performative." If she relished rather than resisted apparent overlaps between her life and work, that was because her off-stage identity, too, was a performance: "I'm going to show what France made of Josephine!" she said returning to the United States in 1935. "I was a little savage before."[115] It would be wrong to suggest, however, that Baker confused fact and fiction: in an earlier show, timed to coincide with the 1931 Exposition Coloniale, she played a series of exotic roles ("la petite tonkinoise," "la jolie martiniquaise") alongside Pierre Meyer's French colonist—until, that is, the two fell out and she immediately had him fired.[116] Not to recognize Baker's agency, however constrained, in the construction of her characters (and the power she derived from manipulating them) would be to do her a disservice.[117] Whatever the critics

114. Andrea Barnwell attempts to rescue Baker from the colonial narratives she told by focusing on moments when she "broke free" from the plot by dancing for herself (and is only coincidentally watched). Examples are found in both *Zouzou* (when she dances on stage, unaware that the curtain has been raised) and *Princesse Tam-Tam* (when, alone in a bar, she recaptures her memories of home in a dance). Barnwell argues: "The sheer joy and personal pleasure of creating this display . . . are significant elements often neglected. . . . By demonstrating her conscious decision to please herself she defies colonialist expectations" ("Like the Gypsy's Daughter, or Beyond the Potency of Josephine Baker's Eroticism," in *Rhapsodies in Black: Art of the Harlem Renaissance* [Berkeley: University of California Press, 1997], 82–99 [quote on p. 85]). As I have shown, there are parallel places in *La Créole*. While I am in sympathy with Barnwell's intentions, however, I cannot agree with her conclusion. Such moments are complicit with a racial determinism, whose consequences on the narrative I have observed. Further, she ignores a wider frame: Zouzou may not know she is being watched in the music hall, but Baker knows she is dancing to a movie audience; indeed, her lack of acknowledgement of our presence heightens the voyeuristic pleasure of the gaze.

115. Gabriel Reuillard, "Joséphine Baker va nous quitter pour les 'Ziegfeld Folies' de New York," *Excelsior*, 28 July 1935, in Ro 15816(6), "Joséphine Baker, 1933–35," Rondel.

116. Georges Martin, "Magie noire?," *Le Petit Journal*, 29 December 1930; Pierre Lagarde, "Il y a rupture entre l'étoile noire et le dieu bleu," *Comœdia*, 1 January 1931 (both are in Ro 18937, "Casino de Paris, 1930," Rondel).

117. I completely agree with Barnwell, therefore, that "confining Baker to the realm of a performer who was solely preoccupied with satisfying colonial fanta-

thought, of course, her wilder moments were not windows on her soul nor on her racial "essence." The frequent mention of *La Revue nègre* was a giveaway: her 1925 "sauvage" had no more authenticity than her 1934 "créole."

The reversions discussed, then, were not atavistic (the ideology of both the tragic mulatto and the soldier and the exotic) but performative: the recovery of a mode of highly physical dance characteristic of an earlier period in her career. And if there never *was* a "savage" Baker to be "civilized," the colonial discourse that sought to view her transformations in such terms collapses. In its place I locate an intelligent actor who pandered to her audience's imaginations at one moment but challenged them at the next. If there remains a certain bitter irony to the way she, in effect, became French by consenting to act out that country's colonial fantasies, it is important to recognize that, in Baker's hands, those illusions were rarely simple; the largest gains may well have been hers.[118] Where, though, did her very versatility—an ability to move at whim among different (often racially defined) roles—leave a politics of identity?

"Don't talk to me about black power," a sixty-four-year-old Baker is reported to have said in 1970: "All power is power. I don't like discrimination. I'm shocked when I hear our own saying 'black people this,' 'black people that.' It just shows you we haven't come very far."[119] Having portrayed in her long career every "exotic" under the sun, racialized identities left Baker cold. Although her role was sometimes important in the American civil rights movement, for the most part she remained a step removed. The reason was certainly practical, in that she continued to live mainly in Europe, but it also had an ideological element: Baker's position emphasized equality more than it recognized difference. While strategic essentialisms have historically been a political imperative in campaigns for racial, national, or gender equality the world over, Baker's refusal to accept such constructions was, in a sense, ahead of its time.[120] The notions

---

sies does not acknowledge her self-agency, autonomy or ability to influence European perceptions of African women" ("Like the Gypsy's Daughter," 85).

118. My point here is not that Baker has complete freedom in her performances as racialized (and later nationalized) subject, or that her "true identity" lies somewhere else. Rather, it is that she is constantly playing with—exploiting, resisting, amending—society's expectations of her in a peculiarly conscious way, even as she cannot help but be shaped by as well as shaping them.

119. John Vinocur, "At 64, Josephine Baker Looks at Black Power," *International Herald Tribune*, 31 August 1970, in 4° Sw 4754(1), "Baker, Joséphine," AdS.

120. See Jules-Rosette, *Josephine Baker*, particularly "Hues of the Rainbow in a Global Village" and "Legendary Legionnaire," 184–242.

of "hybridity" and "mongrelization" may have become clichés of post-colonial literature, but a related concept is irresistible in this context.

Not so long ago, anthropologist Ulf Hannerz proposed that "a concept of creole culture . . . may be our most promising root metaphor" for processes of transmission and transition.[121] "Creolization," as he defines it, is a dynamic process *among* agents rather than one imposed on one by another. It thus holds out the possibility of escaping constructed notions of "authentic" otherness on the one hand and ideas of a homogenizing cultural imperialism on the other. This theoretical use of the term, outside of the language groups and cultures with which it is commonly associated, has proved rather controversial. For some scholars, it risks conflating or confusing biological, ethnic, and linguistic models; for others, ignoring cultural and geographical specificities.[122] However, creolization may serve as a useful reminder that the transformation of *La Créole* was not a one-way process: Baker certainly adapted her persona as she sought to guarantee her longevity as a performer in France, but so too did the "the old man from Cologne" have to be reworked in the spirit of the new age.

Amid all the nostalgia, there was an acknowledgement that Baker's *Créole* was one distinctly renewed. Even André Rivollet, so keen that Baker symbolize "civilization's" rejection of *jazz hot*, noted: "She has not attempted to imitate . . . , but she has created an Offenbach for 1935 by instilling him with new lifeblood, a thrilling youthfulness."[123] On the level of genre, too, several critics noted that Baker had presented a hybrid; as André Cœuroy said: "She transforms the 'divertissement' of the old comic theatre into the frenzy of the modern revue."[124] Not only, in

---

121. Ulf Hannerz, "The World in Creolization," in *Readings in African Popular Culture*, ed. Karin Barber (London: International African Institute in association with James Currey, 1997), 12–18 [originally published in *Africa* 57 (1987): 546–59]. With regard to African, specifically Nigerian, popular culture, Hannerz argues: "The world system, rather than creating massive cultural homogeneity on a global scale, is replacing one diversity with another; and the new diversity is based relatively more on interrelations and less on autonomy" (16). For related discussions, see Hannerz, *Transnational Connections: Cultures, People, Places* (London: Routledge, 1996); and Hannerz, *Cultural Complexity: Studies in the Social Organization of Meaning* (New York: Columbia University Press, 1992).

122. For recent discussions see, inter alia, Viranjini Munasinghe, Ulf Hannerz, et al., "*AE Forum*: Locating or Liberating Creolization," *American Ethnologist* 33 (2006): 549–92; Charles Stewart, ed., *Creolization: History, Ethnography, Theory* (Walnut Creek, CA: Left Coast Press, 2007); and Robert Baron and Ana C. Cara, eds., *Creolization as Cultural Creativity* (Jackson: University Press of Mississippi, 2011).

123. Rivollet, "Du jazz hot à 'La Créole,'" 106.

124. Cœuroy, review of *La Créole*.

other words, was Baker assimilating her role as (almost) French, she was also, at least potentially, expanding notions of French culture itself. In fact, while creolization may have its limitations as an analytical device, its blurring of the boundaries between race, culture, and language paradoxically make it all the more apt a description of the transformations involved in *La Créole*: these confusions are perfectly characteristic of the discourse around Baker, as I have shown. It may be preferable, then, to see Baker's *Créole* as neither contaminated nor commoditized but as fruitfully—gloriously—"creolized."

Such rather utopian ideas of cultural exchange are perhaps what attracted the organizers of an unlikely coproduction of Offenbach's *La Créole* in 2009. Not performed live since a brief revival by Baker in 1940, the piece was again resurrected by L'Atelier Lyrique de Tourcoing, an opera workshop in northern France, and Cantaréunion, a choir from La Réunion (an island in the Indian Ocean, east of Madagascar, that has been a French possession since the mid-seventeenth century, and a département within the French parliamentary system since 1946). The combined forces gave a small number of performances in both Tourcoing (near Lille) and on La Réunion, where some of the lead singers had connections. Holy Razafindrazaka, from Madagascar (itself a French colony from 1896 to 1960) played Crème fouettée, though the role was renamed Quatre épices ("four spices," a common French ingredient); Valérie Yeng Seng, who grew up in La Réunion but trained as a singer in Paris, played Dora (la créole).[125]

The racial politics of the piece do not seem to have been of great concern to participants, perhaps on the assumption that the mixed backgrounds of the performers themselves answered any questions about the operetta's inclusivity. For Jean-Louis Tavan, director of Cantaréunion, who proposed the work, "the message is quite clear: love has nothing to do the color, ethnic or social origins of individuals."[126] Valérie Yeng Seng herself remarked several times that the story was "rather colonial" but nevertheless found it very funny and enjoyed her role:

C'est une histoire très proche, même si elle est un peu vieillotte. La petite créole tombe amoureuse du blanc qui l'abandonne, et qu'elle retrouve. C'est un texte un peu colonial. Au-delà, c'est une opérette très drôle. Dora

125. Programme, "Offenbach, *La Créole*," L'Atelier Lyrique de Tourcoing, Tourcoing Théâtre Municipal, 13–18 January 2009, accessed 5 August 2012, http://reunion .orange.fr/IMG/pdf/progLACREOLE.pdf.

126. David Chassagne, "Jean-Louis Tavan: 'Nou lé [sic] tout couleur et toutes les couleurs sont belles,'" *Clicanoo.com* (La Réunion), 19 April 2009, repr., accessed 6 August 2012, http://www.myspace.com/cantareunion/blog/485260453.

est une femme forte, une femme qui ose dire qu'elle aime et qu'elle est prête à suivre son amour, et l'assume.[127]

It's a story that's very close to us, even if it's a bit dated. The little Creole falls in love with a white man who leaves her, and whom she gets back. It's a bit colonial. Beyond that, it's a very funny operetta. Dora is a strong woman, a woman who dares to say that she's in love and that she's ready to follow her love, and takes it on.

It is striking, however, how similar were some tropes that emerged in the show's reception to those heard in Paris seventy-five years earlier. One critic found the "Creole exoticism" of the production "an excellent elixir," and the "gorgeous" Creole herself, "très Josephine Baker."[128] Another went further, remarking: "Of course, Valérie Yeng Seng has but the tiny voice of an exotic bird [toute petite voix d'oiseau des îles]: the projection is limited, and one barely understands a word; but it's pretty and very musical."[129] In a repeat of an old pattern, then, Yeng Seng became caught between her own understanding of the role as that of a strong-willed young woman, determined to get what she desires, and her audience's tendency to read her performance instead in strongly gendered and racialized terms. This is an oddly fitting testimony to Josephine Baker's legacy. On one hand, it shows her instant name recognition and considerable standing in her adopted country almost four decades after her death. On the other, it suggests that those who follow in her footsteps are no more able than she was truly to escape the colonialist assumptions of the narratives all around her. For Baker as for others, *La Créole* represents an opportunity that is strictly circumscribed.

127. Florence Merlen, "Valérie Yeng-Seng: Y'a de la voix," *Femme Magazine* (La Réunion), 9 April 2009, accessed 5 August 2012, http://www.femmemag.re/?page =article&id_article=659&id_rubrique=3.

128. Jean-Marie Duhamel, "Offenbach à l'Atelier Lyrique: La Créole s'amuse!," *La Voix du Nord*, 15 January 2009, accessed 5 August 2012, http://www.lavoixdunord.fr/ Locales/Metropole_Lilloise/actualite/Secteur_Metropole_Lilloise/2009/01/15/ article_offenbach-a-l-atelier-lyrique-la-creole.shtml.

129. Jean-Marcel Humbert, "La Perle de La Réunion," *Forumopera.com*, 17 January 2009, accessed 5 August 2012, http://www.forumopera.com/index.php?ma ct=News,cntnt01,detail,0&cntnt01articleid=693&cntnt01detailtemplate=gabar it_detail_breves&cntnt01dateformat=%25d-%25m-%25Y&cntnt01lang=fr_FR& cntnt01returnid=54.

4 "That Gypsy in France"

Django Reinhardt's Occupation *Blouze*

Django's Double: *Sweet and Lowdown*

As the unmistakable sound of Django Reinhardt and the Quintette du Hot Club de France fades at the opening of Woody Allen's 1999 film *Sweet and Lowdown* (fig. 4.1), the director himself appears. "Why Emmet Ray?" he asks, the first of several aficionados grappling to explain their fascination not with Reinhardt but with the "second-greatest guitar player in the world": "To me, Emmet Ray was a fascinating character. I was a huge fan of his when I was younger; I thought he was an absolutely great guitar player. And, um, and he was funny, you know, or, or—if funny's the wrong word, then—you know, sort of pathetic in a way. He was flamboyant, and he was, you know, er, boorish, and obnoxious." But the "problem is there's just so little known about him," a second talking head explains. As the film proceeds, brief excerpts of expert testimony (including venerable jazz critic Nat Hentoff's) alternate with filmed sequences illustrating or extending the anecdotes. In contrast to his earlier "mockumentaries" such as *Zelig* and showbiz tributes such as *Broadway Danny Rose*—about a human chameleon and showbiz manager, respectively—Allen keeps the story just within the realms of believability: Ray is eccentric, to be sure, but no more so than many of the characters handed down by jazz lore; the effect is sufficiently convincing to have fooled more than one film critic.[1]

Emmet Ray (Sean Penn) embodies nearly every legend about early jazz musicians. He's a pimp like Jelly Roll Morton; in common with King Oliver, he carries a revolver even on stage. His refusal at first to record for fear people would steal his ideas recalls Freddie Keppard, but his womanizing is most suggestive of Sidney Bechet. Ray's drinking and occasional drug use bring to mind stories about any number of musicians. Longtime jazz

---

1. For example, Shlomo Schwartzberg: "A departure for Woody Allen, 'Sweet and Lowdown' is actually based on a true story, that of Emmet Ray (Sean Penn), widely considered the second-best guitarist in the world in the '30s, after the legendary Django Reinhardt" (review of *Sweet and Lowdown*, *Box Office* 135/11 [November 1999]: 153).

FIGURE 4.1. Publicity for the French release of Woody Allen's *Sweet and Lowdown* (1999) showing the moonstricken Emmet Ray (Sean Penn), his mute girlfriend, Hattie (*left*, Samantha Morton), and his wife, Blanche (*right*, Uma Thurman).

writer Ira Gitler has said: "Emmet Ray . . . really didn't exist. But he could have. He resembles many of the jazz musicians I knew in the 1940s."[2] Most reviewers were more interested in Ray as another substitute for Allen himself.[3] The neurotic, self-obsessed jazz musician is doubtless a char-

2. Ira Gitler, "*Sweet and Lowdown*: A Jazz History Perspective," accessed 25 August 2013, http://www.sonyclassics.com/sweetandlowdown/frames.html.

3. Such comments tended to concern, in particular, Ray's relationship with a mute laundress, Hattie (Samantha Morton), at a time when Woody Allen's relationship with Soon-Yi Previn, the adopted daughter of his former partner Mia Farrow, was still regarded as scandalous. For example, Dave Kehr: "As a fully li-

acter Allen would once have played. But an effect of psychoanalyzing the auteur was to disguise the fact that Ray stands in for no one so much as the musician he holds in awe and trepidation: "that Gypsy in France."[4]

Played brilliantly by Penn, Ray looks a lot like Reinhardt (the sartorial elegance, the trademark moustache), is as unreliable as he was, and has the combination of egocentricity and vulnerability that many attribute to him. Ray exchanges Reinhardt's billiards for pool, and his "mute orphan half-wit" girlfriend, Hattie, replaces his French counterpart's brother as porter of his guitar. While neither Reinhardt nor any other musician to my knowledge had particular fetishes for watching trains, stealing trinkets, or shooting rats at the dump, one of the most outlandish incidents in the film comes straight from his biography: if Ray dreams of descending to the stage sat on a crescent moon, Reinhardt wanted to make his celestial appearance, less modestly still, enthroned on a star. Fear struck both men, but while Ray goes through with his stunt, to disastrous and hilarious effect, Reinhardt backed out, making his entrance closer to the ground, on a small train.[5] Even Reinhardt's alleged cowardice—which, during the war, reputedly had him charging to the bottom of the deepest metro station before the air raid siren sounded—is thematized in Allen's

---

censed, self-destructive genius, [Emmet needs] to mess up his relationship with this innocent, perfectly adoring, very much younger woman. Allen presents this development as tragic but inevitable—as if loneliness were the price of greatness and infidelity the curse of genius. Such things might bode ill for any innocent, perfectly adoring, very much younger women in Woody Allen's life, if there happen to be any" (review of *Sweet and Lowdown*, *Film Comment* 35/6 [November/December 1999]: 76). Similarly, Amy Taubin: "Though Morton never cloys, Allen's misogyny vis-à-vis this character is so blatant that it almost defies mention. (She's beautiful, she's adoring, she can't talk back.) . . . *Sweet and Lowdown* is too slight to accommodate more than one ego—a larger-than-life model of the filmmaker's own" ("Sean Penn's High-Wire Act; Wisconsin Gothic," *Village Voice*, 30 November 1999, accessed 16 September 2013, http://www.villagevoice.com/1999-11-30/film/sean-penn-s-high-wire-act-wisconsin-gothic/).

4. Ray repeats this phrase many times, with admiration as much as antipathy: he seems to model himself on Reinhardt but is too terrified to meet him. In the broader context, "Gypsy Jazz" (or "Jazz Manouche") is widely used for the genre Reinhardt more or less founded, not least among the community's musicians. I thus retain it here, though I am sensitive to the fact that the ethnic descriptor can be employed pejoratively.

5. Charles Delaunay, *Django Reinhardt: Souvenirs* (Paris: Jazz-Hot, 1954), 16, 51; Charles Delaunay, *Django Reinhardt*, trans. Michael James (London: Cassell, 1961; repr., New York: Da Capo, 1982), 115; and Michel Dregni, *The Life and Music of a Gypsy Legend* (New York: Oxford University Press, 2004), 171.

film by Ray's inability to face up to his idol. In other words, *Sweet and Lowdown* stands in for a biopic of Reinhardt rather as Bertrand Tavernier's *Round Midnight* stands in for one of Lester Young and/or Bud Powell, and is all the more satisfying for this ambiguity.

Music emphasizes how Ray at once is and isn't Reinhardt. The nondiegetic soundtrack comprises recordings from the 1930s and 1940s, Reinhardt's prominently among them. For scenes in which Ray himself performs, on the other hand, the music was played afresh—yet in the style of the period, by an ensemble often comprising the clarinet, two guitars, bass, and drums that made up the wartime variant of the Hot Club Quintet. (The Django-esque guitar was played by Howard Alden, who doubled as Penn's guitar coach—tuition that is reflected to varying success in his faking for the camera.) So, as hard as he tries, Ray never quite gets to *play* Reinhardt.

At the same time, the film's episodic structure removes the need for narrative continuity, as Allen has, in various ways, in other movies (most imaginatively, *Mighty Aphrodite*'s Greek chorus). In this sense, *Sweet and Lowdown* becomes an ironic counterpart to documentaries such as, most obviously, Ken Burns's *Jazz*, which appeared at about the same time and to far greater fanfare. Superficially similar to those programs—the to-camera commentary, the historical "footage," the abrupt transitions between events—Allen's movie deflates their claim to history, revealing both how easy it is to convince with a good story and how trivial or romanticized is most we are told.

This narrative playfulness is nowhere so apparent as in a scene we watch three times, as conflicting versions of an "Emmet Ray story"—one of the tall tales about the musician—are heard and duly unfold. Having discovered that his wife, Blanche (Uma Thurman), is having an affair, Ray hides in the back of the lovers' car. He is unwittingly involved in a holdup and car chase, and the episode ends variously in his contemplating suicide, singing to the police, and coming face-to-face with his nemesis, Reinhardt. The recurrence for each take of the same, rather infuriating, tune (German American bandleader Henry Busse and His Orchestra's "Hot Lips") on the soundtrack emphasizes the narrative breach.[6]

Although these escapades in love are one element wholly of Allen's invention, Django Reinhardt's life is particularly susceptible to such imaginative treatment. Biographers have often concluded their laborious work with a series of anecdotes and recordings, and a disclaimer that whole

---

6. Allen's 2004 *Melinda and Melinda* pushes this idea further: for the entire film, tragic and comic versions of a story alternate, as they are imagined by friends at a dinner table; neither version prevails.

periods of the guitarist's life are unaccounted for and that they are little the wiser about his personality.[7] The problem becomes especially insistent during the Second World War: a historical moment whose memory in France is fraught and fractured, yet whose slightest action may be subjected to intense ideological scrutiny. Not only did Reinhardt remain in the country throughout the German occupation, but he also became a great star, the critical respect in which he was already held now matched by popular appeal.

Recognizing Reinhardt in Ray thus heightens rather than undermines *Sweet and Lowdown*'s two central ideas: the opacity of history, and of jazz history in particular, and the amorality of artists—an old Allen theme. The film helps me to make sense, in this chapter, of a historical puzzle: how a Gypsy jazz musician could achieve his greatest fame in Nazi-occupied Paris. Like Emmet Ray, however, Django Reinhardt is often a mere shadow in his own life story, accessed by others' perceptions of him and the meanings attributed to his music. If this gives little sense of Reinhardt's agency or motivation, the compensation, I hope, is a firmer grasp on jazz's historical significance in a time of trauma and compromise. All the same, I am less concerned in this case with establishing definitive answers than I am with sounding alternative possibilities, as I survey accounts of jazz in occupied France from the 1940s to the present day.

Triple Take: Jazz under Occupation

If Django Reinhardt's life resists conventional narration, the same might be said of jazz in wartime France. As soon as the conflict was over, irreconcilable tales began to circulate, and their passage has not slowed. Three basic variants can be recognized, however, sometimes even coexisting within a single text. To borrow a device from Woody Allen, then, I want to present the three—related but incompatible—"takes" on jazz in occupied France that are most commonly heard.

The first take shows that jazz was removed altogether from occupied France; banned by the authorities, it fled the city along with its American performers prior to or early in the war. The few musicians who did not heed warnings were arrested and interned after the United States en-

---

7. Delaunay, *Django Reinhardt: Souvenirs*, 13; Delaunay, *Django mon frère* (Paris: Le Terrain Vague, 1968), 9–10; Dregni, *Gypsy Legend*, 317. For a critical perspective on the problem in general, see Tony Whyton, "Witnessing and the Jazz Anecdote," in *Jazz Icons: Heroes, Myths and the Jazz Tradition* (Cambridge: Cambridge University Press, 2010), 106–26.

tered the conflict. In *Paris noir*, for example, historian Tyler Stovall bluntly states: "Jazz was classified as decadent music and forbidden during the occupation."[8] This sets the stage for its return in a blaze of glory after the war, mirroring its arrival in 1917/18. Stovall argues: "Both because of its intrinsic qualities and because its condemnation by the Nazis during the occupation made it a cultural symbol of antifascism, jazz enjoyed a spectacular birth in Paris after the war."[9] In take 1, then, jazz departs and returns alongside freedom.

The second take associates jazz with a countercultural movement among youths known as *zazous* (or sometimes *swings*). "Negro music and jazz are already out of date," French singer Johnny Hess had explained in "Je suis swing" (1938), "Now to be fashionable, you must have swing"; reason gave out altogether in the chorus, "Zazou zazou zazou zazou hé."[10] The young zazous were distinguished by their somewhat unruly behavior and, particularly, by their conspicuous dress (which owed much to swing-era fashions in the States): for men, oversized jackets but underlong trousers, worn with white socks and thick-soled shoes, high collars with narrow ties, and gloves; for women, large jackets again, short skirts, striped stockings, generous makeup, and similarly clomping shoes (fig. 4.2). Along with unisex accessories such as umbrellas and sunglasses, rain or shine, occasional English words were part of the image, including profuse use of the term *swing* for anything that warranted approval.[11] A harbinger of all things ill for those maintaining the traditionalist—and collaborationist—order of the French government in Vichy, the zazous were hounded

8. Tyler Stovall, *Paris noir: African Americans in the City of Light* (Boston: Mariner Books, 1996), 126.

9. Ibid., 134.

10. "La musique nègre et le jazz hot sont déjà de vieillies machines / Maintenant pour être dans la note, il faut du swing / Le swing n'est pas une mélodie / Le swing n'est pas une maladie / Mais aussitôt qu'il vous a plu / Il vous prend et n'vous lâche plus / Je suis swing oh . . . / Je suis swing / Zazou zazou zazou zazou hé / Je suis swing oh . . . / Je suis swing / C'est fou, c'est fou c'que ça peut m'griser." The word *zazou* seems to have been forged from Hess's impression of the scat singing of Cab Calloway (whose song *Zaz Zuh Zaz* dates from 1933).

11. A commentator in 1941 noted how many things could now be swung: "swing ballet, swing orchestra, swing mustard, swing poetry, [even] swing rutabaga"—the root that became a staple during the war (Jean Laurent, "Le Music-Hall: Du tour de chant à la revue," *Les Nouveau Temps*, 11 March 1941, in R. Supp. 1125, "Le Music-Hall: Variétés et chansons: Chroniques et articles divers," Collection Rondel, Département des Arts du Spectacle, Bibliothèque Nationale, Paris, hereafter cited as Rondel).

FIGURE 4.2. Young "zazou" dancing (© Albert Harlingue / Roger-Viollet).

by the Jeunesses Populaires Françaises, a French counterpart to the Hitler Youth; a press campaign culminated in a *chasse aux zazous*, occasionally facilitated by the police.[12] Although it is not clear how many zazous were actually "caught" and shorn of their long, carefully quaffed hair—or, worse, sent to work in rural France or industrial Germany—the "hunt" served symbolically to crack down on a youthful ebullience that was out of line with the times. William Shack insists, " 'Je suis swing,' the jitterbug, and the swing music Zazous adopted as their raison d'être were an affront to the moral values that the New Order attempted to instill in citizens of occupied Paris."[13] This version of the story therefore recognizes

12. William Shack, *Harlem in Montmartre: A Paris Jazz Story between the Great Wars* (Berkeley: University of California Press, 2001), 119–23; Matthew F. Jordan, "*Zazou dans le Métro*: Occupation, Swing, and the Battle for *la Jeunesse*," in *Le Jazz: Jazz and French Cultural Identity* (Urbana: University of Illinois Press, 2010), 185–232.

13. Shack, *Harlem in Montmartre*, 120.

jazz as the sound of resistance; though present in wartime France, it came under attack.

The third take on jazz in wartime France is the most elaborate. At the Nazi occupation, enthusiasm for jazz broke out spontaneously among the French. While this, again, signaled opposition to the Germans, skillful spin-doctoring by the Hot Club de France kept jazz safe: members established and maintained a collective myth that jazz was a French tradition. As part of this effort, song titles were disguised; "Saint Louis Blues" famously transformed into "La Tristesse de Saint Louis," and "Lady be Good" became "Les Bigoudis" ("The Hair Curlers"). This movement was thus distinct from the zazous with their overt Anglicisms and poor musical taste; its resistance was implicit. The narrative chimes with familiar—if rarely interrogated—notions that jazz may express human dignity and resilience in the face of oppression. In his *Dancing with DeBeauvoir*, for example, Colin Nettelbeck writes: "As a music whose essence was freedom of personal expression, both for the players and those who (clandestinely) danced to it, jazz provided a space to breathe."[14] In this third version, then, France has its jazz and bans it, too.

With some variation, these three takes—expulsion, resistance, and covert persistence—sum up the tale of jazz in wartime France as it has typically been told. The reality, of course, is more complicated than any of them allows (and, to be fair, most accounts go some way to acknowledging this).[15] All three versions, however, share the notion that jazz was anathema to the occupying forces and the Vichy government and that an engagement with this music implied resistance. They also have in common the idea that the war marked a fundamental shift in French jazz culture—in fact, in French culture tout court.

Vichy France is of course one of the most freighted periods in living memory; it is no accident that so many explorations of the intersection of history and memory have located themselves there. None is more important than Henry Rousso's *The Vichy Syndrome*, which argues compellingly that a "myth of Resistance" took hold of France, not suddenly but progressively after the war; it peaked when the head of the Free French,

14. Colin Nettelbeck, *Dancing with DeBeauvoir: Jazz and the French* (Carlton, Victoria: Melbourne University Press, 2004), 54.

15. See also Jeffrey H. Jackson, *Making Jazz French: Music and Modern Life in Interwar Paris* (Durham, NC: Duke University Press, 2003), 190–95; and Denis-Constant Martin, "Le Jazz résiste," in *La France du jazz: Musique, modernité et identité dans la première moitié du XXe siècle*, by Denis-Constant Martin and Olivier Roueff (Marseille: Parenthèses, 2002), 69–76.

Charles de Gaulle, finally became president of the republic in 1959. According to this myth, the whole of France, even Marshal Pétain's government in Vichy, was engaged in resistance to the Germans and committed to the cause of the Allies; collaboration was swept under the carpet.[16] As Ludovic Tournès has suggested, the association of jazz with resistance may be another manifestation of this syndrome.[17] Recent analyses thus mark the characteristic downturn Rousso identifies, paradoxically, as part of the phenomenon: the moment at which formerly sacrosanct "memories" finally become available for investigation as texts from history like all others. In this process, historians of jazz join other writers belatedly investigating the surprising vitality of the arts under Vichy.[18]

Resourceful investigation by Tournès and, especially, Gérard Régnier has set the record straight on many aspects of the story, even as old myths continue to circulate. To begin, the idea of a ban can safely be dispatched. Jazz was never prohibited in France, either in the Nazi-occupied North (and West) of France, or in the nominally free South run by Philippe Pétain's collaborationist government in Vichy. It is true that American musicians in large majority left at the outbreak of war; with one or two exceptions, those remaining were later interned. But there were by this point a good number of talented French musicians lining up to take their place.[19] Whatever the measure—concerts, recordings, record sales, radio broadcasts, fan base—the war was actually rather a lively and successful period for jazz in France, even in the absence of American musicians.

16. Henry Rousso, *The Vichy Syndrome: History and Memory in France since 1944*, trans. Arthur Goldhammer (Cambridge, MA: Harvard University Press, 1991).

17. Ludovic Tournès, "Le Jazz: Un Espace de liberté pour un phénomène culturel en voie d'identification," in *La Vie musicale sous Vichy*, ed. Myriam Chimènes (Brussels: Complexe, 2001), 313–32 (esp. p. 314). A rather longer version of this essay appears as Tournès, "Le Swing des années noires," in *New Orleans sur Seine: Histoire du jazz en France* (Paris: Fayard, 1999), 59–90.

18. See, for example, Myriam Chimènes, *La Vie musicale sous Vichy*; Stéphanie Corcy, *La Vie culturelle sous l'Occupation* (Paris: Librairie Académique Perrin, 2005); Christian Faure, *Le Projet culturel de Vichy: Folklore et révolution nationale, 1940–1944* (Lyon: Presses Universitaires de Lyon, 1989); and Jean-Pierre Rioux, ed., *La Vie culturelle sous Vichy* (Brussels: Complexe, 1990). Throughout, I follow Robert Paxton and most subsequent historians in using the term *Vichy France* to refer both to the occupied northern zone (including Paris) and to the southern zone administered by the French government in Vichy. See Robert O. Paxton, *Vichy France: Old Guard and New Order, 1940–1944* (New York: Knopf, 1972; repr., New York: Columbia University Press, 2001). At the very least, I believe, the similarities between the two regimes outweighed their differences.

19. Tournès, "Le Jazz," 314.

German censorship of musical events in Paris existed to some degree, but its functioning remains opaque even now. No firm instructions are known to have been given by the Propagandastaffel, which reviewed programs, much less a list of forbidden composers or music (such as existed in Germany). The working understanding seems to have been that Jewish composers were not acceptable (so no Gershwin or Irving Berlin) and that English titles were best disguised even if flimsily (though American composers as a whole were not strictly banned).[20] Oversight of radio programming was even more lax, with Régnier concluding from published listings that "American jazz was played without interruption on Radio Paris, most often under camouflaged titles, but not always, far from it."[21] In fact, he has established that the two most commonly cited examples of subterfuge, "La Tristesse de Saint Louis" and "Les Bigoudis," were inventions of the postwar period, never featuring in wartime programs. There, the more literal "Soyez bonne madame" was preferred for the latter, while the former appeared unchanged.[22] Among French musicians, Raymond Legrand's band appeared on Nazi-run Radio Paris some 520 times.[23]

There are other official indications of jazz's success. In an effort to check the escalating fees some artists were able to demand, for example, the Propagandastaffel set a tariff. In December 1943, performers were assigned to different categories, an estimation of their fame or possibly of their talents. Among jazz and swing musicians, Johnny Hess was permitted to charge high fees, and Alix Combelle and Michel Warlop higher. The twenty-three artists with the highest fee cap included Raymond Legrand, Jo Bouillon, and, of course, Django Reinhardt.[24] No sign here, then, of any attempt to suppress jazz.

Unless, of course, the performers were Jewish—Ray Ventura wisely

20. Gérard Régnier, *Jazz et société sous l'Occupation* (Paris: L'Harmattan, 2009), 142–45.

21. Ibid., 151.

22. Ibid., 58–59. Régnier has further discovered that performing rights continued to be collected for composers such as Irving Berlin during this period, and the German authorities informed, although the money was held in a blocked account as "propriété ennemie dans les territoires français occupés"; some funds held by SACEM (Société des Auteurs, Compositeurs et Éditeurs de Musique) for foreign performing rights associations (e.g., ASCAP, PRS) were also confiscated by the German authorities. In neither case does the question of why this music was being performed in the first place seem to have arisen, which Régnier takes as a tacit acknowledgement that no effective censorship was in place (ibid., 155–57).

23. Tournès, "Le Jazz," 316.

24. Régnier, *Jazz et société*, 89.

took his band to South America for the duration of the war—the cultural climate in Vichy France was thus fairly benign. In this context, the zazous' experience is something of a special case, since some certainly were harassed (and worse) by the authorities and collaborating press. The claim Shack and others make, however, depends on the close connection of jazz with the zazous and the zazous with the resistance—a connection that in neither case is clear. In her detailed study of the phenomenon, Emmannuelle Rioux found no direct ties between zazous and the resistance movements, and she doubts furthermore that their behavior signaled opposition to the occupying powers. Rather, Rioux maintains, theirs was a form of youthful rebellion without specific political ends.[25]

If this was so, the zazous were often misunderstood. As much is revealed by *Gringoire*'s quip that their national anthem was "God Save the Swing"[26]—not to mention a lot of much less amusing coverage in the collaborationist press connecting the zazous not only with the Allies but with illicit groups from Jews to black marketeers. But, Rioux points out, even some of the most vociferous writers took pains to exempt swing qua music from their attacks on *les swings*.[27] For example, Pierre Ducrocq wrote in *La Gerbe* in 1942:

> Que l'on ne s'y trompe pas. Nous ne sommes pas contre le jazz, mais contre les "swings." Le swing c'est encore du jazz . . . du jazz décadent, sans doute, mais de la musique allègre. Les "swings" sont une race aigrie, qui naît à quinze ans avec des trépidations politiques stupides, un cœur de vieille trompette bouchée qui veut singer le clairon de Déroulède.[28]

> Let there be no mistake. We are not against jazz, but against the "swings." Swing is still jazz . . . decadent jazz, no doubt, but cheerful music. The "swings" are a bitter race, who are born age fifteen with stupid political tics, and the heart of an old muted trumpet that wants to mimic Déroulède's bugle.

25. Emmanuelle Rioux, "Les Zazous: Un Phénomène socio-culturel pendant l'Occupation" (Mémoire de maîtrise, Université de Paris X-Nanterre, 1987), 165–72. On the essentially apolitical nature of the zazous, see also Régnier, *Jazz et société*, 245–51.

26. Anon., "L'Esprit parisien," *Gringoire*, 31 July 1942, cited in Rioux, "Les Zazous," 138.

27. Rioux, "Les Zazous," 89–91.

28. Pierre Ducrocq, "Swing qui peut," *La Gerbe*, 4 June 1942, cited in Rioux, "Les Zazous," 90.

Although Rioux does not explore it, the concluding allusion here to nationalist writer Paul Déroulède's well-known song, "Le Clairon" ("The Bugle," music by Émile André) seems at once to doubt the zazous' commitment to their supposed cause and to question that cause itself. (Déroulède [1846–1914] wrote his *Chants du soldat* [1872], from which this song comes, in the aftermath of defeat in the Franco-Prussian War, in which he had served. He subsequently campaigned his whole life—finally losing faith in politics and attempting a military coup d'état—for the return to France of Alsace and Lorraine, now lost once more to the Germans.)[29] Ducrocq is not hiding his pro-German sympathies above, therefore, but he expressly removes music from his field of attack. He was far from alone in doing so, even if defending jazz in order to attack *les swings* was a disingenuous move.[30]

As such, scholar Matthew F. Jordan seems to overstate the matter on both counts in the following: "While Vichy writers argued that jazz and swing represented degenerate and un-French forms of enjoyment . . . , the refrains of 'being swing' or 'being Zazou' came to symbolize resistance to the Vichy moral order. . . . As the Vichy media's hyperbolic denunciations of the jazz-loving public became more venomous and caricatured, the Zazous . . . publicly flaunt[ed] their opposition to the voices of Vichy authority."[31] Although Jordan does several times acknowledge that the issue was not the music itself but its young fans, this point gets lost in his rhetorical emphasis on jazz as the music of resistance; "anti-Zazou" slips almost unnoticed into "anti-jazz." To hear jazz exempted from attack as a benign and even enjoyable music, as it is above, contradicts some cherished beliefs.

It is not surprising that recent writers already minded to view jazz as a countercultural music would find the zazous suited to their case. After some pages recounting the departure—or internment—of African Americans and the collapse of both a community and an entertainment industry, William Shack, for example, turns to "the new vogue of anti-Nazi jazz-swing music adopted by young Parisians in defiance of the New Order."[32] As has been common, he then situates the zazous alongside the so-called Swing Kids in Germany who flouted the Nazis' partial ban on jazz (though

29. See Regina M. Sweeney, *French Cultural Politics and Music during the Great War* (Middletown, CT: Wesleyan University Press, 2001), esp. 32–39, 56–64.

30. See, for example, Lucien Rebatet, "La Musique: Jazz, hot, swing and co.," *Je suis partout*, 7 February 1942.

31. Jordan, *"Zazou dans le Métro,"* 186.

32. Shack, *Harlem in Montmartre*, 116.

the political circumstances there were very different, and political action directed against the arts often much more extreme).[33] Even writers who are relatively circumspect about the meanings of jazz during the war seem anxious to retain a notion of its resistance function. While acknowledging that, zazous aside, the French public's response to jazz is "difficult to interpret," still more to measure, Jeffrey H. Jackson nevertheless insists that they turned to jazz "as a means of asserting their independence from the German invaders."[34] Although the evidence for it is remarkably slim, the "feel good" factor of the resistance narrative is difficult to give up. Before examining more closely the realities of jazz's performance during the war, then, I want to consider the story's roots.

Delaunay's Dilemma: *De la vie et du jazz*

The person responsible above all for crafting the story of jazz in wartime France, particularly its more nuanced third form, was the critic, discographer, and wartime director of the Hot Club, Charles Delaunay (also, importantly, Django Reinhardt's manager and later his biographer). Delaunay's several accounts, written over a period of thirty years, differ in significant respects but share a notion of jazz's sudden popularity and his ambition—his duty—to cultivate and inform it: "Why was I delaying so in coming back [to occupied Paris from the 'free' South]?" he asked himself. "The public was showing unprecedented interest in jazz. They needed

33. See Michael H. Kater, *Different Drummers: Jazz in the Culture of Nazi Germany* (New York: Oxford University Press, 1992); and Horst Bergmeier and Rainer Lotz, *Hitler's Airwaves: The Inside Story of Nazi Radio Broadcasting and Propaganda Swing* (New Haven, CT: Yale University Press, 1997).

34. Jackson, *Making Jazz French*, 194. Similarly, Denis-Constant Martin, whose chapter on the war in *La France du jazz* does not fail to observe official tolerance and even deployment of jazz (e.g., on the radio) and describes at some length the surprising presence and popularity of French colonial musicians, nevertheless concludes: "Le jazz, pour les amateurs comme pour les Zazous, s'est trouvé transmué en symbole de ce qui n'entre pas dans les cadres imposés par les autorités vichyssoises ou nazies: au moralisme puritain, il oppose le rythme et la danse; aux carcans autoritaires, à la dictature, il oppose la liberté de l'improvisation; à l'Allemagne, il oppose l'Amérique; à la pureté culturelle et raciale, enfin, la joie de la rencontre et du métissage. Face à la grisaille, à la vert-de-grisaille il ouvre sur un monde irréel de spontanéité et d'intelligence, sur des rêves, des espoirs qui, n'étant pas explicitement politiques, ne sont pas directement susceptibles de répression. Tout cela, bien sûr, n'est pas nécessairement vécu de manière consciente; mais cela joue dans le jazz qui acquiert ainsi, en France, une dimension protestataire. D'autant plus quand les États-Unis entrent en guerre" ("Le Jazz résiste," 75).

me."[35] His explanations for this change in jazz's fortunes vary: from an "unconscious reaction to trauma" and "moral and intellectual oppression," to the "taste of forbidden fruit," to the paradoxical hypothesis that, with the removal of other forms of American entertainment such as film, young people realized that "jazz was really their music" after all.[36]

Where there had been a "fairly small nucleus" of "competent" jazz fans before the war, Delaunay argued, come the occupation "almost all the young people of France became infatuated with jazz within a few days. They spoke of nothing [else]. . . . French musicians became popular immediately."[37] If this sounds a little unlikely, or at least overstated, it should perhaps be understood as a symptom of unease about the prosperous nature of the wartime entertainment industry, or at any rate an acknowledgment that there was a potential for "misunderstanding." In short, Delaunay was intent on constructing the vogue for jazz—and his role in supporting it—as part of the war effort.

The Hot Club, he remembered, however, found itself in a bind: on one hand, they desired to educate jazz's new converts, who were not always too discriminating; on the other, they needed to defend the music in the eyes of the occupiers and the Vichy government. Delaunay therefore invented a "fiction" or "myth," as he later called it, capable of protecting jazz and the association.[38] He presented jazz not as black or American but as a "universal music" with different national traditions. Delaunay also emphasized its origins in New Orleans and its sources in French dance and military music, thus gaining a hold on "German propaganda and Vichy policies, which presented themselves as defenders of national French qualities."[39]

35. Charles Delaunay, *Delaunay's Dilemma: De la peinture au jazz* (Mâcon, Fr.: Éditions W, 1985), 149. A letter from Delaunay to Andrée "Daidy" Boyer, who was minding the Hot Club in his absence, shows Delaunay's genuine fears, prior to returning to Paris, of jazz's suppression (Letter of ca. August 1940, Archives Andrée Davis-Boyer, cited in Anne Legrand, *Charles Delaunay et le jazz en France dans les années 30 et 40* [Paris: Layeur, 2009], 119–20). Boyer took none of the precautions Delaunay advised (which included not only removing the Hot Club's sign and hiding the record collection but also precluding Jews from entering), and musicians used the Club widely as a rehearsal venue and meeting place in the early months of the occupation.

36. Delaunay, *Delaunay's Dilemma*, 185; Charles Delaunay, "L'Histoire du Hot-Club de France (7)," *Jazz hot*, no. 26 (October 1948): 12; Delaunay, "Jazz Abroad: France," *Jazz Forum* (UK), no. 1 (1946): 13–14 (quote on p. 13).

37. Delaunay, "Jazz Abroad," 13.

38. Delaunay, "L'Histoire du Hot-Club de France (8)," *Jazz hot*, no. 27 (November 1948): 16.

39. Delaunay, "L'Histoire (8)"; see also, Delaunay, *Delaunay's Dilemma*, 151.

In line with this principle, Delaunay urged musicians to compose their own music or at least to translate English titles as a form of subterfuge (advice that was not always followed, as discussed above).[40] And he made sure to establish the decadence of its American model compared to its ascendance in France.[41] Already internationally famous before the war, the Hot Club Quintet was central to Delaunay's case, enabling him to show that "French jazz existed, that with Django Reinhardt, for example, we possessed an incomparable artist who truly represented French grace and genius."[42] In their hands, jazz was "an intrinsically French art, proving that our musicians had not developed from America at all."[43]

While there is no reason to doubt that Delaunay's thinking was, in part, strategic, it is clear that the line he took came fairly naturally. Tournès suspects that it was closer to the French writer's own nationalist feelings after his country's military collapse than he was prepared to admit after the war.[44] In fact, Delaunay's view—that jazz is, or could be, French—seems to have predated the occupation altogether: in a letter that had already been published stateside in the *DownBeat* magazine of May 1, 1940, under the title "Delaunay in Trenches, Writes 'Jazz Not American,'" he had taken a universalist approach to jazz and denounced American commercialism. In an early statement of what would become an influential argument on both sides of the Atlantic, Delaunay maintained: "While [jazz] was born in the United States . . . all its originality and promise were first discovered by . . . the French artistic *Avant-garde*. . . . And this discovery took

40. Delaunay, "Jazz Abroad," 13; Delaunay, "L'Histoire (8)"; Delaunay, *Delaunay's Dilemma*, 151.

41. Charles Delaunay, unidentified article [ca. 1941], cited in Mike Zwerin, *La Tristesse de Saint Louis: Jazz under the Nazis* (London: Quartet Books, 1985; repr., New York: Beech Tree Books and William Morrow, 1987), 149–51 (this article cannot be from *Jazz hot*, as Zwerin states, since publication ceased during the war). As if to make my point about the ideological function of wartime jazz, a later edition of Zwerin's book was retitled *Swing under the Nazis: Jazz as a Metaphor for Freedom* (New York: Cooper Square Press, 2000).

42. Delaunay, "L'Histoire (8)."

43. Delaunay, "Jazz Abroad," 13.

44. Tournès, "Le Jazz," 328. However, Tournès also considers how, later in the war, Delaunay used his movement between zones in the course of Hot Club activities to pursue resistance work, for which he briefly landed in jail, and notes the assistance the Hot Club provided to musicians who had been interned. The best account of Delaunay's Resistance activities—which were perfectly genuine—is found in Legrand, "Résistance active," in *Charles Delaunay*, 136–46. The subsequent chapter, "Résistance musicale," 147–54, however, falls into the trap of accepting too easily as fact postwar reconstructions of jazz's implied meaning.

place *more than 10 years before* . . . enterprising [American] businessmen . . . appeared on the scene to exploit this new art."[45] Denouncing the result of a recent poll, which had prized "commercial" musicians above "authentic" ones, he wondered if "jazz [was] condemned to die with the very persons who created it?"[46] The answer was no, but only because other countries, notably France, would continue jazz's mission.

Delaunay had presented these ideas at much greater length in his 1939 book *De la vie et du jazz*, albeit in a style historian Matthew F. Jordan has aptly characterized as a "bumper-sticker existentialism."[47] This curious tome comprises a number of separately dated sections (July 1935 to January 1938), which nevertheless proceed in a more or less linear fashion. *De la vie et du jazz* is notably absent from most discussions of Delaunay's career, perhaps because writers have trouble positioning it in his oeuvre, and particularly in the context of his more practical activities, as discographer, promoter, record producer, and sketch artist.[48] It thus warrants some attention here.

De la vie et du jazz begins with a series of aphorisms, for example "VIVRE pour VIVRE et non VIVRE pour MOURIR" ("LIVE to LIVE, don't LIVE to DIE"), complete with the typographical eccentricities (in terms of text direction, placement, size, etc.) of French poetic practice dating back at least to the symbolists.[49] It may call to mind in particular the artistic man-

45. Charles Delaunay, "Delaunay in Trenches, Writes 'Jazz Not American,'" *DownBeat*, 1 May 1940, 6, 19 (quote on p. 6, italics original) [also abridged reprint as "From Somewhere in France," in Robert Walser, ed., *Keeping Time: Readings in Jazz History* (New York: Oxford University Press, 1999), 129–32].

46. Delaunay, "Delaunay in Trenches," 19. At the risk of repeating himself, Delaunay returned to his theme later on: "For it must be admitted that 10 years before America interested itself in jazz there existed an entire literature and a wide European public which passionately followed the appearance of new records . . . and studied the style of this new Art." The paragraph in which this sentence appears is cut from the reprint in *Keeping Time*, with the effect that Delaunay's "universalist" sentiments in this passage are not interrupted by jingoism.

47. Matthew F. Jordan, "Jazz Changes: A History of French Discourse on Jazz from Ragtime to Be-Bop" (PhD diss., Claremont Graduate School, 1998), 327. Sadly, the phrase was axed from Jordan's book, *Le Jazz*.

48. Even Anne Legrand in her book about the jazz critic alludes to *De la vie et du jazz* only once, in the context of a discussion between Delaunay and his mother about the book's publication (Legrand, *Charles Delaunay*, 117).

49. Charles Delaunay, *De la vie et du jazz* (Paris: Hot Jazz, 1939), 13. Although it bears a copyright date of 1939, the book did not in fact appear until 1941, as the back page explains: "Remis à l'imprimerie NIDOT, le vingt six Juillet mille neuf cent trente neuf. Sorti des presses le treize Mai mille neuf cent quarante et un."

ifestoes of futurists and Dadaists, which were doubtless familiar enough reading in the heady artistic circles in which Delaunay was brought up (as the son of painters Robert and Sonia). Yet his book is not so much a manifesto as it is a quasi-philosophical treatise, caught between fatalism and utopianism, but ultimately revealing an understandable anxiety about what the future holds.

Delaunay's argument is stark: in so-called civilized societies, reason has gained the upper hand on emotions, which are the true source of life. Capitalism is at once the symptom and the cause of this imbalance, since "man owes all of his problems to money."[50] In one of the more elaborate images, the huge *t* of *argent* (money) is fashioned as a dagger stabbing downward to form also the first letter of *tue* (kills).[51] For Delaunay, the world is in a state of decadence and convention, out of touch with life and nature. Art, similarly, has become divorced from its public, and no effort to reunite them has been successful:

Le "naturisme," "nudisme," "futurisme," "surréalisme," "néo-classicisme," etc.... ne sont qu'efforts maladifs, outrés, malsains; appels de névrosés, de malades, de moribonds qui, dans leurs cauchemars, ont entrevu cette "nature," ce "futur," cette "réalité" ..., la Vérité.

Ils ont compris qu'ils se mouraient, et ont voulu retrouver artificiellement le paradis.[52]

"Naturism," "nudism," "futurism," "surrealism," "neoclassicism," etc. .... are only sickly, exaggerated, unhealthy efforts; calls of neurotic, sick, dying people who, in their nightmares, glimpsed this "nature," this "future," this "reality" ..., the Truth.

They understood that they were dying, and wanted to re-create paradise artificially.

Art, although dying, is kept alive by conservatories and academies, which seek to teach skills logically and analytically: "Mais l'AMOUR est exclu des manuels" (LOVE is excluded from textbooks).[53] Real masters forget the rules and cultivate their own styles.

In all quotations from Delaunay's book, simple typographical emphases (uppercase, bold type, and italics) are retained, but further irregularities of font, size, and placement cannot be preserved.

50. Delaunay, *De la vie et du jazz*, 23.

51. Ibid., 25.

52. Ibid., 38 (ellipses original).

53. Ibid., 46.

Here in particular, Delaunay reveals the influence of the neo-Thomist theologian and philosopher Jacques Maritain. In his widely read *Art and Scholastique*, Maritain had denounced the model of the art academy as fundamentally misconceived, believing that artistic talents were a gift that could not be taught systematically, only informally nurtured. Delaunay quotes him in a footnote (as Hugues Panassié had several times in *Le Jazz hot*):

Plaquez la connaissance théorique accomplie de toutes les règles d'un Art sur un énergique lauréat qui travaille quinze heures par jour, mais en qui 'l'habitus' ne germe pas, vous n'en ferez jamais un artiste, et il demeurera toujours infiniment plus éloigné de l'art que l'enfant ou le sauvage pourvu d'un simple don naturel.

Stick the consummate theoretical knowledge of all the rules of art upon an industrious graduate working fifteen hours a day but without a shoot of habit sprouting in him, and you will never make him an artist; he will always remain infinitely farther removed from art than the child or the savage with a simple natural gift.[54]

For Delaunay, as for Maritain, the appropriate model is at once more workmanlike and more spiritual: the medieval artisan who crafts his art in direct contact with a public that perceives its beauty immediately, not upon intellectual reflection.

In this sense, Delaunay's argument as a whole may be directly or indirectly dependent on Maritain, whose ideas circulated widely. The jazz critic's claim that "L'HOMME N'EST GRAND QUE PAR *LE CŒUR*, seul *désintéressé*, et NON PAR *LA RAISON*, spéculatrice" (MAN IS GREAT ONLY IN *HEART*, all that is *disinterested*, NOT IN *REASON*, which speculates), fundamental to his argument, strongly suggests Maritain's preference, following Aquinas and Aristotle, for practical over speculative orders of logic.[55] Putting this in musical terms, Delaunay maintains in *De la vie et du jazz* that the last significant composers are Debussy, Stravinsky, and Satie. Since them, none has been capable of reasserting classical order and balance in music, in which melody is not sacrificed on the altar of compositional procedure.

Into this dispiriting picture of the world and of culture, jazz appears—a little over halfway through the book—as a ray of light:

54. Jacques Maritain, *Art et scholastique* (1920), cited in Delaunay, *De la vie et du jazz*, 46 [translated by J. P. Scanlan, in *Art and Scholasticism, with Other Essays* (London: Sheed and Ward, 1949), 33]. On Maritain and Panassié, see chap. 2.

55. Delaunay, *De la vie et du jazz*, 21.

Au sein même de la décomposition, de la décadence d'une culture millénaire, au début du XXe siècle, en un point du Globe où se sont rencontrées quatre cultures tout à fait différentes; *américaine, africaine, latine* (franco-espagnole) *et anglo-saxonne*: **La Nouvelle-Orléans**, Louisiana, U.S.A., carrefour où trois âges de la civilisation humaine se sont trouvés réunis; l'AGE PRIMITIF (civilisation négro-africaine), la CULTURE LATINE et ANGLO-SAXONNE, et les éléments d'une CIVILISATION NOUVELLE, reposant sur les prodigieux développements de la mécanique, a vu NAÎTRE LE **JAZZ**.

Le jazz tient de la race noire *primitive*: jeunesse, force et enthousiasme; de la *Culture* millénaire du Vieux-Continent il a assimilé la technique musicale et les moyens d'expression; il vit déjà au rythme d'un AGE NOUVEAU.[56]

In the very middle of the decomposition, the decadence of an age-old culture, at the beginning of the twentieth century, at a point on the globe where four altogether different cultures met; [*Native*] *American, African, Latin* (Franco-Spanish) *and Anglo-Saxon*: **New Orleans**, Louisiana, U.S.A., a crossroads where three ages of human civilization came together; the PRIMITIVE AGE (Negro-African civilization), the LATIN and ANGLO-SAXON CULTURE, and elements of a NEW CIVILIZATION, resting on tremendous developments of the machine, saw **JAZZ** BORN.

Jazz gets from the *primitive* black race: youth, strength and enthusiasm; from the age-old *Culture* of the Old Continent it's learned musical technique and means of expression; it lives already in the rhythm of a NEW AGE.

Jazz is direct and unreflective, Delaunay argues, as musicians create it in the moment; it bridges the divide between composer and interpreter and bypasses the associated paraphernalia such as notated parts and rehearsals. Those who have lost touch with life resent its "brutality" and "crudeness," but Delaunay proposes jazz as "an example of life in a murderous time." By now, he argues, jazz is heard the world over, whether on disc, on radio, or performed live. However, the music is already in decline in America, as new players, emphasizing technique, fail to live up to the old-timers. As in the *DownBeat* article discussed above, Delaunay places his hopes for jazz in its international branches, as the music becomes meaningful in different ways. Yet the book's ominous conclusion, dated January 1938, reads: "Jazz . . . is a vast worldwide movement which has imposed despite everything an international means of expression. . . . How-

56. Ibid., 53–55. A footnote on p. 54 confirms that Delaunay is referring to *Native* Americans.

ever, this dreamscape of a world beating the same rhythm is disappearing under dark clouds."[57]

At the very least, then, Delaunay's subsequent statements that his wartime position on jazz was entirely dictated by the conditions of the occupation were short of complete disclosure. While his universalist statements in *De la vie et du jazz* and elsewhere may be understandable, perhaps admirable, dating from a period of incipient global conflict, his denunciation of American commercialism in favor of old European artisanship was in line with a marked vein of anti-Americanism and anticapitalism—even antimodernity—in French jazz criticism of the interwar period. It is possible, therefore, that jazz's retrospective construction as a force of resistance resulted less from its suppression in any direct sense than from the pervasive threats to the better world Delaunay understood it to represent. Before the war, he already feared that the States had betrayed the utopian possibility jazz held out, and that betrayal would appear ever deeper as the extent of a collapse of civilization in Europe became manifest. As I continue, I want to consider how these ideas played out, both in the sphere of Delaunay's Hot Club activities and in the writings of other critics, notably André Cœuroy and Hugues Panassié (both of whom published books on jazz during the occupation). If French jazz continued unabated—indeed, with new energy and confidence—during the war, what symbolic relevance did it assume?

Jazz Goes On: Hot Club de France

Despite the philosophical pretensions of his book, Delaunay turned quickly to practical matters once the occupation set in. Hugues Panassié, though still officially director of the Hot Club, spent the period installed in his country residence in Montauban (near Toulouse in the South of France) and had little input on day-to-day activities. If the new regime offered certain possibilities to promote the music, however, Delaunay would not fail to take advantage of them. Among his primary activities was the organization of concerts, beginning six months into the occupation with a Festival de jazz français at the Salle Gaveau (December 19, 1940). The program booklet featured an editorial in which Delaunay expounded the possibilities for jazz of this new dawn, evoking the "real *spiritual values*" (italics original) of this time, in which "the music of today, that of tomorrow, affirms its virility, its strength, its beauty and its character."[58] French

---

57. Ibid., 95.

58. Charles Delaunay, "Musique de jazz," in program for Festival de jazz français, Salle Gaveau, Paris, December 1940, cited in Régnier, *Jazz et société*, 189.

jazz, Delaunay claimed elsewhere in the program, was inextricably linked to the Hot Club de France, which for ten years had "affirmed the international class of French musicians that is now universally recognized."[59] The concert sold out so quickly that it was repeated a couple of days later.

The three ensembles featured in these first concerts, or variations on them, would be guiding lights of jazz during the war. They were accordionist Gus Viseur et son Orchestre, "un grand orchestre de vedettes de jazz français" (whose core elements would make up Le Jazz de Paris, led by Alix Combelle), and a new formulation of the famous Hot Club Quintet. A good idea of the music of these first concerts can be gleaned from recordings made for the Swing label in the surrounding days. This company, which Delaunay and Panassié had begun in the 1930s, would record almost three hundred records during the occupation, three times as many as they had before the war.[60] (In 1941, the Hot Club de France also released an anthology of classic jazz recordings in order to make up for the lack of American imports.[61])

Most striking of all among these recordings is a track presumably modeled on the concert's finale: an oversized band with Reinhardt and the Quintet at its core play "Festival Swing." There had been large ensembles in France for more than a decade by now, of course, but they were modeled on Paul Whiteman's band (via the English bandleader Jack Hylton's). Few before the war would have been able to tackle a riff-based head arrangement such as this requiring more than a few of the band to take solos. While neither the tune nor the performance give much indication that this is not a band from the United States, Delaunay introduces the players one by one before proudly prefacing the tutti, "Voici le jazz français." Reinhardt, whose playing is so distinctive, partially excepted, the brash and brassy result is singularly lacking in French grace.[62] Ironically, then, an increase in nationalist rhetoric during the war accompanied players ever more able to pass for American.

While the patriotism may feel stylistically out of place, however, the recording was an achievement: a considerable number of improvising French musicians had united for common purpose as their country faced up to occupation. Certainly, the relationship between the individual and the nation, innovation and tradition, was very much on the mind of Mau-

59. H.-P. Chadel [Charles Delaunay], "Festival de jazz français," in program for Festival de jazz français, cited in Legrand, Charles Delaunay, 126.

60. Régnier, Jazz et société, 111.

61. Ibid., 80.

62. Benjamin Givan transcribes and analyzes Reinhardt's solo in The Music of Django Reinhardt (Ann Arbor: University of Michigan Press, 2010), 113–14, 208–9n.

rice Bex while reviewing "Festival Swing" in *L'Information musicale*. The critic's response in this primary music publication in wartime Paris warrants quoting at some length, since it gives a good impression of public discourse about jazz:

> Le genre Jazz, importé en Europe entre les deux guerres et qui passa aux yeux des réfractaires pour un phénomène essentiellement éphémère, pour une mode fugace, s'avère résistant à l'épreuve. Ni les années, ni les bouleversements accumulés n'ont eu de prise sur lui et s'il a évolué, s'il s'est divisé entre différentes chapelles, les unes férues d'obédience puriste, ou les autres entachées d'hérésie, sa vitalité demeure.
>
> Des équipes se sont même constituées chez nous qui, imbues de la doctrine ésotérique, se flattent d'y adapter leur imagination de civilisés de vieille souche sans compromettre leur orthodoxie.
>
> *Festival Swing* (SWX 91) justifie amplement cette prétention. Alix Combelle, qui l'organisa, l'a conçu comme une présentation dont le cérémonial fort simple consiste à donner à chaque exécutant, tour à tour, l'occasion de montrer ses talents. L'instrumentiste désigné se lance, improvise quelques mesures, cède la place au voisin et rentre dans l'ensemble. Ainsi étiquetés, échantillonnés l'un après l'autre, ayant acquis le privilège de sortir de l'anonymat, les instrumentistes rentrent dans la masse et tirent la conclusion de la fête dans un *tutti* multicolore, synthèse sans mystère succédant à une analyse sans complication.[63]

Jazz, which was imported to Europe between the two wars and which passed for an essentially ephemeral phenomenon, for a fleeting trend, in the eyes of the old guard [des réfractaires], has stood the test of time. Neither the years passed nor the upheavals undergone have got the better of it and, if it has evolved, if it has divided into different sects, some keen on purist obedience, others marred by heresy, its vitality remains.

Some outfits have even formed among us that, imbued with the esoteric doctrine, pride themselves on adapting their deep-rooted culture's imagination to it without compromising their orthodoxy.

Festival Swing (SWX 91) amply justifies this pretension. Alix Combelle, who organized it, conceived it as a presentation whose very simple ritual consists of giving each player, in turn, the chance to show his talents. The instrumentalist named steps up, improvises a few bars, cedes his place to a neighbor and returns to the ensemble. Recognized in this way, sampled the one after the other, the instrumentalists, having acquired the privi-

---

63. Maurice Bex, "Disques," *L'Information musicale*, nos. 21–22 (11 and 18 April 1941): 495.

lege of coming out of anonymity, return to the group and reach the conclusion of the festival in a multicolored *tutti*, a synthesis without mystery
following an analysis without complication.

So, it was not in the end the hold-out *réfractaires* (clergy who refused
to swear allegiance to state over church after the Revolution) who were
defending the national cause, but the young musicians who could express
their identities in the language of jazz. Far from behaving improperly, the
musicians were, Bex suggests, demonstrating their commitment to their
country. Was their performance—independent spirited yet community
minded—a model for personal conduct in occupied France?

Whatever the explanation, Delaunay was not mistaken in his postwar
accounts about the music's popularity, even if it represented for audiences
no more than a temporary distraction. The two Hot Club concerts of December 1940 were followed by several at the Salle Gaveau in January 1941,
featuring Alix Combelle's Jazz de Paris. Delaunay described the ensemble
as "the first French orchestra for authentic jazz, an orchestra of musicians
and not a group of musical clowns": at once a recognition of their significance and a dig at show bands such as Ray Ventura's and now Raymond
Legrand's.[64] Finally, in February, Django Reinhardt and the Quintette du
Hot Club de France took the stage at the much larger Salle Pleyel: the first
of many concerts they would play during the war, alongside regular gigs.

As discussed above, Reinhardt and the Quintet were central to Delaunay's claim not simply of French competence in jazz but of true French
inspiration. Since the first Hot Club concert in December, Delaunay had
boasted how:

Après avoir vaincu le ridicule préjugé qui consiste à croire à la seule va-
leur des musiciens étrangers, le Hot Club de France révéla au public de
véritables talents français par d'incessants concerts, émissions radiopho-
niques, enregistrements et manifestations de toutes sortes. . . .

Ce n'est pas sans orgueil qu'il considère le célèbre Quintette de Django
Reinhardt, son enfant, qui fit briller si glorieusement à travers le monde
entier le nom tant envié du Hot Club de France.[65]

64. Charles Delaunay, "Jazz de Paris," in program for Jazz de Paris concert, Salle
Gaveau, January 1941, cited in Legrand, *Charles Delaunay*, 128. Straight after the
war, however, Delaunay admitted: "Their records are in the tradition of the white
American orchestras and obviously have no interest for fans" (Delaunay, "Jazz
Abroad," 14).

65. H.-P. Chadel [Delaunay], "Festival de jazz français," cited in Legrand, *Charles
Delaunay*, 126.

Having overcome the absurd prejudice which consists of believing that only foreign musicians have value, the Hot Club of France revealed true French talents to the public through incessant concerts, radio broadcasts, recordings, and events of all kinds. . . .

It is not without pride that it looks upon the famous Quintet of Django Reinhardt, its baby, which made the much-coveted name of the Hot Club of France shine so brightly across the whole world.

But this was not at all the band known from before the war, with its unique, all-string sound (three guitars, violin, and bass). The original Quintet had found themselves in Britain when the war broke out, and violinist Stéphane Grappelli had chosen not to return. Back in France, Reinhardt had assembled around him not only different personnel but also some different instruments: clarinet (Hubert Rostaing or Alix Combelle, or occasionally both), two guitars (Reinhardt and, most often, his brother Joseph), bass (Tony Rovira), and drums (Pierre Fouad; fig. 4.3).

As was the case with the bigger band discussed above, a paradox is immediately apparent listening to the new recordings: the reformed Hot Club Quintet—so important to the argument for a national jazz—sounds much closer to an American swing group than did its pioneer before the war. While today the Quintet's recordings from the 1930s are well-known for their peculiarly French jazz, a wartime tune such as "Swing 41," albeit it a Reinhardt original, has little to suggest it were not composed and performed in the United States. Even as famous a number as Reinhardt's "Nuages," his first huge commercial success, owes more than a little to swing-era classics such as "Begin the Beguine," which the ensemble also played. Although "Nuages" is typically seen as a characteristic, even archetypal, product of the war years, it was only when words describing a woman bidding farewell to her lover were added that it took on a wartime connotation, and then hardly an exclusive one (fig. 4.4). (A number of Reinhardt's pieces circulated as popular songs in this way during the occupation.)

The less distinctive sound of the reconstituted band did nothing to halt Reinhardt's success, however. February 1941 brought the Gala Django Reinhardt at the Salle Pleyel, featuring him in a triple role as "composer, conductor, virtuoso-guitarist."[66] In the first half of the concert, a still larger ensemble played arrangements of Reinhardt's pieces (expanded forces and, later, expanded forms becoming a fascination of his during the war). Despite his new role, the descriptions in the press were famil-

66. Advertisement and listing for Gala Django Reinhardt, *L'Information musicale*, no. 10 (24 January 1941): 259–60.

FIGURE 4.3. Quintette du Hot Club de France, 1940. On this occasion, Hubert Rostaing (clarinet), André Jourdan (drums), Emmanuel Soudieux (bass), and Ninine Vées (guitar) accompany Django Reinhardt.

iar. "A sympathetic figure this boy, ignorant, M. Delaunay tells us, of the rules of his art" but blessed with "an amazing musical sense"; his "very restrained gestures" as a conductor contrasted with his "nervous virtuosity" as a guitarist, reminiscent "not of master Spanish guitarists but of Gypsy violinists." In the second half of the concert, the musical forces having pared down, the new Quintet played a series of "tiny concerto[s] for guitar and clarinet"—a kind of "swing chamber music" that this writer found "particularly successful."[67]

And so it went: jazz concerts were held roughly twice as often during the war as in the preceding years, Tournès calculates, and in bigger venues.[68] Before long, Reinhardt and others were also regular features in the

67. Henri Petit, "Django Reinhardt (2 février)," *L'Information musicale*, no. 14 (21 February 1941): 346.
68. Tournès, "Le Jazz," 315.

FIGURE 4.4. Sheet music for Django Reinhardt's "Nuages," as sung by Lucienne Delyle to words added by Jacques Larue, 1942.

music halls, which of necessity reduced their spectacle during the war, to the benefit of straightforward musical acts. Reviews suggest little need to hide jazz's roots, at least at this early stage, while at the same time boasting a distinctive "native" idiom. When Jazz de Paris played the ABC music hall, for example, Jean Laurent praised "an excellent program that Alix Combelle directs in a style at the same time swing and classical."[69] In "New Tiger Rag," the ensemble's trumpeter didn't match Louis Armstrong, whose high register had "a fullness of sound that no trumpeter in the world has succeeded in imitating." Nevertheless, "without copying anyone, Jazz de Paris played this classic jazz number with a color and a spontaneity that perfectly fitted the drive of the melodic line." Laurent continued: "A French swing orchestra, that used to seem as unbelievable to me as a witty line in a song by [comic actor] Fernandel"—a gibe which

69. Jean Laurent, "Le Music-Hall: À Paris dans chaque faubourg," *Les Nouveaux Temps*, 25 March 1941, in R. Supp. 1125, "Le Music-Hall: Variétés et chansons," Rondel.

the critic liked so much that he used it again a few months later in a review of the Hot Club Quintet at the same theatre:

Le quintette du Hot Club de France, avec le célèbre guitariste Django Reinhardt, ce Gitan qui a parcouru toutes les routes de France dans une roulotte, est aujourd'hui presque aussi classique que n'importe quel orchestre de musique de chambre. Rien d'agressif dans leur interprétation, mais un instinct musical infaillible, un sens de l'improvisation, spontanée ou non, qui semble jouer à cache-cache avec la ligne mélodique. . . . Un orchestre français swing . . .[70]

The Quintet of the Hot Club de France, with the famous guitarist Django Reinhardt, this Gypsy who has traveled all the roads of France in a caravan, is today almost as classic as no matter which chamber orchestra. There is nothing aggressive in their performance, but an infallible musical instinct, a sense of improvisation, spontaneous or not, which seems to play hide and seek with the melody. . . . A French swing band . . .

Even Gustave Fréjaville, scarcely a fan of jazz on stage, enjoyed "a repertoire from which various compositions stand out by their delightful soft and subtle effects." Aware of his limitations and of the sharp tongues of the jazz critics, however, he was "cautious about misidentifying the spells that enchant the ear and the imagination on hearing 'Stockholm,' 'Oiseaux des îles,' 'Nuages,' 'Féerie,' performed by the composer and his companions."[71]

In view of these commentaries (which were by no means unusual), Matthew F. Jordan's recent claim that Delaunay's *De la vie et du jazz* was "one of the last publicly pro-jazz writings in France until 1942" again seems rather puzzling.[72] Not that there weren't hostile reviews of jazz, or even the Hot Club Quintet, during the war, of course. Author Georges Gabory in *L'Information musicale*, for example, was "not at all attuned" to the Quintet, which he found "deadly boring, dull, terribly snobby [snobard]."[73] But

70. Jean Laurent, "Le Music-Hall: Un Tour d'horizon," *Les Nouveaux Temps*, 15 November 1941, in R. Supp. 1125, "Le Music-Hall: Variétés et chansons," Rondel.

71. Gustave Fréjaville, "Variétés et chansons: Tours de chant, variétés et orchestres, à l'A.B.C.," *Comœdia*, 8 November 1941, in R. Supp. 1125, "Le Music-Hall: Variétés et chansons," Rondel.

72. Jordan, "*Zazou dans le Métro*," 188.

73. Georges Gabory, "Critique des music-halls: A.B.C.," *L'Information musicale*, no. 47 (21 November 1941): 371.

expressing such views was hardly de rigueur. In fact, Gabory's opinion was sufficiently out of line with the consensus that an editorial footnote all but disowned it, promising different views of Reinhardt to come. Without a doubt, the Hot Club Quintet had a higher profile during the war than in the preceding decade; this conclusion may be extended to jazz as a whole. In a talk in May 1941, Charles Delaunay made the case that "the music of today evinces [explique] perhaps the birth of a new order and the painful separation from a decaying past."[74] Was he simply an uncommonly skilled media operator, as he subsequently wanted it to be believed, or are there other reasons that the war might have offered shelter for jazz in France?

A French Tradition? Nationalizing Jazz

The coexistence of positive discussions of "French jazz" in the press on the one hand, and an uncompromisingly American style in performance on the other calls for explanation. It may be tempting to locate resistance precisely in the gap between the American music and the nationalist rhetoric: to recognize, as Delaunay would have it, an attempt to hide jazz in full view, and to see in the reviews quoted above so many signs of his success in convincing the gullible media that jazz was (or could be) truly French. I do not want to rule out the possibility that, for some players and listeners, the music held such a rebellious charge. Nevertheless, more straightforward explanations for jazz's success during the war should not be ignored. In the absence of Americans, French musicians could no longer be outdone as purveyors of swing, nor did they have to play differently from the visitors in order to justify their presence on stage. Moreover, diligent research over the last two decades has revealed that people not only listened to more jazz during the war; they also attended the theatre and the cinema more often and read many more books.[75] There was time to pass, and the French were eager for distraction—undermining any claim for the special significance of jazz's success.

It must also be borne in mind that the occupying forces were typically prominent members of the audience, in the Hot Club concerts, at the music hall, and particularly in the cabarets. As Régnier has noted, *Pariser Zeitung* detailed the city's delights for German officers without skimping on jazz, notably "der weltberuehmte Django Reinhardt und das Quintett

74. Salle Gaveau, 13 May 1941, cited in Régnier, *Jazz et société*, 189.

75. See, for example, Rioux, *La Vie culturelle sous Vichy*, particularly François Garçon, "Ce curieux âge d'or des cinéastes français," 293–313, and Serge Added, "L'Euphorie théâtrale dans Paris occupé," 315–50.

des Franzoesischen Hot-Club" (the world-famous Django Reinhardt and the Quintet of the French Hot Club).[76] Thus when William Shack writes that the first Hot Club concerts were "a protest against the German boot, trampling the Parisian culture of jazz," that statement at least needs to be qualified by the fact that some Germans trampled no farther than their seats in the auditorium.[77]

Germans were notably absent from Charles Delaunay's later accounts of the war.[78] In the two versions published soon afterward, however, he stated quite frankly that they participated in the Hot Club, and that some of them were quite knowledgeable;[79] "their complicity," as he put it, had its rewards in American records received by way of Sweden or Switzerland.[80] Delaunay gives special mention to Luftwaffe officer Dietrich Schulz-Köhn, a fan and collector he knew prior to the war, whose information helped him finish the fourth edition of his *Hot Discographie* in 1943.[81] While the necessity to demonstrate jazz's (and Delaunay's) resistance credentials was apparent even straight after the conflict, memories of the Germans (good and bad) were still sufficiently present that they could not be written out of the story altogether: members of the Hot Club "acted with unquestionable deference and consideration towards the occupying authorities," Delaunay wrote, "among whom, let it be said, certain individuals really liked jazz and were amazed at the extraordinary quality of French musicians."[82] By the time of Delaunay's more familiar later writings, however, the resistancialist myth, as Rousso calls it, had become so engrained that the German acceptance of, and even participation in, the Hot Club activities could be more or less ignored. These were complexities of the wartime period people no longer wanted to hear.

There are other examples of Delaunay's selective memory with regard to his dealings with the authorities. For example, he recounts in some detail his efforts to have "La Demi-Heure du Hot Club de France" broadcast on Poste Parisien when he was mobilized during the Phony War (the period before German hostilities had begun).[83] But he omits to mention that

76. Advertisement for Kabarett "Le Nid," *Pariser Zeitung*, 6 February 1942, cited in Régnier, *Jazz et société*, 88, and reproduced in appendix 7, n.p.

77. Shack, *Harlem in Montmartre*, 117.

78. Charles Delaunay, "Le Jazz en France (1932–1944)," *Jazz hot*, no. 250 (May 1969): 26–29; Delaunay, *Delaunay's Dilemma*.

79. Delaunay, "Jazz Abroad"; Delaunay, "L'Histoire (8)."

80. Delaunay, "Jazz Abroad," 14.

81. Charles Delaunay, *Hot Discographie* (Paris: Hot Club de France, 1943).

82. Delaunay, "Jazz Abroad," 13.

83. Delaunay, "L'Histoire (7)."

he continued to prepare scripts and select records for a similar program on Radio Paris, after the station had been taken over by the Germans.[84] Both Hugues Panassié and Delaunay also devised broadcasts about American jazz musicians for Radiodiffusion Nationale (a station run from the "free zone" though broadcast also from Paris), in which neither performers nor all of the titles were disguised.[85]

Both jazz and, more specifically, the Hot Club made substantial inroads into the provinces during the war, too. There were regular tours by artists and an expansion of clubs across both free and occupied zones (from just five chapters in 1939 to twenty-nine in 1944).[86] Delaunay continued the prewar practice of organizing competitions for amateur bands from around the country. The war, however, brought new rules, such as an insistence that all composers were French (no American tunes, even disguised) and signed declarations that no member was Jewish—a position that Régnier suggests may have been less a precaution than a result of Delaunay's own prejudice (despite the fact his mother was Jewish).[87]

Nor did the discourse Delaunay later claimed he had created to defend French jazz during the war require great powers of invention. As discussed in chapter 2, large bands such as Ray Ventura's had taken an explicitly nationalist line from the early 1930s, and writers had provided lively testimony to the intrinsic Frenchness of jazz beginning even earlier. Some had located jazz's roots in "an old stock of French love song," nurtured by colonists and their slaves in Louisiana.[88] Others looked to the etymology of *jazz*, finding its roots in the old French word *jaser*, meaning "to chatter," "to babble," "to gossip,"[89] or asked whether the importance of the saxophone didn't prove that "jazz is a French invention!"[90]

Evidence of the continued currency of this discourse is found in col-

84. Régnier, *Jazz et société*, 55–56.

85. Ibid., 72–75.

86. Tournès, "Le Jazz," 320.

87. Régnier, *Jazz et société*, 128–31.

88. Maurice Delage, "La Musique de jazz," *Revue Pleyel*, no. 31 (April 1926): 18–20 (quote on p. 19). See also, for example, Fortunat Strowski, "Petites Hypothèses: Et si le jazz était français? Nous aurions apporté aux nègres les mélodies, et eux leur auraient donné le rythme," *Paris-Midi*, 20 March 1928, in Ro 585, "Le Jazz et les spectacles nègres," doc. 50, Rondel.

89. See, for example, Irving Schwerké, "Le Jazz est mort! Vive le jazz!," *Le Guide du concert*, 12 and 19 March 1926, reprinted in *Kings Jazz and David (Jazz et David, rois)* [bilingual] (Paris: Presses Modernes, 1927), 13–30. Schwerké was actually an American journalist living in Paris.

90. Adolphe Sax, "Aimez-vous le jazz?," *Le Soir*, 16 June 1926, in Ro 585, "Le Jazz," doc. 24. Sax was the Belgian inventor's son.

laborationist critic André Cœuroy's 1942 *Histoire générale du jazz: Strette, hot, swing*. As his subtitle reveals, nationalization required a linguistic intervention: *Jazz* itself, *swing*, and *hot*, Cœuroy could admit, but he preferred *strette* in place of *straight*, *brec* (break), and *blouze* (blues).[91] Terminology was just the beginning. Cœuroy thought Panassié had erred in *Le Jazz hot* (1934) in asserting jazz's independence from European music; rather it was merely located on a "peninsula" of Europe, with "no border, no customs post separating it." Hence the raison d'être of Cœuroy's book could be boldly stated:

> On a longtemps cru que le jazz était spécifiquement nègre. La thèse présente est tout à l'opposé. Le jazz n'a été noir que par hasard. Les principaux éléments qui le composent, sont venus des blancs, et des blancs d'Europe. Par son histoire, par sa matière, le jazz est nôtre; son avenir est dans nos mains.[92]

> It was long thought that jazz was specifically Negro. The present thesis is precisely the opposite. Jazz was black merely by chance. Its principal elements came from whites, and whites from Europe. By its history and by its substance, jazz is ours; its future is in our hands.

This reorientation of jazz history is revealed even in the chronology that Cœuroy appended to his *Histoire générale du jazz*. It begins with the arrival in the New World of "Dutch Pilgrims" (1620) and "Puritans from Scotland" (1628) and includes French possession and sale of the Louisiana territories (1682–1803). Yet it makes no mention of indentured slaves, or indeed of the English.[93] In the main text, the psalms (as represented in seventeenth-century sources) reveal the origins of jazz's melodies, and the practice of "lining out" (teaching them by rote) lies behind African American call-and-response, rather than the African retention that is commonly supposed. Cœuroy also cites an improbable law of 1675 that limited the accompaniment of psalms to the drum, trumpet, and Jew's

91. André Cœuroy, *Histoire générale du jazz: Strette, hot, swing* (Paris: Denoël, 1942), 34.

92. Ibid., 24. Cœuroy's position was particularly ironic given his collaboration on ethnomusicologist André Schaeffner's pioneering *Le Jazz* (1926). As I noted in chapter 2, however, the two men do not ever seem to have agreed: Schaeffner's concern was with African roots; Cœuroy's with white bands such as Paul Whiteman's.

93. Cœuroy, *Histoire générale du jazz*, 223.

harp, and strictly forbade the violin as the devil's instrument. Here he locates both the "embryo of the jazz band" and the idea that the violin was not a proper jazz instrument. And in case his readers missed the point: "[Jazz's] origins are not in a deliberate choice of the Negro: it was imposed on him by the white man, according to directives from Europe."[94] Thus jazz was not only European in origin, Cœuroy insisted, it was also religious.

Ludovic Tournès has presented Cœuroy's *Histoire* as a sui generis product of the war, written by a collaborationist critic trying to "annex jazz to the Nazi cultural project whose objective is the emergence of a new European culture under German influence."[95] As with Delaunay's supposedly strategic argument, however, Cœuroy did not have to go much further, if any, than the discourse of the twenties and thirties in order to make his point. Indeed, his book was opportunistic in more than a political sense: whole sections are, not only based on, but more or less cut and pasted from earlier publications by other authors. As such, Cœuroy's *Histoire* could even be considered an, admittedly partisan, survey of the prewar field.

Some of Cœuroy's choices are predictable, in view of his thesis above. For example, in the "Elements of Jazz" chapter, he quotes at length from Arthur Hoerée's writings of the mid-1920s, which argued that jazz was not black but rather "a Negro interpretation of an art of white stock [de race blanche] and of European origin."[96] Sometimes acknowledging his debt, other times not, Cœuroy succeeds in the difficult task of making Hoerée's argument blunter. He maintains, for example, that an "accent déplacé" (displaced/shifted accent) Hoerée had identified in a Scottish folk song "is the hidden source of all jazz music. The Negro received, developed, exaggerated it—without inventing it."[97] Cœuroy goes on to pro-

94. Ibid., 38–40 (quote on p. 38). This fabricated law, which is widely cited in early writings on American music, originated in Rev. Samuel Peter's *A General History of Connecticut by a Gentleman of the Province* (1781). It was exposed by Percy Scholes in "The Truth about the New England Puritans and Music," *Musical Quarterly* 19 (1933): 1–17. Cœuroy doubtless derived it from Esther Singleton, "États-Unis d'Amérique," *Encyclopédie de la musique et dictionnaire du conservatoire*, part 1, *Histoire de la musique*, ed. Albert Lavignac and Lionel de la Laurencie, vol. 5, *Russie, Pologne, Finlande, Scandinavie, . . .* (Paris: Librairie Delagrave, 1922), 3245–332 (esp. p. 3281), accessed 18 September 2013, http://gallica.bnf.fr/ark:/12148/bpt6k1237270/f770, which he appropriates widely in this section.

95. Tournès, "Le Jazz," 329; Tournès, *New Orleans sur Seine*, 85.

96. Arthur Hoerée, "Le Jazz," *La Revue musicale* 8/11 (1 October 1927): 213–41 (quote on p. 221), cited in Cœuroy, *Histoire générale du jazz*, 52.

97. Cœuroy, *Histoire générale du jazz*, 53.

pose Hoerée's examples of "oppositions rhythmiques" (momentary poly-rhythms) in classical music as precedents of familiar characteristics in jazz, although the author himself had described them as existing in an "embryonic state."[98] Similarly, Hoerée's detailed (if obfuscatory) harmonic explanations boil down, in Cœuroy's hands, to claims that "harmonically, jazz doesn't teach us anything new. It modulates as in Europe, because it is of Europe." And of its form, that "there's nothing as European and historical."[99] "Il n'y a rien de nègre" ("It has nothing Negro") is the book's refrain.

Paradoxically, however, other sources on which Cœuroy draws greatly are in complete disagreement with his case. Notable among such writers is André Schaeffner whose 1926 book, *Le Jazz*, Cœuroy obviously felt particularly free to appropriate given that he had appeared as its co-author (although he in fact only contributed a small part); the survey of respondents with which *Le Jazz* concludes is reprinted in *Histoire générale du jazz*. Indeed, interleaved between the sections on borrowings from European rhythm and harmony derived from Hoérée are a number of pages on "Rythme noir" taken more or less straight from Schaeffner, to whom Hoérée was originally responding. The disjunction is apparent, but juxtaposing such different ideas may give the impression of rounded expertise; Cœuroy seems to sift evidence before arriving at his foregone conclusion. Thus, for example, lengthy sections on African practices and their manifestations are followed by one on "Le frein européen" (the European brake) in which he explains that "Negro jazz owes it to Europe that it did not lose itself in the inextricable extravagance of the primeval forest" (*Histoire générale du jazz*, 72). Yet the bibliography for this chapter, made of accounts by explorers in Africa and the Americas beginning in the seventeenth century, is lifted directly from Schaeffner's book, and the sources listed against other chapters draw on it extensively.

Having alternated between Schaeffner's and Hoerée's opposed arguments, Cœuroy brings his chapter on the "Elements of Jazz" to a close thus:

On peut alors conclure que le jazz a trouvé son unité en cristallisant, dans le moule européen de la variation ou du concerto: une technique harmonique *européenne* (de Liszt à Ravel en passant par Debussy), une mélodie issue du *choral protestant*, une rythmique mi-*blanche*-mi-noire, et un usage spécifique des instruments. Le jazz n'est pas un art nègre: il est,

98. Hoerée, "Le Jazz," 227.
99. Cœuroy, *Histoire générale du jazz*, 58–59. Subsequent citations in text.

comme dit Hoérée [*sic*], en marge de cet art. Ceux qui détestent l'art nègre
peuvent donc ne point détester le jazz. Il est aux blancs comme aux noirs.
Si les noirs en ont d'abord tiré le meilleur usage, aux blancs de prendre
leur revanche. Elle est déjà commencée. (75, italics original)

One can thus conclude that jazz has found its unity by crystallizing, in
the European mold of variations or the concerto: a *European* harmonic
technique (from Liszt to Ravel passing through Debussy), a melody from
Protestant hymns, a rhythm that is half-*white*-half-black, and a particular
usage of instruments. Jazz is not a Negro art: it is, as Hoérée [*sic*] says, on
the margins of this art. Those who hate Negro art can hardly thus hate
jazz. It belongs to whites as to blacks. If blacks at first made the best use
of it, it is for whites to get even. This has already started.

Cœuroy's view of jazz history is therefore of the progressive reclama-
tion of Europe's birthright. While he is broadly in favor of "hot jazz,"
he maintains that it was anticipated in Europe by everything from the
24 Violins of King Louis XIII to the improvising actors of *Commedia
dell'Arte* (81). Moreover, he prefers the tamer Chicago style to the rawer
New Orleans original. Familiar racial stereotypes, of the rational white
gaining supremacy over the emotional black, are rife in this comparison.
Cœuroy recognizes as well the attempts of both Paul Whiteman and Jack
Hylton to "escape the Afro-American specter," but he thinks that Whiteman tried too hard to be "symphonic" and Hylton became too showy
(176). Even as he was determined to prove jazz white, then, Cœuroy,
sought to establish its authenticity against the ravages of pretension or
commercialism.

As they were for Delaunay, Reinhardt and the Quintet are central to
Cœuroy's case. Before the war, he argues, the Quintet had "shocked fans
who saw but a distant connection to the Negro music of Harlem. It was
true. But they presented as a criticism what should have been understood
as a deliverance. Today we are less intransigent" (149). Cœuroy concludes
that the Quintet brought to jazz a "European spirit," which represents a
"victory for whites" (193). Reinhardt's playing in particular is "hot" but
not "nègre"—"a model of what could be, parallel to black hot, a white
hot suited to the European sensibility" (192). New Orleans and Chicago
styles are over, he thinks; now is the time of the "style Paris" (198). As I've
shown, however, most everything in Cœuroy's book was actually cribbed
from prewar writings, suggesting that the discourse had not changed as
substantially as some have thought. This dream of a French jazz, whether
by birth or adoption, had been around for a long time: the war may have

furthered this aspiration but it certainly did not create it.[100] How would the Hot Club respond?

Common Ground? National Regeneration

Cœuroy's *Histoire générale du jazz* must have left Hot Club critics in a quandary, since in some ways it merely amplified their own recent rhetoric. Linguistically at least, they might even have gone further: at one point the Hot Club had proposed a competition to find French words for "Hot Jazz" and "Swing-Music."[101] Nevertheless, Delaunay's review was frank and dismissive: "The author does not know his subject. It is just a superficial mass without unity. There are many contradictions and errors. Perhaps to try and remain in step with the current political state of affairs, the author adopted a thesis which he pushed to the absurd. He tries to prove that everything worthwhile in jazz is European, he portrays Negroes as clowns, he ridicules black music. This is really shocking."[102]

Hugues Panassié felt even less constrained in his response. Having honed his critical muscle enforcing a strict separation of what was "hot" from what was not in his 1934 book *Le Jazz hot*, Panassié's definition of "real jazz" had narrowed still further after a trip to the United States in 1938–1939;[103] the occupation did nothing to change this. In two wartime volumes, he argued more forcibly than ever that jazz was not a product of American genius but specifically of black Americans.[104] Panassié's review of Cœuroy's book in *Le Figaro* affirmed once more that jazz was "neither European nor American; it's a music created by blacks." Cœuroy's argument about jazz's roots in European folk song and hymnody was, for Panassié, like using the pretext that Racine drew his subjects from Euripides

100. Philippe Gumplowicz situates Cœuroy's and Panassié's writings in the context of their prewar publications and politics in "Musicographes réactionnaires des années 1930," *Le Mouvement social*, no. 208 (2004): 91–124.

101. *Bulletin du Hot Club de France* [henceforth, *BHCF*], no. 1 [December 1940?], cited in Régnier, *Jazz et société*, 189.

102. Charles Delaunay, review of *Histoire générale du jazz: Strette, hot, swing*, by André Cœuroy, unidentified periodical [ca. 1942], cited in Zwerin, *La Tristesse de Saint Louis*, 151 (this review cannot be from *Jazz hot*, as Zwerin states, since publication ceased during the war).

103. See Hugues Panassié, *Le Jazz hot* (Paris: Corrêa, 1934); and Panassié, *Cinq mois à New York (octobre 1938—février 1939)* (Paris: Corrêa, 1947).

104. Hugues Panassié, *The Real Jazz*, trans. Anne Sorelle Williams (New York: Smith and Durrell, 1942); Panassié, *La Musique de jazz et le swing* (Paris: Corrêa, 1943). The former book did not appear in French until after the war, as *La Véritable Musique de jazz* (Paris: Robert Laffont, 1946).

to argue that the French author represented Greek literature: "You see the absurdity of this proposition. The subject matters little, whether in literature, painting or music, everything is in *the manner* of treating it" (italics original). Rearticulating his stance on jazz's unconventional instrumental and vocal usage, on swing (which term, he complained, had been "ridiculously misappropriated"), and about the primacy of performance over score, Panassié explained that

> les jugements de M. Cœuroy sur le jazz sont malencontreusement soumis à des conceptions qui, parfaitement légitimes pour la musique classique, sont sans valeur lorsqu'il s'agit de cette musique des noirs, musique qui ne prétend nullement supplanter les autres, ni même s'opposer à elles mais qui, fraîche et savoureuse, comme tout art créé par des primitifs, mérite d'être aimée pour ses vertus propres au lieu d'être condamnée ou méconnue sous prétexte qu'elle n'a pas les vertus, toutes différentes, de la musique classique ou moderne européenne.[105]

> Mr. Cœuroy's judgments about jazz are inappropriately acquiescent to concepts that, perfectly legitimate for classical music, are useless when it concerns this music of blacks, music that in no way proposes to supplant the others, nor even to conflict with them but which, fresh and delectable, like all art made by primitives, merits to be liked for its own virtues instead of being condemned or neglected under the pretext that it does not have the, quite different, virtues of classical or modern European music.

Such was his vexation that Panassié added an appendix to his own book *La Musique de jazz et le swing* (1943) in which he sought to undermine Cœuroy's critical voice by revealing his plagiarism of earlier texts (aligning like passages in columns). While Panassié's list was far from complete, however, he ran the risk of confirming that Cœuroy's book represented a critical consensus, even if it did not attend well to scholarly etiquette.

In some ways, Panassié's position was more akin to Cœuroy's than might be anticipated, and not only because the latter had appropriated his writings. On the role of African Americans, of course, the two authors could never have agreed. But both were patriotic Frenchmen, even if they saw their duty during the war differently. Where "Anglo-Saxons," as Panassié had long called gentile Americans and Brits, had no special facility for jazz, he had always believed that the French were the most talented among Europeans. Now he went further, suggesting that they were more

105. Hugues Panassié, "Situation du jazz dans la musique," *Le Figaro*, 11 August 1942.

naturally suited for the music than white Americans.[106] Panassié's explanation exceeded even the culturalist reasoning of Cœuroy and others,
maintaining that the open-minded French had mixed not just their music but their blood more with African Americans in the southern States
than had the Anglo-Saxons: African Americans were, at root, French![107]
He also compared their orally based culture to that of the peasantry, revealing a nostalgia for rural roots that matched Cœuroy's and—as Ludovic Tournès has pointed out—the Vichy authorities'. The same could
be said of his increasing religious references (Panassié was a devout, and
conservative, Catholic): *La Musique de jazz et le swing* is cast as a dialogue
between the layman ("le profane") and the swing fan ("le swingfane"),
one that Tournès suggests was modeled on catechism.[108]

In his invaluable recent account of wartime jazz, Gérard Régnier defends Panassié against Tournès's charge that his ideas were allied to Vichy's. He acknowledges Panassié's extreme right-swing sympathies but
insists: "As far as his relations with the occupier are concerned, nothing
can be held against him, no more in his conduct than in his writings."[109]
Régnier seems, though, to confuse ideas and politics, in as much as he
defends the jazz critic against a charge of collaboration that Tournès had
not in fact made. Tournès remarks upon Panassié's ideological compat-
ibilities and rhetorical consistencies with notions propagated by the Vichy authorities, but in the context of 1940s France, these superficial similarities are not in themselves surprising. Such discourse about traditional
French values and culture may have peaked during the war, but it did not
begin with it, nor was it limited to circles loyal to the Vichy government.
As historian Julian Jackson explains, "People who made different choices
[during the war] often did so in defence of similar values" and "antago-
nists might share as many assumptions with their enemies as with those

106. Panassié, *La Musique de jazz et le swing*, 20.

107. Ibid., 22. I am not, of course, doubting the continued influence of French
culture in New Orleans, or the extent of "racial" mixing, merely highlighting Panassié's insistence on the superior potency of the French over the Anglo-Saxons.

108. Tournès, "Le Jazz," 324–26.

109. Régnier, *Jazz et société*, 100. In a rare misstep, Régnier also cites Boris Vian
as evidence that Panassié's structuring of *La Musique de jazz et le swing* as a dialogue
suggests not religious models (and thus the National Revolution), as Tournès had
suggested, but the standard mode of teaching within the Hot Club. This both
misses the extent to which Panassié had, precisely, cultivated this infantiliza-
tion of jazz fans and, more oddly, the fact that Vian is not merely exhibiting this
style but parodying it (Boris Vian, "Le Vrai Jazz et le public des cabarets," *Style de
Paris* [April 1947], reprinted in Vian, *Œuvres*, vol. 8, *Jazz 3*, ed. Claude Rameil [Paris:
Fayard, 2001], 274–75, cited in Régnier, *Jazz et société*, 96).

on their own side."[110] The striking fact about Panassié's book is not the moralistic tone but the subject matter—and this only because the story of jazz's resistance to wartime authority subsequently became pervasive. Celebrating jazz's resistance or denouncing its collaboration is not only simplistic but anachronistic in the context of a period when politics were not so much polarized as they were all multicolored hues.

One way this may be observed is in the convergence of writers with little else in common around ideas of national regeneration. This is a notion that, in the broader political sphere, could signify overt collaboration as much as active resistance but typically implied one of the many shades between: it was more important, for many, that France recover than under what regime she do so.[111] Witness, for example, a slightly earlier book by André Cœuroy, whose collaborationist credentials were of course impeccable. *La Musique et le peuple en France* was published in 1941, the year before Cœuroy's history of jazz, in a series of *Études françaises*. These studies of French national identity aimed to "respond to the need for truth that our country feels after the most complete and humiliating defeat in history";[112] other authors' volumes included one on definitions of France and another on literary depictions of the Gallic peasant. Traditional folk song had disappeared all over France, Cœuroy complained, where an individualistic spirit had deposed the "collective soul" that music both arose from and addressed:[113] France had lost the war because she could not sing. The solution lay in education, both in schools and in the wider community. Choirs had to be formed, religious music fostered, urban and rural workers alike reunited with their music, which would restore discipline:[114] folk song's revival was crucial to "national reconstruction."[115]

Jazz is mentioned only once in *La Musique et le peuple*, but that mention is important. In Germany, Cœuroy argues, music education is still effective because creativity and improvisation have remained key. Among familiar examples (organ improvisations, cadenzas, etc.) jazz too, he contends, is a "living force" that could show the way for the renewal of French

110. Julian Jackson, *France: The Dark Years, 1940–1944* (Oxford: Oxford University Press, 2001), 4.

111. For detailed accounts of this mode of thinking, its evolution, its politics, and its contradictions, see Andrew Shennan, *Rethinking France: Plans for Renewal, 1940–1946* (Oxford: Clarendon Press, 1989); and Debbie Lackerstein, *National Regeneration in Vichy France: Ideas and Policies, 1930–1944* (Farnham, UK: Ashgate, 2012).

112. André Cœuroy, *La Musique et le peuple en France* (Paris: Stock, 1941), 6.

113. Ibid., 61.

114. Ibid., 129–30.

115. Ibid., 9.

folk song (la chanson populaire).[116] This is a jarring moment, in such a reactionary context, given the oppositional function this music is often believed to have served. Yet Cœuroy's argument is not, of course, out of line with Delaunay's *De la vie et du jazz*, which predated the conflict altogether, as I have observed. Both authors thought jazz would restore life to the lackadaisical and decadent French. Panassié, too, located jazz's roots among the people and, in the process, squared the circle between African American tradition and French jazz.

Once more, Django Reinhardt was central to Panassié's theory: "It is interesting to note that Django, one of the rare white musicians comparable to the Negroes, belongs to a race which has remained very primitive, for in truth the Gypsies' lives and customs are closer to those of the Negroes than those of the whites."[117] In this interpretation, then, it was not Reinhardt's French civilization but precisely his lack of it that warranted celebration. Where Cœuroy followed some prewar critics in seeing the Quintet as a model of "white hot" that might supersede its black counterpart, Panassié dismissed such an idea (as he had before the war) and was concerned only with how the French might aspire to black genius. But the authors came together, and also met with official Vichy discourse, in their emphasis on the music's roots in folk culture and among humble rural people. This is the sense in which Tournès notes Panassié's compatibility with Vichy ideology, not to denounce his collaboration, as Régnier seems to suppose.

Most revealing, in fact, is not how Panassié's writings changed to accommodate the climate of the occupation, but how similar they could remain. His denunciations of British and American musicians, for example, certainly take on a different inflection in the context of war, but to read them in such light may be to do him a disservice: he was still bemoaning the commercialism that had afflicted jazz in his eyes before the war; the world had changed around him. Now the venom Panassié had previously reserved for Anglo-Saxon purveyors of straight jazz, and their ill-informed audience, was extended to the zazous:

Le snobisme de ces jeunes écervelés dits "zazous zazous" et "swing" a achevé de compliquer le malentendu qui pèse sur la musique de jazz dans notre pays. À vrai dire, ce fléau n'est pas nouveau. Il a sévi tout d'abord en Amérique. Il y a quelques années. Là-bas les zazous s'appelaient "jitterbugs." . . . Comme nos zazous, ils prétendaient aimer une musique à

116. Ibid., 135.
117. Panassié, *The Real Jazz*, 143–44.

laquelle ils ne comprenaient rien et s'extasiaient devant les mauvais orchestras de jazz bien plus que devant les bons.[118]

The snobbery of these young featherbrains called "zazous zazous" and "swing" has managed to complicate the misunderstanding that weighs on jazz music in our country. To tell the truth, this scourge is not new. It raged first in America. That was a few years ago. Over there the zazous were called "jitterbugs." . . . Like our zazous, they claimed to love a music about which they knew nothing, and got much more excited in front of bad jazz orchestras than good ones.

Panassié would happily ban the "pseudo-jazz" that the zazous most enjoyed. But to attack the music of Reinhardt or Grappelli, Armstrong or Ellington, on account of a noisy minority would be like refusing to acknowledge Debussy because a few "snobs" as well as musicians liked him. Doubtless the zazous' counterculturalism appealed little to Panassié, a Royalist opposed even to universal suffrage, but this was actually an old battle for the cause of "real jazz," which had retained its primitive authenticity.

A final, unlikely consequence of this quasi-folkloric reading of jazz—sponsored in different ways by all the writers discussed above—was that it became possible to imagine other groups expressing their unique characteristics in the "international" language of jazz. Hence the altogether unexpected spectacle of the Hot Club de France sponsoring a Festival de musique nègre featuring the so-called Hot Club Colonial at the Salle Pleyel in December 1943. Colonial chapters of the Hot Club had been set up before the war, notably in North Africa. But this particular title was merely a ruse to give musicians established in Paris a degree of legitimacy (and no doubt for the association to benefit from doing so).

So the story goes, the Cameroonian drummer and bandleader Fredy Jumbo came to Paris after demobilization keen to make his living playing music. Finding French club owners reticent to hire him, he secured the support of members of the occupying forces impressed by his German language skills (Cameroon had passed into French hands only in the Treaty of Versailles and German was still widely spoken). With a Nazi attestation, he and his band found a regular gig at La Cigale in Montmartre

118. Hugues Panassié, "Êtes-vous sûr de savoir ce qu'est le jazz?," *Radio nationale*, 11–17 October 1942, reprinted in Christian Senn, *Hugues Panassié: Fondateur, président du Hot Club de France* (Lutry, Switz.: privately published, 1995), 99 (where it is incorrectly marked 1944).

where Delaunay heard them and invited them to make some recordings. He, however, ejected Jumbo himself and replaced him with Harry Cooper (an African American married to a French woman and naturalized French).[119] Régnier writes:

> Que ces musiciens noirs, se soient produits sans problème pendant l'Occupation, à Paris . . . et dans plusieurs villes de France . . . dans le cadre d'un Festival de musique nègre, demeure encore pour beaucoup l'une des énigmes de l'histoire du jazz sous l'Occupation. C'est oublier qu'avec eux la référence n'est pas américaine. Il s'agit cette fois de musiciens de couleur français, originaires des Antilles, colonie française qui, avec son folklore propre, représente un retour à la tradition. La biguine et autres musiques de danse du folklore antillais se situent tout à fait dans la ligne culturelle de la politique de rénovation nationale en phase avec l'idéologie de Vichy.[120]

> That these black musicians appeared without problems during the Occupation in Paris . . . and in several towns in France . . . in the context of a Festival of Negro Music still remains for many one of the enigmas of the history of jazz under the Occupation. This is to forget that with them the reference is not American. This time it concerns French musicians of color, from the Caribbean, a French colony which, with its own folklore, represents a return to tradition. The beguine and other dance musics of Caribbean folklore are quite in line with the cultural politics of national renewal consistent with the ideology of Vichy.

This curious episode from wartime Paris has gifted a fascinating picture of Luftwaffe officer and jazz fan Dietrich Schulz-Köhn, one that has sometimes been reproduced in the literature with his own gloss: "Here I am, in uniform, with a Gypsy, four Negroes, and a Jew" (fig. 4.5).[121]

Looking Back: Jazz and Liberation

The image of a Nazi officer posing with visible minorities in the cause of wartime jazz risks to be a reductive end to a chapter that has been keen to nuance accounts of the music's fortunes during the occupation. In its

---

119. Régnier, *Jazz et société*, 62–63, based in part on information provided to him by trombonist Albert Lirvat.

120. Ibid., 188.

121. Zwerin, *La Tristesse de Saint Louis*, facing page 54.

FIGURE 4.5. *Left to right:* Django Reinhardt, Dietrich Schulz-Köhn, and musicians in Paris during the occupation (courtesy of the Institute of Jazz Studies, Graz, Austria).

horror and its glory, the photo forces the viewer to confront the topic in a peculiarly visceral way, but it should not encourage hasty conclusions that trivialize wartime suffering. Nevertheless, it is surely time to recognize popular notions of jazz's suppression and resistance potential as, above all, a postwar construction. Jordan, for example, makes a bold claim that the war changed perceptions to such a degree that no French subsequently dared sound antijazz sentiments for fear of being labeled a collaborationist: "Embraced as a part of a shared cultural heritage, jazz now floated above the question of national origin and became congruous with postwar notions of Frenchness and representative of a 'true' France grounded in the wartime experience of resistance."[122]

The immediate situation at the liberation, as throughout the war, was much more complex and paradoxical, however. Indeed, Jordan himself goes on to cite the young critic and musician André Hodeir's *Le Jazz, cet inconnu* (1945) in an attack on "the abhorrent and ridiculous 'zazous,' whose futility and bad taste are evident": language that, had it been

122. Matthew F. Jordan, "Assimilation, Absence, and the Liberation of French Discourse on Jazz," in *Le Jazz*, 233–46 (quote on p. 234).

written during the occupation in a collaborationist paper might, for Jordan, have signaled antijazz discourse.[123] While still a Paris Conservatoire student during the war, Hodeir had played jazz violin under the name Claude Laurence, in André Ekyan's Sextet and in recordings with Django Reinhardt's brother Joseph. In his book, Hodeir notes how the campaign against the zazous, while mostly lighthearted, became spiteful and that "politics weren't always absent" from it.[124] Personally, he found the zazous "inoffensive in their stupidity," but he thought it "important to be harsh toward them," because "they constituted the most harmful, the most unsympathetic [incompréhensif] public for jazz," pushing the musicians toward exhibitionist playing:

C'est pourquoi nous insisterons spécialement sur cette vérité élémentaire: *la musique de Jazz n'est nullement solidaire des "petits swings."* Les véritables amateurs de Jazz sont presque toujours des gens intelligents, sensibles, cultivés (dans le bon sens du mot). Qu'une bande de jeunes snobs parfaitement grotesques ait cru devoir manifester en faveur du "swing" (du faux-swing, le plus souvent), ne doit nullement influencer notre attitude vis-à-vis de la musique de Jazz elle-même.[125]

This is why we insist especially on this basic truth: *jazz music has no connection to these "little swings."* Real jazz fans are almost always intelligent, sensitive people, cultured (in the good sense of the word). That a group of perfectly grotesque young snobs have made a show of being in favor of "swing" (false swing, most often), should in no way affect our attitude to jazz music itself.

By this point, post-liberation, attacks on the zazous by jazz critics could no longer of course have been made to protect the music, as a matter of political expediency. Rather, this attitude signaled a defense of Hodeir's own taste and his cultural (and musicianly) capital. Delaunay took a similar line, complaining that the first signs of jazz from America were not good: "American jazz has followed the tendencies it was showing be-

123. André Hodeir, *Le Jazz, cet inconnu* (Lyon: Éditions France-Empire, 1945), 9. Although the book was obviously drafted during the occupation, the preface in which this line appears is dated December 1944, four months after the liberation; Hodeir refers to his "révision soigneuse à la lumière des quelques nouveaux éléments d'appréciation nous étant parvenus des États-Unis depuis septembre dernier" (11).

124. Ibid., 50.

125. Ibid., 51–52, italics original.

fore the war, that's to say commercialism and exhibitionism." The most popular orchestras (Harry James's, Glenn Miller's, etc.) were cultivating the spectacular and the "symphonic," he argued. They were imitated in this even by formerly "hot" bands such as Jimmie Lunceford's and Count Basie's, resulting in a "contamination" of swing and a loss of jazz's "purity, inspiration and vitality."[126] During the war, it seems, it was France not the United States that had kept the flame of true jazz alive.

Meanwhile—and more ironically still—several French commentators noted the sudden reduction of jazz on the radio against its prevalence during the war. "Now we've been liberated of the constraints of the occupier," one wrote, "Radiodiffusion Française is coming progressively to apply the pan-German cultural plan."[127] Another observed archly: "We will finally be free of jazz, this hateful product of German genius."[128] Gérard Régnier, in his recent history, concludes quite rightly that "the image of an enormous surge of jazz in France liberated by the Americans is as misleading as that of the lead weight falling on jazz with the entry of Germans into Paris."[129]

As I have shown in this chapter, the varied attitudes toward jazz during the war were not, for the most part, imposed from outside but grew quite naturally from interwar French discourses. In place of the simple break in French culture, jazz culture in particular, suggested by each of the three takes on the story with which I began, more useful may be historian Pascal Ory's understanding of Vichy as a period of both "rupture and continuity."[130] I do not mean to suggest by this that the closed nationalism of Vichy was, in any sense, an inevitable outcome of the prewar years (a position I contested in chap. 1). On the contrary, I am interested in how a range of possibilities were retained into the occupation, particularly perhaps in popular culture: though subject to some degree of censorship, this was not dependent on state coffers. In the case of jazz at least, Vichy cultural policy might be considered less as a set of rigid precepts than of discursive possibilities, through which familiar debates could be reengaged. What I *am* suggesting, albeit somewhat tentatively, is that, for a short while in the early 1940s, it was possible for French at all points of the political spectrum to believe both that the future of jazz was theirs,

126. Charles Delaunay, "Jazz 45," *Jazz hot*, new series, no. 1 (n.d. [1945]): 4.

127. Georges Brisson, "La Radio française contre le jazz," *BHCF*, no. 3 (n.d. [1945]): 4, 14 (quote on p. 14).

128. Jean Michaux, "La Radio," *BHCF*, no. 2 (n.d. [1945]): 14.

129. Régnier, *Jazz et société*, 262.

130. Pascal Ory, "La Politique culturelle de Vichy: Ruptures et continuités," in Rioux, *La Vie culturelle sous Vichy*, 225–39.

DJANGO REINHARDT
vedette des disques "Swing"

FIGURE 4.6. Django Reinhardt, star of Swing Records.

and, more troublingly, that this would be the music of a new France in a new Europe. Far from the music of resistance in any real sense, then, jazz it seems could be the music of national regeneration, or even—Vichy's catch term—National Revolution.[131]

Where does this all leave Django Reinhardt (fig. 4.6), so often appropriated in these discourses and a popular figure, on stage and on record, throughout the occupation? A force of resistance? An active collaborator? A hapless bystander? A conservative estimate of the number interned as "nomads" in France during the war is 6,000–6,500, of whom a minority were transferred to extermination camps in Germany, but many more died in the harsh conditions.[132] Reinhardt's fame was probably his pro-

131. A word of caution may be in order here: I am not arguing that such views were necessarily widespread, or that propagating jazz was a deliberate policy of the Vichy authorities (although, as in Nazi Germany, some use was made of the music on radio). Rather, I am showing how it was possible, for writers and promoters who were so inclined, to defend and even advance jazz's cause with little interference—and to do so within the terms of Vichy cultural discourse and of prewar jazz criticism.

132. Marie-Christine Hubert, "The Internment of Gypsies in France," in *The Gypsies during the Second World War*, vol. 2, *In the Shadow of the Swastika*, ed. Donald Kenrick (Hatfield, UK: University of Hertfordshire Press), 59–88 (esp. pp. 76, 85–87). Donald Kenrick and Grattan Puxon give a figure of thirty thousand Roma

tection. Opportunistic he certainly was, playing for French, German, and finally American audiences with equanimity; in the early years of the war, he was living the high life in a luxurious apartment on the Champs-Élysées.[133] Nevertheless, Reinhardt seems largely to have avoided playing on Nazi-run Radio Paris and successfully to have evaded a trip to Germany mandated by the Nazis.[134] At the liberation, he busied himself performing for and with American military personnel, including members of Glenn Miller's Army Air Force Band (whose leader was missing in action) and the Army Transport Command Band under Sgt. Jack Platt, with broadcasts going out on the the the Armed Forces Network. Not so long afterward, Reinhardt embarked on a US tour (fig. 4.7).

If the story of jazz in wartime France is not as wholesome as some have wanted to believe, in other words, the answer is not to relocate the music on the collaborationist "side"—as if the politics of wartime France were as black and white as some of its writers would make the history of jazz. Without a doubt, the majority of the occupied French lived their lives during the conflict in what Philippe Burrin has called "the vast grey area that produces the dominant shade in any picture of those dark years."[135] Several recent historians have, in their different ways, attempted better to understand this zone. Particularly useful may be a term Burrin coins in his *Living with Defeat* for describing the activities of everyday French (bakers, barkeepers) who were neither truly resisters nor active collaborators: "accommodation." Without especial willingness, or especial acrimony, people got by as well as they could, doing what they did. Reinhardt may have played under bright lights, but he lived in the grey zone, "accommodating" the regime, as, perhaps more surprisingly, it chose to "accommodate" him.

Ethical dilemmas, as well as historical ones, are picked up in Woody Allen's depiction of Django's double, Emmet Ray, to whom I want briefly to return. In a scene late in *Sweet and Lowdown*, Ray looks up his old girlfriend, Hattie, whom he had left, without a word, sometime earlier. Ray's selfishness and duplicity we well know, but Hattie, who is mute, is "good-hearted—a genuinely sweet person," in Ray's own words; in the topsy-turvy world of the film, she is the moral grounding. Nevertheless, one

internees, a majority of whom perished (*The Destiny of Europe's Gypsies* [New York: Basic Books, 1972], 103).

133. Delaunay, *Django Reinhardt*, 111.

134. Delaunay, *Django Reinhardt: Souvenirs*, 50; Dregni, *Gypsy Legend*, 182.

135. Philippe Burrin, *Living with Defeat: France under the German Occupation, 1940–1944*, trans. Janet Lloyd (London: Arnold, 1996), 3.

FIGURE 4.7. Portrait of Django Reinhardt, Aquarium, New York, NY, ca. November 1946 (William P. Gottlieb Collection, Library of Congress).

movie critic has raised an intriguing possibility: that Hattie may be lying when she indicates to Ray—for her own, or perhaps his, protection—that she is now married, with kids.[136] In a film whose deliberate blurring of fact and fiction can be read as an ironic comment on jazz historiography, this makes still more explicit Hattie's obvious function as a metaphor for the silence of history.

I do not wish to overburden Allen's charming comedy and know there is nothing less amusing than a joke explained. Nevertheless, the more common experience of history is not, of course, that it is mute, but on the contrary, how very noisy it is: as soon as familiar narratives are put aside,

136. Jonathan Romney, "Sweet and Lowdown," *Sight and Sound* 10/7 (July 2000): 55–56.

voices compete to make themselves heard over the hubbub of others, and that is how it should be. It is only when a certain version of history, particularly a history as fraught and complex as that of occupation France, comes to silence others that there is cause to worry. So the next time, in another rerun of Ken Burns's *Jazz*, French filmmaker Bertrand Tavernier (b. 1941) recounts how jazz in occupied France was "a way . . . of fighting against conformism . . . the spirit of Vichy . . . the German atmosphere" and, of course, "a symbol of the resistance,"[137] just think of it as one more "Emmet Ray story": as unstable and precarious as he was, aboard his crescent moon.

137. Ken Burns, dir., *Jazz* (Burbank, CA: PBS DVD, 2001), episode 7, "Dedicated to Chaos," track 49.

5 Remembrance of Jazz Past
Sidney Bechet in France

On a Negro Orchestra: Ansermet Gets Animated

Among the many tributes to the New Orleans reedman Sidney Bechet, following his death in Paris in 1959, the least likely may be the most telling: *Tintin*, "the magazine for the young, aged 7 to 77," made the great man its cover story (fig. 5.1).[1] While the iconic tufty-haired boy and his dog peer down from atop the weekly magazine, a rosy-cheeked Bechet leads a cartoon band inspired to the point of ecstasy or even possession. In the foreground, a rack of gleaming white teeth and a bright red tongue set off a familiar "Satchmo" pose. But, standing farther back, Bechet is relaxed and composed; unlike his band mates', his eyes remain open, addressing the reader benevolently. Is his right hand gesturing to an unseen musician? Or does it serve merely to draw us in, to a music whose secrets he will kindly share with us (as he had with so many in France)? Soon, we anticipate, those large, podgy hands will raise the soprano saxophone to his lips, and the jazzman will once more channel through the instrument the sounds of New Orleans.

Inside, cartoon panels of Bechet's life extend across four pages (two blazingly multicolored, like the front cover; the others simpler, in black, white, and red). Like Bechet's autobiography (which I discuss below), the comic begins by journeying back "a long way," to the plantations of the Old South. "After a day's hard labor," the first caption explains, "the blacks got together and sang" white hymns, in their own peculiar fashion. Later, in New Orleans, "all the blacks were crazy about music," none more so than the family Bechet (fig. 5.2). Even Maman joins in their homemade band on her washboard, before the children run off to hear a funeral parade ("Chic! Un enterrement! Un enterrement!!"). Seeing his older brother Leonard charm a sick man with music, Sidney makes away secretly with his clarinet; next, the young boy surprises everyone when he is able to fill the renowned George Baquet's shoes. (Leonard's miracle

1. "Sidney Bechet," *Tintin: Le Journal des jeunes de 7 à 77 ans* 11/580 (3 December 1959): 1, 4–7.

FIGURE 5.1. Sidney Bechet as cover story of a comic magazine (*Tintin*, 3 December 1959).

cure—and Baquet's mysteriously white skin—apart, these are versions of the truth.)

Bechet's next few years elided in the cartoon, he is soon off to Europe, with the Southern Syncopated Orchestra under Will Marion Cook. In London, classical musicians take an interest, among them Swiss conductor

FIGURE 5.2. *Above*, Bechet's childhood as imagined by *Tintin* (3 December 1959).

FIGURE 5.3. *Left*, Ernest Ansermet's review of Bechet's performance in London, 1919 (*Tintin*, 3 December 1959).

Ernest Ansermet (whose pointed beard could not yet have been as white as depicted here). One "longhair" says to another, "Have you seen what Ansermet wrote about this black musician?: 'He's an extraordinary virtuoso. He shocks by the richness of invention, force of accent, and daring of novelty'" (fig. 5.3).[2] Yet fame and fortune are not forthcoming: despite

2. "Sidney Bechet," 7. Truncated but perfectly correct in the comic strip, this famous passage reads in full: "Il y a au Southern Syncopated Orchestra un extraordinaire virtuose clarinettiste qui est, paraît-il, le premier de sa race à avoir *composé sur la clarinette* des *blues* d'une forme achevée. J'en ai entendu deux qu'il avait longuement élaborés, puis joués à ses compagnons pour qu'ils en puissent faire l'accompagnement. Extrêmement différents, ils étaient aussi admirables l'un que l'autre pour la richesse d'invention, la force d'accent, la hardiesse dans la

FIGURE 5.4. Bechet's triumph at the Paris Jazz Festival, 1949 (*Tintin*, 3 December 1959).

some short-lived success, Bechet is famously reduced during the Depression to running a Harlem tailor's shop. Not until his return to Europe—to France—after the war, the cartoon suggests, is his true worth again recognized and celebrated (fig. 5.4). In this final chapter of *Paris Blues*, I want to reexamine the tenor of Bechet's pictorial obituary, with its emphasis not only on youthful epiphanies but also on international recognition. Prizing apart some interlocking myths, I hope to suggest a more complex and contested, self-conscious, and, finally, more musical account of Bechet's assimilation to France, as well as that of jazz all told.

It is not a surprise to find Ansermet's well-known review recalled here, even in this least scholarly of sources. In London with the Ballets Russes, the conductor heard Cook's large band several times and quizzed the musicians about their playing; he subsequently wrote a lengthy article, "Sur un orchestre nègre" (1919), for the Swiss journal *La Revue romande*. As astute as it is generous, the text has been more widely cited, discussed, and anthologized in the jazz literature than almost any other. Gunther Schuller terms it "the first intelligent criticism" of jazz,[3] while Bechet's British biographer John Chilton still considers it "one of the most incisive examples of jazz analysis ever conceived." Chilton finds it "bizarre," however, that such "expert acclaim" had not been forthcoming in the States, revealing how trusty a symbol Ansermet's text has become of Eu-

nouveauté et l'imprévu" ("Sur un orchestre nègre," *La Revue romande* 3/10 [October 1919], reprinted in Ernest Ansermet, *Écrits sur la musique* [Neuchâtel, Switz.: Baconnière, 1971], 171–78 [quote on p. 177, italics original]).

3. Gunther Schuller, "The Influence of Jazz on the History and Development of Concert Music," in *New Perspectives on Jazz*, ed. David N. Baker (Washington, DC: Smithsonian Institution Press, 1990), 9–23 (quote on p. 15).

ropean prescience about jazz.[4] American self-flagellation has been even more severe. When the text appeared in the 1947 book *Frontiers of Jazz*, for example, editor Ralph de Toledano chided his readers: "It cannot be too often repeated, to our shame, that Europeans realized the importance and value of jazz many years before the Americans who originated it. . . . Ernst-Alexandre Ansermet . . . was able to make mature and still-valid pronouncements of the nature of jazz in 1919."[5] Even James Lincoln Collier, in his spirited rebuttal of jazz history's "two myths," as he calls them, of American neglect and European respect, has to admit Ansermet was "prescient" (while also maintaining that "American commentators . . . were making much more informed appraisals of the music two years earlier").[6] And the most prominent recent history of jazz features Ansermet as representative of high culture's endorsement of Bechet, and of jazz, in the conventional fashion.[7]

The best of Ansermet's review is indeed startlingly perceptive. Noting the musicians' African descent, for example, he identifies musical retentions of various orders: a nuanced rhythmic sense incorporating, in addition to syncopation, fractional delays and anticipations; a tendency to employ pitches that lie outside the diatonic system, particularly around the third and seventh scale tones (i.e., "blue notes"); and unconventional instrumental and vocal techniques, which allow for a wide range of attacks and great timbral variation. Collectively, he believes, such stylistic traits—still textbook material today—reflect "a racial genius."[8] He also recognizes how compositions are mere sketches filled out in performance,

4. John Chilton, *Sidney Bechet: The Wizard of Jazz* (New York: Oxford University Press, 1987; repr., New York: Da Capo Press, 1996), 39–40. Similarly, critic Henry Pleasants complimented the article's "analytical insight and prophetic vision," remarking that "it was characteristic of America's view of its own music that it should be a European, Ansermet, who would react so appreciatively and acutely to what he heard. . . . American awareness of jazz . . . has come largely as a result of enlightenment from abroad" ("America's Impact on the Arts: Music," *Saturday Review*, 13 December 1975, reprinted in *Music Educators Journal* 62/9 [May 1976]: 43–51 [quote on p. 49]).

5. Ralph de Toledano, ed., "Bechet and Jazz Visit Europe, 1919" [Ansermet's "Sur un orchestre nègre," trans. Walter E. Schaap], in *Frontiers of Jazz* (New York: Oliver Durrell, 1947), 115–22 (quote on p. 115).

6. James Lincoln Collier, *The Reception of Jazz in America: A New View* (Brooklyn, NY: Institute for Studies in American Music, 1988), 1, 52. On Collier, see the introduction above.

7. Scott DeVeaux and Gary Giddins, *Jazz* (New York: W. W. Norton, 2009), 105, 310.

8. Ansermet, "Sur un orchestre nègre," *Écrits sur la musique*, 175.

and he is "inclined to think that the genius of the race is manifested most strongly in the Blues."[9] Ansermet admires the Southern Syncopated Orchestra's "astonishing perfection, highest taste and fervor of playing" and even appreciates how their physical body movements interact with the music.[10]

Less often acknowledged is that Ansermet's biological determinism extends beyond such innocuous praise. Finding the Southern Syncopated Orchestra's harmonic language derivative, despite their innovative approach to rhythm and melody, for example, he suspects that this is "an element that enters into musical evolution only at a stage that the Negro art has not yet attained."[11] Even the dynamic nature of the performance ultimately betrays to him that this is "a perfect example of what is called folk art [l'art populaire]—an art which is *still in its period* of oral tradition" (my italics). While the orchestra's director, Will Marion Cook, was no neophyte—he had studied composition with Dvořák at the National Conservatory of Music in Washington, DC, and violin with Joachim in Berlin— "the Glinka of Negro music," Ansermet supposes, was yet to arrive.[12]

Ansermet's assessment of Bechet is likewise marred by this "evolutionist" ideology. Although he reserves his highest praise for the clarinetist, famously calling him an "artist of genius," the conclusion to which this leads him is troubling:

Quand on a si souvent cherché à retrouver dans le passé une de ces figures auxquelles on doit l'avènement de notre art—ces hommes des XVIIe et XVIIIe siècles, par exemple, qui avec des airs de danses faisaient des œuvres expressives et ouvraient ainsi le chemin dont Haydn et Mozart ne marquent pas le point de départ, mais le premier aboutissement—quelle chose émouvante que la rencontre de ce gros garçon tout noir, avec des dents blanches et de front étroit, qui est bien content qu'on aime ce qu'il fait, mais ne sait rien dire de son art, sauf qu'il suit son "own way," sa propre voie, et quand on pense que ce "own way," c'est peut-être la grande route où le monde s'engouffrera demain.[13]

When one has so often tried to rediscover in the past one of those figures to whom we owe the advent of our art—those men of the seventeenth and eighteenth centuries, for example, who made expressive works of

9. Ibid., 177.
10. Ibid., 172.
11. Ibid., 176.
12. Ibid., 177.
13. Ibid., 178.

dance airs, thus opening the path on which Haydn and Mozart do not mark the starting point but the first milestone—how moving it is to meet this very black, fat boy, with white teeth and a low brow, who is very glad one likes what he does, but who can say nothing of his art, save that he follows his "own way," and then one thinks that his "own way" may be the highway the world will rush along tomorrow.

While he is prescient about jazz, the racial stereotypes Ansermet employs patently do not describe the light-skinned Bechet, perhaps even recalling ideas from physiognomy or craniometry (e.g., his "low brow").[14] As Ted Gioia and others have discussed, the notion that such "natural" musicians (read "primitives") cannot put into words—or even fully understand—what they are doing is an insidious myth of jazz criticism.[15] More than this, Ansermet seems to think he is catching the evolutionary process in action: he wonders not only what will become of jazz once it has "grown up," but what Bechet and his fellow musicians may teach about the lost musical past. Conflating cultural and historical difference in this way, his interest in the end may be ethnological as much as it is musical.

As has occasionally been noted, Ansermet's bright view of jazz anyway dimmed in later years. When a reunion with Bechet was engineered in Chicago in 1948, the conductor was happy to see him again but brutally honest in assessing the music: "The days of jazz are over. It has made its contribution to music. Now in itself it is merely monotonous."[16] Even

14. The first translator, Walter E. Schaap, rendered "front étroit" not as "low brow" but as "narrow forehead," which I do not think captures its implication. Similarly, his final phrase, "the highway the whole world will swing along tomorrow" was a poetic translation (of "la grande route où le monde s'engouffrera demain") that perhaps overplays the positive in Ansermet's prediction (Toledano, *Frontiers of Jazz*, 122).

15. See Ted Gioia, "Jazz and the Primitivist Myth," in *The Imperfect Art: Reflections on Jazz and Modern Culture* (New York: Oxford University Press, 1988), 51–71 [also reprinted in *Musical Quarterly* 73 (1989): 130–43]. Gioia dates the rise of the myth to the early French jazz critics but does not address Ansermet. In another passage, Ansermet writes of the whole ensemble: "Je ne saurais dire si ces artistes se font un devoir d'être 'sincères,' . . . s'ils sont persuadés de la 'noblesse' de leur tâche, . . . ni d'ailleurs s'ils sont animés d'une 'idée' quelconque. Mais je vois bien qu'ils ont un sens très précis de la musique qu'ils aiment, et un plaisir à la faire qui se communique à l'auditeur" (Ansermet, "Sur un orchestre nègre," *Écrits sur la musique*, 172). Again, although ostensibly complimentary, Ansermet seems to doubt the musicians' capacity for abstract thought.

16. Ernest Ansermet, remarks from Chicago reunion, cited in Clyde H. Clark, "Overseas News," *Jazz Notes* (Adelaide), no. 83 (April–May 1948): 13–16 (quote on p. 13).

the two psalm settings that Bechet proudly presented to Ansermet were damned with faint praise: "naïve but beautifully melodic."[17] Asked, in the 1950s, to explain his change of heart since 1919, Ansermet insisted:

L'art négro-américain ne m'a pas déçu; je continue à penser que son avènement est un fait musical historique d'une signification considérable.... Mais j'ai mieux compris par la suite que sa nature même de *folklore* . . . en limitait d'avance le développement possible. C'est sur ce point . . . que les fanatiques du jazz se font, je crois, des illusions. La *croissance historique* est le fait de la musique de *culture* (ce qu'on appelle la "grande musique"); elle n'est pas le fait d'un folklore, qui est ce que j'appellerais une musique des *mœurs*. Un folklore naît, constitue des "types," puis se perpétue.[18]

The Negro-American art has not disappointed me; I continue to think that its advent is an event of considerable significance in music history. . . . But I have better understood since then that its very nature as *folklore* . . . limited from the beginning the development that was possible. It's on this point . . . that, I believe, jazz fans are mistaken. *Historical growth* is the act of music of *culture* (that which we call "art music"); it is not the act of folklore, which is what I call a music of *conventions*. A folk practice is born, forms "types," then just lives on.

As I have indicated, this was not so far out of line with Ansermet's earlier article as most have supposed. Nevertheless, one important change had occurred in his thinking: where previously Ansermet had imagined that jazz might evolve into something akin to art music, now he had concluded that such a transformation was impossible; lowly jazz, like other vernacular styles, was incapable of development or of the higher orders of meaning available only to Western art music.[19]

17. Ernest Ansermet, exchange with Raymond Mouly, in Mouly, *Sidney Bechet, notre ami* (Paris: La Table Ronde, 1959), 41–44 (quote on p. 43).

18. Ibid., 41–42 (italics original). For a similar explanation, see Ernest Ansermet and J.-Claude Piguet, *Entretiens sur la musique*, 2nd ed. (Neuchâtel, Switz.: Baconnière, 1983 [first published 1963]), 41–43.

19. For a view of this point in the context of Ansermet's evolving philosophy and his changing views of Stravinsky's music in particular, see J.-Claude Piguet, *La Pensée d'Ernest Ansermet* (Lausanne, Switz.: Payot, 1983), 12–16. Even around the time of the original review, Ansermet made a very clear distinction between popular source and artistic transformation, describing Stravinsky's relocation of syncopation—"telle que l'ont exploité les nègres dans les limités étroites de l'art populaire"—to a harmonic context devoid of ragtime's "banalité" (Ernest Ansermet, "L'Œuvre d'Igor Stravinsky," *La Revue musicale* 2/9 [1 July 1921]: 3–27 [quotes

Ansermet's theories about music—and about race—eventually came together in his two-volume *Les Fondements de la musique dans la conscience humaine* (*The Foundations of Music in Human Consciousness*), published in 1961.[20] Seeking a phenomenological approach to musical understanding, he combined elements of cognitive science, mathematics, and philosophy; but he also borrowed from "historians of civilizations" heavily marked by racial ideology, such as Oswald Spengler and Houston Stewart Chamberlain (whose French translator, Robert Godet, was Ansermet's friend and dedicatee in memoriam of *Fondements*).[21] The result was an all-embracing theory of musical and social development based around "three ages of man": eras of history that were in large part racially defined.

In the first age (preantiquity), primitive man experimented with music, according to intuition alone, but had no way to codify it. In the second age, ancient civilizations systematized knowledge, including the foundations of music, but intelligence took over from imagination, leading to stagnation and rigidity. The third age in effect brought together intelli-

---

on pp. 10, 12]). On this issue, see also "La Composition musicale" (1931), in Ernest Ansermet, *Les Compositeurs et leurs œuvres*, ed. J.-Claude Piguet (Neuchâtel, Switz.: Baconnière, 1989), 11–20.

20. Ernest Ansermet, *Les Fondements de la musique dans la conscience humaine*, ed. J.-C. Piguet, 2nd ed. (Neuchâtel, Switz.: Baconnière, 1987 [first published 1961, 2 vols.]). The ambiguity of the French word *conscience* (meaning both "consciousness" and "conscience") aptly encapsulates the at once scientific (or scientistic) and theological or moral character of the book but is unfortunately lost in translation.

21. Houston Stewart Chamberlain, *La Genèse du XIXme siècle*, trans. Robert Godet, 2 vols. (Paris: Librairie Payot, 1913) (includes a long and rather circumspect "Préface de la version française" by Godet, vii–lxvi). Playing his cards close to his chest, Ansermet cites Houston Stewart Chamberlain and Oswald Spengler only once in *Fondements* (pp. 402, 574–75), in both cases to disagree with them, though their effect on his thinking was obviously profound. For more on this, see Jean-Jacques Langendorf, "Pourquoi une approche phénoménologique de la musique par Ernest Ansermet?," in *Euterpe et Athéna: Cinq Études sur Ernest Ansermet* (Geneva: Georg Editeur, 1998), 123–39, particularly 125–29. For an overview, see J.-Claude Piguet, *La Pensée d'Ernest Ansermet*. There are also strong parallels with various strains of anthropological thought, particularly that fostered in the United States by Lewis Henry Morgan and his students, although in this case the connection appears to be indirect. See Adam Kuper's influential account, now revised, *The Reinvention of Primitive Society: Transformations of a Myth*, 2nd ed. (New York: Routledge, 2005); and Steven Conn, *History's Shadow: Native Americans and Historical Consciousness in the Nineteenth Century* (Chicago: University of Chicago Press, 2004), which usefully attends to archeological as well as anthropological thought.

gence and intuition, but the specific union Ansermet defines—of Socratic thought with the revelation of Christ—renders this an exclusively Western phenomenon: other cultures, including contemporary ones, were left behind, in the second or even the first ages of man. In the manner of such tomes, it is paradoxically Ansermet's global reach—his aspiration to the universal—that most clearly betrays the insularity and Eurocentricism of his thought: Enlightenment philosophy, nineteenth-century anthropology, and modern racialism form an unholy alliance, which Husserl's phenomenology (read through the lens of Sartre) does nothing to break apart.

A book at once so colossal in scope, so convinced of its merits, and so frequently lacking in rhyme or reason attracts bon mots. Louis Andriessen and Elmer Schönberger find it the work of "an incorrigible schoolteacher," which is most memorable for "its rancour, its convulsiveness, its ideological fanaticism and its anti-Semitism," albeit "wrapped in phenomenological terminology."[22] Michel Philippot, the polymath French composer (and theorist, musicologist and aesthetician) who was one of the few people with a serious chance of understanding the book in more than one of its many aspects, nevertheless wondered in a contemporary review whether it amounted to "an extraordinary miscalculation, an ingenious hoax, a great and universal mistake, or a masterpiece."[23] It is surely not Ansermet but Philippot, however, who relishes its large component of "nonsense";[24] the conductor, who spent fifteen years writing these volumes, is nothing if not sincere.

If Ansermet's book does not, therefore, lend itself easily to summary, its subtext is less difficult to grasp. Leaving aside its ostensibly psychological or even physiological basis, *Fondements* is ultimately a defense of tonality against serialism, electronics, non-Western traditions, and any other intruder in the temple of Music. This is witnessed most particularly in Ansermet's lengthy "proof" that twelve-tone music is an aberration, the creation of a "stupid Jew," whom he compares to *Die Meistersinger*'s Beckmesser.[25] Ansermet's position on jazz is also confirmed: Despite its

22. Louis Andriessen and Elmer Schönberger, *The Apollonian Clockwork: On Stravinsky*, trans. Jeff Hamburg (Oxford: Oxford University Press, 1989), 191–92.

23. Michel Philippot, "Ansermet's Phenomenological Metamorphoses," *Perspectives of New Music* 2/2 (Spring/Summer 1964): 129–40 (quote on p. 129).

24. Ibid., 135.

25. Ansermet, *Les Fondements de la musique*, 530, 534. Ansermet ascribes the offensive phrase to the Jewish composer Ernest Bloch, which is disingenuous but not impossible given Bloch's "complex relationship to Judaism" that sometimes manifested itself in anti-Semitic outbursts (Bloch, like Ansermet, was a friend of

recent provenance, jazz is a remnant of an earlier age, like non-Western traditions around the world. As time in jazz is circular not linear, repetition is its only option—a statement that applies equally to its internal form and to its prospects for evolution.

While the consequences of Ansermet's ideas are too easily lost in *Fondements* among the dense theoretical prose—and logarithms—they are stated in balder form in a series of in-depth interviews on Swiss radio (subsequently published), which sought to expose his views to a wider audience. Asked about contemporary composers' use of non-Western scales in their works, for example, Ansermet replies that a "return to intervals of music of the second age" is "very far from being progress"; those who employ such unnatural sounds put at risk tonal music's privileged position as the only "universally communicable" language.[26] Most composers simply evoke exotic musics superficially, he argues, which does no harm, but Messiaen's use of techniques from Indian music, for example, goes too far, "breaking with our language and regressing to an earlier and outmoded stage of history." Ansermet could explain the confusion:

Nous vivons à une époque où, aux Nations Unies, les peuples du deuxième âge sont mis sur le même pied que ceux du troisième âge, et l'on est enclin à mettre aussi sur le même pied les musiques des civilisations antiques et la musique occidentale. On se dit que leurs systèmes de sons sont aussi légitimes que le nôtre. On ne voit pas que notre système tonal est celui auquel devait aboutir la musique, si celle-ci devait devenir un langage immédiatement compréhensible et compréhensible à tous.[27]

We live at a time in which, at the United Nations, peoples of the second age are put on the same footing as those of the third age, and one is inclined to put musics of ancient civilizations and Western music on the same footing too. It is said that their systems of sounds are as legitimate

Godet's). See Klára Móricz, "Ancestral Voices: Anti-Semitism and Ernest Bloch's Racial Conception of Art," in *Western Music and Race*, ed. Julie Brown (Cambridge: Cambridge University Press, 2007), 102–14 (quote on p. 104). Ansermet's anti-Semitism, as it intersected with antimodernism on the issue of serialism, is discussed by Michael Steinberg in "Jewish Identity and Intellectuality in Fin-de-Siècle Austria: Suggestions for a Historical Discourse," *New German Critique*, no. 43 (Winter 1988): 3–33 (esp. pp. 11–13); and Mark Carroll, *Music and Ideology in Cold War Europe* (Cambridge: Cambridge University Press, 2003), 145–49.

26. Ansermet and Piguet, *Entretiens sur la musique*, 115.

27. Ibid., 116. The preceding pages, 109–16, are a straightforward (if bizarre) exposition of Ansermet's three musical ages, only the last of which is "historical."

as ours. It is not recognized that our tonal system is the one music must achieve, if it is to become a language that is immediately comprehensible and comprehensible by all.

Brazen as this is, Ansermet's prejudices may not in themselves be so remarkable. Though more thoroughly—obsessively—theorized by Ansermet than by others, such an attitude toward non-Western musics, and toward serial music, is not exceptional for a classical musician in the twentieth century. What is more surprising is that jazz history has, for generations, celebrated the text of a man who not only was fairly ambivalent about the music but whose racialized historiography and pseudoscience trapped jazz, along with those who created it, in a premodern age. As I have noted, some observations in Ansermet's "Sur un orchestre nègre" are as good a witness to his extraordinary musicianship as are his fascinating recordings. But the conductor's keen ear was not matched by as open a mind. So when, in good faith, one recent anthologist explains that the conductor found jazz "different from European concert music yet not inferior to it," the misapprehension is rather akin to recognizing Wagner for his interest in Meyerbeer and Mendelssohn.[28] Ansermet's canonization in jazz criticism notwithstanding, "primitive" jazz figured for him, as it has done for many, not as an alternative tradition but rather as a foil for European art music.[29]

A further irony: Ansermet's 1919 article remained, for almost twenty years, wholly unknown. French discourse of the 1920s and 1930s never made mention of it, though the small coterie of jazz writers frequently referenced one another's work. It was not until 1938—as Ansermet's ideas were "maturing" into something less palatable—that his text was rediscovered and republished, with a fawning preface and parallel English

28. Robert Walser, ed., "A 'Serious' Musician Takes Jazz Seriously" [extracts from Ansermet's "Sur un orchestre nègre," trans. Walter E. Schaap], in *Keeping Time: Readings in Jazz History* (New York: Oxford University Press, 1999), 9–11 (quote on p. 9).

29. It seems unlikely as well that Ansermet would have approved of Bechet's transition to the soprano saxophone. In a peculiar section on sonority and instrumentation in *Fondements*, he writes: "Le seul instrument nouveau qui soit entré dans la famille depuis l'époque classique est le saxophone, et encore n'y apparaît-il qu'occasionnellement, à cause de la qualité sensible trop accusée de son timbre. Le caractère sensuel et phallique de ce timbre vouait le saxophone à la musique de plaisir: dans le jazz, le chant du saxophone-ténor traverse sans broncher les syncopes, comme le phallus les spasmes du coït, et avec la même sorte de corporéité" (Ansermet, *Les Fondements de la musique*, 109).

translation, in *Jazz hot*.[30] Although it had been written in London by a Swiss, French jazz critics immediately adopted Ansermet as their fore-runner; his text was subsequently celebrated almost despite its author. As well as serving as a reminder of Bechet's early visits to Europe, it lent support to a growing sense of superiority among the French writers about their pioneering acumen. The composer and critic André Hodeir went as far as to dedicate his first book, *Le jazz, cet inconnu* (1945), to Anser-met. In this roundabout way, then, Sidney Bechet came forever to be as-sociated with the arrival of jazz in a prescient and appreciative Europe, and France's youth would eventually learn about Ansermet's text in their weekly installment of *Tintin*.[31]

Bechet's Blues: Living the Revival

The rediscovery of Ansermet's text was timely. Years later, Bechet would proudly recall Ansermet's fascination with him and the Southern Synco-pated Orchestra in his autobiography: "This man, he was trained for clas-sical, but he had a real interest in our music. There was just no end to the questions he could think to ask about it."[32] But if Bechet had indeed paved the road the world would travel, he too often had been pushed aside in the rush. Not until the late 1930s did the New Orleans Revival Movement finally bring him the regular, sometimes even lucrative, small-group gigs and recordings in New York and Chicago that would ensure his place in jazz history. While Ansermet's text served Bechet's cause well, writing him back into that story from the beginning, his newfound success was not attributable to the conductor. Nor was it correct to infer, as was some-times imagined, that Bechet had been reputed in Europe throughout the

30. Ernest Ansermet, "Sur un orchestre nègre" [with parallel English transla-tion by Walter E. Schaap], *Jazz hot*, no. 28 (November–December 1938): 4–9.

31. Laurent Cugny mounts a sturdy defense of Ansermet in "Did Europe 'Dis-cover' Jazz?," in *Eurojazzland: Jazz and European Sources, Dynamics, and Contexts*, ed. Luca Cerchiari, Laurent Cugny, and Franz Kerschbaumer (Boston: Northeast-ern University Press, 2012), 301–41 (esp. pp. 308–10). He misunderstands me, though—on the basis of the text of a spoken paper I shared with him—in suggest-ing that I hoist the Ansermet of 1919 on a petard the conductor did not construct until 1961 (334n27). My point, as will be apparent from the longer account above, is that there were already strong hints of this kind of racialized theorization in the 1919 text, even as it was in some other ways rather perceptive; in any case, nobody seems to have paid attention to the article for almost twenty years, by which time Ansermet's position was hardening.

32. Sidney Bechet, *Treat It Gentle: An Autobiography* (New York: Twayne Publish-ers, 1960; repr., New York: Da Capo Press, 1978), 127.

intervening decades. Pigheaded, itinerant, and unlucky, he had no more triumphed there than he had in the States.

Bechet's movements in the twenties and early thirties are still somewhat difficult to piece together.[33] He played with the Southern Syncopated Orchestra, its spin-offs, and other ensembles in London (and around the United Kingdom), Paris (at the Apollo), and Brussels, before being briefly imprisoned and then deported from Britain in November 1922.[34] He returned to Europe in 1925, first to Paris with *La Revue nègre* and then further afield, including a tour of Russia. The year 1928 found Bechet back in Paris—at Bricktop's nightclub, then at the Ambassadeurs (with Noble Sissle's first, hastily arranged band), and finally Chez Florence.[35]

Although he was often featured as a soloist, Bechet did not gain great celebrity during this period. Rather, he was a gigging musician, moving somewhat itinerantly where work and fortune took him. Nor did he always receive a warm welcome. As much is shown by a newspaper report of Bechet's arrest in Paris, in December 1928, after a shooting incident involving a fellow African American musician, Mike McKendrick. Wondering if Montmartre had moved to the Wild West, the author explains the scene:

> Huit heures du matin, rue Fontaine. . . . Sur le trottoir, deux nègres qui ont fini leur journée de travail—c'est-à-dire leur nuit—dans un orchestre de jazz-band. . . . L'un s'appelle Mike Mac Kendrich [sic], l'autre Sidney Bechet. . . . Une fusillade en pleine rue. Mais ils tirent mal, ces deux nègres. . . . Ce sont les passants qui reçoivent les projectiles. Et parmi eux, tout d'abord un nègre—un troisième, nommé Cambdon [sic]. Que de nègres à Montmartre! . . . *Ah! qu'il était beau mon Paris.*[36]

> Eight o'clock in the morning on the rue Fontaine. . . . On the sidewalk, two Negroes who have finished their work for the day—that's to say for the

33. For a valiant attempt to do so, however, see Guy Demole, *Sidney Bechet: His Musical Activities from 1907 to 1959*, 3rd ed. (Geneva: privately published, 2006); I am grateful to the author for sending me this invaluable chronicle. The best of several biographies of Bechet, in French and English, remains Chilton's *Sidney Bechet*. Unless otherwise stated, these two volumes are my sources on Bechet's life and career.

34. Differing accounts of this incident are offered by Chilton (*Sidney Bechet*, 53–54) and by Bechet himself (*Treat It Gentle*, 129–33).

35. Chilton, *Sidney Bechet*, 81.

36. Georges Claretie, "Un Matin à Montmartre," *Le Figaro*, 3 January 1929 (italics original).

night—in a jazz band. . . . One is called Mike Mac Kendrich [*sic*], the other Sidney Bechet. . . . A gunfight in the middle of the street. But they're bad shots, these two Negroes. . . . It is passersby who get hit. And among them, first of all a Negro—a third, called Cambdon [*sic*]. So many Negroes in Montmartre! . . . *Oh! how beautiful my Paris was.*

The last line is a pointed reference to "Mon Paris," a Lucien Boyer and Vincent Scotto song nostalgically evoking the city at a time when "Everyone spoke but one language."[37] Bechet would have understood the tenor of it: recounting this incident in his autobiography, he admits wrongdoing but also insists that, as a foreigner without means, his guilt was assumed, his plea of self-defense went unheeded, and even his lawyer betrayed him; the injustice of the trial, he claims, troubled him more than the next eleven months in jail.[38] On release, Bechet was required to leave the country. He went first to Berlin then, a year later, back to New York. He seems to have returned once more to Europe (including Paris, his ban notwithstanding) with Sissle's band in 1931, but he did not stay long and would not come back again for almost two decades.

What's baffling is how, throughout this period, Bechet moved beneath the radar of the French critics. Recognized now as a New Orleans pioneer second only to Louis Armstrong—perhaps ahead of him in France—he is more or less absent from their celebrated early histories of jazz. Bechet rates only a single passing mention in Robert Goffin's *Aux frontières du jazz* of 1932 and again in Hugues Panassié's *Le Jazz hot* of 1934. Neither author is sure how to spell his name. After a lengthy discussion of the alto and soprano saxophone playing of Johnny Hodges (who had learned from Bechet), Panassié writes simply: "Incidentally, we note that there is another remarkable soprano saxophonist, Sidney Béchet (it is perhaps spelled Bashay). We don't know his style well enough to give a description."[39]

Unlike most of the musicians whose playing Panassié described in colorful detail, Bechet had played in Paris a number of times during the 1920s and early 1930s, and for quite extended periods, as I have shown. So focused were the early critics on the few discs they were able to obtain, it seems, that an extraordinary musician who was right under their noses went unnoticed. More important, Bechet's near absence from the histori-

37. Correctly, the refrain is "Ah! Qu'il était beau mon village, / Mon Paris, notre Paris."

38. Bechet, *Treat It Gentle*, 150–56. The third musician involved was Glover Compton.

39. Hugues Panassié, *Le Jazz hot* (Paris: Corrêa, 1934), 137. See also Robert Goffin, *Aux frontières du jazz* (Paris: Sagittaire, 1932), 193.

cal record makes clear one surprising fact: by this point, his star had risen no higher in French than in foreign skies. His glory was yet to come.[40]

Back in the States, the 1930s were hard for Bechet, as they were for many musicians, but he was still in work as a musician more than he was out of it (albeit mainly with Noble Sissle's less-than-inspiring band), and he spent no time behind bars. His second career as tailor did not actually occupy him for long, and he never had to act on his other ideas of working as an undertaker or short-order cook. More is the point, in the last years of the decade, Bechet became sufficiently well-known to give up his job with Sissle in search of more interesting fare; hence began his most intensive period of performances and recordings. By the time that Hugues Panassié—impresario as well as critic—sought to record Bechet with Panassié's old friend Mezz Mezzrow in New York in 1938, he found him under contract to another label. The recordings went ahead, but they had to be released under the name of the trumpet player, as Tommy Ladnier and His Orchestra.[41]

Before war broke out, then, a fair collection of discs by the music's older stars (whether reissued or newly produced) was already circulating, in Europe as in the United States. Whereas the New Orleans Revival took off for real in America during the early forties, in France it coalesced during the war but gained wide influence only after it. The adventurous French performers who sought to learn the style by imitating the new recordings of Bechet or the older ones of King Oliver were typically very young students (often not twenty years old) with, at the beginning, more enthusiasm than ability. Nevertheless, performers such as Claude Luter and Pierre Braslavsky quickly built up considerable support, and the *caves* (cellar bars) of theatres and restaurants in the Saint-Germain-des-Près area on the Left Bank soon became filled with their sophomoric playing in the "new" idiom. Boulevard Saint Germain is often compared, with

40. Witness Charles Delaunay, recalling the period, in 1949: "Pour la clarté des faits, rappelons que c'est peu avant la dernière guerre mondiale que certains critiques de jazz commencèrent à 'découvrir' quels avaient été les véritables créateurs du jazz. . . . Ce n'est qu'en 1938 qu'on découvrait le génie de Sidney Bechet et qu'à sa suite on mobilisait à nouveau dans les studios d'enregistrement les derniers survivants de la Nouvelle-Orléans" ("Le Cas Claude Luter: Comment se pose le problème," *Jazz hot*, no. 30 [February 1949]: 6–7 [quote on p. 6]).

41. Chilton, *Sidney Bechet*, 113. Chilton sees the early part of 1937 as the turning point in Bechet's career, marked by articles in *DownBeat*, in which Paul Eduard Miller recognized his achievements and historical importance, and well-received recordings by Noble Sissle's Swingsters (a small group from within Sissle's band that often featured Bechet as soloist) (ibid., 103–6).

some justification, to New York's 52nd Street, in the same period: as was the case there, a series of small venues in close proximity allowed multiple performers and jazz styles to coexist.[42]

So, when artists such as Bechet began to consider returning to France in the late forties, there was already considerable interest in their music, a growing body of local players, and an audience of sufficient size to make such a venture commercially viable. Although Bechet's flurry of fame in the States had, by this time, settled down into a comfortable living rather than an extravagant one, bringing him to France involved some tricky negotiations. In 1948, Panassié twice tried unsuccessfully to coax Bechet over: the first time, the financial terms were not satisfactory to the musician; by the second, for the Nice Jazz Festival, he was amid a long run in Chicago and sent his young student Bob Wilber instead (fig. 5.5).[43] It took a much more generous offer from Panassié's estranged colleague Charles Delaunay, for his own Paris Festival of Jazz the following year, to get Bechet on the plane: he was hardly anxious for French endorsement.[44] Still, Bechet's decision to participate in the 1949 festival—alongside Charlie Parker, a young Miles Davis, and many others—was fortuitous. Although this was not the first time since the war that celebrated American musicians had visited, or even the first jazz festival, no previous event had approached its range, scale, or cost; the international reputation of the French jazz scene can arguably be dated from here.

The 1949 festival was also a kind of "coming out" party for the Fédération des Hot Clubs Français. This new association of local chapters of the fan club had been set up by Delaunay to rival the Hot Club de France after an acrimonious split with Panassié. The causes of this dissolution were an inextricable mix of the aesthetic and the personal. Having long been concerned to police the definition of jazz, Panassié had, since the war, taken a hard line against bebop, arguing for New Orleans as the only authentic style. The ensuing battle with Delaunay and some younger critics had resulted in his resignation as editor of the magazine *Jazz hot* and the division of hot clubs across two competing organizations. The critics' differing principles were reflected in the festivals they arranged:

42. Ludovic Tournès, *New Orleans sur Seine: Histoire du jazz en France* (Paris: Librairie Arthème Fayard, 1999), esp. 103–5, 309–13, 340–42, and 363–64. See also Patrick Burke, *Come in and Hear the Truth: Jazz and Race on 52nd Street* (Chicago: University of Chicago Press, 2008).

43. Chilton, *Sidney Bechet*, 205–6.

44. Walter E. Schaap, who was working on Delaunay's behalf, explained the circumstances in a letter to John Chilton of June 12, 1985, reproduced in Chilton, *Sidney Bechet*, 213–14.

FIGURE 5.5. Portrait of Bob Wilber and Sidney Bechet, Jimmy Ryan's, New York, NY, ca. June 1947 (William P. Gottlieb Collection, Library of Congress).

Panassié's, in Nice in 1948, featured high-profile visitors (most notably, Louis Armstrong) but no bebop musicians and only two French bands (Claude Luter's and the original, reunited Hot Club Quintet); Delaunay's, in Paris a year later, made a point of welcoming musicians in varied styles from America, France, and across Europe. The dispute, then, was less between traditional and modern styles than it was between "closed" and "open" notions of the jazz tradition; it also involved a healthy slice of professional jealousy.[45]

This context would have been at once familiar and strange to the visiting musicians. As has been well discussed, there had been long-running

45. On the history of the Hot Club movement and the Panassié/Delaunay dynamic, see Tournès, *New Orleans sur Seine*, particularly 91–117, 141–94.

FIGURE 5.6. Charlie Parker and Sidney Bechet en route to the Paris Jazz Festival, 1949 (Frank Driggs Collection / Getty Images).

critical disputes in the States about styles of jazz.[46] In New York, Bechet and Parker had recently shared a stage in a mock battle between bebop and traditional jazz—one of several attempts to profit on the publicity generated by the debate. There was little personal animosity, however, and the two men knew one another, socialized occasionally, and for a while even shared an agent (fig. 5.6).[47] Not that Bechet much enjoyed playing sup-

46. See, for example, Bernard Gendron, "Moldy Figs and Modernists" and "Bebop under Fire," in *Between Montmartre and the Mudd Club: Popular Music and the Avant-garde* (Chicago: University of Chicago Press, 2002), 121–57. More comprehensive discussions of American jazz criticism may be found in John Gennari, *Blowin' Hot and Cool: Jazz and Its Critics* (Chicago: University of Chicago Press, 2006); and Bruce Boyd Raeburn, *New Orleans Style and the Writing of American Jazz History* (Ann Arbor: University of Michigan Press, 2009).

47. Chilton, *Sidney Bechet*, 212.

port act to the young lions. Orin "Hot Lips" Page reported how Bechet conspired with him to show up the "be-bop boys" on arrival in Paris, leaving them haplessly waving dollars when the older men had already exchanged theirs for francs.[48] Bechet did not want it forgotten that he had not only age over the bebop musicians but worldly knowledge, too.

Bechet need not have worried. If both he and Parker were embodying music already known on disc, it was the older man whose stature grew most in live performance; Bechet rather than Parker was the revelation of the festival. One writer, noting that Luter's and Braslavsky's bands were not up to the task of playing with Bechet, could nevertheless barely contain his excitement: "His fire, impossible to put out, even at his age . . . 52 years old . . . his air of distinction . . . his ideas . . . his swing . . . and this fire, this fire . . . ," he spluttered.[49] Composer and critic André Hodeir, himself more inclined toward modern jazz, nevertheless agreed:

Le grand triomphateur du Festival fut sans nul doute Sidney Béchet, dont chaque apparition sur scène a suscité une énorme vague d'enthousiasme. Il faut dire que Béchet, parfois décevant en disque, possède cette qualité si rare qu'est la "présence." Il joue avec une telle foi, une telle jeunesse, en dépit de ses cheveux blancs. . . . Les plus difficiles ont été conquis par la spontanéité et la perfection du jeu de Béchet. . . . Je n'ai pas entendu une seule note discordante à son propos.[50]

The great triumph of the [Paris Jazz] Festival was without any doubt Sidney Bechet, whose every appearance on stage sparked off a huge wave of enthusiasm. It must be said that Bechet, who is sometimes disappointing on record, possesses this quality that is so rare of "presence." He plays with such commitment, such youthfulness, despite his white hair. . . . The most difficult [to please] were won over by the spontaneity and the perfection of Bechet's playing. . . . I didn't hear a single note of disagreement about him.

It was true. Almost without exception critics marveled at Bechet, regardless of where they stood on the jazz debate. The closest to dissent came from the musician and writer Boris Vian, an important chronicler of jazz in France in the postwar years. Although he was delighted to see

48. Oran "Hot Lips" Page, "Kanas City Man," interview by Kay C. Thompson, *Record Changer* 8/12 (December 1949): 9, 18–19 (esp. p. 19).

49. "Le Festival de Pleyel: Les Impressions de Johnny 'Scat' James," *La Revue du jazz*, no. 6 (June–July 1949): 188 (ellipses original).

50. André Hodeir, "Le Festival 1949," *Jazz hot*, no. 34 (June 1949): 7, 9 (quote on p. 7).

this belated recognition of Bechet's talents, Vian was baffled that the French public was "twenty-five years behind the times." Recalling that Bechet had first visited France some thirty years ago, he feared it would take a similar period before Parker received the same attention.[51] In the process, Vian captured the paradox in which Bechet—and his music—were at once new and old, familiar and unfamiliar:

> Les auditeurs familiarisés depuis plusieurs mois avec la musique Nouvelle-Orléans ne seront sans doute pas surpris par le style de Béchet; mais ils le seront par l'esprit qui anime ce grand chef de file, aussi vert à cinquante ans qu'au temps de sa première tournée en Europe, en 1919.[52]

> Listeners accustomed for several months to New Orleans music will not by any means be surprised by Bechet's style; but they will be by the spirit that animates this leader in the field, as sprightly at fifty as at the time of his first European tour, in 1919.

Or at least so Vian—who was not born at the time of Bechet's now-legendary visit—imagined. Thanks in large part to the rediscovery of Ansermet's article, French audiences could congratulate themselves for long ago having appreciated the importance of an artist they had only recently come to know.

Monsieur Bechet: Cultivating a New Audience

Recognizing that Bechet had struck a chord at the 1949 festival, Delaunay hastily arranged a follow-up tour of France for him later in the year. In order to take up the opportunity, Bechet absconded from his regular gig (at Jazz Limited in Chicago) and, so as to travel the country in style, shipped with him his brand new Cadillac.[53] During this second visit, Bechet laid down the first of his huge catalog of French recordings, made both with local musicians and with other visiting Americans. In particular, he cut a number of sides for Charles Delaunay's newly formed Vogue label, in the process guaranteeing its long-term prosperity. The big hit was "Les

51. Boris Vian, "Retour sur . . . le festival du jazz," *Spectacles*, no. 8 (1 June 1949), reprinted in Vian, *Œuvres*, vol. 8, *Jazz 3*, ed. Claude Rameil (Paris: Fayard, 2001), 97–99. See also Vian, "Réflexions en l'air," *Combat*, 10 June 1949, reprinted in *Œuvres*, vol. 7, *Jazz 2*, ed. Claude Rameil (Paris: Fayard, 2000), 171–73.

52. Boris Vian, "Ne crachez pas la musique noire," *Radio '49*, no. 238 (13 May 1949), reprinted in Vian, *Œuvres*, 8:109–11 (quote on p. 110).

53. Chilton, *Sidney Bechet*, 219–20.

Oignons," a catchy if trivial tune based on an old Creole folk song, which, over the next ten years, came to be Bechet's signature; by the time of his death in 1959 it had sold well over a million copies.[54]

As is often the case with hit songs, the extent of the popularity of "Les Oignons" is, in retrospect, a little hard to fathom. Certainly, this music does not place great demands on the listener, its simple tune little more than a riff, repeated time and time again. On the other hand, perhaps it made the perfect introduction to traditional jazz, whose noisy polyphony can leave newcomers perplexed. The tune of "Les Oignons" is stated and restated before any variations on it are made; the counterpoint is of the simplest kind, mostly in rhythmic unison with the melody; and even the breaks have nothing tricky to fill them—rather, silence in anticipation of the return of the theme. When, finally, Bechet takes a solo, the same tune continues underneath; having caught listeners' attention by soaring high, he constructs his line from brief motives that fit the melody's rhythmic syntax. In short, this is a form of ragged march, reconstructing in coarse but not unappealing terms the earliest days of jazz. For French fans it had a further attraction: you could dance to it "like a bourrée."[55]

Similar numbers on French folk songs (or their ur-type) would follow, many of them becoming jukebox hits. Of course, Bechet was far from the first to add a Gallic tinge to jazz: at least since the early thirties, French bands such as Ray Ventura's had swung local songs. But Bechet lent the enterprise a legitimacy that it had previously lacked: as one writer put it in 1956, he provided at once "a style of jazz more accessible to Latin ears" and an attachment to "the authentic and passionate music discovered by black Louisiana slaves."[56] What is more, he pandered to a long-standing French desire to lay their hands on jazz. Describing the origins of jazz, Bechet once said: "The rhythm came from Africa, but the music, the foundation, came from right here in France."[57]

In another song recorded in the same session, "Buddy Bolden Story," Bechet went further to establish his credentials as an originator of the New Orleans style. At the beginning, he and Claude Luter engage in some lighthearted banter (in French). Bechet remarks that playing the blues

54. Tournès, *New Orleans sur Seine*, 289.

55. Mouly, *Sidney Bechet*, 10.

56. J. P., "À l'Alhambra: Sydney Bechet: Musique d'abord," *Franc-Tireur*, 23 January 1956, in 8° Sw 80, "Alhambra, 1951–1960," vol. 2, Département des Arts du Spectacle, Bibliothèque Nationale, Paris (hereafter cited as AdS).

57. Sidney Bechet, interview, in Blake Ehrlich, "Old Man with a Horn: Sidney Bechet, at Sixty-one, is America's Most Renowned Expatriate Musician," *Esquire*, July 1958, 95–98 (quote on p. 95).

takes him back to his earliest days in New Orleans. But he laughs off Luter's suggestion that he was already performing with jazz pioneer Buddy Bolden at age six or seven, modestly insisting this was not until he was twelve or thirteen. Given that Bolden had been admitted to a psychiatric hospital by the time Bechet was ten, it is possible the young musician could have heard the trumpeter play but not that he had joined his band:[58] it was a tall tale designed to authenticate Bechet as a living record of the earliest jazz.

Between these two songs and others, Bechet achieved a careful balancing act: he was a New Orleans jazzman but also a Creole who had, in a sense, come "home" to France and was happy to play a Gallic-inflected repertoire. In a review of these recordings in *Jazz hot*, Gérard Pochonet remarked how his "delightful accent [savoureux accent]" speaking French and his "striking inspiration" made these "the best souvenirs . . . of Bechet's visit to France."[59] What the musician (or perhaps his new manager, Delaunay) had been quick to realize was that it was not only exoticism or "authenticity" that underlay his appeal but a feigned familiarity, too.

One more tune he recorded for the first time in 1949 and adopted into his "French" repertoire was the old Maurice Yvain song "Mon homme" (cut at the tail of a session with a band of American expatriates, reduced in this track to a trio of drummer Kenny Clarke, pianist Charlie Lewis, and French bassist Pierre Michelot). This was another canny choice. While the song was indelibly associated in France by then with the music-hall star Mistinguett, it had also been familiar in the States since Fanny Brice sang it in the *Ziegfeld Follies of 1921*. As "My Man," the song had subsequently been adopted as a jazz standard, performed and recorded famously by Billie Holiday among many others.

"Mon homme" suited Bechet well: his version owes more, I'm sure, to Holiday than to Mistinguett, still less to Fanny Brice, but in France it played as a tribute to their own great artiste, who had rerecorded it as recently as 1938 (eighteen years after her first version). This said, Bechet's famous vibrato—broadening even, in his last decade—is not of Holiday's pretty, ornamental kind, used to "tickle" long notes once she finally reaches the vowel, but rather a strong, sometimes raucous effect, which is more or less constant in his sound. Is there not a trace of the street singer turned cabaret star Mistinguett—or even Edith Piaf—to be heard in that distinctive timbre? Frank Ténot noted:

58. On Bechet's possible encounter with Bolden, see Chilton, *Sidney Bechet*, 5.

59. Gérard Pochonet, "Les Disques: Vogue, Bechet-Luter," *Jazz hot*, no. 40 (January 1950): 16.

Outre ses vertus propres, cette face donnera peut-être l'occasion de faire apprécier le mécanisme de l'improvisation dans le jazz à de nombreux profanes. Bechet reste ainsi le meilleur des vulgarisateurs de cette musique—mais un vulgarisateur sans vulgarité.[60]

Besides its own virtues, this side will perhaps provide the opportunity for many uninitiated listeners to learn to appreciate the improvisation process in jazz. Bechet remains in this way the best of the popularizers of this music—but a popularizer without populism.

If Bechet, too, became a successful music-hall "turn," "Mon homme," with its rhetorical slow introduction preceding an up-tempo bounce, provides a clue why. For once, he does not have other horns to steer a path around and can give free rein to his powerful, throaty saxophone; New Orleans tradition notwithstanding, it was as an unrivaled soloist that Bechet was most comfortable and played at his best. The last few bars of the song, in slower tempo again, are pure showboating. Bechet had returned "Mon homme" to France—though most listeners probably never knew it had been away.[61]

Already by October 1949, *Jazz hot* was reporting that Bechet's renown in the jazz community was crossing over into mainstream success; the general public was falling for Bechet, despite their customary disinterest bordering on animosity about jazz.[62] The next month, André Hodeir tried to explain the broad base of his appeal:

Sidney Béchet réussit ce miracle de passionner à la fois l'amateur de jazz, le musicien et le profane. Au premier, il apporte toutes les joies que celui-ci attend du jazz. Il étonne le second par sa maîtrise d'un instrument

---

60. Frank Ténot, "Les Disques: Vogue, Sidney Bechet," *Jazz hot*, no. 40 (January 1950): 16.

61. Mistinguett's own account of hearing Bechet perform the song is priceless: "As I sat sipping my 'pastis,' an old Negro with stubby jewelled fingers put his saxophone to his lips and began to play. . . . I did not recognize the tune at first. It was a sad tune and everyone was looking at me. Then before I knew it my eyes filled with tears. The Negro was called Sidney Bechet. He was playing *Mon homme*. I put on my dark glasses. Others were crying too, pretty girls, who leaned their faces on their hands as they sat listening" (*Mistinguett: Queen of the Paris Night*, trans. Lucienne Hill [London: Elek Books, 1954], 239).

62. Jazz hot [pseud. for the editors], "Armstrong et Béchet en France," *Jazz hot*, no. 37 (October 1949): 1.

ingrat entre tous. Enfin, le côté sentimental et un peu facile de sa musique séduit le dernier.[63]

Sidney Bechet pulls off the miracle of enthralling at once the jazz fan,
the musician, and the uninitiated listener. To the first, he brings all the
joys expected of jazz. He stuns the second with his mastery of the least
sympathetic of instruments. Finally, the sentimental and slightly facile
side of his music appeals to the last.

And so it was that, over the next few years, paunchy, grey-haired Bechet
became an unlikely national celebrity in France. For a while, he shipped
his Cadillac back and forth with him from the States, but by 1951, when
his wedding in the south of France was celebrated with a re-creation of a
New Orleans Mardi Gras parade, Bechet's move had become permanent.
Aside from his regular performances in St. Germain clubs (beyond both
the price range and the comfort zone of many record fans) and occasional
concerts, Bechet would come to play on mixed bills at the music hall.
Though not a new practice among jazz musicians in France (far from it),
this signaled a continued desire to reach out to audiences, rather than to
accept a niche appeal.

Music-hall critics commonly praised Bechet's performances, even as
they admitted knowing next to nothing about jazz and caring even less for
its arcane wrangles. However, their lack of vocabulary for the music left
them grasping for metaphors, which capture an important (if troubling)
aspect of Bechet's allure. His "coppery stream of black lyricism" came with
"the nice, broad smile of old Uncle Tom," thought one writer.[64] For another, more extraordinarily, Bechet had succeeded in turning the hall into
"a New Orleans tavern, in the same way that Vivien Leigh [in *Gone with
the Wind*] took us, galloping on her horse, back to the Civil War."[65] Indeed,
the musician seems to have tapped into a deep vein of nostalgia, in the
1950s, for simpler times (a theme to which I shall return). Asked one more
reviewer, in 1955:

N'est-ce pas du soleil, des fleurs, de l'eau, du ciel que vous parle ce nègre
aux cheveux blancs et au masque plissé comme un marron glacé—du

63. André Hodeir, "Popularité de Louis Armstrong," *Jazz hot*, no. 38 (November
1949): 1.
64. G. Joly, "À l'Olympia: Mouloudji et Sidney Bechet," *L'Aurore*, 4 September
1954, in 8° Sw 106, "Olympia, 1954–1960," vol. 2, AdS.
65. Jean Bouret, "Les Variétés: Music-Hall Saint-Germain-des-Prés," *Franc-
Tireur*, 4 September 1954, in 8° Sw 106, "Olympia, 1954–1960," vol. 2, AdS.

Montmartre et du Montparnasse de naguère, de La Nouvelle-Orléans de jadis? N'est-ce pas la joie de vivre et l'amour qu'il vous souhaite dans le cri strident de sa clarinette?[66]

Is it not the sun, the flowers, the water, the sky of which this Negro with white hair and a face wrinkled like a chestnut speaks to you—of Montmartre and of Montparnasse of recent times, of New Orleans of yesteryear? Is it not joie de vivre and love that he wishes you in the strident cry of his clarinet?

It would be wrong to think that this was simply a matter of nostalgia, however, or that Bechet's fans were all "of a certain age." In fact, his success was only the most conspicuous sign of a more general change in audience patterns—and behaviors. Ludovic Tournès, whose extraordinary history of jazz in France is richest in detail about the twenty years after the war, has traced a dramatic rise in audiences in the 1950s. Following a slump to just ten thousand attendances at jazz events in Paris per year during 1944–1946, numbers rose to an average of around four times that in 1947–1951 and peaked at greater than three hundred thousand in 1954.[67] This audience was typically young and educated, often still studying—50 percent of respondents to a survey in the French monthly *Jazz Magazine* in 1959 were aged fifteen to twenty[68]—although it did extend into middle age. Broadly speaking, their tastes seem to have broken down like this:

Le jazz Nouvelle-Orléans, par sa franchise brutale et ses thèmes faciles, plaît aux très jeunes et . . . aux plus de cinquante ans, qui y trouvent une survivance d'un passé déjà lointain. Le jazz moderne, lui, touche la génération intermédiaire, qui se complaît dans cette musique où tout est recherche et raffinement.[69]

---

66. Unidentified editorial in *Pourquoi pas?* (Belgium), n.d., cited in Boris Vian, "Revue de presse," *Jazz hot*, no. 96 (February 1955): 33, reprinted in Vian, *Œuvres*, vol. 6, *Jazz 1*, ed. Claude Rameil (Paris: Fayard, 1999), 455–56.

67. Tournès, *New Orleans sur Seine*, appendix 4, 465–67 (esp. p. 467). The figures I cite here are attendances not unique attendees and include music-hall shows featuring jazz as well as concerts. Tournès focuses his discussion (pp. 333–34) on concert audiences alone, hence his interpretation reads slightly differently to mine, but the statistics are all his.

68. Tournès, *New Orleans sur Seine*, 336.

69. Unidentified article, *Le Figaro*, 17 July 1958, cited in Tournès, *New Orleans sur Seine*, 337.

New Orleans jazz, by its rude spontaneity and its simple themes, appeals to the very young and . . . to the over fifties, who find in it a vestige of an already distant past. Modern jazz reaches the generation in between, who take pleasure in this music in which all is studied elegance and refinement.

The ages of the audiences, as well as perhaps the styles of performance, produced different behaviors. Concerts of New Orleans music were, far from historical re-creations, often riotous affairs, once described by trombonist Mowgli Jospin as "a battle between the bands and the public to find out which one could make the most noise."[70] In a bizarre but real way, the older New Orleans musicians and the young French pretenders experienced, for a while in the early to midfifties, the adulation and hysteria that would soon be reserved for rock 'n' roll stars. Gate-crashing, overcrowding, and a degree of hysteria were evident at Bechet's Paris concerts as early as 1950.[71] Tournès has even coined a term for the phenomenon: "Bechetmania."[72]

Matters came to a head at a free concert Bechet gave at the Olympia music hall in 1955 to celebrate the sale of his millionth record. While three thousand fans crushed into the hall, up to the same number who had not gained entry ran amok outside. One hundred police arrived, twenty people were arrested, and two were injured. The photo story in *Paris-Match* spoke of a "maladie du jazz."[73] *Jazz hot* meanwhile congratulated Bechet heartily on his success and role in the diffusion of jazz but deplored how

l'enthousiasme—le mot est faible—excessif des très jeunes gens qui constituaient l'essentiel de l'auditoire se soit transformé en une espèce de furie dévastatrice absolument inexcusable. Nous savons bien que les vrais amateurs de jazz ne sont pas parmi ceux-là, mais il est à craindre que le "grand public" à la suite des actes de vandalisme commis à l'Olympia n'enfourche à nouveau le fameux cheval de bataille "de la musique de sauvages" et cela pour le plus grand préjudice du jazz.[74]

70. Mowgli Jospin, interview, *Le Figaro*, 12 March 1956, cited in Tournès, *New Orléans sur Seine*, 364.

71. Chilton, *Sidney Bechet*, 236.

72. Tournès, *New Orleans sur Seine*, 285–90.

73. Anon., "Les Fans de Paris sacrifient à leur dieu Bechet en saccagant un music-hall," *Paris-Match*, no. 342 (29 October 1955), cited in Tournès, *New Orléans sur Seine*, 365, which account of the event I draw on here.

74. Anon., "Sidney Bechet millionnaire," *Jazz hot*, no. 104 (November 1955): 38.

the excessive enthusiasm—the word is inadequate—of the very young people who made up the core of the audience turned into a violent rage that was absolutely inexcusable. We know for sure that the real jazz fans were not among those involved, but we fear that the general public, following the acts of vandalism committed at the Olympia, will get on its high horse again about "the music of savages," and that to the greatest detriment to jazz.

Critics need not have worried. By the end of the decade, concerts of rock 'n' roll would displace those of jazz as the venue of such displays of ebullience bordering on unrest: jazz fans were growing up and their younger siblings would find new outlets for their energy and adulation. According to Tournès's analysis, when rock 'n' roll began to vie with jazz in the midfifties, its audience tended to be still younger and was also typically less educated. Meanwhile, students remained prominent among the jazz audience, which in addition was largely middle class. From that point forward, jazz musicians could but wish their performances would be interrupted by clamoring young fans.[75] For the moment, though, the crowd's "excessive enthusiasm" was enough to ensure a large police presence at Bechet's concerts.

But Is It Authentic? Critical Disputes

If the public and mainstream press loved Bechet, the attitude of specialist critics during his last decade in France was much more mixed—a situation that is only partly explained by the postwar factionalization of the French jazz community. As Tournès has discussed at length, the dynamics of jazz criticism in postwar France were complex and personal; I can only sketch them here. Bechet is an interesting case, however, as reactions to him sometimes ran contrary to established positions, revealing what was truly at stake. Paradoxically, the "progressive" *Jazz hot* critics were ultimately sympathetic to the saxophonist, albeit with reservations. Bechet's more natural champion, Hugues Panassié, turned his back, suspicious of the musician's very popularity, his divergence from New Orleans classics, and—perhaps particularly—his management by Delaunay.[76]

75. Tournès, *New Orléans sur Seine*, 365–69.

76. *Jazz hot* was not reticent about taking credit for its role in reestablishing Bechet's career: "En quelques années, Sidney Béchet est devenu l'une des figures les plus populaires du continent et le musicien de jazz le plus populaire en France. C'est en grande partie grâce à notre revue et par la reproduction dans ces colonnes d'un article d'Ernest Ansermet (décembre 1938) découvert par notre collaborateur

In Panassié's record reviews of the 1950s, a pattern emerged in which reissues of Bechet's prewar and immediate postwar recordings (which had sometimes been supervised by the critic) were celebrated, while those made "after the fall" (on occasion for Delaunay) were derided. He played "dreadful 'baloney'" (affreux "saucissons") and corny old tunes (rengaines) that he did not swing but warbled—"as antijazz as possible."[77] To begin, Panassié's distaste could still be overcome, by a disc in which the musician's "magnificent inspiration" shone through, or in which "on retrouve le grand Bechet."[78] But, as time passed, such occasions became increasingly rare; his most successful recordings just stank, to the critic, of commercial compromise.

In preference, Panassié turned back to one of his early informants about jazz, the Chicago clarinetist and self-proclaimed White Negro, Mezz Mezzrow, whose autobiography, *Really the Blues*, had recently done much to cement a view of black life as one of "natural" depravity (fig. 5.7). Before the war, the critic had taken great pains to win Mezzrow the chance to record with Bechet. Ten years later, Panassié was celebrating Mezzrow's musical "authenticity" over Bechet's "corruption." *Really the Blues* had been immediately translated, in part by Panassié's longtime "companion," Madeleine Gautier. It was, the Frenchman insisted, essential reading: "the finest, truest book that has ever been written on our music" and a "message of life and of hope . . . to all men, white or black, jazz fans or not."[79] Mezzrow's playing, too. Panassié had "scarcely heard jazz, even in the United States, that swung as intensely"; Mezz's was "true jazz, jazz in its pure state."[80] The approbation ran both ways, with the musician himself enlisted (translated by Gautier again) to attack the "pseudo-critics" and to sing Panassié's praises. In an impure and cynical world, only one organization, the Hot Club de France, and its director kept the faith, "across all

Michel Andrico, que l'attention des amateurs fut attirée sur ce grand musicien. . . . Dès lors, sa réputation ne cessa de s'affirmer et il est aujourd'hui universellement considéré comme l'un des plus grands musiciens de la Nouvelle-Orléans" (Pierre Cressant, "Sidney Bechet," *Jazz hot*, no. 65 [April 1952]: 16–17 [quote on p. 16]). The same article complains of Panassié's "conspiration du silence" about Bechet (17).

77. Hugues Panassié, "Les Disques: Bechet," *Le Bulletin du Hot Club de France* [henceforth, *BHCF*], no. 1 (October 1950): 12.

78. Hugues Panassié, "Les Disques: Bechet," *BHCF*, no. 1 (October 1950): 12; Panassié, "Les Disques: Bechet-Luter," *BHCF*, no. 6 (March 1951): 8.

79. Hugues Panassié, "Les Livres: *La Rage de vivre*," *BHCF*, no. 1 (October 1950): 13.

80. Hugues Panassié, "Mezz et Luter au Vieux Colombier," *BHCF*, no. 12 (November 1951): 5.

FIGURE 5.7. Portrait of Mezz Mezzrow in his office, New York, NY, ca. November 1946 (William P. Gottlieb Collection, Library of Congress).

the obstacles, all the humiliations, all the years"; Panassié was Mezzrow's "friend, a gentleman and a scholar."[81]

Finally, Mezzrow's and Bechet's records began going head-to-head in Panassié's criticism. Mezzrow's recording of "Black and Blue" was the only one worth hearing after Louis Armstrong's and "far superior to Sidney Bechet's."[82] A few months later, Panassié complained that Bechet's recordings were becoming "less and less good." He proposed to his readers an experiment:

81. Milton "Mezz" Mezzrow, "Le Jazz et ses parasites," *BHCF*, no. 14 (January 1952): 3–4 (quotes on p. 4).

82. Hugues Panassié, "Les Disques parus en France: Milton 'Mezz' Mezzrow– Claude Luter," *BHCF*, no. 14 (January 1952): 13.

Après avoir entendu toutes ces exécutions de Bechet, écoutez immédiatement après celles enregistrées par Mezz pour Vogue avec le même orchestre de [Claude] Luter. C'est le jour et la nuit. Il y a autant de vie, de
swing, d'ambiance jazz dans ces enregistrements de Mezz-Luter qu'il y
en a peu dans ces nouveaux Bechet. Pour ne rien dire de l'inspiration de
Mezz, si supérieure à celle de Bechet.[83]

After having heard all these performances by Bechet, listen straight
away to those by Mezz for Vogue with the same band of [Claude] Luter.
It's like night and day. There's as much life, swing and jazz atmosphere
in the new recordings of Mezz-Luter as there is little of it in the new
Bechet. Not to say anything about Mezz's inspiration, so superior to that
of Bechet.

Mezzrow, whose last dealings with the saxophonist had ended with Bechet
pulling a knife on him to retrieve some disputed money, was doubtless
happy to agree about his "corruption." But by insisting musicians reproduce old styles and repertoire exactly, Mezzrow and Panassié had arrived
at a position similar to that of Ernest Ansermet, if by a different route.
The parties agreed that the core of jazz was strongly resistant to change.
Where Ansermet believed that jazz could not evolve, however, Mezzrow
and Panassié insisted it *should* not—and that if it did, the result would
no longer be jazz. Regarding jazz as the folk music of a deprived minority, they considered its transformation its degeneration and an abandon-
ment of its cultural roots. In other words, they sought not just to describe
or define but also to delimit African American musical expression.[84]

At the same time, Panassié was goading the *Jazz hot* critics, whose "incompetence" he never hesitated to advertise, into a response: "Zazotteux,"

83. Hugues Panassié, "Les Disques parus en France: Bechet-Luter," *BHCF*, no. 18
(May 1952): 9. For the *Jazz hot* position, see Cressant, "Sidney Bechet," 17.

84. Panassié reiterated the comparison when recordings of Bechet's and
Mezzrow's concerts at the Salle Pleyel early in 1952 were released. Not only was
Mezz's performance better but even his audience seemed more connoisseuring
("l'air plus connaisseur") ("Les Disques parus en France: Bechet-Luter," *BHCF*,
no. 22 [December 1952]: 13). Panassié was still making the point at the decade's end:
"Bechet revint en Europe en 1949 et, devant le gros succès qu'il remporta auprès
du public français, ne tarda pas à se fixer dans notre pays. Ce succès le gâta quelque peu, d'ailleurs. Abusant des effets faciles sur l'instrument 'séduisant' qu'est le
saxo soprano, Bechet joua de moins en moins pour les amateurs de jazz et de plus
en plus pour le public de variétés, évidemment beaucoup plus nombreux. Mezz,
au contraire, resta fidèle au jazz pur" (Panassié, *Histoire du vrai jazz* [Paris: Robert
Laffont, 1959], 192).

as he called the offending writers (combining *Jazz hot* with *zazou*, the wartime term for swing fans, to imply youthful foolishness), were under strict instructions to be "béchetolâtre" (Bechet-ites).[85] Having refused to spend column inches debating with him, the *Jazz hot* writers finally hit back in a one-off issue of a supposed new journal, in July 1952. Designed to resemble Panassié's *Bulletin du Hot Club de France*, it took the name *La Revue du jazz*, under which he had for a time published (1949–1950, until the director of that journal himself defected and distributed *Jazz hot* instead). Its rhetoric was no subtler than his, stating up front that its purpose was to counteract Panassié's "sometimes dangerous" writings.[86]

Aside from predictable complaints about the critic's exclusion of modern jazz—which extended, they claimed, as far as sabotaging concerts—his tastes in the traditional music and their motives came under attack: Panassié had organized a huge "press campaign" for Mezzrow but maintained a "veritable conspiracy of silence" about Bechet.[87] This might not, Delaunay speculated, be unconnected to Panassié's financial interests in the former's success (a hypocritical remark, given Delaunay's own stake in the latter's). Meanwhile, other writers denounced the critic's "megalomania," and his "refusal of the name jazz to all that does not evoke the Louisiana black stooped under a bail of cotton."[88] André Hodeir, in slightly melodramatic fashion, identified in Panassié's attacks on him not only partisanship and a lack of technical understanding but "l'ENVIE et la HAINE" (ENVY and HATRED).[89] The pièce de résistance of the team's special magazine was a copy of a letter from Bechet to Panassié complaining that the critic's dispute with Delaunay was making musicians' lives difficult and bemoaning in particular his mention in print of Bechet's earlier expulsion from France: "I wouldn't have treated a dog like that."[90] If, ostensibly, the two organizations and their respective publications differed on musical grounds, their debate about Mezzrow's and Bechet's merits

85. Hugues Panassié, "Livres: *Les Maîtres de jazz*, de Lucien Malson," *BHCF*, no. 26 (March 1953): 25.

86. *La Revue du jazz*, "2ᵉ série, no. 1" (July 1952): 2.

87. Charles Delaunay, "Autrefois les amateurs . . . ," ibid., 2–4 (quotes on p. 4).

88. Lucien Malson, "Panassié mégalomane," ibid., 5–6; Jacques B. Hess, "Panassié: archéologue ou viellard?," ibid., 6.

89. André Hodeir, "Une Réfutation de 'l'irréfutable,'" *La Revue du jazz* (July 1952): 8–14 (quote on p. 14).

90. "Quelques Lettres peu connues: Une Lettre de Sidney Bechet," *La Revue du jazz* (July 1952): 14. Panassié responded briefly in "Revue de la presse," *BHCF*, no. 20 (August–September 1952): 22; and "Mise en point au sujet de Big Bill et Bechet," *BHCF*, no. 21 (October 1952): 17.

suggest that this was a misleading symptom of a condition that was at once more generalized and more superficial.

Nevertheless, in the face of the *Bulletin*'s critical onslaught, even from a writer with decreasing influence, affirmations of Bechet in *Jazz hot* sometimes sounded a little defensive. Thus, in a very positive review of his 1952 Salle Pleyel concert, Gérard Pochonet insisted:

> Bechet est toujours aussi vert, aussi dynamique, et sa flamme communicative est tout simplement admirable. Il reste un VRAI ET GRAND musicien qui n'a pas usurpé sa réputation, et honore grandement le style New-Orleans. Sidney et son soprano ne font qu'un. Quant aux années, elles sont sans effet sur cet extraordinaire instrumentiste qui force l'admiration du plus endurci.[91]

> Bechet is as sprightly, as dynamic as ever, and his infectious fervor is quite simply admirable. He remains a TRUE AND GREAT musician who richly deserves his reputation and greatly honors the New Orleans style. Sidney and his soprano are but one. As for the passing years, they have no effect on this extraordinary instrumentalist who commands the strongest admiration.

Over time, *Jazz hot*'s reviews, too, became more circumspect. A group of critics for the journal even got together to discuss "Le Cas Sidney Bechet" in 1955, without however reaching any firm conclusions. One, René Urtreger, thought Bechet's appeal lay in his extraordinary presence: "He looks like a grandfather and he plays like crazy [comme un fou]."[92] But this did not explain why André Hodeir's mother "who doesn't like jazz, loves Sidney Bechet": there was just something about his playing that was "very close to the French temperament," Kurt Mohr said.[93] Familiar issues were sounded, including the varied and sometimes incompatible audiences he attracted: New Orleans jazz fans, who demanded the traditional repertoire, and music-hall goers, who wanted to hear him play familiar popular songs. These writers also believed that Bechet's reception as a New Orleans jazz musician had more to do with his city of birth than with his playing: his instrument, his compositions, and even his stylistic

---

91. Gérard Pochonet, "Sidney Bechet, Claude Luter à Pleyel," *Jazz hot*, no. 64 (March 1952): 19.

92. André Clergeat, André Hodeir, Kurt Mohr, Michel de Villers, and René Urtreger, "Le Cas Sidney Bechet," *Jazz hot*, no. 101 (July–August 1955): 9–10 (quote on p. 9).

93. Ibid., 9, 10.

inclinations all had reinvented tradition, even before he left the States. Nobody accepted that Bechet's playing had faded over time, though his output had been mixed. André Hodeir concluded:

Le double faux personnage que l'on a fait de Sidney Bechet: la vedette de music-hall et le champion-du-vrai-jazz-New-Orleans ne devrait pas nous dissimuler le véritable Bechet. Espérons qu'il se trouvera des amateurs en nombre suffisant pour l'inciter à jouer plus souvent la musique qu'il aime et, par là, à rester un créateur authentique.[94]

The two bogus figures that have been made of Sidney Bechet—the music-hall star and the champion-of-true-New-Orleans-jazz—should not conceal from us the real Bechet. Let's hope that he will find a sufficient number of enthusiasts to encourage him to play the music that he likes more often and, in this way, to remain a true artist.

For Hodeir, then, neither populism nor re-creation truly described—contained—Bechet's style; he was too vibrant a musician to be frozen in nostalgia for a timeless past. Bechet would not have disagreed; he disdained the "fossilization" of the tradition into standard arrangements that he saw among some of the white Dixieland revivalists: "You know, there's this mood about the music, a kind of need to be moving. You just can't set it down and hold it. Those Dixieland musicianers, they tried to do that; they tried to write the music down and kind of freeze it. . . . The music, it's got this itch to be going in it—when it loses that, there's not much left."[95] Nevertheless—as Bechet would repeatedly emphasize—the story he wanted to tell with his music went back "a long way."[96]

Telling His Own Story: The Long Song

Despite his success, Bechet's life and music had become a screen onto which were projected quite different sets of expectations and desires, capable of generating in turn nostalgia, excitement, and even disdain. It is little surprise, then, that Bechet grew increasingly concerned, over his last few years, to wrest back some control of his representation. His attempts to shape his history—and his music's—are nowhere more apparent than in his extraordinary autobiography, *Treat It Gentle*. This book is rightly celebrated as one of the most evocative depictions there are of

94. Ibid., 10.
95. Bechet, *Treat It Gentle*, 95–96; see also pp. 114–15.
96. Ibid., 4.

a "jazz life," and it has been well mined. A degree of caution is required, however, given the book's convoluted journey to publication, as well as Bechet's own capacity to fictionalize.

In as understated a claim as one is likely to find in jazz writing, John Chilton notes in a short introduction to his biography of Bechet that his "findings do not always tally with Sidney's own account of events."[97] Only at the very end of his book does Chilton return to explain the long and difficult gestation of the autobiography, which was finally published posthumously in 1960 with the less-than-inspiring declaration that "among those who helped record and edit the tapes on which this book is based are Joan Reid, Desmond Flower, and John Ciardi." This is not a unique problem in jazz testimony, of course, but where it is possible to track, for example, Alan Lomax's rendition of Jelly Roll Morton's autobiography back to its source in the Library of Congress recordings, Bechet's trace is thin: only parts of the last interviews with Desmond Flower are available in public collections; the rest are presumed lost, along with any manuscripts.[98]

American poet John Ciardi, who first met Bechet in Paris in 1950, provides the most complete explanation. According to him, when Bechet learned that Ciardi was a writer and an editor, he proffered a manuscript of his autobiography. The document turned out to have been compiled, from taped interviews and monologues, by Joan Reid (née Williams), whom Bechet called his "secretary," complete with her own interjections. In preparation for publication, Ciardi removed the intrusions and filled in details, particularly of later years, from conversations with Bechet that he himself held in Paris and later Boston. At this point, Reid insisted that the work was hers and threatened to sue the prospective publisher, Twayne, who shelved the project.[99] Years later, however, British writer Desmond Flower procured Ciardi's manuscript from Twayne, and conducted his own interviews with Bechet, a process that was not complete when the musician died. The extent of Flower's intervention, like Reid's, is unclear,

97. Chilton, Sidney Bechet, xv.

98. The still incomplete story is told in ibid., 290–92. See also Desmond Flower's foreword to Treat It Gentle.

99. John Ciardi, "Writing Treat It Gentle: A Letter to Vince Clemente, September 22, 1985," in John Ciardi: Measure of the Man, ed. Vince Clemente (Fayetteville: University of Arkansas Press, 1987), 82–83. Ciardi apparently conveyed similar information in correspondence with John Chilton (Chilton, Sidney Bechet, 291–92). Traces of Reid's questions and commentary that were excised by Ciardi are found in the extracts of the book published as "Souvenirs de Sidney Bechet," trans. Boris Vian, Jazz hot, no. 63 (February 1952): 12, 20.

but Ciardi himself insisted at the time of the threatened suit that "in the finished manuscript *no word of [Reid's] appears: not one*. It's all Sidney's talk and," he continues, tellingly, "talk I have put into his mouth."[100] Ciardi further believed that "the first eighty-five or ninety percent" of the book as it was eventually published, under Flower's name, was "just as I had set it down."[101]

So the waters are muddy. What seems clear is that Ciardi did not hear the original tapes on which Reid's manuscript was based, did not always employ a recording device himself, and was confident in his ability to render material convincingly in Bechet's voice. Both Ciardi and later Flower stated independently that Bechet had approved their completed texts, albeit with the caveat by the time of Flower's that he wanted to add more detail about the later years.[102] Even if these self-serving claims are true, however, Bechet would have been unlikely to object, given his sympathetic portrayal, failing health, and long-held desire to see his story in print. He never did get the chance to update it fully, and *Treat It Gentle* remains strongly weighted toward Bechet's early career (indeed, to his origins as he saw them), merely sketching his last years in France. Still, it is from the perspective of those last years, when the reminiscences were recorded and the book written, that I want to consider it here—reading the story, as Bechet et al. narrate it, back through the lens of the fifties to early jazz in New Orleans.[103]

Despite all the interventions, the voice that speaks from Bechet's biography is a powerful one, resonant with an oral storytelling tradition. This is the case in particular of the opening chapter—for good reason, as it turns out. In a long, rambling tale, Bechet locates the source of his musical gift, as well as of the whole jazz tradition, with his slave grandfather Omar. Omar's story is extraordinary and is not easily reduced to a plot. Deferring for the moment its music and poetry, however, its essential events are these: An admired musician and dancer, Omar falls in

---

100. Ciardi, letter to Jack Steinberg, 16 April 1952, John Ciardi Papers, Library of Congress, Washington, DC, cited in Edward M. Cifelli, *John Ciardi: A Biography* (Fayetteville: University of Arkansas Press, 1997), 154 (italics original).

101. Ciardi, "Writing *Treat It Gentle*."

102. Ibid.; Flower, foreword to *Treat It Gentle*.

103. Given the text's complex history, it would be foolhardy to give much weight to the shape of the book, as if it were constructed by its subject with not only rhetorical prowess but also structural oversight. Nevertheless, the device, repeated several times, of positioning the reader in Paris with Bechet in later life (e.g., *Treat It Gentle*, 1–3, 45), foregrounds the act of remembering in this distillation of the musician's wisdom.

love with a young slave girl, Marie, whom he sees in Congo Square. Her master is jealous and shoots Omar, who loses an arm. Falsely accused of raping the master's daughter, he hides out in the bayou, with a voudou woman and runaway slaves. A manhunt follows; eventually Omar is betrayed and killed by a fellow slave, leaving Marie pregnant with Bechet's father.

The story, told over thirty pages, was not a mere stretching of the truth. According to John Chilton's research, Bechet's real paternal grandfather, Jean Becher (Beschet, Beshé, Bechet; b. ca. 1802) was a carpenter and a free man, whose mother, Françoise Cocote, had moved south from Illinois. Jean married Marie Gabrielle and Bechet's father, genuinely called Omar (Omer, Homer), was born circa 1855; one of six surviving children, he would become a cobbler.[104] What is more, Bechet's tale was well-known in African American folklore as the legend of Bras Coupé, the one-armed man; it had even been published in multiple versions, notably (as a story within a story) in George Washington Cable's *The Grandissimes* (1880),[105] and, most surprising of all, transformed into a blackface opera, Frederick Delius's *Koanga* (1897).

Of greater interest than the fact that Bechet's narrative is not literally true, however, is his motivation to craft it. Accustomed as he was to discographers pestering him for minutiae of the distant past, Bechet must have known that his tale would be open to challenge. But he did not allow this to inhibit him. *Treat It Gentle* is a book that seems peculiarly aware of the imagination involved in the act of remembering and of the truth inherent in myth. Most likely, I think, is that Bechet understood the power of Bras Coupé's story and was happy to appropriate it for his purposes— not because he thought he would be believed but because he wished to share its poetic insights with readers. In the process, he revealed much more about his music and philosophy than would have done a simple account of his family history.

In a recent essay, literary scholar Bryan Wagner traces the checkered history of Bras Coupé, a real outlaw of the 1830s. His notoriety, Wagner finds, was the ironic outcome of fearmongering by the New Orleans police, eager to justify their contested weapons and powers. After he lost first his arm and then his life at the hands of the police, Bras Coupé became a folk hero among African Americans. The scene in Congo Square that is Bechet's start-off point was actually a late addition to the story, notably in Cable's version: where the story had formerly concluded with the ex-

104. Chilton, *Sidney Bechet*, 1.

105. George Washington Cable, *The Grandissimes: A Story of Creole Life* (New York: C. Scribner's Sons, 1880).

hibition of Bras Coupé's corpse at the Place d'Armes, now he was literally captured, by lasso, while dancing in the square. Yet Bras Coupé is central to the description of music and dancing at Congo Square in Herbert Asbury's *The French Quarter* (1936). This celebrated book (still in print) was in turn the source, Wagner demonstrates, of accounts of the music's primal scene in early jazz histories—though there such depictions appear minus the one-armed man himself. In other words, the violence and suppression that were at the heart of the black experience in the United States had been progressively written out of the origins of jazz. "What does it mean," Wagner wonders, "to find, as the absence at the origin of jazz historiography, a slave maimed by the police?" *Treat It Gentle*'s "unstated yet unmistakable intention," he argues, "is to write Bras-Coupé back into the history of jazz."[106]

This must be overstating the case on the level of intention, but it does capture the effect. Bechet's book, which at one point was called *Where Did It [Jazz] Come From?*,[107] repeatedly insists on the racial violence that he considers intrinsic to jazz's history. This is less, perhaps, to determine the music's essence than to indicate the range of human experience it engages—a range much wider than found in the brothels where, Bechet also insists more than once, jazz may sometimes have been played but not where it was born.[108] In other words, Bechet won't allow jazz's supposed roots in Congo Square to be couched in terms of nostalgia for an exoticized—eroticized—Old South. Rather, he conveys the danger of the music, in terms both of how it was perceived and of the circumstances in which it was produced.

What is striking, however—and where Bechet's version of the legend differs from many—is that it moves toward a point of reconciliation. Although Bechet portrays the slaveowner who shoots Omar as a brutal man, he also finds him tormented, and the shock of Omar's death elicits a remorse that sees Marie allowed to bring up Bechet's father in the master's house, with his support and kindness: "That girl, Marie, she had a child. And my grandfather being dead, she had no name for it, nothing to christen it by. . . . The master and his wife told her to take their name, Bechet. . . . And after that they let her alone. . . . She had this child, and it was Omar, too. She had a name from each side of her memory to give this

106. Bryan Wagner, "The Strange Career of Bras-Coupé," in *Disturbing the Peace: Black Culture and the Police Power after Slavery* (Cambridge, MA: Harvard University Press, 2009), 58–115 (quotes on p. 105).

107. Announcement of forthcoming Bechet autobiography, *Melody Maker*, 13 October 1951, cited in Chilton, *Sidney Bechet*, 291.

108. Bechet, *Treat It Gentle*, 53–54, 205.

child. Omar Bechet, he was my father."[109] Thus, Marie bears a child who represents the hope of a new beginning in which warring groups may be reconciled. In the account as published, Omar junior's birth directly precedes the emancipation of slaves, which is for Bechet what unlocks the music's potential: "That one day the music had progressed all the way up to the point where it is today, all the way up from what it had been in the beginning to the place where it could be itself."[110]

In Bechet's poetic narrative, then, jazz is born at the intersection of black and white communities, between African and European languages, and at the moment when desperation turns to hope. What is more, by reintroducing Bras Coupé, in the form of his "grandfather," to Congo Square, Bechet lays claim to jazz history in a rather literal sense, suggesting that the transition from the old traditions to the new style took place through the body of his family member: "It was Omar started the song. Or maybe he didn't start it exactly. . . . But it was Omar began the melody of it, the new thing." He continues to explain how, of all the musicians he encountered around the world, "if they was any good, it was Omar's song they were singing," before adding, more circumspectly, "They all had an Omar, somebody like an Omar, somebody that was *their* Omar."[111]

Thus Bechet has it both ways at once. It is clear that Omar is a symbolic figure, representing the generation who would create the earliest sounds of jazz. At the same time, Bechet insists on the direct familial connection between a good "musicianer" and his ancestors and locates himself in the central line of that tradition. The story is at once shared and personal, history and myth, true and not true, remembered and created, believed and performed. Logically nonsensical, his words—connecting the arrival of jazz with the coming of emancipation—are intuitively correct and rhetorically persuasive: "Maybe that's not easy to understand. White people, they don't have the memory that needs to understand it. But that's what the music is . . . a lost thing finding itself. . . . That's where the music was that day [of emancipation]."[112]

109. Ibid., 46–47. Similarly, "those people there, the man and his wife, they were trying to make it up to her. It was almost like they were trying to tell her without putting it into words that they wanted her to come over to them and do their forgetting. Time changes a man, and that master he acted a very different way after all that trouble. It was like some part of the evil had been washed away out of him by all that had happened; and the evil had left a kind of sorrow in its place, a gentler thing" (49).

110. Ibid., 48.

111. Ibid., 202.

112. Ibid., 48.

Composing History: Memories and Memorials

Memory is a topic that has generated some interest in jazz studies recently. In *Race Music* (2004), for example, Guthrie P. Ramsey Jr. considers how music helped to sustain community and tradition at the local level, across generations of his own family in working-class Chicago.[113] In *Monk's Music* (2008), by contrast, Gabriel Solis investigates how the legacy of Thelonious Monk has been negotiated and inscribed by younger musicians who have played his compositions and learned from his idiosyncratic piano style.[114] My interest here is rather different: I am concerned, on the one hand, with how Bechet himself sought to write—and play—his way into the very foundation of jazz's history and, on the other, with how his "rememories" (to borrow a term from Toni Morrison) helped to reinforce a rather rose-tinted view of France's historical relationship to jazz.

In another intriguing reading of *Treat It Gentle*, Nicholas Gebhardt describes Bechet's autobiography as a "remytholigization," which, by assigning an origin myth to jazz, attempts to relocate its social meaning in the space between slavery and freedom. Thus Bechet's task, in words as in music, is to explain the logic of the one condition (indentured servitude) in the terms of the other (free-market capitalism). This renders it an impossible act and makes Bechet's position, as a keeper of the tradition serving entertainment to the market, intractable. But jazz must keep trying to capture the change in black consciousness brought about, slowly rather than suddenly, in the transition between social and economic systems at which its history is located. (Where Gebhardt's reading of jazz performance differs from many is that he describes it not as a process of individual self-expression within the constrictions of the group but rather as a collective act made within social constrictions.)[115]

In a more fundamental way, Bechet's text and music reveal to Gebhardt the "master-slave" dynamic of American society (after the Civil War as much as before it). Dissecting accounts of jazz's roots in the intersection of African and European practices, Gebhardt observes how they elide the Middle Passage (the way in which African and European practices came together in the first place). He—like Bechet, in his way—insists

---

113. Guthrie P. Ramsey Jr., *Race Music: Black Cultures from Bebop to Hip-Hop* (Berkeley: University of California Press, 2003).

114. Gabriel Solis, *Monk's Music: Thelonious Monk and Jazz History in the Making* (Berkeley: University of California Press, 2008).

115. Nicholas Gebhardt, "Sidney Bechet: The Virtuosity of Construction," in *Going for Jazz: Musical Practices and American Ideology* (Chicago: University of Chicago Press, 2001), 33–76.

upon it: "The history of black American music is itself symptomatic of a fundamental and irresolvable antagonism between white and black, between master and slave, and finally between Africa and Europe; and this antagonism, as such, is the inexplicable and irreducible fact of the jazz act that few wish, or even bother, to explain."[116] Thus, Bechet's remythologization of jazz paradoxically requires moments in its prehistory to be understood, retrospectively, in terms of what they came to mean. As Bras Coupé's story was not that of a slave meaninglessly killed but rather one who died fighting for a prefigured freedom, so Bechet's description of jazz's emergence in the context of racial violence paradoxically holds a utopian vision for the future.

Even as he insists on accounting for music in terms of its production rather than its reception,[117] however, Gebhardt gives little sense of what this evolving black consciousness—failing better every time to resolve impossible contradictions—might actually sound like. Bechet is rarely more precise, but he does give a few pointers. In a parallel that is surely too neat to take at face value, he repeatedly sought in *Treat It Gentle* to position his move to France late in life as reuniting jazz's diverse elements, in the same way that Omar Bechet had first brought them together. The most creative example: "I felt when I settled in France that I was nearer to Africa, and I suppose too that being there is nearer to all my family and brings back something I remember of Omar and my father too. So I started to record some lovely Creole tunes that I remembered from when I was young and *some I made myself out of the same remembering*."[118]

This intriguing statement could, of course, represent an attempt to justify decisions made for commercial reasons (as Panassié might have suggested), but so effectively does it sum up Bechet's concerns in the book that it has a ring of truth—or at least the familiarity of a well-rehearsed story. Certainly, jazz scholar David Ake has sought to reposition Bechet in the specific context of French Creole culture in New Orleans. By playing the blues, he argues, Bechet was committing a political act: "playing . . . into being" a "blacker" identity by aligning himself with his African rather than his European heritage.[119] If this is the case, I wonder if Bechet's "French" recordings might not be heard as attempts to play—or

116. Gebhardt, *Going for Jazz*, 67.

117. Ibid., 6.

118. Bechet, *Treat It Gentle*, 194–95 (my italics).

119. David Ake, " 'Blue Horizon': Creole Culture and Early New Orleans Jazz," in *Jazz Cultures* (Berkeley: University of California Press, 2002), 10–41 (quote on p. 36). See also the review by Gabriel Solis in *Ethnomusicology* 47 (2003): 392–95, which is circumspect about Ake's account of the racial context.

play back—into being a self-consciously creolized identity, one which by this time had much more to do with Paris than it did with New Orleans.

Striking in particular in the quotation above is Bechet's description of remembering as a generative as well as a regenerative act. An example might lie in his famous composition "Petite Fleur," a tune that has no deep roots but somehow sounds as if it must. In form, it's a thirty-two bar song: AABA. The first section feels rather earthbound, Bechet's bluesy melody competing with stabbed chords from an ensemble that seems to owe more to the Old World than to the New. In the second section, by contrast, Bechet reaches for the skies, the ensemble supporting him from beneath with sustained harmonies. The first time through the chorus, the effect is heightened when Bechet cuts off the repeat of A after only two bars. He soars straight onto B, which is elongated to fourteen bars and accompanied by rapturous runs in the piano as well as the sustained chords. By sequence, he slowly eases back down to the ground. Bechet plays through that surprise move to B with such rhetorical force that it is tempting to hear this revelatory moment itself as an act of remembering, or at least its invocation; what follows is of an emotional expansiveness that was quite unknown to the first section. (Only later is the B section heard at its "proper" length.)

In a beautiful, evocative discussion of "remembering" in music, Bechet wrote:

> You take when a high note comes through—lifting and going and then stopping because there's no place else for it to go. That's stepping music—it's got to rush itself right off your voice or your horn because it's so excited. You can feel it. . . . All the music I play is from what was finding itself in my grandfather's time. It was like water moving around a stone, all silent, waiting for the stone to wear away. . . . It's like the Mississippi. It's got its own story. There's something it wants to tell."[120]

Granting, for the moment, Bechet's wish to relinquish agency, is this the soaring high note that rushes off his horn—ahead of time—in "Petite Fleur" (and in other such moments that those familiar with Bechet's music will immediately recognize)? It is not an improvised gesture but a studied one whose trace in memory far outlasts its immediate visceral impact.

Far from merely generating nostalgia for the past, however, in such ways as this, Bechet's music of the 1950s is still envisioning the future: where in "Les Oignons" his bluesy playing scarcely gets off the ground,

120. Bechet, *Treat It Gentle*, 46.

here he appears to break through the clouds above to a better place. If that place is France, it is not the France Bechet lived in, even with the fame he had latterly garnered, but rather an imagined France, viewed from afar: a location of which a shackled slave, an immobile sharecropper, or even a humble Creole cobbler like Bechet's father might dream; the place to which, if not this time, then next time, jazz might finally break through.

Meanwhile, French reactions would have brought him back down to earth with a jolt. Far from speaking of future freedoms, Bechet's music increasingly elicited a wistful longing in his adopted country for times past. Before the famous musician came to Paris, one writer observed, in 1957, "he was already our cousin from the country [de province]."[121] Another thought Bechet could "revive with his instrument the poetry of the blacks of Mississippi, that which floats over the bayous, the cotton or sugarcane plantations, and even the 'show-boats' moored along the swampy rivers of America's former Old France."[122]

Such colonial nostalgia—at once affectionate and paternalistic—continued even after Bechet's death, in 1959. Some of this was purely sentimental: Bechet's love of children, his appeal across barriers of age and race, his happy life in Paris (that he had, for years, divided his time between two ménages—his wife's and his child's mother's—was, of course, discreetly ignored). As well as eulogizing the musician as a "vedette française" (French star) and "Français de nom et de cœur" (French in name and heart), however, there were some imaginative renditions of his past.[123] According to one writer, he was born "a little Creole with French blood mixed with his black blood," grandson to a man who "had been adopted by Monsieur Bechet, a French settler on whose plantations, of corn and cotton, the family worked."[124] But for this "jovial patriarch escaped from 'Uncle Tom's Cabin,'" France was the best country "because he had complete freedom": "between segregation and exile, he chose exile."[125]

121. Christian Mégret, "De tout un peu," *Paris-Variétés*, 13 March 1957, in 8° Sw 84, "Bobino Music-Hall, 1933–1960," vol. 7, AdS.

122. Serge, "En écoutant Sidney Bechet," *Les Nouvelles Littéraires*, 14 March 1957, in 8° Sw 84, "Bobino Music-Hall, 1933–1960," vol. 7, AdS.

123. François Millet, "Jazz: Sidney Bechet, vedette française," *L'Express*, 21 May 1959; Lucien Malson, "Mort d'un grand jazzman," *Arts*, 20 May 1959 (both are in 8° Sw 1232, "Bechet [Sidney]: Articles biographiques et critiques le concernant publiés de 1949 à 1959," AdS).

124. Robert Chaix, "'Nuit silencieuse' pour Sidney Bechet," *Ici Paris*, 20 May 1959, in 8° Sw 1232, "Bechet (Sidney)," AdS.

125. Raphaël Valensi, unidentified clipping; Robert Chazal, "Mort à 63 ans, le jour de son anniversaire, le grand saxophoniste Sidney Bechet," *France-Soir*, 15 May

Such was the people's attachment to him that his passing was "almost a national bereavement."[126]

"Between the French and Bechet," one last writer thought, "it was love at first sight: he settled in Paris like a native, even buying a beret."[127] Although the relationship was, as I have shown, a rockier one than this suggests, there is no doubt that Bechet died a well-loved celebrity in France, at the end of the most successful decade of his career. Nevertheless, it is the gap between Bechet's self-representation (albeit self-serving, albeit mediated) and representations of him in the French press that is, in the end, most telling. The sheer power of his music meant that Bechet could never be fully contained by the Uncle Tom caricatures he sometimes condescended to play, and his autobiography is always fighting against his location in a romanticized past, reliving instead the suffering, which could only fleetingly be overcome. To believe some in his adopted country, however, Bechet had, in 1919, escaped American racism to reclaim his historic birthright as a son of Greater France, in whose metropolis he had died a hero, some forty years on. This ignored not only the abortive nature of those early visits, and the happenstance of Bechet's much later return, but also the often intense debates, about art and about race, that jazz had generated in the interim. The gap between his perspective and theirs may also, therefore, allow some light to shine on the historiography of jazz in France.

In retrospect, the rediscovery of Ansermet's text in 1938 was a signal event, although it had to wait a decade before its symbolic importance was fully realized. Nevertheless, it was surely this perspicuous article, much more than the few lines penned by Jean Cocteau and others in the 1910s and 1920s, that informed Charles Delaunay's claim as early as 1940 that the French avant-garde had recognized the "originality and promise" of jazz *"more than 10 years before"* the Americans.[128] Soon even American

---

1959; Alain Guerin, "Sidney Bechet: Le Chant interrompu" (all are in 8° Sw 1232, "Bechet (Sidney)," AdS).

126. Millet, "Jazz: Sidney Bechet, vedette française."

127. Anon., "Sidney Bechet à l'agonie," *Tribune de Genève*, 14 May 1959, in 8° Sw 1232, "Bechet (Sidney)," AdS.

128. Charles Delaunay, "Delaunay in Trenches, Writes 'Jazz Not American,'" *DownBeat*, 1 May 1940, 6, 19 (italics original) [also abridged reprint as "From Somewhere in France," in Walser, *Keeping Time*, 129–32]. Compare Walter E. Schaap in the American edition of Delaunay's discography: "Although a distinctly American art form, [jazz] achieved intellectual recognition only when endorsed by European critics, who did the work our own writers should have done, but lamentably failed to do, some ten years earlier" (Schaap, foreword to Charles Delaunay, *Hot Discog-*

authors, such as Rudi Blesh in his *Shining Trumpets* (1946), were calling France "the first country to accord intellectual recognition to jazz."[129] And Boris Vian reproached the Americans for "not tackling the challenge of jazz in the same way as they treated the challenge of the bomb."[130]

Meanwhile, Bechet began to find jazz history as it was evolving to be too static in its perception of the music; it is this, he said, that prompted him to record his autobiography: "I began to think there's a whole lot of people, all they've been hearing is how ragtime got started in New Orleans, and as far as they know it just stopped there. They get to think in a memory kind of way all about this Jazz; but these people don't seem to know it's more than a memory thing. They don't seem to know it's happening right there where they're listening to it, just as much as it ever did in memory."[131]

One way to understand Bechet's French recordings, then, may be as an attempt to remake New Orleans jazz from the ground up—to re-create what it "felt" like rather than merely to reproduce its ossified sound. Taking French folk songs (real or imagined) and adding his own bluesy sound, Bechet was in effect restaging in fifties' France the hybridization of musics to which turn-of-the-century Louisiana had borne witness. If in one sense Bechet told the French what they wanted to hear, at the same time his presence—and his music—was productive of impossible memories: he "played them into being" to borrow David Ake's evocative phrase.[132] Still, Bechet's most attentive audience may yet have been those crazed teenagers who heard the music of a man more than three times their age not as a reconstruction of the past but rather as an anticipation of the popular music of the future. That, of course, is to speak with the benefit of hindsight, but I think this much may safely be said of Bechet's "French jazz" of the 1950s: what seems at first a music out of time and out of place turns out to be peculiarly closely *of* its time and place, a music in which nostalgia for the past combines with a commitment to the moment and the knowledge that remembering too is an act conducted in the present tense.

raphy [New York: Commodore Music Shop, 1940 (first published, Paris: Jazz Hot, 1938)], n.p.).

129. Rudi Blesh, *Shining Trumpets* (New York: Alfred A. Knopf, 1946), 8.

130. Boris Vian, "Le Jazz et sa critique" (unpublished, n.d.), *Œuvres*, 8:355–61 (quote on p. 359).

131. Bechet, *Treat It Gentle*, 2.

132. Ake, "'Blue Horizon,'" 36.

Epilogue

Paris Blues (1961) closes with a potent image. As Lillian (Joanne Woodward) waits anxiously at the station for Ram (Paul Newman), bill posters are hanging a new advertisement (fig. E.1). The day before, the aspiring composer had met with a respected musical authority. He'd admired Ram's creative playing and "genuine gift for melody" but warned him that "there's a great distance between [your improvisations] and an important piece of serious music." Ram needed to study—"composition, harmony, theory, counterpoint." Chastened but determined, Ram arrives to tell Lillian he cannot return with her to the States: "I gotta follow through with the music, I gotta find out how far I can go." Throughout the film, posters of Wild Man Moore (Louis Armstrong) all around the city have been an obsessive focus of his attention (fig. E.2). Now, without him appearing to notice, the biggest one of all is covered over with an advertisement for a French publishing house (fig. E.3). Ram's mind, like the billboard, has moved onto higher things.

The adaption of Harold Flender's novella *Paris Blues* to film at first seems to elide the question of race in France, as I discussed in the introduction. In fact, the issue is not so much removed as it is relocated to the dimension of art. From its opening, with Ram composing through the night, to its close, with his decision not to board the boat-train with Lillian, *Paris Blues* is concerned above all with one white man's quest. Yet it is actually the music of Duke Ellington and Billy Strayhorn on the soundtrack that signals Ram's potential. At the very end, as Connie and Lillian disappear on the train, the "Paris Blues" theme we heard Ram compose is enveloped by one of Ellington's characteristic train songs, all pounding drums and spluttering saxophones. "The pretensions of the white musician who wants to rise above jazz," Krin Gabbard writes, are "overwhelmed with rousing African American rhythms and harmonies," thus "subtly destroy[ing] the film's dichotomies of jazz and art."[1] I wonder how

1. Krin Gabbard, "*Paris Blues*: Ellington, Armstrong, and Saying It with Music," in *Uptown Conversation: The New Jazz Studies*, ed. Robert G. O'Meally, Brent Hayes

FIGURE E.1. Lillian (Joanne Woodward) waits for Ram, *Paris Blues*, dir. Martin Ritt (1961).

FIGURE E.2. Ram (Paul Newman) with a poster of Wild Man Moore (Louis Armstrong), *Paris Blues*, dir. Martin Ritt (1961).

FIGURE E.3. Ram as solitary artist, *Paris Blues*, dir. Martin Ritt (1961).

many more scenes Ellington might not be heard to "misread" if only his music were not sometimes turned down so low in the mix as to make it inaudible.

Jazz's evolving status as an art form had long been at stake in jazz films, as Gabbard has shown. To take Louis Armstrong's movies alone, however, from *New Orleans* (1947) and *A Star is Born* (1948) to *The Glenn Miller*

Edwards, and Farah Jasmine Griffin (New York: Columbia University Press, 2004), 297–311 (quotes on pp. 307, 308). This is an extended revision of a reading that first appeared in Gabbard's *Jammin' at the Margins: Jazz and the American Cinema* (Chicago: University of Chicago Press, 1996), 192–203.

FIGURE E.4. Wild Man
Moore's image is erased,
final frame, *Paris Blues*, dir.
Martin Ritt (1961).

Story (1954) and *The Five Pennies* (1959), it is not the trumpeter himself who "elevates" jazz within the narrative. Rather, he confers his wisdom and authenticity—more, his "phallic power"—on a young white musician, pushing him toward maturity, artistic or sexual.[2] Armstrong brings greater range to this ancestral role in *Paris Blues*, not only jamming with Ram but also advising him on his compositions. Nevertheless, he is finally transcended—indeed, erased—as he always had been (fig. E.4). The film's ending, then, reasserts several distinctions that the story had sometimes placed in doubt: improvised jazz (black, feminized, commercial) is repatriated to the States; learned composition (white, masculine, artistic) remains in the capital of culture.

The context for this ambivalent relationship with black music in civil rights America is not difficult to see, particularly given a film industry that was at once anxious to do the right thing and queasy about doing so. But the movie also captures more about France's relationship to African American music and musicians than I think is often recognized. In that country, too, debates ostensibly about art often disguised ones about race, and virulent nationalism hid its head as mere patriotism. A powerful myth of French acceptance of jazz has led, I fear, to some untested assumptions and (dare I say?) a degree of self-satisfaction. In this book, I've tried to provide a more nuanced account of the French reception of black music from the 1920s to the 1950s by contextualizing it in ongoing debates about race, nation, and culture.

The turn of the 1960s marks the end of this study, but it did not of course signal the last of jazz in Paris. In some ways, it was just the beginning: a regular circuit of clubs and festivals for musicians touring Europe now made African American performers a commonplace. After the deaths of Django Reinhardt (1910–1953) and Sidney Bechet (1897–1959), the principal actors in the last two chapters, however, jazz would never

2. Gabbard, *Jammin' at the Margins*, 117–23, 222–25 (esp. pp. 224–25).

regain the mantle of popular music in France, nor would homegrown music ever achieve such international recognition as the Quintette du Hot Club de France. Paradoxically, then, French jazz culture already became tinged with nostalgia for a lost time. Something like an official view of the history of African American music in France began to take hold, one in which an often fraught relationship in the first half of the twentieth century was reimagined as a perfect alliance.

French writers, performers, and audiences certainly did show an early interest in, sometimes even a respect for, African American music. This is witnessed in their extravagant marveling at performers, from Florence Mills to Duke Ellington. However, their desire to understand was often undercut by one to appropriate, and that wish to possess occasionally then undone by one to be. From Ray Ventura to André Hodeir, French musicians and critics remade jazz in their own image, whether musically or rhetorically. Sometimes they attempted a compromise with the music's creators; other times they brazenly assumed it as their birthright. Narratives of jazz's Frenchness peaked during the Second World War, whether for strategic reasons or nationalistic ones. At this time, the absence of American performers and the demands of audiences for entertainment were a boon to French musicians, of whom Django Reinhardt is only the most celebrated. These wartime experiences did not, to my mind, guarantee jazz's acceptance in the postwar period, however. Disputes rumbled on, notably when Sidney Bechet reinvented the music as a form of youth culture.

At times, throughout, African Americans found themselves caught up in discourses of race that today seem arcane if not ridiculous. This was the case in particular of performers in the almost forgotten tradition of black musical theatre, whose shows both reflected and responded to quasi-scientific theorizations of race: the turn from primitive to hybrid in their reception at once suggested greater understanding and revealed increasing suspicion. I recognize as well the pervasive colonial ideology in such discourses (particularly on Baker's *Créole*) and its rhetorical use for the purposes of appropriation. Yet where some see cosmopolitism and tolerance giving way quite abruptly to close mindedness and bigotry in the interwar period, I see an intertwining of liberal and conservative opinions throughout these years, racial attitudes being one prominent forum.

Race is far from the only issue at stake, however. Jazz engages too many touchstone issues of the twentieth century for any simple explanation to do justice to its very complex reception, which embraces modernity, technology, and global reconfigurations of power, cultural as well as political. In Jack Hylton's case, the audacity of presenting black music (albeit its "whitest" version) in *the* symbol of French musical culture, the Opéra, was at once heightened and offset by another confluence of "high" and "low": an arrangement of Stravinsky. Similarly, as both Louis Douglas and Josephine Baker climbed the ladder of genres, they flattered French taste while staking their claim for recognition. Later on, French critics began to exert powerful control over their country's history with the music. This was especially the case with regard to jazz during the occupation, as a benign interlude for French musicians was successfully constructed as one of their suppression and resistance. Following the triumph of some early jazz styles in the late 1940s and 1950s, it became possible, too, to reimagine the interwar period as one when jazz had received a much warmer welcome than was in fact the case.

Although the lives of the musicians onto whom were projected France's hopes and fears have not themselves been my focus here, French writers did not act alone in shaping the story, nor did they have it all their own way. African American performers, too, were able to make good use of these narratives. As I've shown, both Josephine Baker and Sidney Bechet played on and with their imagined connection to France: Baker performed colonial roles that blurred (but did not erase) her difference; Bechet used his Creole roots to write himself into both the prehistory of jazz in New Orleans and its re-created tradition in his adopted home. The musicians' causes were not the same as their hosts', however, and it is to oversimplify the issues if French writers and African American performers seem to speak as one.

I have been concerned throughout to illustrate the continuing relevance of issues from the first half of the twentieth century to representations and discussions today. Even in as recent a scholarly volume as *Eurojazzland* of 2012, for example, one may read an impassioned insistence that "melody, harmony, scales and modes, notation, rhythm, timbre, form, and even improvisation have much to do, in jazz, with European musical roots, as do instruments. Besides the banjo and the xylophone, which come from Africa, and the drums . . . all the most popular instruments in jazz are, in fact, European instruments: the saxophone . . . was patented before the second half of the nineteenth century by Belgian instrument maker Adolphe Sax." Later, and more controversially, one learns how "improvisation didn't start at all with jazz: European classical music is so rich in terms of improvisation that we could probably infer that jazz improvisation mostly comes from the European tradition."[3]

3. Luci Cerchiari, introduction to *Eurojazzland: Jazz and European Sources, Dynamics, and Contexts*, ed. Luca Cerchiari, Laurent Cugny, and Franz Kerschbaumer (Boston: Northeastern University Press, 2012), vii–xviii (quotes on pp. viii, x–xi).

Of course, the basic facts presented here are not in doubt (though the idea that jazz improvisation owes more to the church organist than the blues singer is a curious one). I worry, though, when the presence of European as well as African or African American traits in this American music—which has never been disputed—serves to minimize black invention. This may in turn be used to justify the music's appropriation in and by Europe, with an insufficient "paying of dues." It is one thing to speak of a specific and meaningful European contribution to jazz; quite another to suggest that this displaces African American roots. However far this may be from the author's intention, a distant echo of the racialized, nationalist discourses of the last century is heard when such similar points are sounded in the present day.

Mine is not an example of the "so-called Afrocentric point of view" this writer describes as partially responsible for an emphasis on African over European roots. On the contrary, I believe that the interaction of different ethnic groups within and without the United States is one of the most important areas of current research. And I recognize that, even to sympathetic critics in Europe, the American music industry often seems to exert hegemonic control. But nor is it precisely the case that "jazz has always been regarded as a typically twentieth-century expression of the broader African American contribution to world music history."[4] In fact, that recognition was hard won, and many of the writers cited in the preceding chapters would have denied entirely jazz's contribution to music history, let alone the input of African Americans. If it may seem churlish to point these things out in what is, I am sure, a well-meaning volume, what's extraordinary after a century of jazz history is that I should have to. I hope that putting these ideas into historical perspective may yet help to alleviate some cross-cultural misunderstanding.

Such issues explain what makes the legacy of a figure like Hugues Panassié so complicated. On the one hand, he recognized the African American contribution to jazz as preeminent. On the other, he increasingly denied the role of other groups and, moreover, sought to delimit the contribution younger musicians could make. Conversely, internationalist positions, such as that adopted by Charles Delaunay before the war, tend finally to be undercut by nationalist agendas: less reciprocity than appropriation (witness again the examples above, now extended to the whole of Europe). In seeking today to remove signs of racial determinism, it must surely not be forgotten that the music *was* fostered primarily among the

---

I propose this as a critique of a point of view, not of a particular author or group of authors.

4. Ibid., viii.

African American community (broadly conceived) as the social and racial prejudice that would confine it there very slowly fades from view.

Paris Blues, the movie, continues this traffic across time and space, both in creating a vision of France for Americans in the early 1960s and in reproducing that vision today. The ideas it engages—of the racial equality and artistic recognition offered African Americans and their music in Paris—are as familiar today as they were fifty or even one hundred years ago. If the complexities of relations among races in France broached (if hardly investigated) in the book are lacking from the film, however, the substitution as a theme of jazz's position vis-à-vis Western art music reveals yet again how closely discourses of race and of art are linked. Beneath a surface of mutual respect, assimilation, and exposure, I find a darker story about racial anxiety, appropriation, and erasure. Paradoxically, I suggest, it is in the movie's very ambivalence or instability that it comes closest to capturing the range of signification, if not necessarily the real experience, of African American music and musicians in France.

Index

Italicized page numbers indicate figures, and boldface page numbers indicate music examples.